Mon. Dec 1.

12:45 - 2:45

Same Room

A Creative Approach to

Music Fundamentals

with CD-ROM

Eighth Edition

William Duckworth
Bucknell University

THOMSON
SCHIRMER

Australia • Canada • Mexico • Singapore • Spain • United Kingdom • United States

THOMSON
SCHIRMER

Publisher, Music: Clark Baxter
Development Editor: Sharon Adams Poore
Assistant Editor: Stephanie Sandoval
Editorial Assistant: Eno Sarris
Technology Project Manager: Jennifer Ellis
Marketing Manager: Mark D. Orr
Marketing Assistant: Kristi Bostock
Advertising Project Manager: Brian Chaffee
Project Manager, Editorial Production: Emily Smith
Print/Media Buyer: Rebecca Cross
Permissions Editor: Sarah Harkrader
Production Service: Johnstone Associates
Autographer: Ernie Mansfield
Compositor: TBH Typecast, Inc.
Cover Designer: Ark Stein
Text and Cover Printer: Webcom

Printed in Canada

1 2 3 4 5 6 7 07 06 05 04 03

For more information about our products, contact us at:
Thomson Learning Academic Resource Center
1-800-423-0563

For permission to use material from this text, contact us by:
Phone: 1-800-730-2214
Fax: 1-800-730-2215
Web: http://www.thomsonrights.com

Library of Congress Control Number: 2003103807

ISBN: 0-534-60345-9

Wadsworth/Thomson Learning
10 Davis Drive
Belmont, CA 94002-3098
USA

Asia
Thomson Learning
5 Shenton Way #01-01
UIC Building
Singapore 068808

Australia/New Zealand
Thomson Learning
102 Dodds Street
Southbank, Victoria 3006
Australia

Canada
Nelson
1120 Birchmount Road
Toronto, Ontario M1K 5G4
Canada

Europe/Middle East/Africa
Thomson Learning
High Holborn House
50/51 Bedford Row
London WC1R 4LR
United Kingdom

Latin America
Thomson Learning
Seneca, 53
Colonia Polanco
11560 Mexico D.F.
Mexico

Spain/Portugal
Paraninfo
Calle/Magallanes, 25
28015 Madrid, Spain

For Will, Katherine, and Alison

who grew up with many of the songs in this book.

Contents

Preface

To Students

The more things change, the more they remain the same. We have all heard that adage since childhood, and nowhere is it more true than in music. How should we begin our study of music in the 21st century when we have instant access to the music of the world through media ranging from CDs to web radio to MP3s? So many different musical styles have emerged in the recent past—from dissonant 12-tone music, to improvised jazz, to rock, to music written by chance—that it is often difficult to know where to begin. When we look at the potential for the music of this new century—including computer music, new sounds of synthesizers, ambient, hip hop, and music on the Web—the confusion compounds itself.

So, how do we begin? Today? How can we start to learn about music when there are so many possible places from which to begin and so many different directions we can take? Fortunately, all of these styles, plus others that haven't been mentioned—including classical music—use the same basic set of building blocks, or elements, or fundamentals. These fundamentals always stay the same. It is the many different ways that composers use and combine them that changes. To put it more succinctly, musical styles change, the fundamentals don't. No matter what kind of music you are interested in, and want to write and play, the way to begin is to learn the fundamentals, because you will always be able to apply them to any style of music, including ones that haven't even been imagined yet.

The Package

That is where this book, and the material packaged with it, can help you. It is about the fundamentals of music, and it is designed to help you get off to a good start. In addition to the text, which includes written examples to test your musical intelligence, aural examples to help you practice your musical skills, and periodic quizzes to measure your progress, there is a fold-out keyboard at the back of the book to help you learn the notes, and a CD-ROM, called *Focus on Fundamentals,* containing practice material that you can use on your computer, and sound files of some of the examples in the book that you can listen to on both your computer and your CD player.

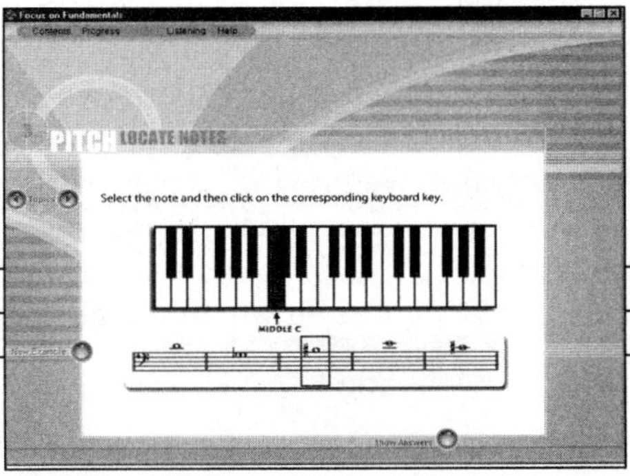

Locate Notes

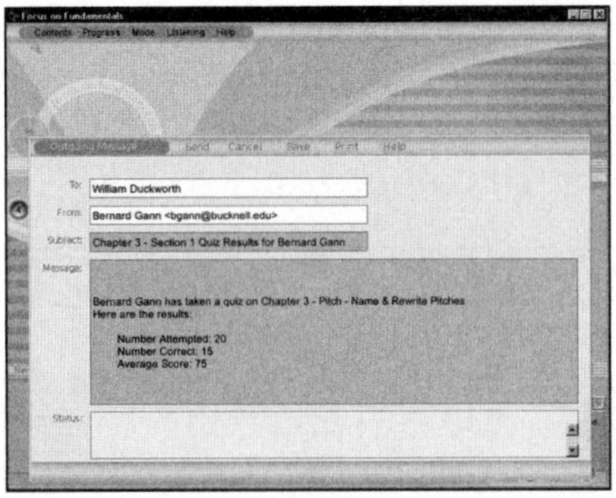

You can e-mail your quiz results directly to your instructor.

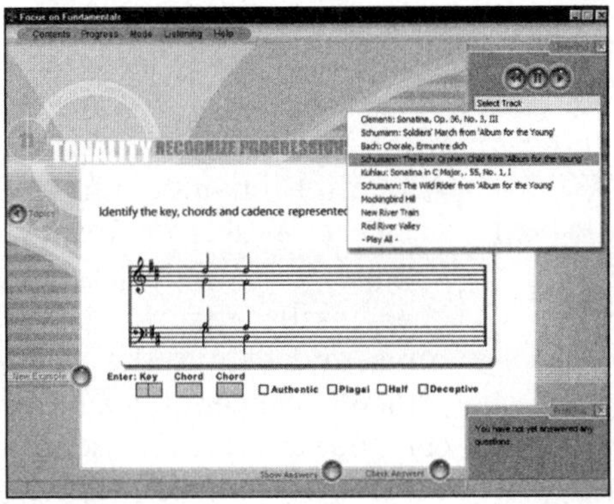

Recognize Progressions

The reason for including these additional exercises and interactive activities is to give you the opportunity to learn the fundamentals of music in an individualized way that better matches your own unique set of skills and abilities. Because no two people ever learn music in the same way, or at the same speed, you will find that you may need more work on some skills and less on others. Those needs are different for each member of the class. So this additional material can help you individualize your work. Now you can supplement your class work with as much individual practice as you need.

The Schirmer Music Resource Center http://music.wadsworth.com presents this textbook's companion site and other tools to aid in learning the fundamentals. *The Schirmer Audio Dictionary of Music* contains hundreds of terms and definitions that include interactive audio, images and links to related terms.

What about the music of the future, for someone just beginning to study music? What new skills might be needed as the century progresses? And what is the best way to prepare for a new musical world? The answer is both simple and complex. Certainly, new kinds of music are coming along that will require the development of as-yet-unimagined musical skills. We must all be prepared, as 21st-century musicians, to assimilate new musical knowledge continually throughout our lives. To do this, we must first develop a solid foundation in the fundamentals. Then we can build upon that knowledge when we approach the musical unknown.

To Instructors

This new eighth edition of *A Creative Approach to Music Fundamentals* has been designed to encourage your students to begin making, and interacting with, music as quickly as possible. The first three chapters have been reorganized and integrated into a new first chapter on the basics of music. This new Chapter 1 introduces keyboard skills from the beginning, and delays the more difficult concepts such as compound meter and ties until after simple meters and basic note values have been practiced and understood. Additionally, many of the rhythms and melodies from Appendices A, B, and D have now been integrated into the text and the appendices themselves have been graded for difficulty. To help illustrate that the fundamentals of music apply to all styles of music, this new edition now includes expanded musical examples taken from television, advertising, and film, as well as from the classical repertoire, plus the inclusion of the music of other cultures.

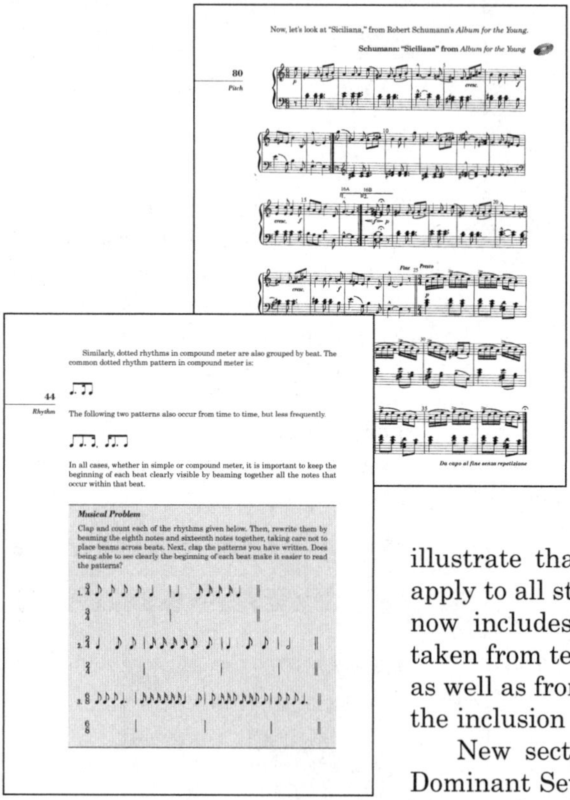

New sections titled "Inversions of the Dominant Seventh Chord" and "Triads in a Musical Context" have been added to Chapter 10, Triads. And as always, there are a wealth of Musical Problems in every chapter that help your students put their newly acquired knowledge of music to practical use.

Teaching Package

An **eBank Instructor's Manual** is available for instructors that includes answers to the exercises in the text, suggested classroom activities, and more.

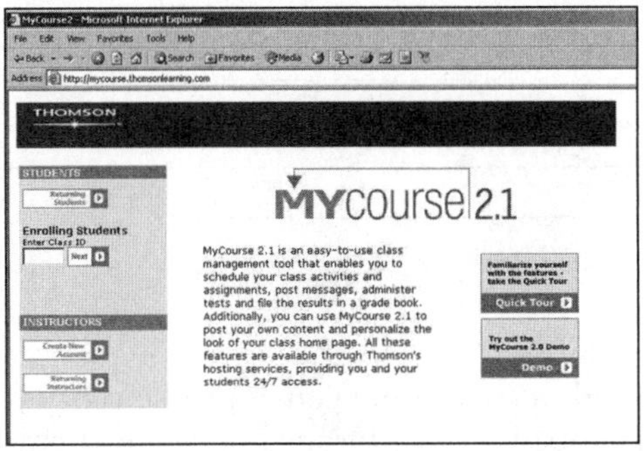

My Course 2.1 is available free to instructors who want a simple solution for a customized Web site that allows you to assign, track, report on student progress, and more. Visit http://mycourse. thomsonlearning. com for details.

InfoTrac© College Edition can be chosen as a package with the text, and you and your students will receive four months FREE anywhere/anytime access to this online library. Articles are available from almost 4,000 diverse sources, including the *Journal of the American Musicological Society, Music Week, Opera News,* and thousands more.

Acknowledgments

I would like to thank the following reviewers for their input in revising the text: Christy Dana, University of California at Berkeley; Andrew N. Guthrie, Tulane University; Daniel Luzko, Irvine Valley College; Susan Wilson Mills, Frostburg State University; James Sodke, University of Wisconsin–Parkside; David Starkweather, University of Georgia; Jennifer Sterling, University of Maryland.

Introduction

Musical Talent, Musical Knowledge

The distinction between musical talent and musical knowledge can be confusing. Some people think there really isn't much of a difference between them. But there is, and it is important to understand what it is because that is the first step toward becoming a better musician.

All of us know people who can play or sing extremely well but who have a hard time explaining in words how they do what they do. Often these people are able to play pieces of music that they have heard only a few times or to write music of great charm and subtlety with seeming ease. Yet these same people sometimes find it very difficult to talk about their obvious natural abilities. On the other hand, some people can easily put into words what they think about a piece of music, or what they hear happening in it technically, but they may not be able to perform particularly well, or to compose. For some reason the ability to "understand" music does not seem to make them better as performers or composers.

Why is this? What is the basic difference between these two types of musical people? Each has a unique skill that the other sometimes desires. And, surely, both wish to know as much as possible about the music they love. The answer is that the first type of person relates to music primarily on the basis of innate musical talent, while the second type relies on a learned knowledge of music that has been acquired through study. Both kinds of musicianship are necessary to becoming a complete musician. Nurture and develop both as much as you can. It is not a reasonable option to develop one talent or skill and discard the rest as boring or unnecessary. You will need them all if you really want to make it in the complex world of music today.

Everyone reading this book has some musical talent. All of us do. But the extent to which this talent has been developed probably varies greatly from person to person. Some of you may just be learning to play an instrument, or plan to learn to play, or hope to write a song some day. Others may already play and sing, and some may even be writing songs "by ear." No matter what the current range of your musicianship, it's fairly safe to assume that you have not yet explored the full range of your musical talent.

This book, however, is not about developing your talent but about building on your musical knowledge. It will help you to learn the *facts* about music. Fundamentally, this is a book about skills. Musical skills. Skills that are shared, in varying degrees and combinations, by *all* successful musicians. For some of you, this book will help you learn concepts and terms for the music you can already perform. For others, working with this material will help you to develop faster as a performer or composer than you otherwise might. For all of you this book will at times be hard work. The work may even become frustrating, since developing new skills in any area always requires a great deal of practice and repetition. The thing to keep in mind is that becoming more musical requires your active and continued commitment and participation. You can't do it merely by reading the book. You have to physically clap and play the rhythms, sing the melodies, and listen to the examples. You also need to complete the exercises and go through all the musical problems as they occur. It may take a bit longer, but you'll see the results more quickly.

This book is designed to go beyond a mere set of drills and exercises. There is more to music than that! If you study the book carefully and do the exercises thoughtfully, you will gain the knowledge and vocabulary you need to enhance your basic understanding and enjoyment of music. It will encourage you to listen to music rather than just hear it, and enable you to discuss music objectively rather than simply to describe your emotional responses. It will also open the door to how music *works*—knowledge that will, in turn, contribute both to better performance and to greater musical understanding.

A Theory of Music

What is music theory, and why is it necessary? How do "facts" about music sometimes make us better musicians? These questions are not easy to answer. Like the person who plays by ear, the music theorist sometimes understands the answers to these questions in ways that cannot be easily or completely expressed in words.

On one level, music theory is the planned and systematic study of how a particular type of music works. This is equally true whether we are talking about Western European art music, American popular music, or music from another culture such as Bali, Morocco, or Japan. No matter what type of music is being studied, basic music theory examines the various parts, or elements, of the music—melody, harmony, rhythm (studied in this book) and timbre, texture, form (studied in later classes)—and the ways in which these individual elements combine and interact to create a piece of music. Many of you may have had the experience of wanting to learn more about the music you listen to but not knowing where to begin, or of wanting to explain something about music you can perform, but not knowing what to say. These kinds of frustrations illustrate the value of a theory of music and the need for a book such as this.

The question of how factual information about music makes us better musicians is more difficult to answer. While theoretical knowledge will undoubtedly help you become a "better" musician, it does not automatically mean that you will be able to write, play, or sing any better. It will probably happen that way; it does for most people. But don't assume that it will happen magically. The best approach it to set goals for yourself. What do you want to be able to do musically by the end of this course? By the time you graduate? In ten years? If you do this, it will give you a standard against which to measure your progress. As you proceed from exercise to exercise and chapter to chapter, keep your goals in mind and try to see how each topic relates to helping you carry out your plan.

Remember, all fine musicians, no matter what style of music they play, are their own unique blend of musical talent and musical knowledge. No two are alike. As you grow and learn, you too will develop a musical personality that is distinctly your own. As you begin, keep in mind that musical talent and musical knowledge are two distinctly different things. Both must be encouraged and developed, and both require hard work. As you proceed, use your innate musicianship to make the work in this book less difficult and more musical. Let your musical knowledge grow and accumulate. Before long, this new information will begin to influence and inform your talent. You can't be sure exactly how or when this will happen, but you'll know it when it begins. When it starts, it never stops. Becoming a good musician is a lifelong journey. There is more to learn, no matter how accomplished you are.

Chapter 1

The Basics of Music

Although music is a broad, complicated, and subtle form of artistic expression, it contains a few basic elements that, when understood, will not only make learning more about music seem easier but will also make it come alive for you. And that, after all, is the real purpose of the class you are taking and of this book—to give you some understanding and control over the basic elements of music so that you can make your own music in whatever style you choose. This chapter could just as easily have been titled "The Three Things You Really Need To Know," because that is what it is—an introduction to the three basic building blocks of tonal music. These basic building blocks are the place where almost everyone begins their study of music, because no matter what kind of musician you plan to be, you're going to need to know the basics. You will need to be able to manipulate pitches, to maneuver through rhythms, and to develop some way to visualize sound, in our case through the use of the piano or the synthesizer keyboard. This chapter introduces these three topics. And, although these topics will be covered in more detail later in the book, the purpose of introducing them here is to get you on the road to making music as quickly and efficiently as possible.

Rhythm

We are going to begin our study of music with the element of rhythm. All music has a rhythmic component. Sometimes the rhythm is front and center, sometimes it is in the background. But whether fast and aggressive or slow and subtle, rhythm always represents a measuring and a parceling out of time. When we talk about rhythm, we are talking about how music flows through time.

For some reason, most beginning music students feel more secure with their rhythmic skills than they do about their ability to hear and sing pitches. Perhaps it is because our pitch skills seem more individual, and therefore more personal. Also, since it is often thought of as easier, rhythm is sometimes given less attention and drill than pitch. Perhaps for this reason many people, even those with a lot of musical training, have misconceptions about rhythm's place in and contribution to a piece of music. As you begin, keep in mind that rhythm plays a fundamental role in all of the world's music, and that a mastery of rhythm (no matter what the style) and of rhythmic notation (for most Western styles) is a necessary first step in becoming a musician.

So what is musical rhythm? All of us can feel it when it's happening. It's one of the things we really respond to. Most of us can even single out the instruments most involved in creating the rhythm. But, when asked to define rhythm, we have trouble; we give only a partial definition. And while each definition contributes to the understanding of musical rhythm, none by itself explains the concept entirely. A true explanation of musical rhythm is complex, changes from culture to culture, and involves the interaction of a large number of rhythmic components, or elements.

We will begin by discussing each of these rhythmic elements individually, both here and in the chapter that follows. What you will soon discover is that all of these rhythmic components—the pulse, meter, measure, note values, dotted notes, or ties—are relatively simple concepts when studied individually. The difficulty comes with trying to combine these simple concepts into an accurate and sufficiently complex definition of musical rhythm. Equally difficult is applying these definitions to the rhythm of an actual piece of music in an effort to understand how it works. As you continue with this chapter and the next, remember that all of the individual rhythmic elements combine within a piece of music to produce a rhythmic feeling unique to that piece. Remember also that most of us already have a high degree of sensitivity and an intuitive appreciation of those rhythmic qualities. There is the place to begin.

Musical Problem

Listen to a piece of music that you have heard many times before. It may be a solo work, or a piece for a small or large ensemble. It can be something from the past such as a symphony or string quartet, or something more current such as a pop song, rap, or dance mix. What is important, whatever style you choose, is that it be a piece you "know." When listening this time, however, try to concentrate only on the rhythm, shutting out the melody (and lyrics), the harmony, and the sounds of individual instruments. Are you able to direct your musical attention this selectively? If you have never tried this before, it may take several tries before you are successful.

How different does the piece sound when you listen to it this way? Do you hear things in it that you have never really paid attention to or thought much about before? Is there a steady beat? Can you hear rhythmic patterns? Do these rhythmic patterns repeat? Are there a lot of different patterns, or just a few? Try to put your thoughts and feelings about the *rhythmic* qualities of this piece into two or three sentences. Ask various people to read their sentences to the class. Does everyone agree?

Now, with help from your teacher or another student, choose a piece of music from another culture and listen to it, again paying particular attention to the rhythm. Are there obvious rhythmic similarities or differences between this and the more familiar piece you heard first? Do the questions for the first piece apply to this style of music? Can you summarize your thoughts about the rhythmic qualities of this unfamiliar piece?

Pulse

Most music that we hear around us every day has a steady beat, or **pulse**. The pulse, which is both constant and regular, can be felt when you tap your foot to music. This steady beat in your foot can be represented visually by a line of whole notes.

It can also be represented by half notes, quarter notes, or eighth notes.

The point is that any note value can be used to visually represent the pulse. This even includes dotted notes, which we will study later.

But regardless of the note value chosen—the quarter note is probably used most—what is important to remember is that a steady, proportional relationship is established by the pulse, against which the combination of sounds and silences that makes up the actual music moves.

Meter

As you listen to and feel the pulse in various pieces of music, you will notice that some pulses sound stronger than others. This combination of strong and weak pulses forms a recurring pattern known as the **meter.** When musicians talk about the meter of a piece, they are referring to a particular pattern of strong and weak pulses. The most common patterns or meters are duple meter, triple meter, and quadruple meter. As the following illustration shows, in **duple meter,** the pulse is divided into a recurring pattern of one strong and one weak beat; **triple meter** divides the pulse into a recurring pattern of one strong and two weak beats; and **quadruple meter** divides the pulse into one strong and three weak beats.

duple meter 

triple meter 

quadruple meter 

The sign > is an **accent mark.** It indicates that the note under which (or over which) it appears is to be given more stress than the surrounding notes.

Musical Problem

Clap each of the metrical patterns shown above twice—first slowly, then faster—giving an accent to the notes indicated. Notice that the speed you choose does not in any way alter the meter. What matters is that you keep the pulse steady and put the accents in the proper places.

Measures

As you performed the musical problem, you may have lost your place momentarily in one of the lines. Even if you didn't, you can see that it would be hard to play a long piece of music without losing one's place. For this reason, music is divided into **measures** with vertical lines called **bar lines**.

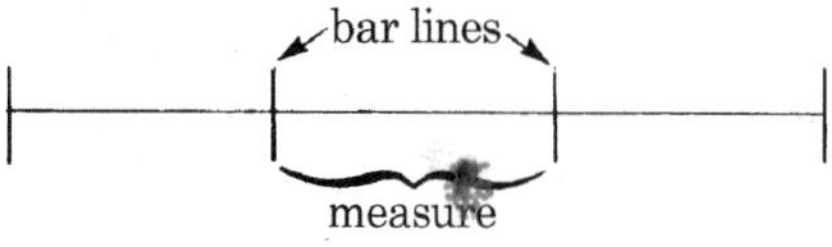

A bar line occurs immediately before an accented pulse. Thus, duple meter has two beats per measure, triple meter has three beats per measure, and quadruple meter has four beats per measure. The following example shows the common meters again, this time with bar lines included. Notice how much easier it is to read and perform the meter when it is written in this way.

duple meter 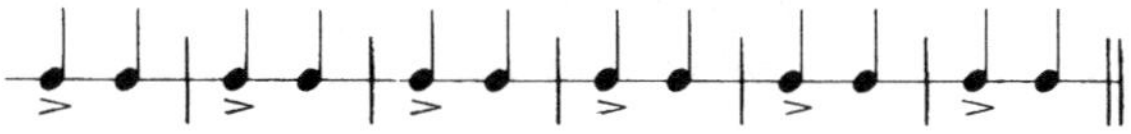

triple meter 

quadruple meter 

Double bar lines have a special meaning: Their two most common uses are to signal the beginning of a new section in a large work and to mark the end of a work. You should put double bar lines at the end of any exercises or pieces you write.

> ***Musical Problem***
>
> As members of the class listen, clap a steady pulse without any noticeable accents. Slowly change the pulse to duple, triple, or quadruple meter. You may want to have a contest to see how quickly members of the class can detect the shift to a measured pulse.

Note Values

Learning to read music involves mastering two different musical subsystems: pitch notation and rhythmic notation. Pitch is indicated by the placement of a note on a five-line staff. (The higher the note on the staff, the higher the pitch.) You will learn about that later in this chapter. Rhythm, on the other hand, is written with note-value symbols, which show duration. The following note values are the most commonly used:

whole note 

half note 

quarter note 

eighth note 

sixteenth note 

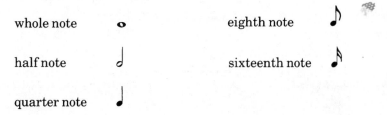

Notice that only the whole note exists as a notehead. Half notes and quarter notes consist of both a notehead and a stem,

half note quarter note

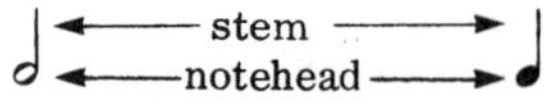

while eighth notes and sixteenth notes consist of a notehead, a stem, and either one or two flags.

eighth note

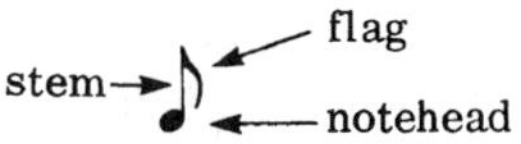

sixteenth note

By combining these note values into various rhythmic combinations, the steady pulse of a piece of music is subdivided into an endless variety of patterns. The following example shows both the steady pulse and a rhythmic division of that pulse. Can you see how one line appears to support and strengthen the other?

quadruple meter

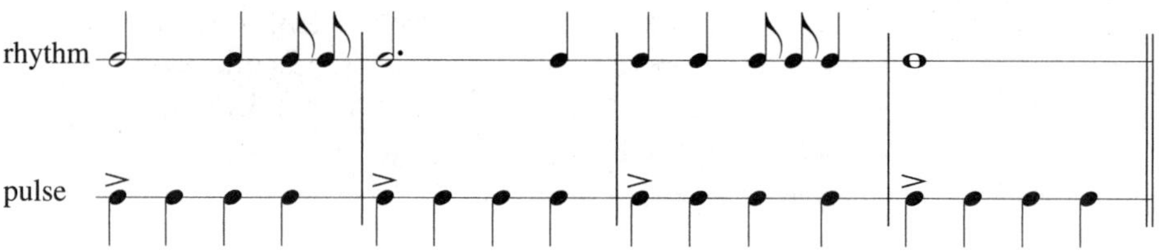

When several notes with flags occur together, the flags are usually replaced by beams that join the notes together at the tops of the stems. Generally, these note groupings are put into combinations of two, three, four, six, or eight. This is done to reflect the location of the pulse in relation to the rhythm. That is, a new beam is used at the beginning of each pulse. This makes it visually easier to tell where the beats are.

When beams are used, they indicate the rhythmic value of the notes in the same way as flags do for individual notes.

eighth notes beamed together 

sixteenth notes beamed together 

Sometimes sixteenth-note beams stop in the middle of the pattern and then begin again. This is usually done to make the rhythm clearer to the eye and does not affect the value of the notes in any way. The rule is that if a stem is touched by a beam, it becomes that value, even if the beam touches only one side of the stem. Thus, in the following example, the two sixteenth-note patterns would sound identical, even though they look slightly different, because each stem is touched by two beams.

Once you begin working with rhythms of different note values you will notice that short, incomplete beams are often used.

In this example, the second and fourth notes are sixteenth notes, and the first and third are eighth notes (the function of the dot will be explained later in this chapter). Just remember that if a stem is touched by a beam, it becomes that value, and you should not have any trouble deciphering the rhythmic patterns that appear throughout the rest of this book.

EXERCISE 1•1

Before proceeding further, you should practice drawing note values. This is not difficult but it does require some practice if you have not worked with them before. Keep the following points in mind:

1. Note heads are oval rather than round.
2. The flags on eighth and sixteenth notes always point to the right, no matter which side of the note the stem is on.
3. Notice also that when the stem points down it is always located to the left of the notehead, and when it point up it is always on the right.

Now try some on your own. Remember to draw examples of the stems both above and below the notes.

whole notes 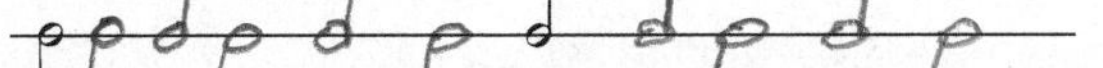

half notes

quarter notes 

eighth notes 

sixteenth notes 

Regardless of the speed (tempo) at which a piece of music moves, the note value symbols are proportionately related to each other. Thus, if the quarter note receives one beat, the half note will receive two beats and the whole note four beats. This proportionality can be illustrated in the following way:

One whole note is equal in duration to four quarter notes.

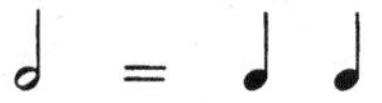

One half note is equal in duration to two quarter notes.

Notes of lesser value than the quarter note are proportioned in the same way:

Two eighth notes equal one quarter note in duration.

Four sixteenth notes equal one quarter note in duration.

Different note values can represent the pulse. If, for example, the eighth note receives one beat, then the quarter note will get two beats and the half note four beats. Similarly, if the half note receives one beat, the whole note will get two beats and two quarter notes will be needed to complete one beat.

Musical Problem

Your instructor will select five examples from the rhythmic patterns given on the next page and play them on the piano. In the space provided, indicate whether the examples are in duple, triple, or quadruple meter. Remember to listen for the basic, underlying pulse.

1. ______________________________
2. ______________________________
3. ______________________________
4. ______________________________
5. ______________________________

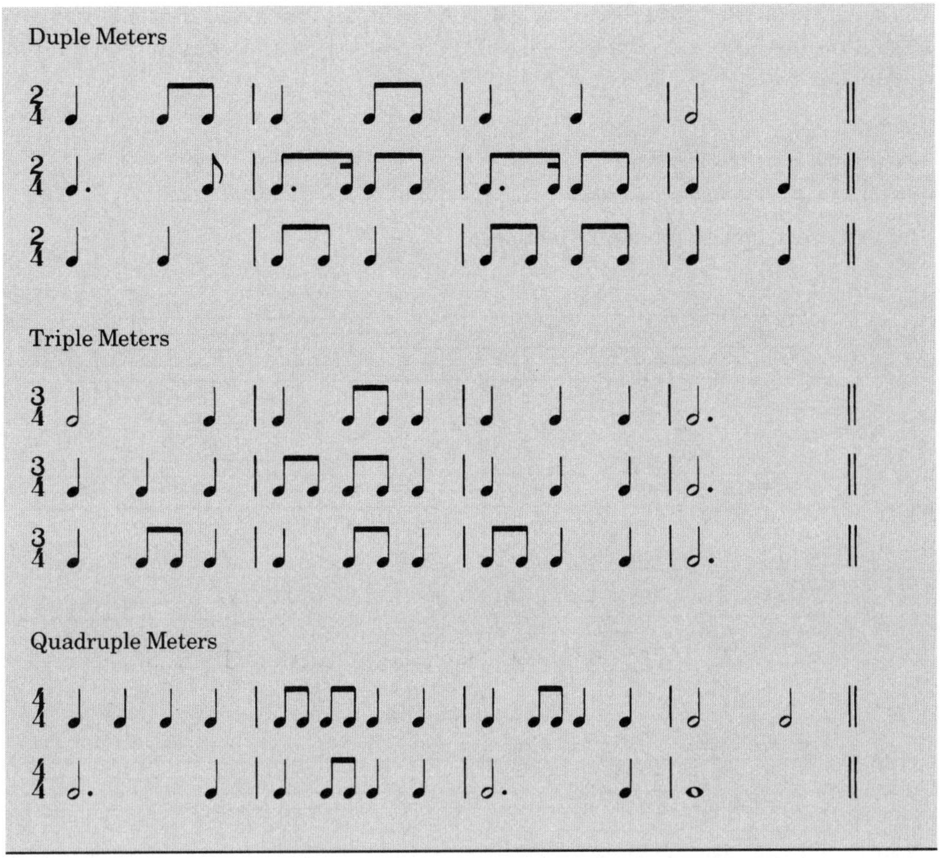

Rests

Just as the symbols for note value represent duration of sound, **rest** signs are used to indicate durations of silence. Each note value has a corresponding rest sign.

whole rest (fourth line of staff)	𝄻
half rest (third line of staff)	𝄼
quarter rest	𝄽
eighth rest	𝄾
sixteenth rest	𝄿

The whole rest is often used to indicate one complete measure of silence. It can serve this purpose for any meter, and when used in this way it is centered within the measure.

EXERCISE 1•2

Practice drawing the following rest signs:

whole rests

half rests

quarter rests

eighth rests

sixteenth rests

Dotted Notes

When you first begin to study dotted notes, they can seem very confusing. But if you will keep in mind that the dot always means the same thing, you will have less trouble. A dot to the right of a notehead gives that note a longer duration. Furthermore, the dot always increases the time value of that note by one-half. For example, a half note is equal in value to two quarter notes.

𝅗𝅥 = ♩ + ♩

When a dot is placed beside a note, this new note, called a **dotted note**, becomes equal to the original value plus one-half the original value. In the case of our half note, adding a dot creates a dotted half note with a time value equal to three quarter notes.

𝅗𝅥. = ♩ + ♩ + ♩

Rests as well as notes can be increased in value by adding a dot, although dotted rests are used less often than dotted notes. As with notes, a dot placed to the right of a rest increases its value by one-half.

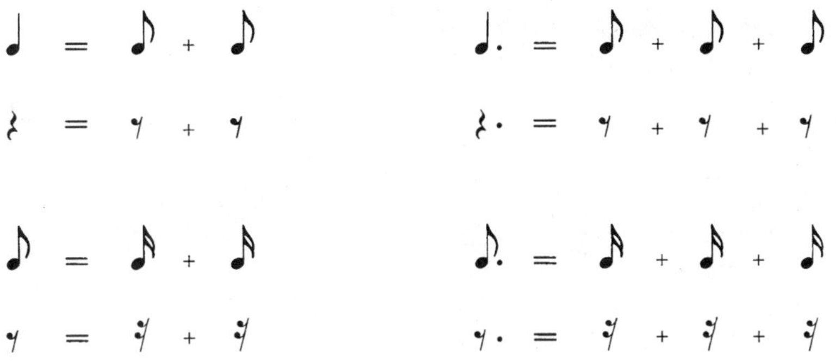

Time Signatures

The **time signature,** or **meter signature** as it is also called, is made up of two numbers, one above the other. It always appears at the beginning of a piece of music. The time signature gives us two different pieces of information: The top number tells us the meter of the piece; the bottom number identifies the note value that represents the pulse. For example, in the time signature $\frac{3}{4}$:

- **3** indicates triple meter—that is, three pulses, or beats, per measure.
- **4** identifies the quarter note as the pulse beat.

Remember that although the quarter note represents the pulse for many pieces, other note values can also serve this purpose. Both the eighth note and the half note are frequently used.

Here is an example of triple meter with the eighth note representing the pulse,

while this is a triple meter with the half note representing the pulse.

Notice, incidentally, that the meter signature is *never* written as a fraction: $\not{3/4}$.

EXERCISE 1•3

Identify the meter and indicate the note value that represents the pulse for each of the meter signatures below.

EXAMPLE: $\begin{matrix}4\\4\end{matrix}$ quadruple meter / quarter-note pulse

1. $\begin{matrix}2\\8\end{matrix}$ duple meter / eighth-note pulse
2. $\begin{matrix}3\\4\end{matrix}$ triple Meter / quarter-note pulse
3. $\begin{matrix}4\\2\end{matrix}$ quadruple meter / ________
4. $\begin{matrix}3\\8\end{matrix}$ ________ / ________
5. $\begin{matrix}2\\4\end{matrix}$ ________ / ________
6. $\begin{matrix}4\\8\end{matrix}$ ________ / ________
7. $\begin{matrix}3\\2\end{matrix}$ ________ / ________
8. $\begin{matrix}2\\2\end{matrix}$ ________ / ________

EXERCISE 1•4

For each of the following sequences, determine the meter and the note value that represents the pulse. Then, divide each example into measures by placing bar lines in the appropriate places. Remember to put double bar lines at the end.

8. 

9. 

10. 

When you have correctly placed the bar lines in each of these examples, practice playing each rhythmic passage on the instrument you play or on a keyboard. If you sing, choose a comfortable pitch in the middle of your range. Remember to hold each note its full value.

EXERCISE 1•5

The following rhythmic passages are barred and notated correctly. Study them carefully and write the meter signature for each in the appropriate place.

1. 

2. 

3. 

4. 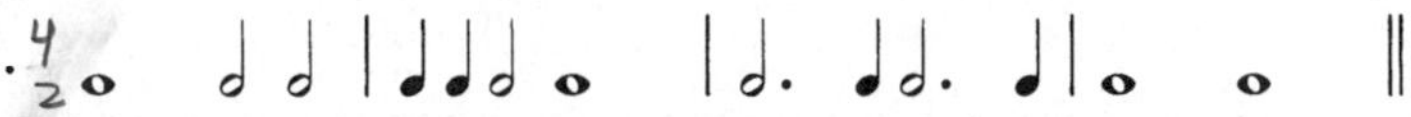

5. 

6. 

7. 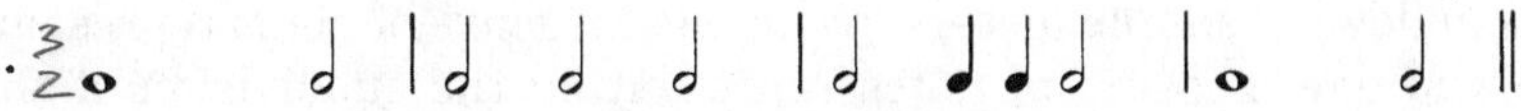

8. 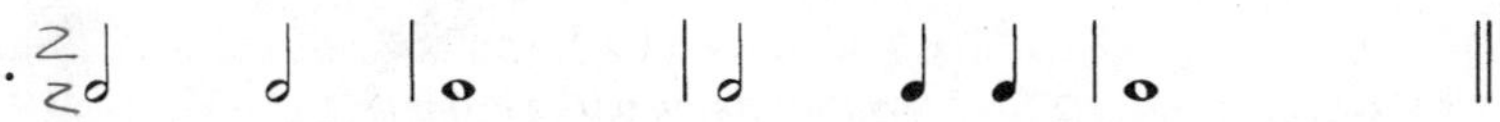

When you have correctly identified the meter signature of each example, practice playing the passages on the instrument you play or on a keyboard. If you sing, choose a comfortable pitch in the middle of your range.

Simple Meter

Thus far, our discussion of meter has dealt entirely with simple meter. In **simple meter,** the basic pulse or beat is normally subdivided into two equal parts. For instance, in $\frac{2}{4}$ meter each quarter note (the note representing the pulse) is divisible into two eighth notes:

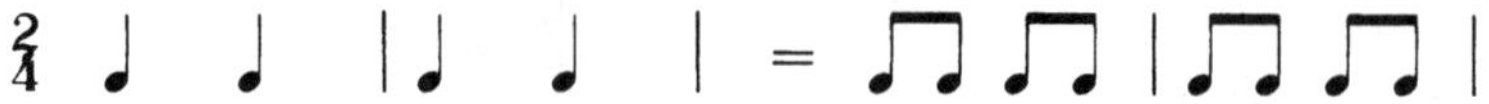

This subdivision of the basic pulse into two equal parts is the mark of a simple meter. Metrical patterns such as $\frac{3}{8}$ and $\frac{3}{2}$ subdivide in this way:

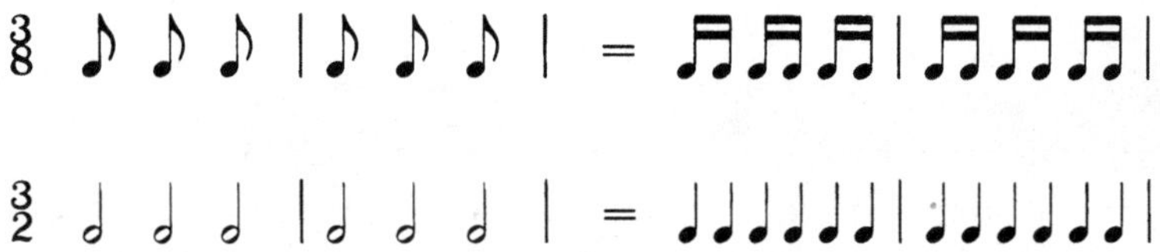

The common simple meters are:

simple duple	$\frac{2}{8}$	$\frac{2}{4}$	$\frac{2}{2}$
simple triple	$\frac{3}{8}$	$\frac{3}{4}$	$\frac{3}{2}$
simple quadruple	$\frac{4}{8}$	$\frac{4}{4}$	$\frac{4}{2}$

Note that in all cases the top numeral indicates the number of pulses in each measure, and the bottom numeral indicates the note value that represents the pulse.

EXERCISE 1•6

For each of the following simple meters, write one measure of notes representing the pulse and one measure of notes representing the subdivision of the pulse. Follow the example.

EXAMPLE: *Pulse* *Subdivision of the Pulse*

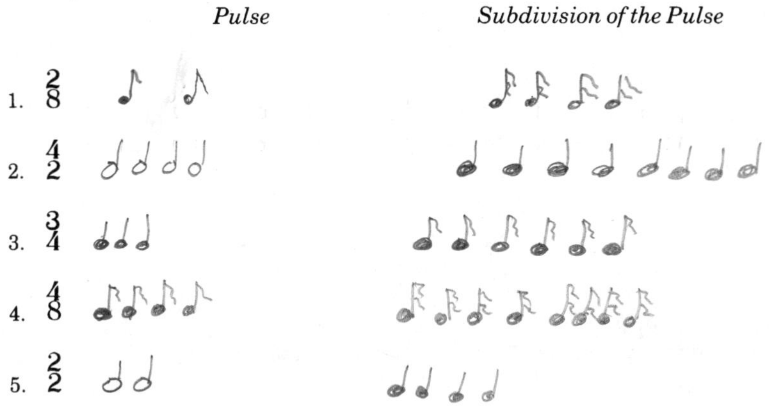

A Counting Method for Simple Meters

In learning rhythms, it is helpful to know a method of counting that can be spoken aloud as you are clapping rhythms. The value of such a system is that it can be transferred to "mental" counting when you are playing or singing actual music. Although several systems are in use, the following one is recommended.

The Basic Beat

In this system, the basic beat is identified by the numbers "one, two, three, four," as needed. (This is true for both simple and compound meter, which we will learn later.) Practice counting the following examples in simple meter until you feel comfortable with the basic beat. Remember to always keep the beat steady.

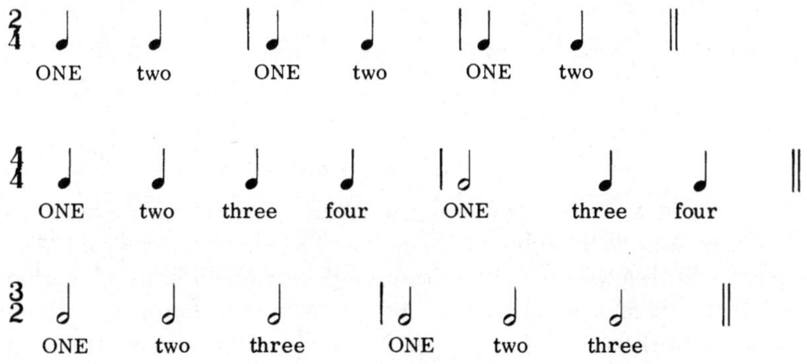

Subdivisions of the Beat

When dividing simple meters, *and* is used to indicate the division of the beat. Practice the following examples until they feel comfortable.

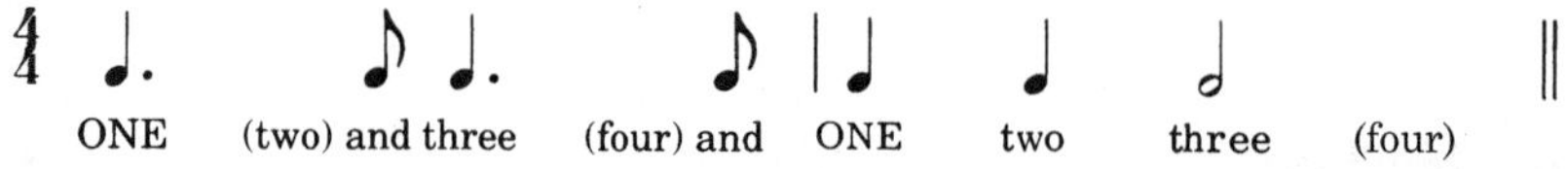

When a further subdivision is needed—that is, if you need to indicate one-quarter of the basic beat—the syllables to use are "e" and "a" (or "da"). Here are some examples to practice.

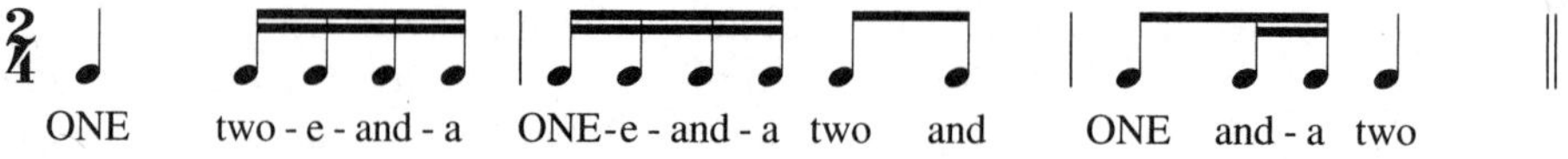

EXERCISE 1•7

Individually and as a class, clap and count the following rhythmic examples taken from folk songs. You will probably know some of these pieces and that will help you decide whether you are doing them right or not. Begin by saying two measures of the divided beat (1-and 2-and) aloud before clapping. When you are comfortable with the counting system, also try playing the rhythms on an instrument or keyboard while counting mentally. Remember to always keep the basic beat steady.

"America"

1. 

"She'll Be Coming Round the Mountain"

2.

"The Yellow Rose of Texas"

3.

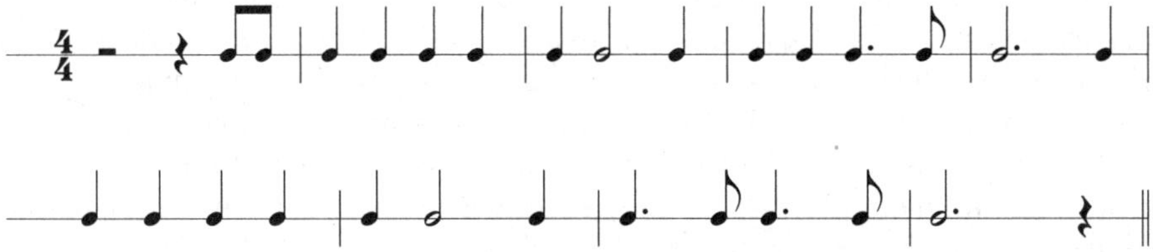

Pitch

The Staff

In western music, pitch is written on a **staff**. The music staff (pl., *staves*) consists of a group of five parallel lines. In music notation, the five lines, the four spaces between the lines, and the spaces above and below the staff are all utilized. The lines and spaces are numbered from bottom to top: the lines 1 through 5, the spaces 1 through 4.

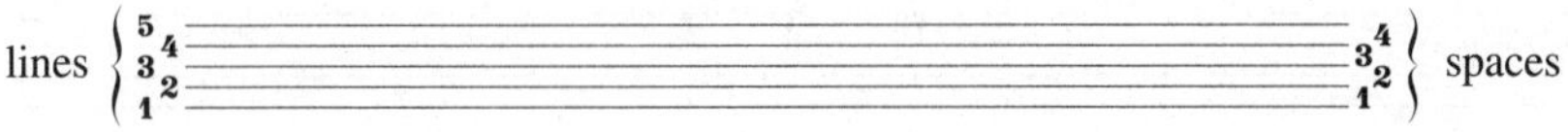

Noteheads

The lines and spaces of the staff, from the bottom to the top, indicate successively higher pitches. In technical terms, **pitch** is the frequency at which a given sound vibrates. The faster the vibration, the higher the pitch is said to be. (A more detailed explanation of the physical characteristics of sound is given in Appendix H.)

Noteheads are the small oval shapes drawn on the staff to represent particular pitches. They may appear either on a line or in a space, as in the following staff. Notice that the second notehead represents a slightly higher pitch than the first one, since the third space is above the third line.

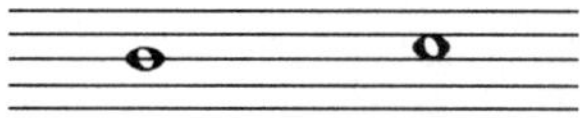

EXERCISE 1•8

In Exercise 1-1, you were asked to practice drawing notes on a single line. Look back at that effort now. Are your noteheads clearly on the line? In order to indicate pitch, noteheads must be placed exactly on a line or in a space. Practice notehead placement once more, this time on the staff, by drawing the following noteheads. Remember to make the noteheads oval rather than round, and to draw them small enough so that they sit clearly centered either in a space or on a line.

1.

2.

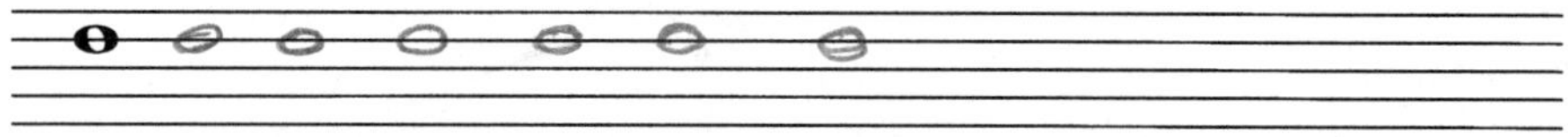

3.

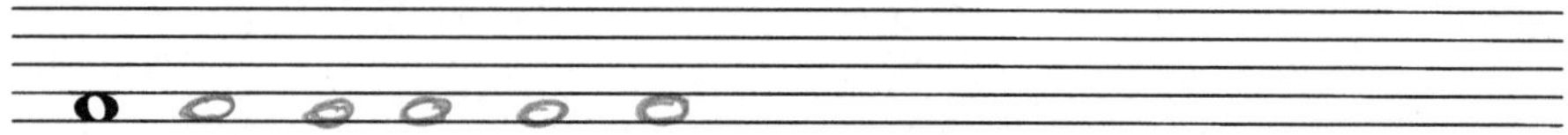

4.

1. L H
2. L L–?
3. H H
4. L H

I L ⅄H
 L L
 H ⅃H
 H L

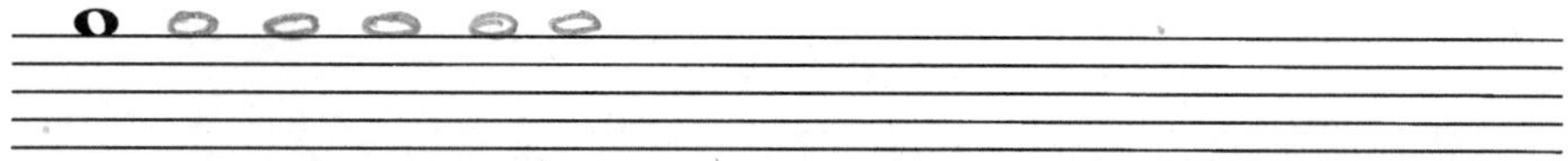

Musical Problem

Your instructor will play, in random order, various two-note sequences from examples 1 through 12 below. Listen carefully to each of the sequences, and indicate in the numbered spaces below the examples whether the second note is higher in pitch (*H*) or lower in pitch (*L*) than the first. Remember, these examples are being played in random order.

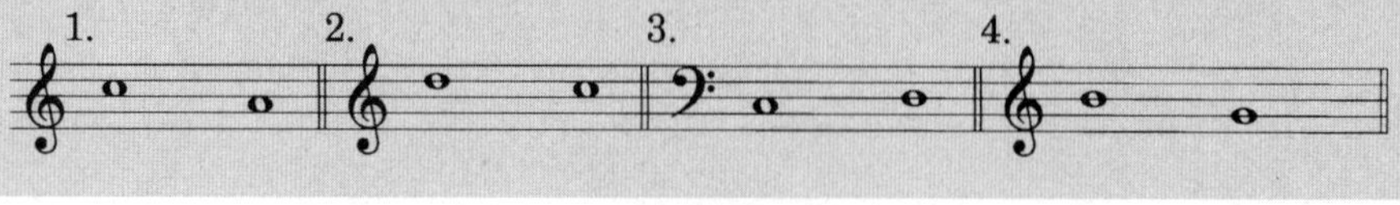

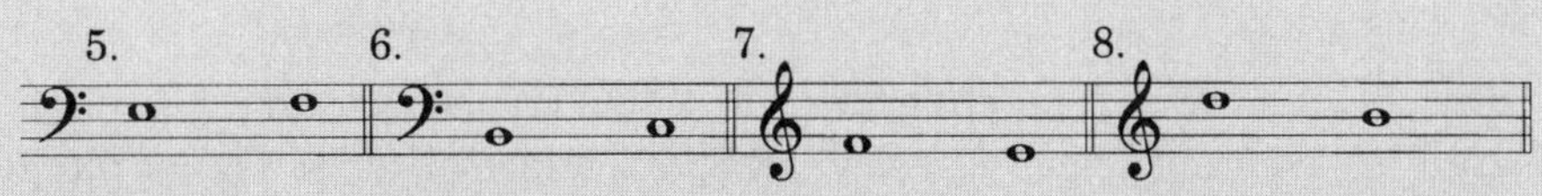

1. ______
2. ______
3. ______
4. ______
5. ______
6. ______
7. ______
8. ______
9. ______
10. ______
11. ______
12. ______

Musical Problem

Your instructor will randomly select and play various three- and four-note sequences from those given below. Listen carefully to each of the sequences, and in the spaces below the examples, indicate whether the last note is higher in pitch (*H*) or lower in pitch (*L*) than the first.

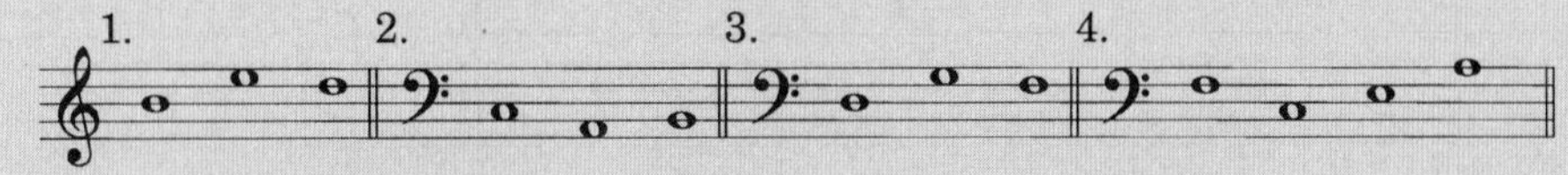

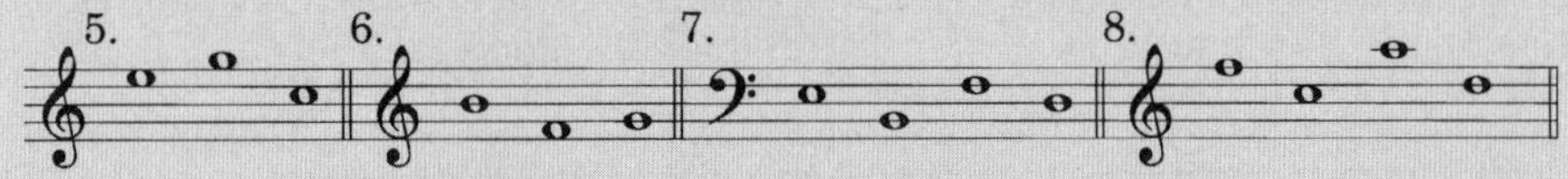

1. ______
2. ______
3. ______
4. ______
5. ______
6. ______
7. ______
8. ______
9. ______
10. ______
11. ______
12. ______

Clefs

The first seven letters of the alphabet (A through G) are used to name pitches. The staff by itself does not represent any particular set (or range) of pitches; this is the function of **clef** signs. Each clef sign locates a particular pitch on the staff. Two clef signs are used the most: treble clef and bass clef.

The Treble Clef

The **treble clef,** or **G clef,** identifies the second line of the staff as the location for the note G that is five notes above middle C (the C approximately in the middle of the piano keyboard). Notice that the lower part of the treble clef sign encircles the second line:

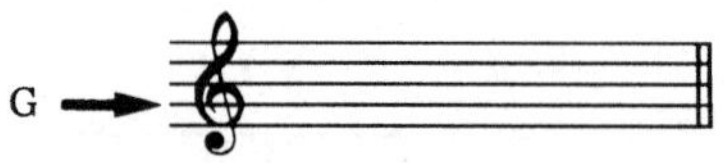

EXERCISE 1•9

Practice drawing the treble clef sign. It is made by first drawing a vertical line and then drawing the remainder of the clef, starting at the top of the vertical line. Remember to encircle the second line with the lower part of the clef.

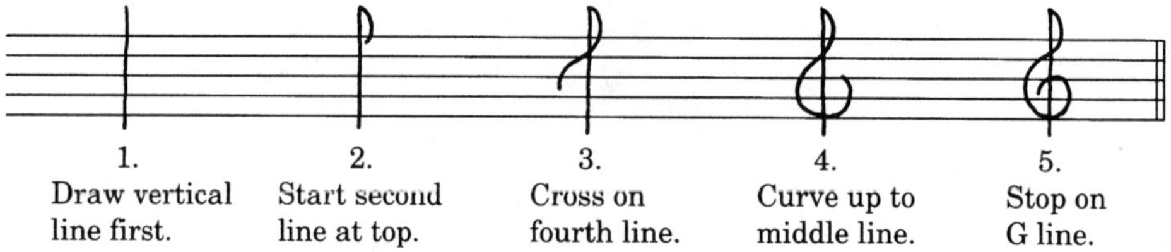

Once a particular pitch is identified on the staff by a clef sign, the other pitches on that staff follow automatically in alphabetical sequence. Remember, only the first seven letters of the alphabet are used. After that, the sequence of letters repeats.

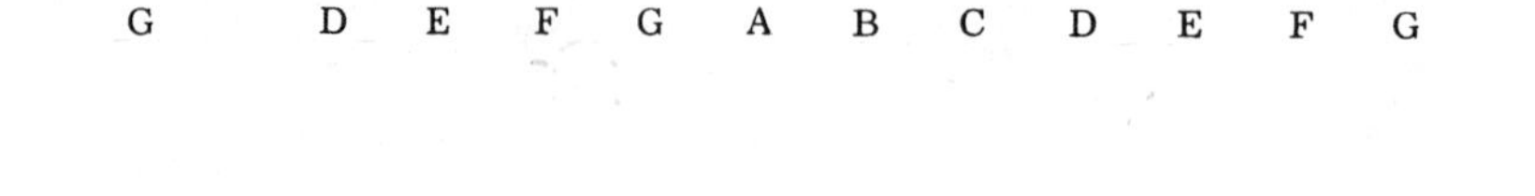

EXERCISE 1•10

Identify by letter name the following pitches in the treble clef.

1. 

G A B F E D C D E F

2. 

G B D F E C A F D E

3. 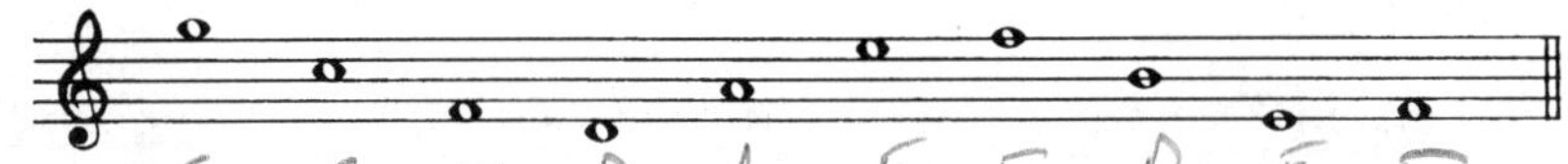

G C F D A E F B E F

EXERCISE 1•11

Identify by letter name the pitches of the following songs.

"Down in the Valley"

1. 

G C D E C C E D C D

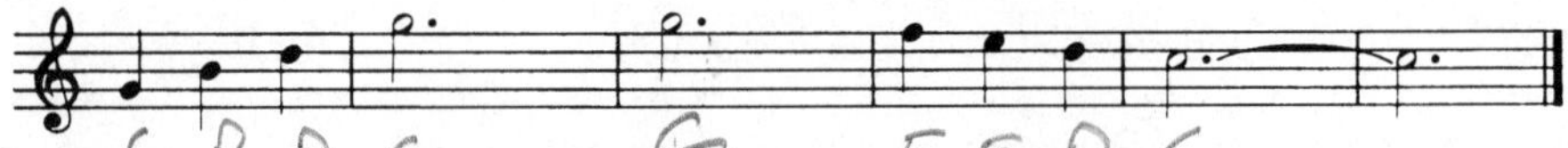

G B D G G F E D C

Foster: "Camptown Races"

2. 

G G G E G A G E E D E D G

G G E G A G E D D E D C

"Wayfaring Stranger"

3.

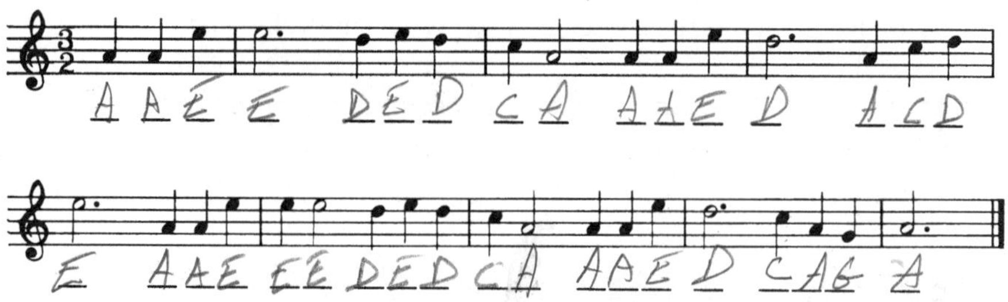

> ### *Musical Problem*
>
> Sing the songs in Exercise 1–11 using the syllable *la.* Then try singing them, in rhythm, with letter names. For each song, see whether some pitches occur more frequently than others, and identify the pitch that seems to produce the most restful feeling or clearest sense of completion. Once you are comfortable singing these melodies, try playing one or more of them at the keyboard. Your teacher or another student in the class may be able to provide an accompaniment while you play.

The Bass Clef

The **bass clef,** or **F clef,** identifies the fourth line of the staff as the location for the note F that is five notes below middle C on the piano.

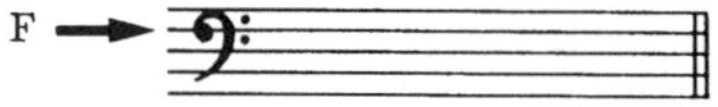

EXERCISE 1•12

Practice drawing the bass clef sign. It is made by first drawing a dot on the fourth line; then drawing the curved sign, beginning at the dot; and finally placing two dots to the right of the sign, one just above the fourth line and one just below.

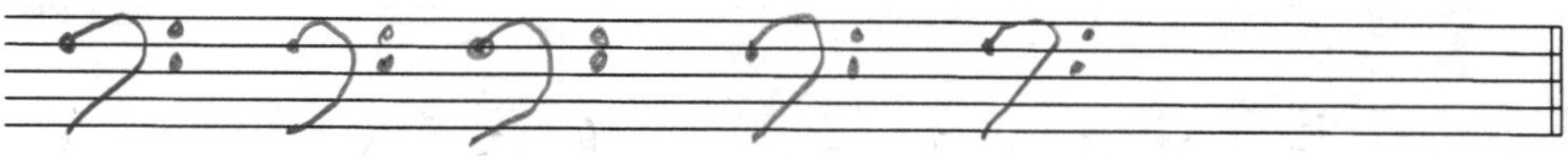

As with the treble clef, the pitches of the bass clef are arranged in alphabetical sequence.

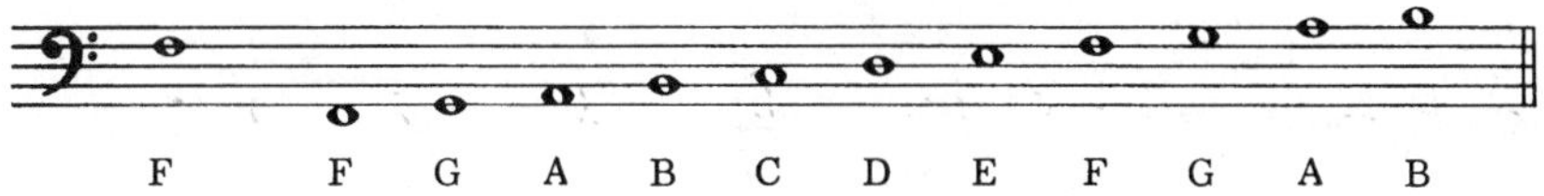

EXERCISE 1•13

Identify by letter name the following pitches in the bass clef.

1. 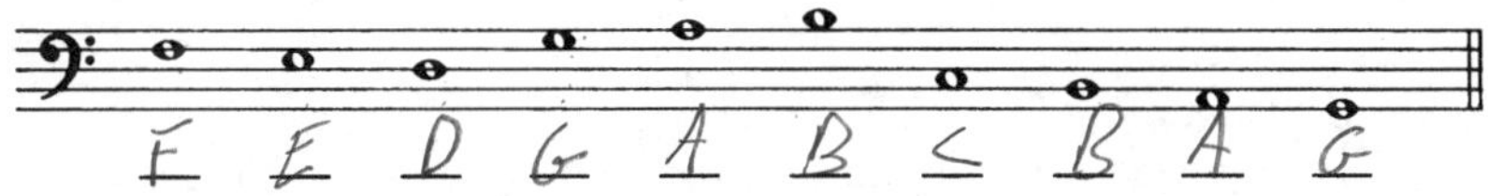

2. 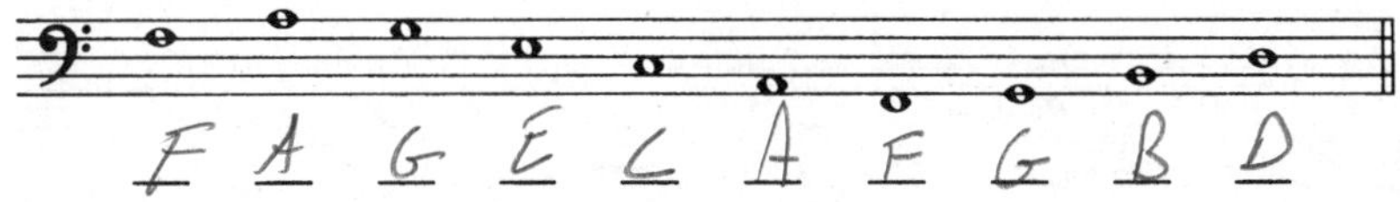

3. 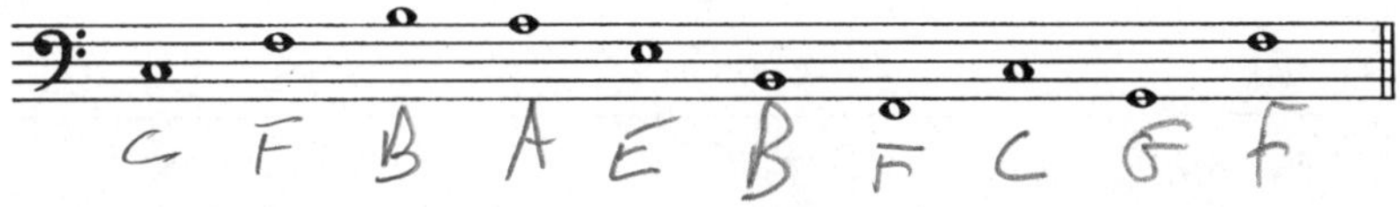

EXERCISE 1•14

Identify by letter name the pitches of the following songs.

"Nine Hundred Miles"

1. 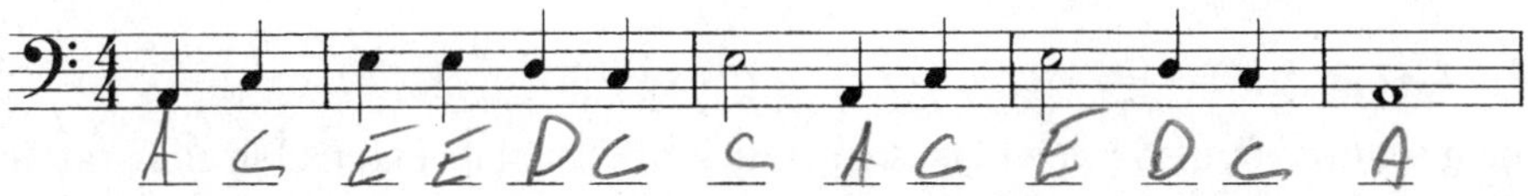

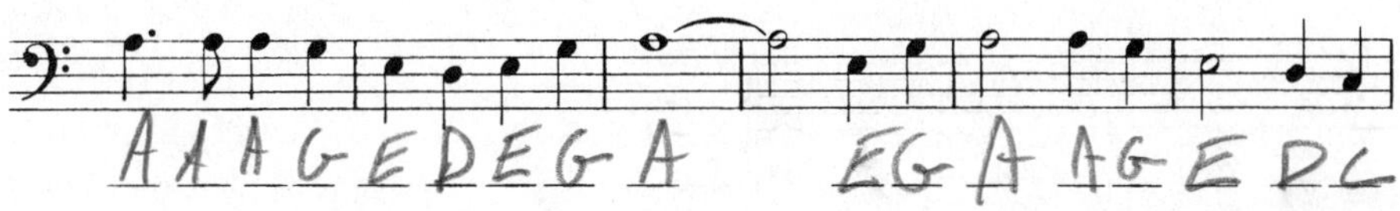

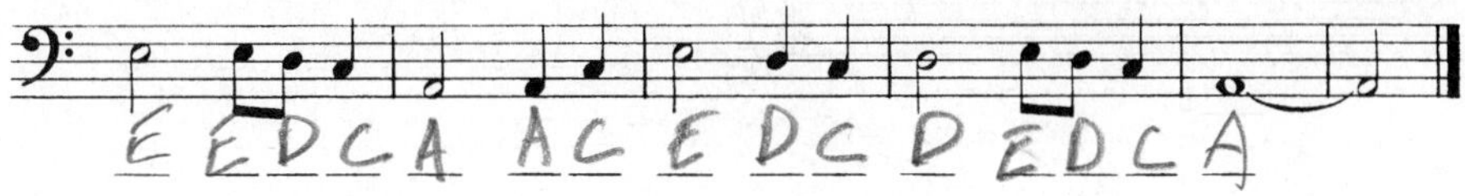

"Skip to My Lou"

2. 

"Mexican Folk Song"

3. 

> ***Musical Problem***
>
> Sing the songs in Exercise 1–14, first using the syllable *la,* then with the letter names in rhythm. In each song, identify the pitch that seems to produce the most restful feeling or clearest sense of completion. Then, try playing one or more of these songs at the keyboard. Your teacher or another student may be able to provide a suitable accompaniment.

The Great Staff

The **great staff,** also known as the grand staff, consists of a treble clef staff and a bass clef staff joined together by a vertical line and a brace.

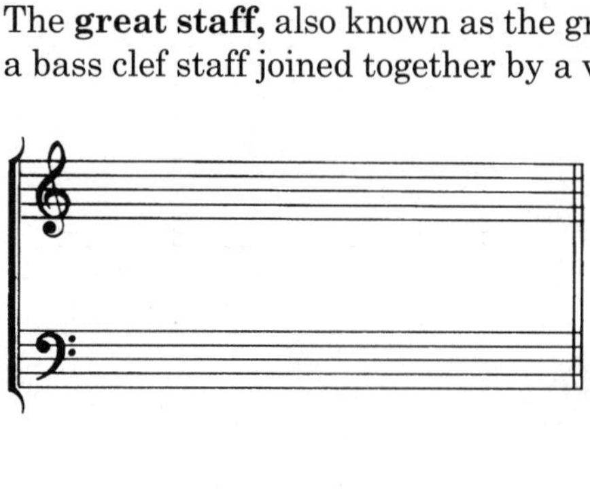

The great staff is used primarily for piano music. It is also sometimes used for choral music or any other type of music requiring a range of pitches too wide for a single staff.

In the following example, notice that one pitch, *middle C*—so-called because of its location in the middle of the piano keyboard and of the great staff—does not touch either staff. Instead, it sits on a short line, called a *ledger line*, that is not part of either staff. Ledger lines are explained in more detail on page 68.

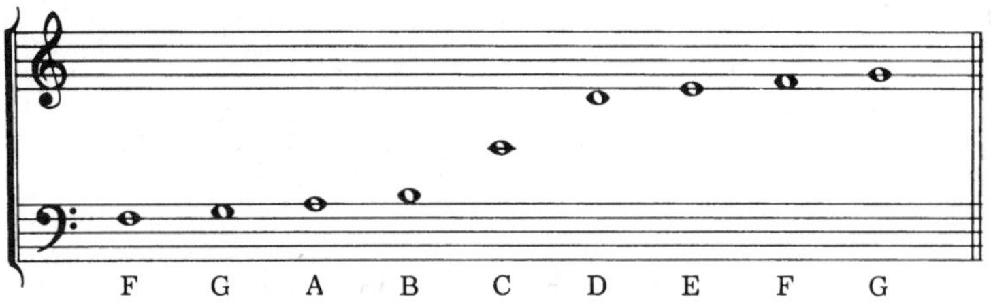

In actual music, however, middle C does not appear, as it does here, in the center of the great staff. Rather, it is located closer to one staff or the other.

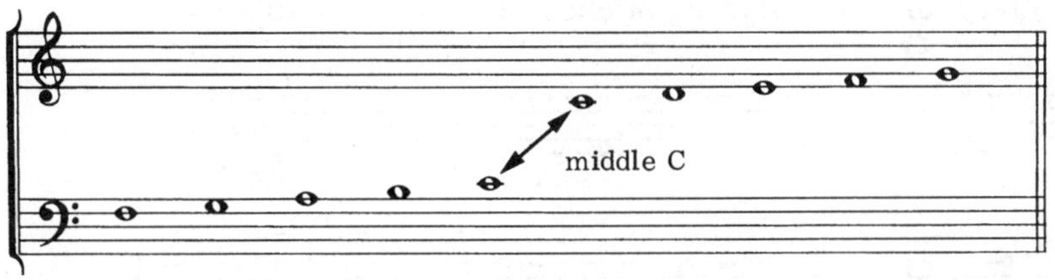

In piano music, the notes on the treble staff are usually played by the right hand, and the notes on the bass staff are played by the left hand. As shown in the following example, the location of middle C indicates which hand is to play it.

Bach: Courante from French Suite No. 2

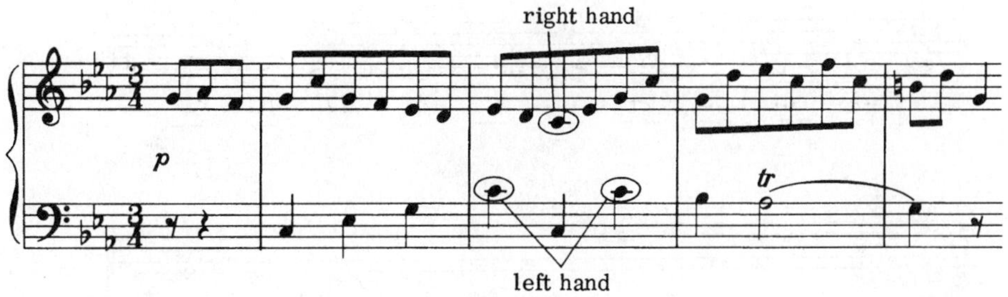

In choral music, the location of middle C indicates which voice should sing it.

Bach: Chorale from Cantata No. 180

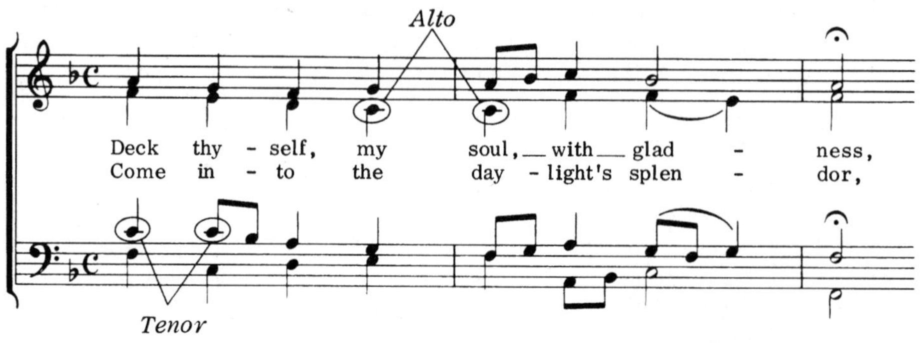
Alto
Deck thy - self, my soul, — with — glad - ness,
Come in - to the day - light's splen - dor,
Tenor

EXERCISE 1•15

Identify by letter name the following pitches on the great staff.

1.

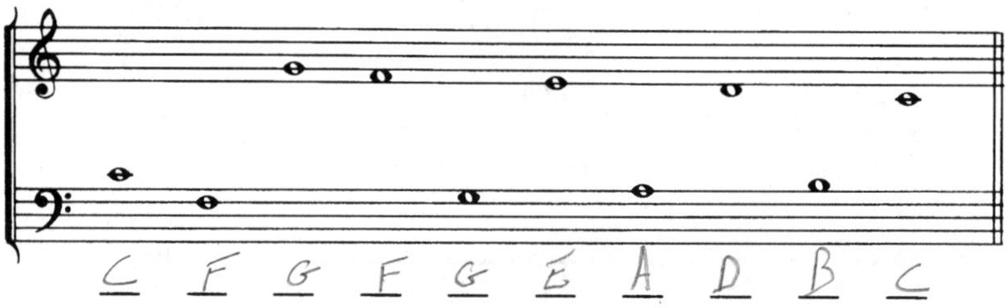
C F G F G E A D B C

2.

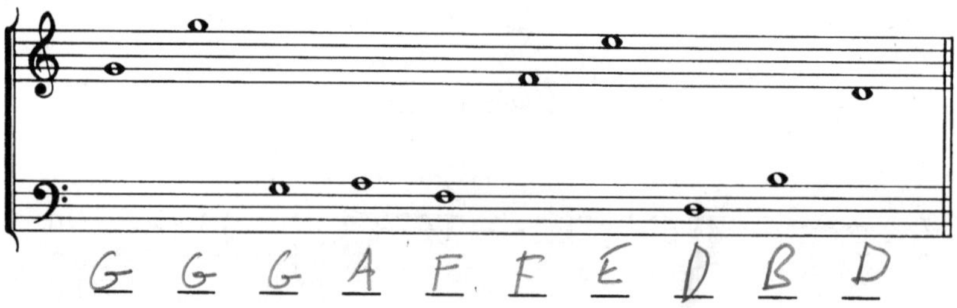
G G G A F F E D B D

3.

A C F B G C B F C E

The Keyboard

When you first begin to learn music theory, it is enormously helpful to know your way around the keyboard. Either the piano or the electronic keyboard will do well. With either of them you will be able both to hear and see concepts of musical sound like intervals, scales, and triads. While it is possible to do this to some extent on other instruments, such as the fingerboard of the guitar, it is far easiest to work with these concepts at the piano keyboard. This section will introduce the keyboard and help you begin to understand it. Future chapters will frequently refer to the keyboard when clarifying particular points. Some exercises will help you become familiar with the keyboard.

The standard piano keyboard has 88 keys: 52 white ones and 36 black ones. (Synthesizers and electronic keyboards are generally smaller, commonly five-and-one-half octaves, as opposed to slightly more than eight octaves for the piano.) The black keys on both pianos and synthesizers are arranged in alternating groups of twos and threes. Moving from right to left on all keyboards produces successively lower pitches, while moving from left to right creates successively higher ones.

The White Keys

As explained earlier, only the first seven letters of the alphabet are used to name pitches. These seven letters name the white keys of the piano, beginning at the left end of the keyboard with A and successively repeating the sequence A through G up to the other end of the keyboard.

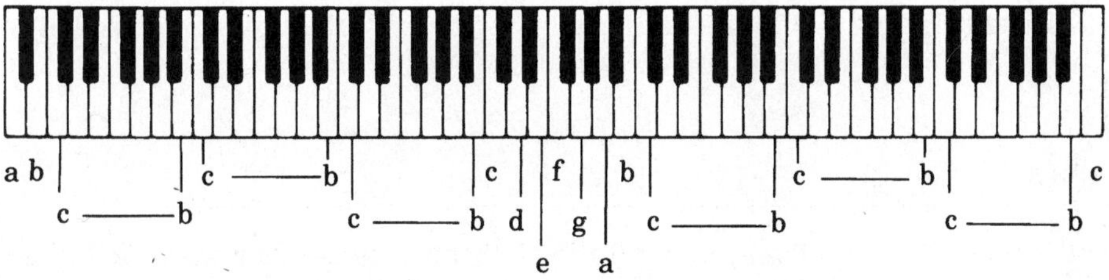

Learning the keyboard can be made easier by locating and remembering two landmarks. The first is the note C. In the following illustration, notice that the note C always occurs immediately to the left of a group of two black keys. The pitch called *middle* C is the one approximately in the middle of the keyboard.

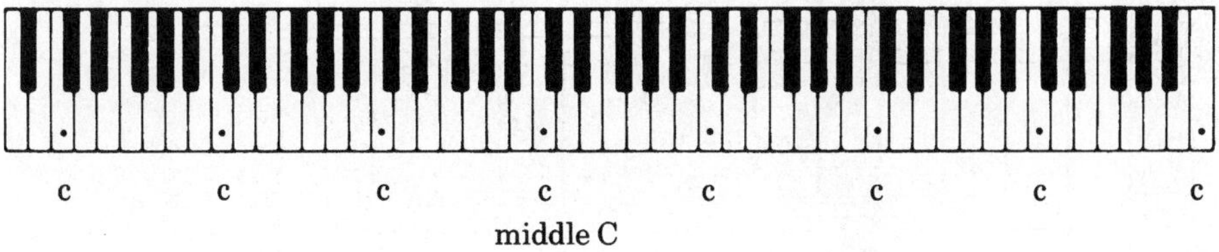

The second landmark to locate is F. This is the pitch that occurs immediately to the left of a group of three black keys.

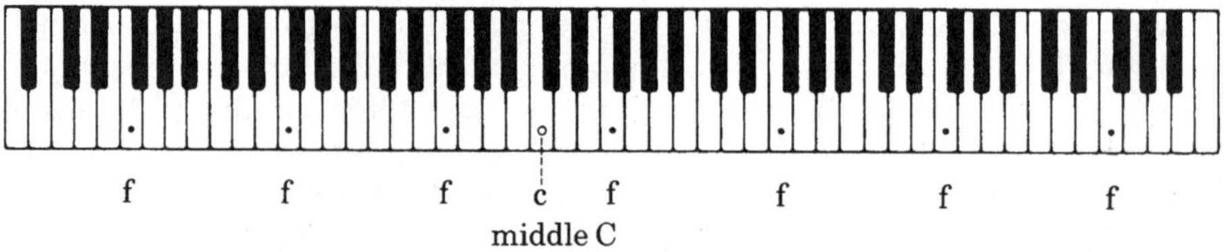

With these two landmarks you should be able to learn the rest of the keyboard more easily. Remember, too, that only the letters A through G are used, and that the alphabetical sequence runs from left to right.

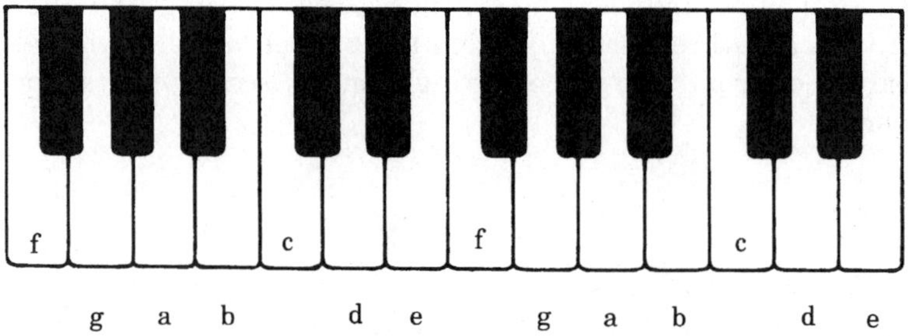

It is sometimes helpful to memorize other landmarks such as G or B. But be careful not to rely too heavily on landmarks at the expense of learning all of the keys equally well. Landmarks are convenient at the beginning, but you only know the keyboard when you can name any key at random.

EXERCISE 1•16

Locate and write each given pitch on the keyboard. Remember that each pitch will occur more than one place, since these keyboards are greater than an octave. When you have written all the pitches, practice finding and playing them on the piano.

1. f, c, g, d, b

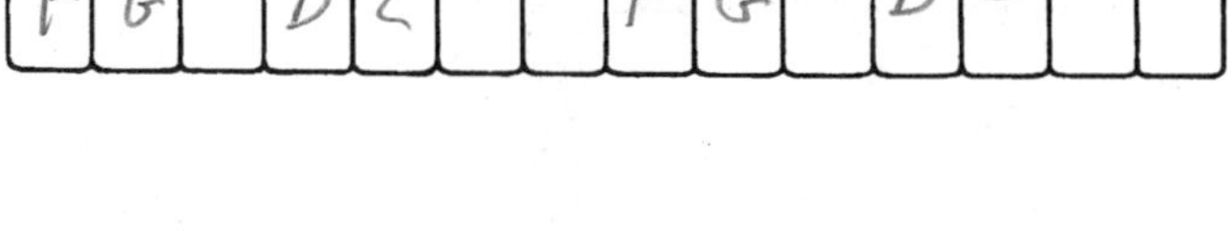

2. g, d, e, a, c

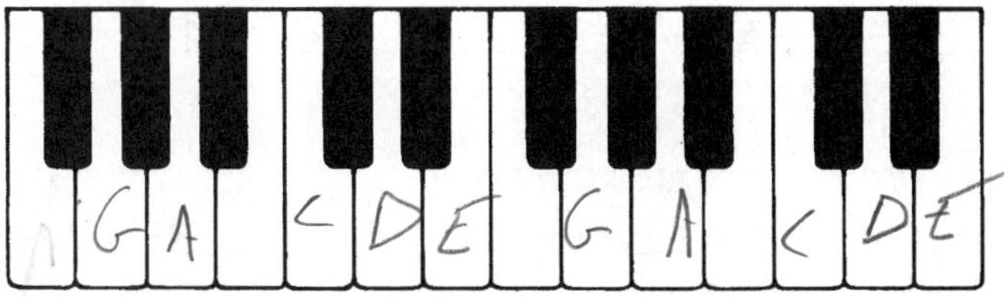

3. a, e, b, f, d

Musical Problem

The following pitch sequences are the opening notes of four songs you may know. Find and play these pitches at the piano, and name each song if you can. When you have completed your work at the piano, practice singing each song fragment with letter names.

Name ______________________

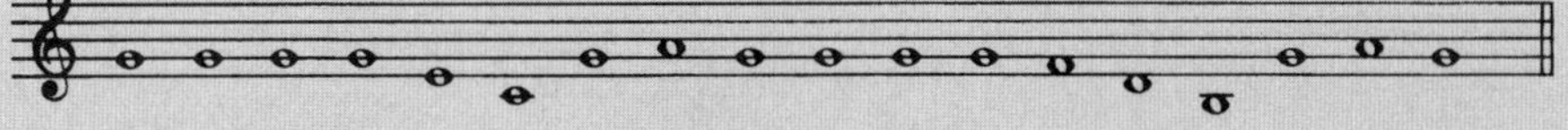

Name ______________________

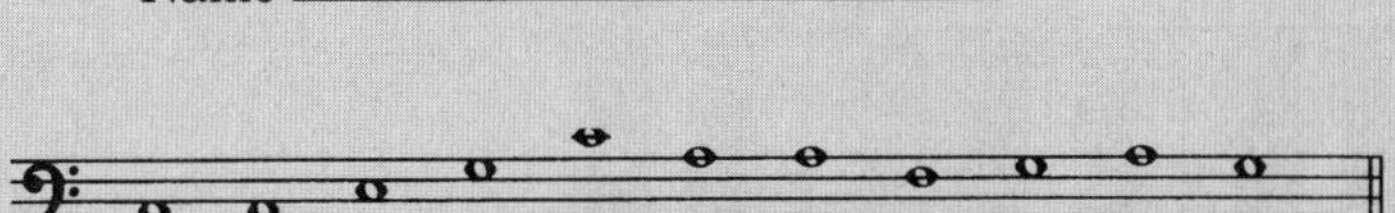

Name ______________________

(continued)

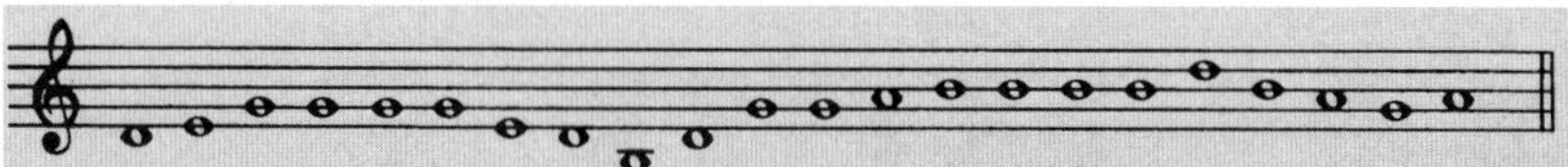

Name ____________________

EXERCISE 1•17

Identify by letter name the pitches given. Then, write each pitch once on the keyboard that follows. Finally, find and play each of the pitches at the piano.

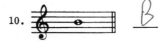

1.  D

2.  F

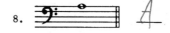

3. 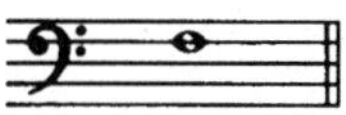 F

4.  A

5.  B

6.  C

7.  G

8. 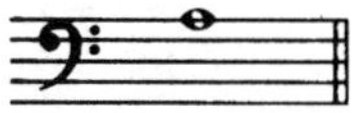 A

9.  E

10. 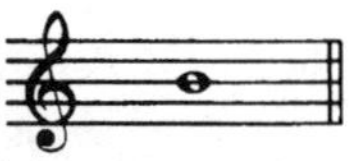 B

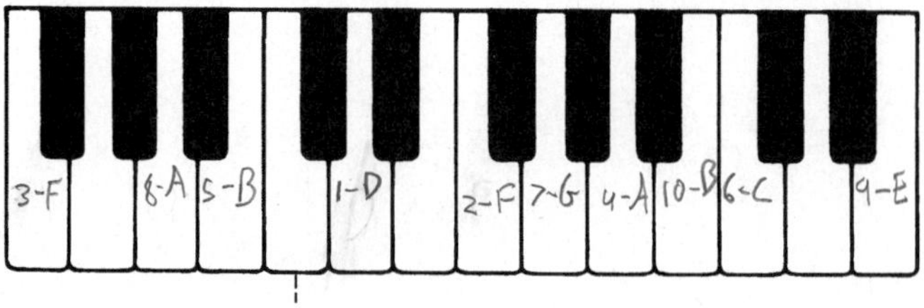

Middle C

The Black Keys

The black keys of the piano are named in relation to the white keys that they stand between. Furthermore, each black key can be identified by two different names. For instance, the black key between F and G is called either *F sharp* (F♯) or *G flat* (G♭). F sharp identifies that black key as the pitch *above F*, while G flat tells us it's the pitch *below G*.

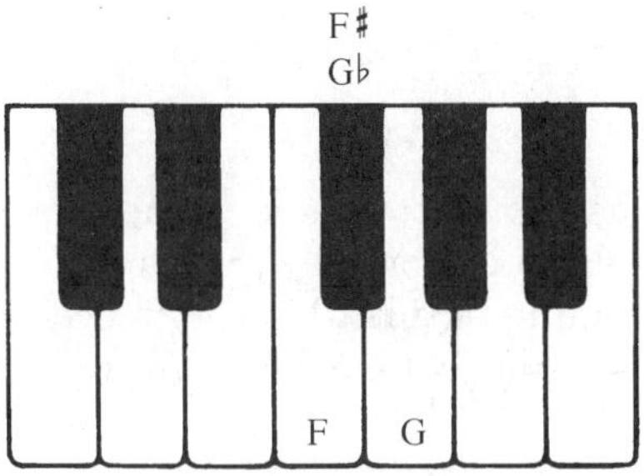

EXERCISE 1•18

Locate the following pitches on the black keys of the keyboard by drawing a line from each pitch name to the appropriate places on the keyboard. Remember that each pitch will occur in more than one place, since these keyboards are greater than an octave. When you have located all the pitches, practice finding and playing them on the piano.

1. C♯, G♭, B♭

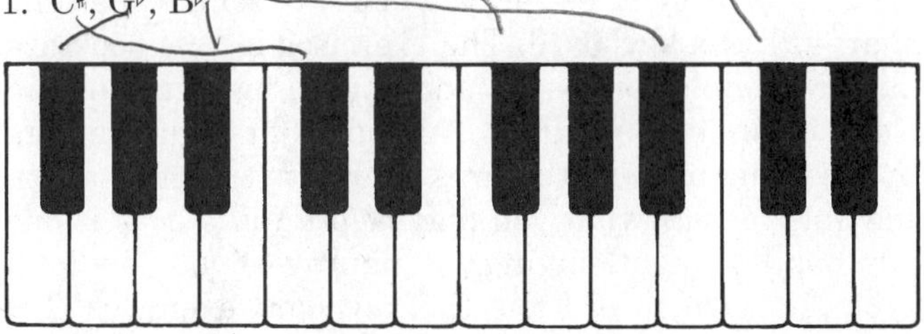

2. E♭, F♯, A♭

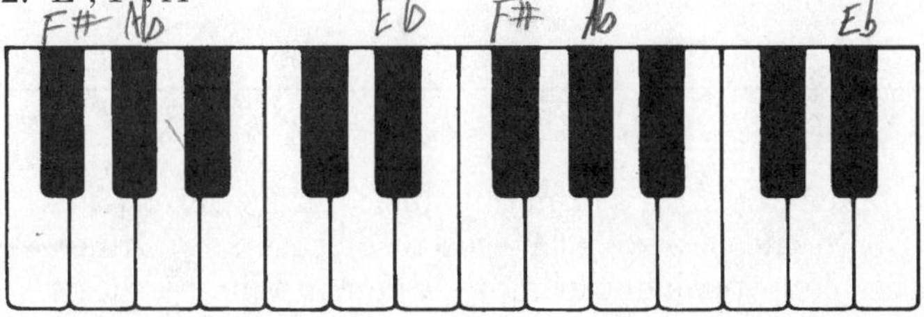

3. D♭, D♯, G♯

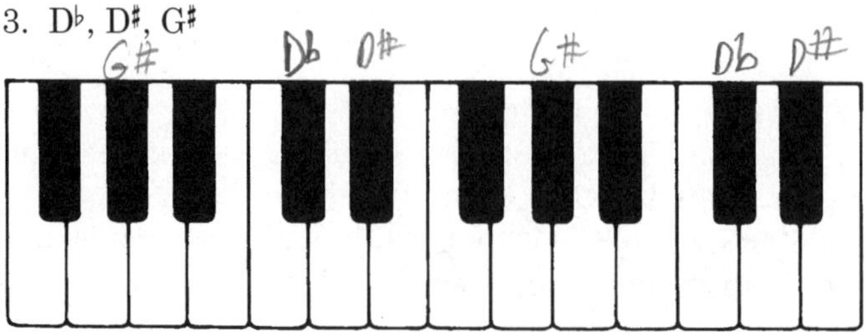

Focus

When music is written down on paper it can be thought of as a storage and retrieval system. In this system, musical information is stored by the composer in a code of shapes and symbols. A performer wishing to turn this written code back into sound must understand not only which musical elements are being dealt with but also how they are encoded.

The key to reading and writing Western music is to realize that the written music of our culture focuses on and encodes two major musical elements: pitch, which is the basis of melody and harmony; and duration, through which the rhythm flows. While a lot of additional information is given in music notation, these two elements—rhythm and pitch—are the primary ones.

As you probably are aware by now, the piano or electric keyboard is extremely useful in helping us visualize abstract musical concepts like intervals, scales, and chords. Knowing the keyboard is also important for a number of other reasons, such as understanding harmony, learning voicing for arranging, and composing. Many musicians study piano or synthesizer as a second instrument because of this versatility. These people feel that improving their abilities on the keyboard helps them to *understand* the music better.

Even if you do not play piano or synthesizer, you should spend some time each day becoming familiar with the keyboard. The exercises in this book are useful for this purpose, as are simple songbooks and beginning sight-singing books. Another good place to begin is Appendix D, "Melodies for Sight-Singing and Playing." Remember, becoming musical requires your active participation. Remember, too, that being able to *hear* what you play *before you play it* is one sign of a good musician. Your skill at sight-singing will improve if you do it for a few minutes each time you sit down to practice the keyboard exercises. Try singing each exercise before you play it. Then play it. Then sing it again. This may seem difficult at first, but you will get better as you practice, and the skill you will learn will be invaluable.

Musical Problem

Bring to class a piece of music borrowed from the music library or a friend. Your teacher may wish to choose several pieces to discuss as a group. Which musical symbols can you identify at this point? What do they mean? What is their purpose? Can you see that reading a piece of music is in some ways similar to reading a map?

Musical Problem

The following rhythms and melodies are taken from Appendices A, B, and D. Clap and count the rhythms, and try to sing the melodies using a neutral syllable such as *la.* (In Chapter 4 you will learn another way to sing melodies called moveable *do.*) After you have tried to sing these melodies, play them on the keyboard to check for accuracy. These three appendices contain a lot of practice material. As you continue with this book, it would be extremely helpful to practice one or two rhythms and melodies at the beginning of each study session.

Rhythms

1. 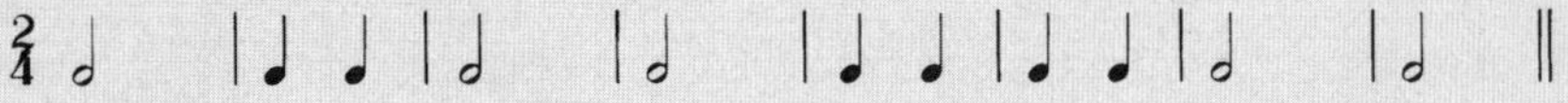

2. 

3. 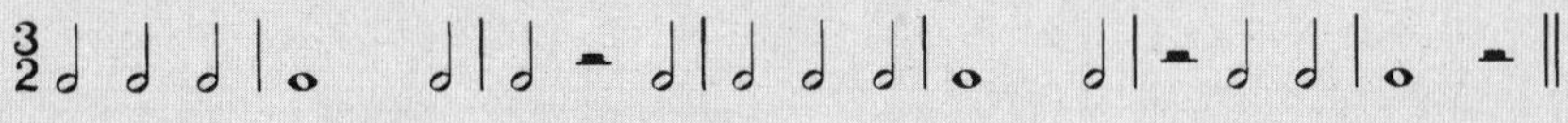

4. 

5. 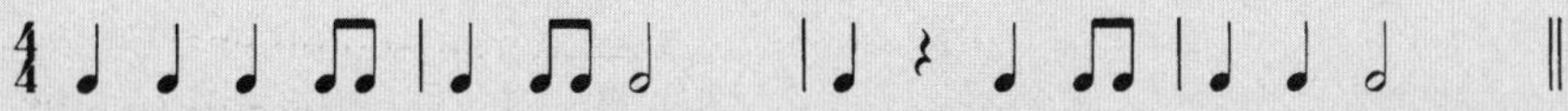

Moderate **Asia**

6. 

Fast African

7. 

Melodies

1. 

2. 

3. 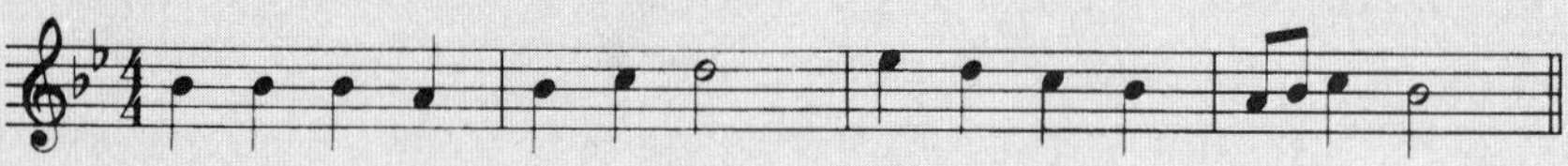

4. 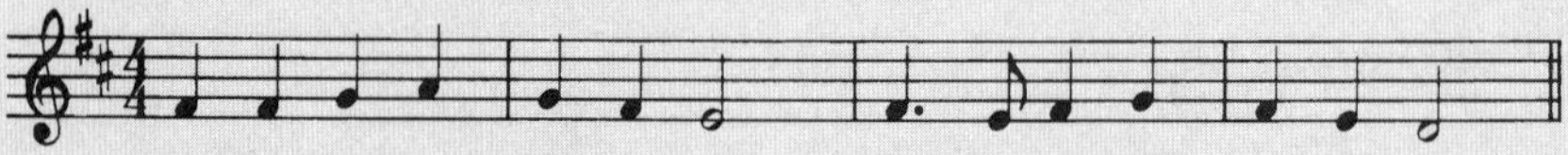

5. 

Chapter 2

Rhythm

Compound Meter

In addition to the two-part subdivision of simple meter that we learned in Chapter 1, there is another common way to subdivide the pulse. This is a subdivision into three equal parts, and is called **compound meter**. The most common compound meter is $\frac{6}{8}$.

Compound meter may be confusing at first because the $\frac{6}{8}$ meter signature seems to indicate that there are six beats in a measure and the eighth note gets a beat. This is true, but the way $\frac{6}{8}$ meter is normally played groups the six eighth notes into two sets of three. As a result, $\frac{6}{8}$ meter "feels" like duple meter, with the pulse represented by a dotted quarter note and with each beat divisible into three parts:

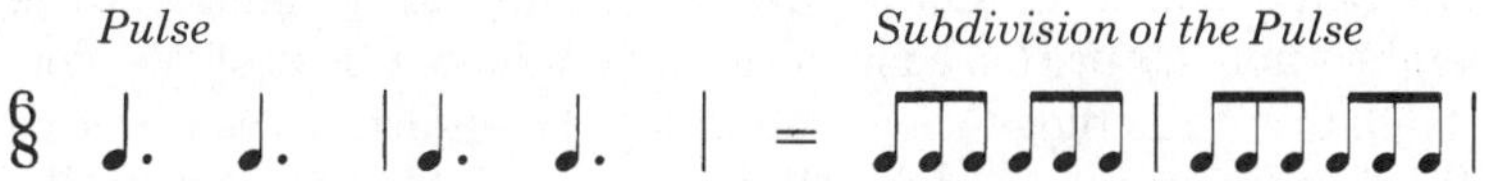

The correct term for $\frac{6}{8}$ meter, therefore, is *compound duple*.

Practice clapping the following pattern in $\frac{6}{8}$ meter. It will help you begin to feel the subdivisions of compound duple meter. Be sure to emphasize the accented notes.

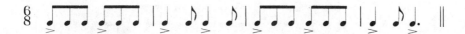

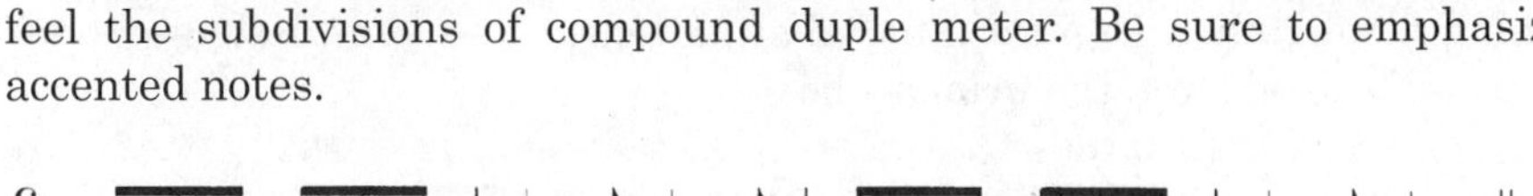

A problem that often arises is how to distinguish between $\frac{3}{4}$ meter and $\frac{6}{8}$ meter, since both contain six eighth notes. The difference is in how the pulse is accented, and can be clearly seen in the following illustration:

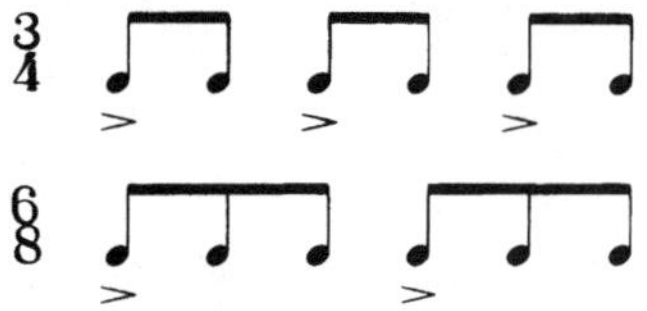

Simple meter: eighth notes (and accents) grouped in twos

Compound meter: eighth notes (and accents) grouped in threes

In a similar way to $\frac{6}{8}$ meter being compound duple, $\frac{9}{8}$ meter is *compound triple* and $\frac{12}{8}$ meter is *compound quadruple*:

$$\frac{9}{8} \quad \text{♩. ♩. ♩. } | \quad = \quad \text{♫♫♫♫♫♫} |$$

$$\frac{12}{8} \quad \text{♩. ♩. ♩. ♩. } | \quad = \quad \text{♫♫♫♫♫♫♫♫} |$$

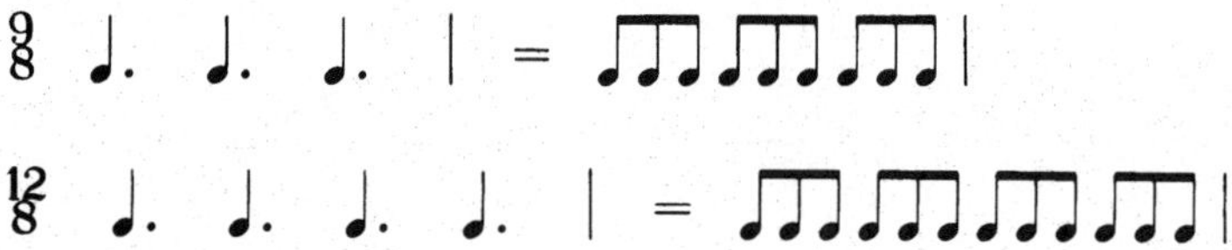

The common compound meters are:

compound duple	$\frac{6}{16} \, (\frac{2}{\text{♪.}})$	$\frac{6}{8} \, (\frac{2}{\text{♩.}})$	$\frac{6}{4} \, (\frac{2}{\text{♩.}})$
compound triple	$\frac{9}{16} \, (\frac{3}{\text{♪.}})$	$\frac{9}{8} \, (\frac{3}{\text{♩.}})$	$\frac{9}{4} \, (\frac{3}{\text{♩.}})$
compound quadruple	$\frac{12}{16} \, (\frac{4}{\text{♪.}})$	$\frac{12}{8} \, (\frac{4}{\text{♩.}})$	$\frac{12}{4} \, (\frac{4}{\text{♩.}})$

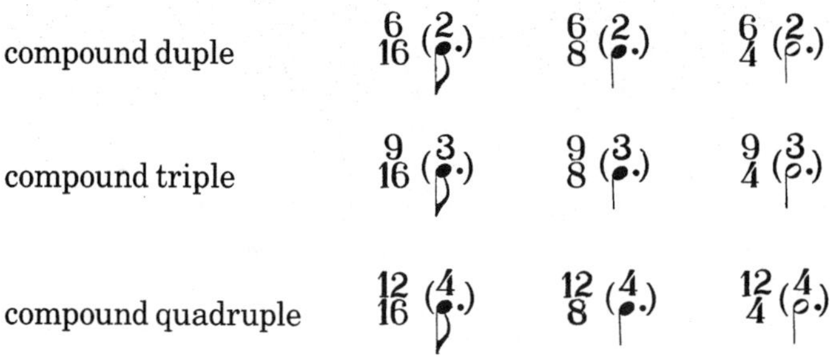

The interesting thing about compound meter, of course, is that there are really two different beats going on simultaneously inside of it. There is the faster beat of six eighth notes, but there is also a bigger, slower beat of two dotted quarters in a measure. This bigger beat combines the eighth notes into two groups of three. While this may be a difficult concept to understand initially, most people can hear it very easily. Look at the rhythm to "For He's a Jolly Good Fellow," which follows. Have some class members sing the melody while others clap either the eighth-note beat or the dotted-quarter beat. Notice how everything fits together. In most musical situations, the slower dotted-quarter beat is usually considered the primary beat.

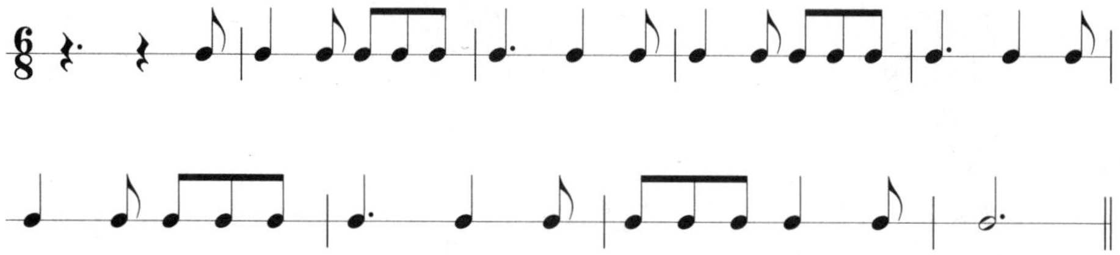

> **Musical Problem**
>
> Try to sing the melody to "For He's a Jolly Good Fellow" (or some other melody in compound meter), while beating the eighth notes on your desk with one hand and the dotted quarters with the other. This is not easy at first, but an understanding of these interlocking qualities of rhythm makes our performances smoother and more musical.

EXERCISE 2•1

Identify the meter and indicate the note value that represents the pulse for each of the following compound meter signatures.

EXAMPLE: 6/8 duple meter / dotted quarter-note pulse

1. 6/4 duple meter / dotted 1/2 note
2. 12/4 quadruple meter / dotted 1/2 note
3. 6/16 duple meter / dotted 1/8 th note
4. 12/16 quadruple meter / dotted 1/8 note
5. 9/8 triple meter / dotted 1/4 note
6. 9/4 triple meter / dotted half note
7. 12/8 quadruple meter / dotted 1/4 note
8. 9/16 triple meter / dotted 1/8 note

EXERCISE 2•2

For each of the following compound meters, write one measure of notes representing the pulse and one measure of notes representing the subdivision of the pulse. Follow the example.

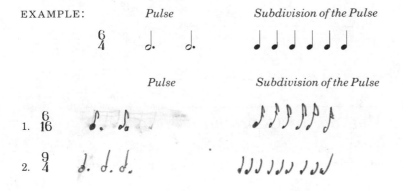

EXAMPLE: *Pulse* — *Subdivision of the Pulse*

6/4

Pulse — *Subdivision of the Pulse*

1. 6/16

2. 9/4

3. 12/16

4. 12/4

5. 9/16

EXERCISE 2•3

In each of the following sequences, identify the meter name and the note value that represents the pulse. Then indicate measures by placing bar lines in the appropriate places in each example. When you have finished, either play each rhythmic pattern on the piano or other instrument, or sing it.

1. 6/4 

2. 9/8 

3. 6/16 

4. 9/4 

5. 12/8 

	Meter Name	*Note Value*
1. 6/4	____________	____________
2. 9/8	____________	____________
3. 6/16	____________	____________
4. 9/4	____________	____________
5. 12/8	____________	____________

A Counting Method for Compound Meters

Remember from our discussion of simple meter that the basic beat in either simple or compound meter is counted the same: "one, two, three, four."

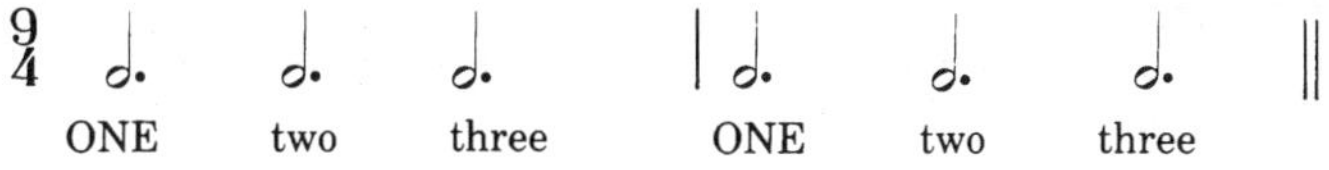

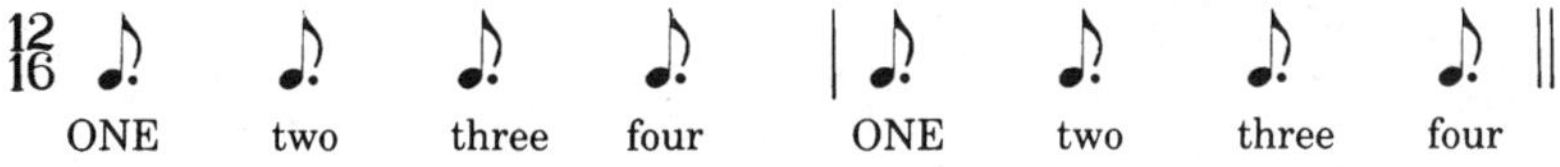

Subdivisions of the Beat

Since compound meters are divided into three equal parts rather than two, a different set of syllables is used. These are *la* and *le*. Practice counting the following examples in compound meter until you feel comfortable with them. Remember that this is a different system from the one used to count simple meters. It may be confusing at first, but it will become easier with practice.

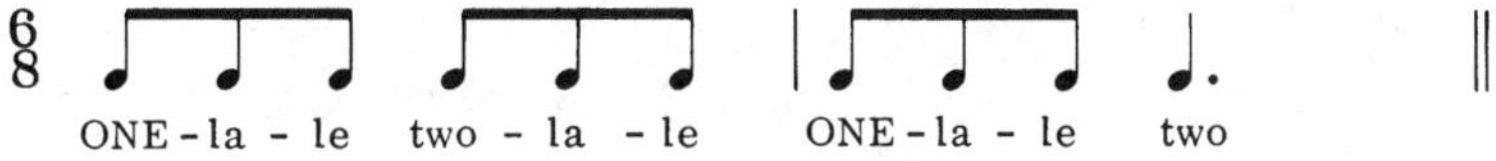

Some people prefer to count the eighth-notes (or other pulse value) in compound meter. In $\frac{6}{8}$ in this system, for instance, you would say <u>1</u>–2–3–<u>4</u>–5–6, emphasizing the 1 and 4.

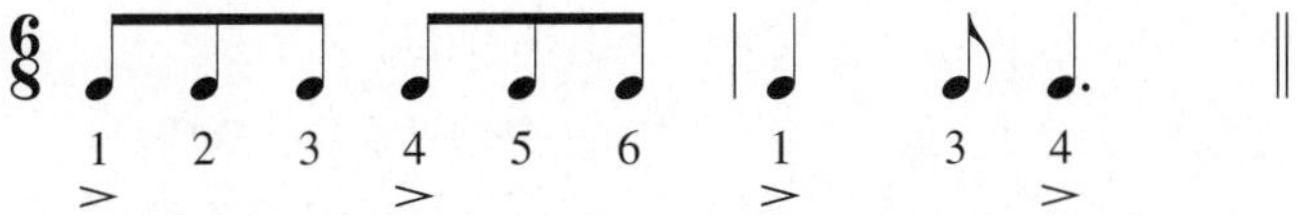

We will continue to use *la* and *le,* but either system works equally well, and you should use the one that your teacher prefers.

When a further subdivision of the beat in compound meter is required—that is, when you need to indicate one-sixth of the beat—the syllable *ta* is used.

The following examples can be tongue twisters at first, but will grow easier as you practice them.

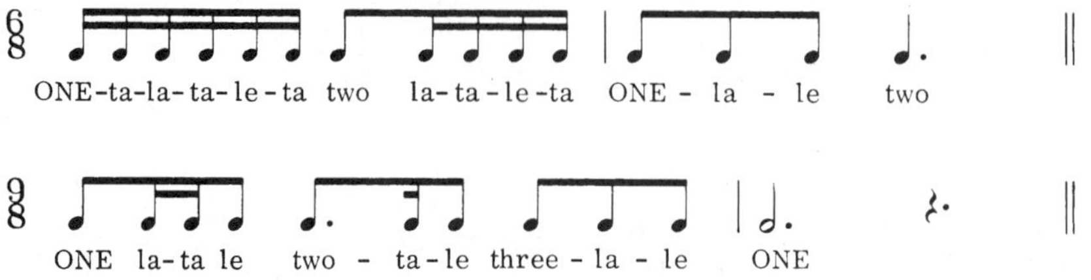

EXERCISE 2•4

Individually and as a class, clap and count the following rhythmic examples in compound meter. You probably know these pieces and that should help you decide whether you are performing them correctly or not. Begin by saying two measures of the divided beat (1-la-le 2-la-le or $\overset{>}{1}$-2-3 $\overset{>}{4}$-5-6) aloud before clapping. When you are comfortable with the counting system, also try playing the rhythms on an instrument or keyboard while counting mentally. Remember always to keep the basic beat steady.

"For He's a Jolly Good Fellow"

1.

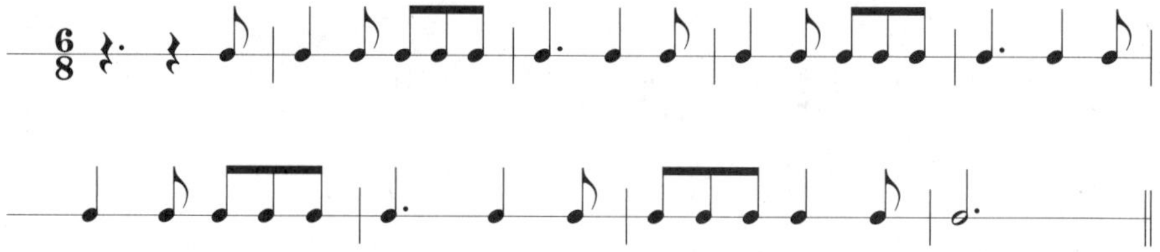

"Down in the Valley"

2.

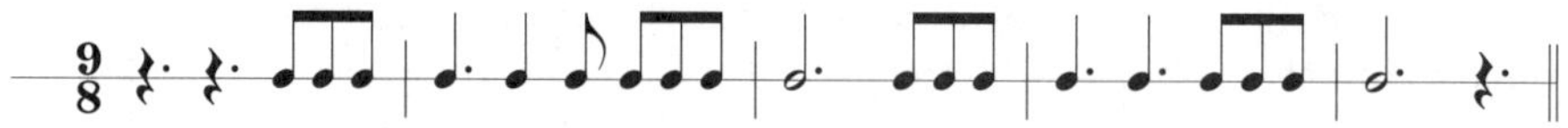

"Home on the Range"

3.

EXERCISE 2•5

Write in the counting syllables for each of the following rhythms. Then, practice clapping and saying the syllables aloud. Be sure to keep the beat steady.

1. 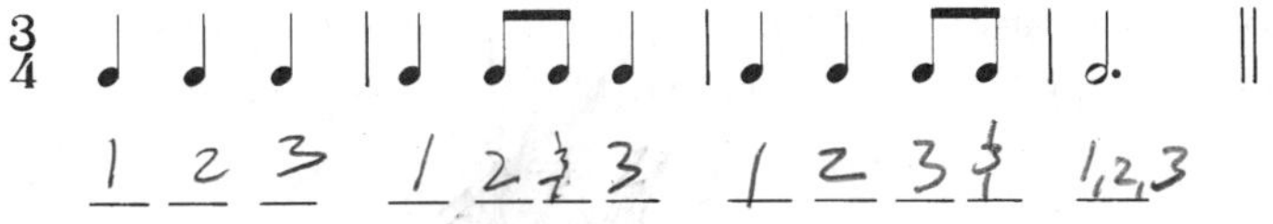

2. 

3. 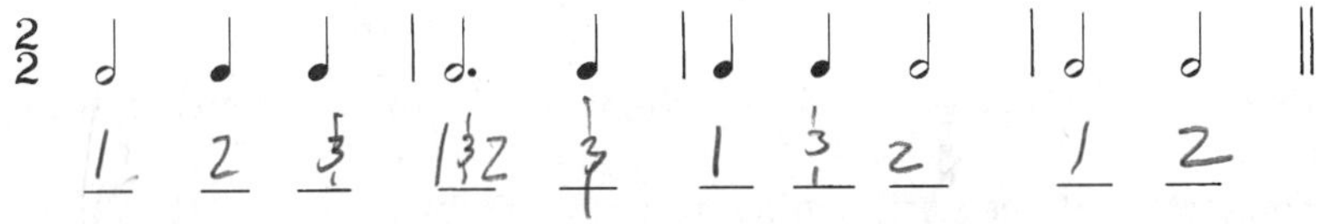

4. 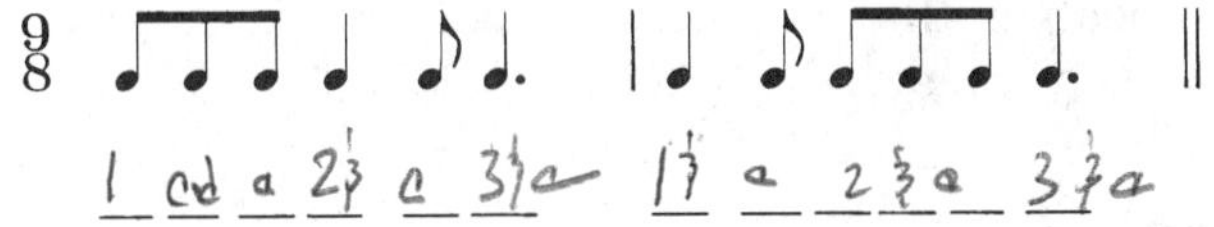

5. 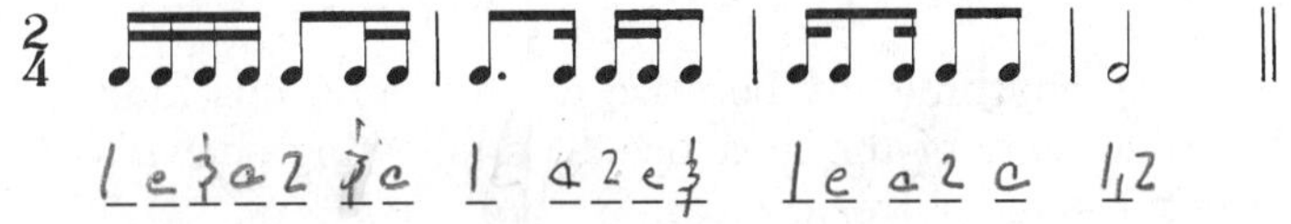

EXERCISE 2•6

Give the correct terminology for each of the following meter signatures.

EXAMPLE: $\frac{3}{2}$ simple triple

1. $\frac{3}{4}$ ____________________
2. $\frac{4}{2}$ ____________________
3. $\frac{6}{8}$ ____________________
4. $\frac{4}{4}$ ____________________
5. $\frac{12}{16}$ ____________________
6. $\frac{6}{4}$ ____________________
7. $\frac{12}{4}$ ____________________
8. $\frac{2}{2}$ ____________________
9. $\frac{9}{4}$ ____________________
10. $\frac{2}{8}$ ____________________

Notational Problems

Although it is still common in vocal music—where it is important to align notes precisely with the lyrics—to see individual eighth notes or sixteenth notes with separate flags, in instrumental music these notes rarely appear individually. Instead, two or more eighth or sixteenth notes will be grouped together, according to beats, with a connecting beam. A vocal rhythmic pattern such as

will appear in instrumental music as

Notice that eighth notes are grouped by a single beam, and sixteenth notes by a double beam.

When connecting notes with beams, it is important in all but the simplest patterns to begin each beat with a separate beam. A musician trains his or her eye to see such patterns of beats within a measure. A poorly written arrangement, such as the following, is momentarily confusing:

This pattern is confusing rhythmically because the beaming has hidden the second, third, and fourth beats of the measure. The following shows a much clearer way of writing the same pattern:

Here, each of the four beats begins with a new beam. Remember, the reason we beam notes together is to make the rhythmic patterns easier to recognize, not more difficult.

Extra care must be taken when beaming irregular divisions of the beat, particularly dotted rhythm patterns, since these can be especially tricky. The first step is to decide whether the pattern is in simple or compound meter. Knowing this will tell you whether the basic beat is divided into subgroups of two or three. After that, try to determine where each basic beat begins. This is more or less a process of adding up the note values. Finally, combine groups of notes so that each basic beat is beamed together. Make sure, however, that you do not combine two beats into one group. Each beat should be beamed separately.

The following examples may make the above explanation clearer. In a simple meter, such as $\frac{2}{4}$, the basic beat is the quarter note. This quarter note can be divided into two eighth notes or four sixteenth notes.

But the quarter note can also be divided into any combination of eighth notes and sixteenth notes that total one beat. In simple meters, for instance, there are three ways that the combination of one eighth note and two sixteenth notes can be written.

Notice that in each case the combination of notes is equal to one beat in simple meter. Notice also that the beaming (one beam for eighth notes, two for sixteenth notes) clearly indicates the beginning of each beat.

The beaming of dotted notes in simple meter is simply an extension of this same principle. Since a dotted eighth note is the equivalent of three sixteenth notes, the dotted-eighth-and-sixteenth pattern is frequently found and can be written one of two ways.

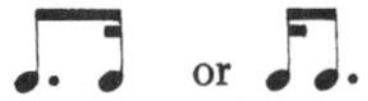

Notice that in both cases a complete beat is combined under one beam.

A similar process is employed in compound meter, with one major difference: The basic pulse is divided into three parts rather than two. In a compound meter such as $\frac{6}{8}$, the basic pulse is normally felt as two beats per measure, and the note representing this beat, the dotted quarter note, is divisible into three eighth notes or six sixteenth notes.

As in simple meter, any combination of eighth notes and sixteenth notes that adds up to a complete beat should be beamed together. The following are some of the more common combinations:

Similarly, dotted rhythms in compound meter are also grouped by beat. The common dotted rhythm pattern in compound meter is:

The following two patterns also occur from time to time, but less frequently.

In all cases, whether in simple or compound meter, it is important to keep the beginning of each beat clearly visible by beaming together all the notes that occur within that beat.

Musical Problem

Clap and count each of the rhythms given below. Then, rewrite them by beaming the eighth notes and sixteenth notes together, taking care not to place beams across beats. Next, clap the patterns you have written. Does being able to see clearly the beginning of each beat make it easier to read the patterns?

1. 

2. 

3. 

EXERCISE 2•7

Rewrite the following rhythmic patterns by beaming the eighth notes and sixteenth notes together. Remember not to place beams across beats. Remember also that dotted eighth and sixteenth notes that occur within one beat are joined in one of the ways shown in the example.

EXAMPLE:

1.

2.

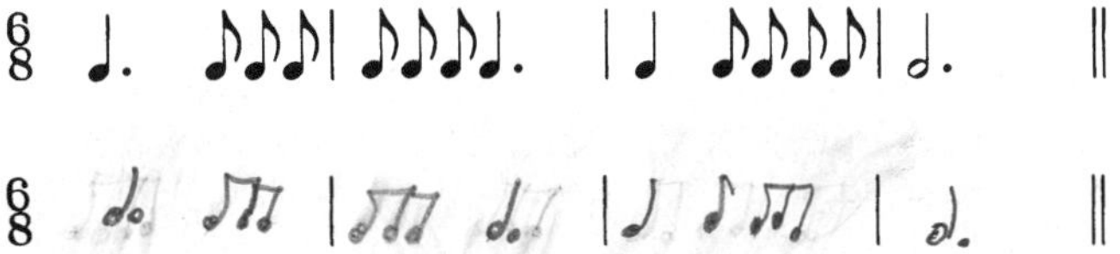

3.

4.

5.

6.

7. 

8. 

Triplets and Duplets

Sometimes, a note in simple meter is subdivided as if it were in compound meter. That is, a note normally subdivided into two equal parts is now momentarily subdivided into three equal parts. This is called *borrowed division.*

 normal subdivision

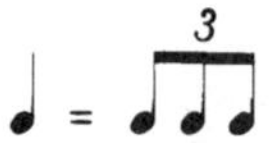 borrowed division

The *3* above the beam indicates that three even eighth notes occur within the time normally taken by two. When a borrowed division of this type occurs, it is called a **triplet.** A note of any value may be subdivided into a triplet. The three most common are:

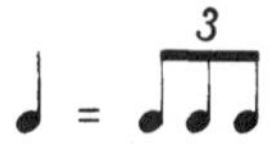 eighth-note triplet

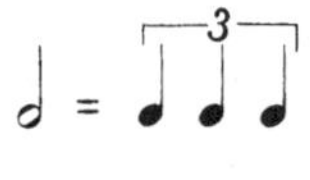 quarter-note triplet

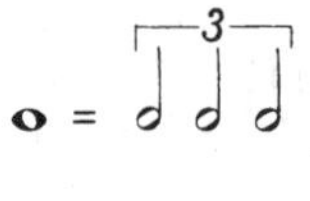 half-note triplet

Less frequently, a note in compound meter is subdivided as if it were in simple meter:

 normal subdivision

 borrowed division

When this occurs, it is called a **duplet**. The two most common duplets are:

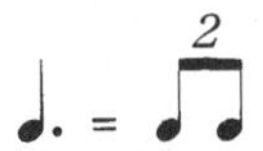
eighth-note duplet

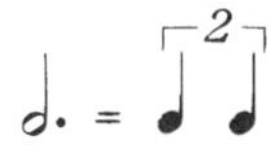
quarter-note duplet

Notice that (1) in both duplets and triplets a numeral is used to alert the performer to an unusual subdivision, and (2) where no beam exists, a bracket indicates exactly which notes belong to the triplet or duplet figure.

Triplets and duplets are best employed as rhythmic exceptions, to be used sparingly in a particular piece of music. If more frequent use is necessary, it makes more sense for the entire piece to be written in the corresponding compound or simple meter.

A Counting Method for Triplets and Duplets

The way most people count triplets is to momentarily shift their thinking from simple meter into compound meter. Notice in the following example that the syllables change from those of simple meter to the ones for compound meter at the point where the triplet occurs.

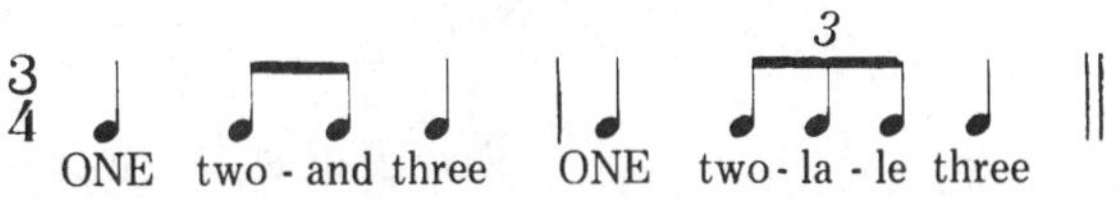

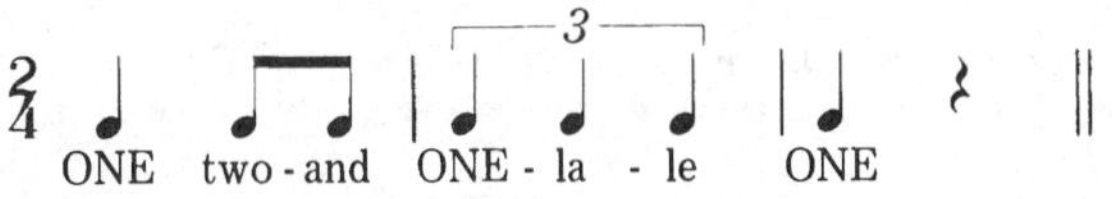

Duple rhythms work the same way, only in reverse. Duple rhythms normally occur in compound meters. So at the point where they occur, the thinking (and the syllables) change from the ones for compound meter to the ones for simple meter.

EXERCISE 2•8

Clap and count the following rhythmic examples. Pay particular attention to the triplet or duplet, and be sure to switch syllables for it. When you are comfortable counting, try playing the rhythms on an instrument or keyboard while counting mentally. Remember to always keep the basic beat steady.

Henry Tucker: "Sweet Genevieve"

1. 

"Havah Nagilah"

2. 

"Sometimes I Feel Like a Motherless Child"

3. 

Swedish Folk Song

4. 

Musical Problem

As a class, clap and count the following rhythmic examples. Begin by saying two measures of the divided beat (1-and 2-and for simple meters; 1-la-le 2-la-le for compound meters) aloud before clapping. Experiment with a variety of speeds. When you are comfortable with this counting system, also try playing the rhythms on an instrument or keyboard while counting mentally.

"All the Pretty Little Horses"

1. 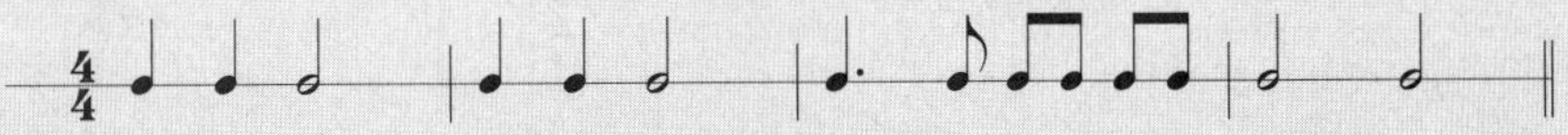

Eskimo Folk Song

2. 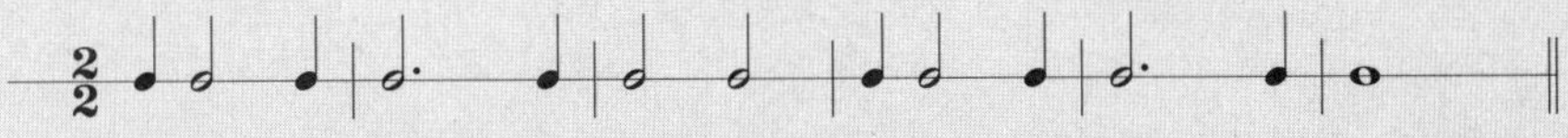

Irish Folk Song

3. 

Welsh Folk Song

4. 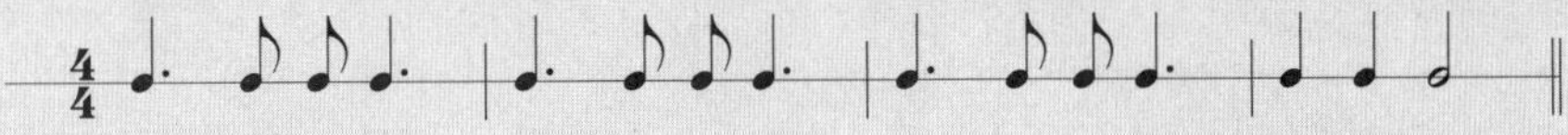

Brazilian Folk Song

5. 

Danish Folk Song

6. 

Henry C. Work: "Grandfather's Clock"

7. 

(continued)

Slovakian Folk Song

8. 

English Folk Song

9. 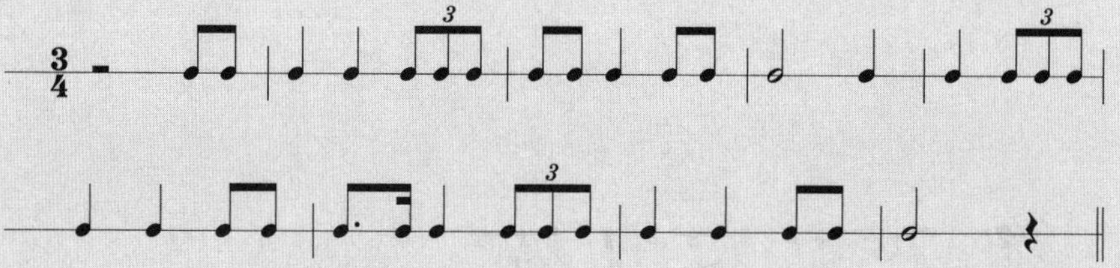

English Folk Song

10. 

Musical Problem

Your instructor will choose three of the rhythmic passages given in the preceding musical problem and play them for you several times. You will be told the meter of each example. Listen carefully to each passage, and try to notate it in the space provided below. If the passages seem too long, your instructor can divide them into shorter segments. Use the counting method to help clarify the rhythmic patterns you hear.

1. ______________________________

   ____

2. ______________________________

   ____

3. ____

____

____

Musical Problem

As a class, clap the following two-part examples, with half the class clapping the top part and half the bottom part. Then, by yourself, try tapping the examples on a desk or tabletop, one part per hand.

1. 

2. 

3. 

4. 

Ties

Often, a composer will want to hold a note beyond the end of a measure in a particular meter. Suppose, for example, we want a note to last four beats in $\frac{3}{4}$ meter. Obviously, four beats will not fit into a single three-beat measure. To permit the note to last four beats, we use a **tie,** which extends the note into the next measure. As shown in the following example, the tie is a curved line connecting the notehead to be prolonged with the same notehead in the next measure.

In performance, the second note will not be sounded separately. Instead, the first note will be held through the time value of the second, producing a single sound, four beats in duration.

Ties are not only useful for creating notes of longer duration than the number of beats in a measure, they are sometimes also needed at the end of a measure. In the following illustration, for example, the tie is needed because a half note cannot occur on the last beat of the first measure.

Another use of ties is to help make clear metric groupings, both within the bar and over the bar line. Notice in the following example that the use of ties allows the normal grouping in 6/8 to be maintained.

Ties are very similar in appearance to slurs, which are used to specify a smooth, connected style of playing. **Slurs** always connect different pitches, and may extend over several pitches at once, whereas ties always connect two notes of the same pitch.

EXERCISE 2•9

Rewrite each of the following rhythmic patterns in the meter indicated. To do this you will have to divide some notes (for instance, 𝅗𝅥 into ♩♩) and use ties.

EXAMPLE:

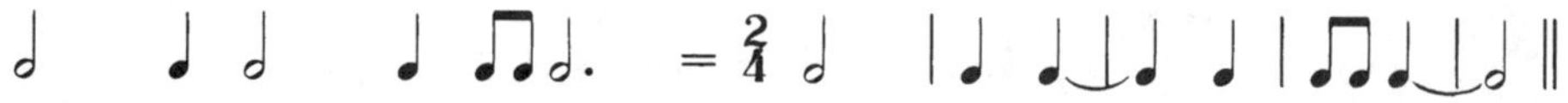

1. 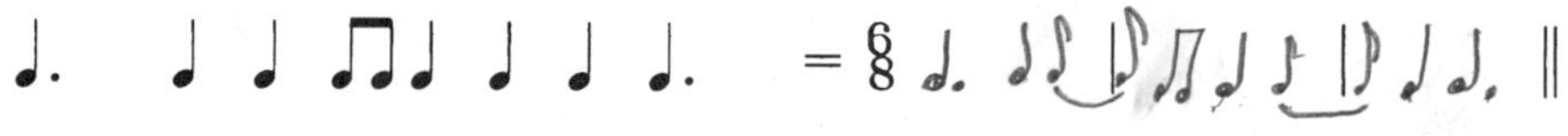

2. 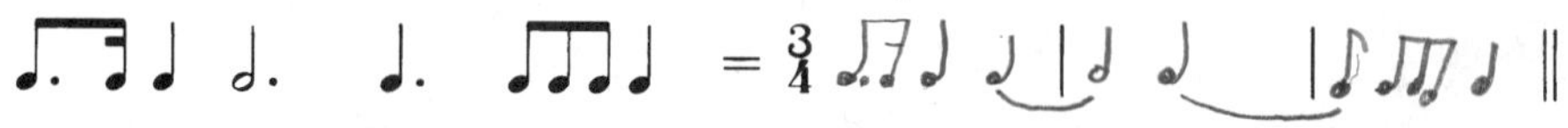

3. 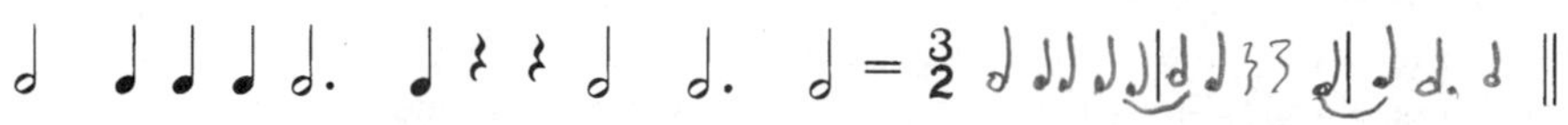

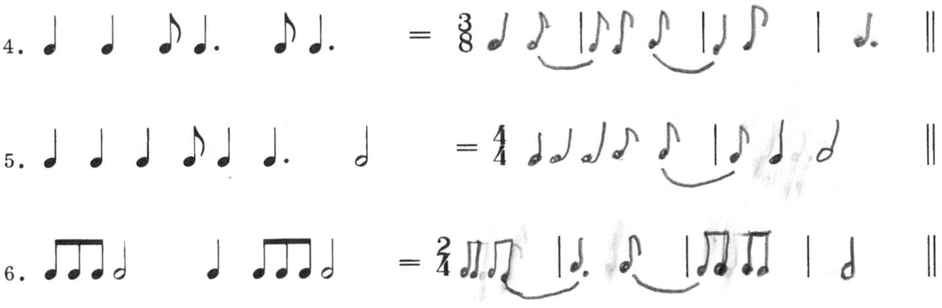

Syncopation

In some styles of music, an accent is frequently placed on what would otherwise be a weak beat. When this occurs, it is called **syncopation**. Clap and count aloud the following example:

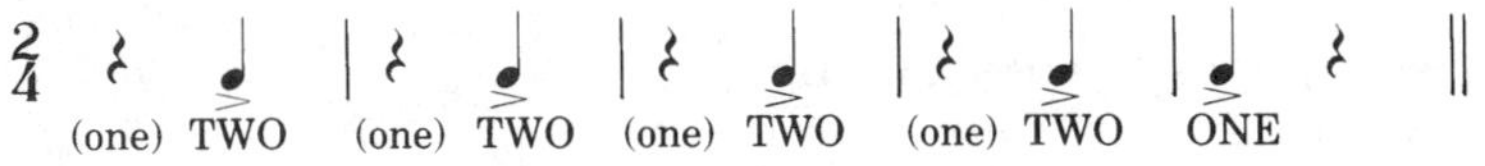

Notice that even this simple example of syncopation creates more rhythmic drive and energy. This is why some styles of music use syncopation so extensively. Here are several more examples.

A seemingly endless number of different syncopation figures are possible. In fact, almost every culture in the world has a group of these rhythms embedded somewhere in their traditional music. And what all syncopations have in common is a stressing of the weaker beats (or the weaker subdivisions of a beat) in order to produce more rhythmic tension. Some Western styles of music, such as jazz and rock, make extensive use of syncopation, while others, such as symphonies and string quartets, usually do not.

Repeat Signs

Occasionally, composers want several measures in a composition to be repeated immediately. They can do this either by writing all of the measures again or by using **repeat signs**. Although it is easy enough to rewrite a few measures, for longer passages repeat signs are more convenient.

Repeat signs are two large dots, one above the other, that appear at the beginning and the end of the measures to be repeated. Double bar lines generally accompany the repeat signs at the beginning and the end of the repeated measures in order to call attention to the repeat signs.

This example, when performed, will sound like this:

If the repeated measures include the first measure of the composition, the repeat sign occurs only at the end of the section to be repeated and is omitted from the beginning. For example,

when performed, will sound like

Musical Problem

Clap and count the following rhythms, individually and as a class. Pay particular attention to the repeat signs and ties. It will also be helpful if you sing the rhythms or perform them on an instrument. Be sure to hold each note for its full value.

1. 

2. 

3. 

4. 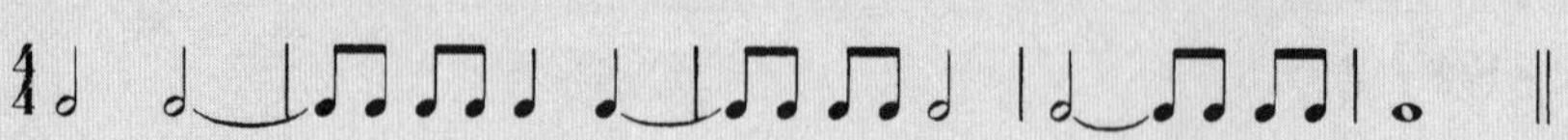

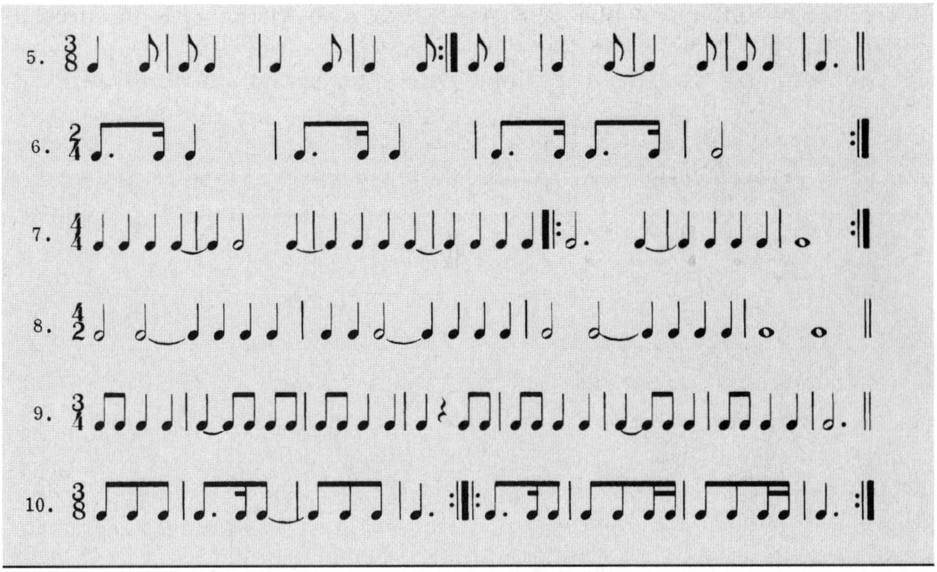

Tempo

How fast the pulse of a piece of music moves is called the **tempo**. Whereas today we might use the terms *fast* and *slow* as indications of speed, many pieces of music use Italian terms to assign the tempo. The following is a list of the most important terms and their meanings:

Slow Tempos

largo	*broad, very slow*
lento	*slow*
adagio	*slow*

Moderate Tempos

andante	*walking speed*
moderato	*moderate*

Fast Tempos

allegro	fast
vivace	quick, lively
presto	very fast

In addition, the following two terms are important because they indicate gradual changes of tempo:

ritardando (*rit.*)	gradually becoming slower
accelerando (*accel.*)	gradually becoming faster

Although these terms give a general indication of how fast a piece of music should be performed, they are open to a certain amount of interpretation. A more precise method of setting tempo is to use metronome indications. The metronome is an instrument invented in the early 1800s that produces a specific number of clicks per minute. Each click represents one beat. The metronome indication is given at the beginning of a composition. It looks like this:

♩ = M.M.60 or ♩ = 60

This particular indication means that the metronome will produce sixty clicks in one minute, and that each click is to be considered the pulse of one quarter note.

Conducting Patterns

The rhythmic patterns you have been asked to clap in this chapter can be performed by the class without a conductor. To perform more complicated patterns, or patterns consisting of three or four separate parts, you would probably need a conductor to keep everyone together. Indicating the beats and keeping the group together are important functions of the conductor.

The conductor indicates the beat with movements of the right arm. The following are the basic arm movements for duple, triple, and quadruple meters.

two-beat pattern

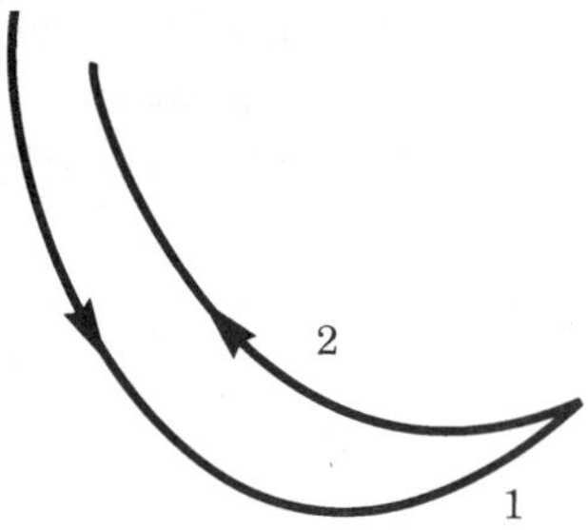

three-beat pattern

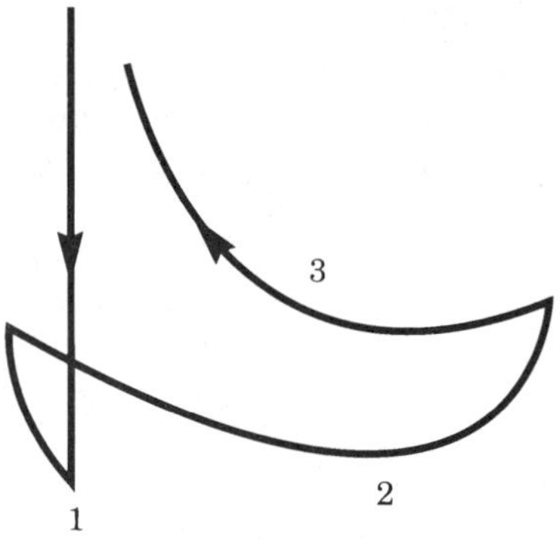

four-beat pattern

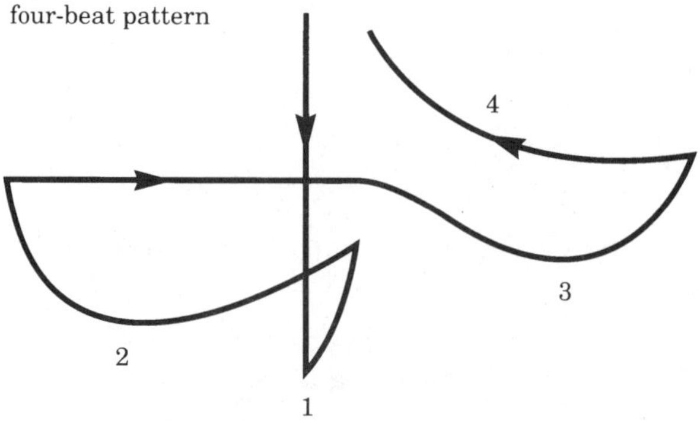

When practicing these patterns, remember the following points:

1. The beat pattern is always performed by the right arm only. This is true even if you are left-handed.
2. Always practice standing up. It is difficult to conduct correctly while sitting down, and almost no one does.
3. The first beat of each pattern is called the **downbeat;** the last beat is called the **upbeat**.
4. Keep the beat pattern high enough for everyone to see. The center of the pattern should be level with your chest, not your waist.
5. The arm motion should always be fluid and smooth. Never let the arm come to a complete stop.
6. When beginning a pattern, always prepare for the first beat of the exercise by giving the beat that comes directly before it. Assume, for instance, that you are going to conduct an exercise that uses a three-beat pattern starting on the downbeat. To begin, you would give the previous upbeat as a preparation. This is called the *preparatory beat.*

Musical Problem

The following melodies are in duple, triple, and quadruple meters. Practice conducting each of these melodies while your teacher or another student plays them. Then practice conducting while you yourself sing each of them on *la.* Keep practicing until you are comfortable singing and conducting simultaneously.

"Hush, Little Baby"

1.

"Scarborough Fair"

2.

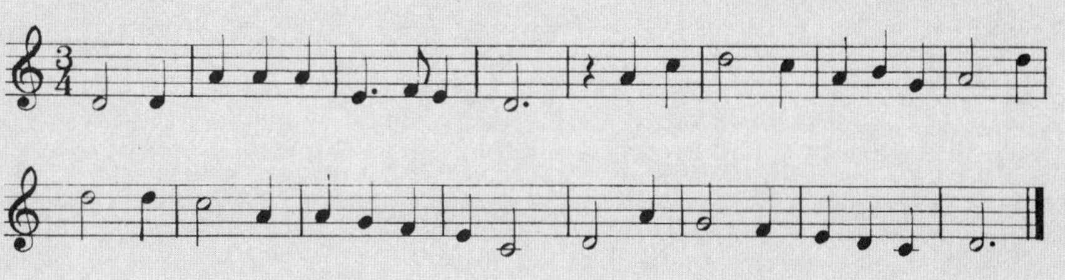

(continued)

"Oh Dear, What Can the Matter Be"

3. 

Musical Problem

Clap or perform on instruments the following two- and three-part rhythmic examples with one member of the class conducting and the other members taking the parts. You may wish to practice some of the simpler exercises in Appendix A first.

Allegro

1. 

Moderato

2. 

Andante

3. 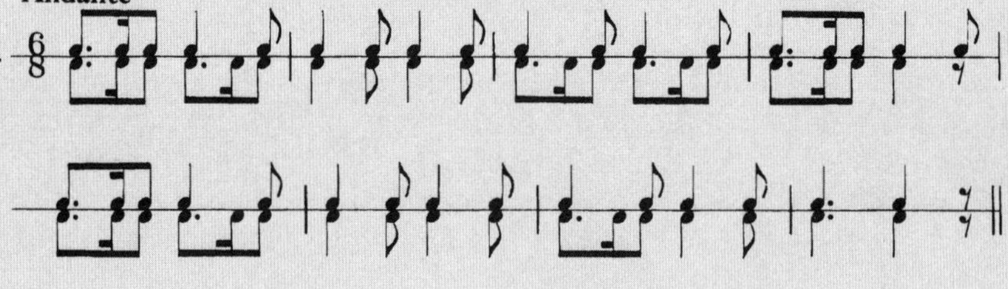

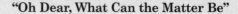

Musical Problem

Experiment with tapping out the two-part examples from the preceding musical problem on a desk or tabletop, one part per hand.

If you are particularly adventurous, you might also like to try tapping out the three-part examples. To do this, tap out the top part with your right hand, the middle part with your left hand, and the bottom part with one foot. You will probably find the three-part examples extremely difficult at first. (This kind of rhythmic coordination is what organists and trap-set drummers must use every day.)

Musical Problem

Below are melodies from a minuet by Bach and a folk song from Russia. You may have heard one or both of these pieces before. Clap the rhythm of each melody several times. Then, in the space provided, write a second rhythmic part that, when clapped with the rhythm of the melody, will complement it and create a two-part clapping piece. Perform these clapping pieces in class, and discuss their strengths and weaknesses.

Bach: Minuet in G Minor

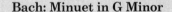

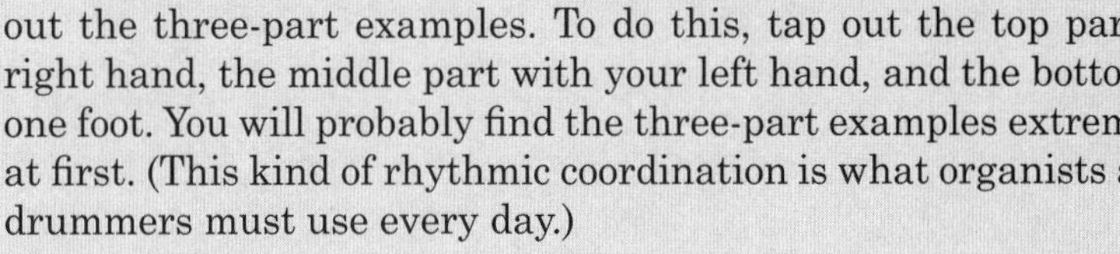

(continued)

Russian Folk Song

Musical Problem

As a class, choose several songs that everyone knows. These may be folk songs, popular songs, or the theme songs from your favorite movies. For each song, say the words aloud several times until you have the rhythm created by these words clearly in mind. Then, decide the meter of this rhythm. Finally, determine where the downbeat occurs. To do this, begin by deciding whether the *first* word begins on the downbeat or on some other beat of the measure. After you have done this, try writing the rhythm suggested by the words. Here, there is no one absolutely correct way of doing things, although your rhythms should always sound natural, not awkward.

Focus

Chaper 1 began with the question, What is musical rhythm? Are we now ready to begin to formulate an answer to that question? So far, we have discussed the individual rhythmic elements, but not how these parts interact within an actual composition. It is this interaction that gives a piece of music its unique rhythmic character. On one level, this interaction is relatively easy to describe: Musical rhythm is the inherent flow and tension between the steady pulse of a particular meter and the irregular note values that occur within that meter. Unfortunately, this simplistic definition, while true, ignores the more subtle and complex aspects of the rhythm of most pieces of music.

In a real composition, a number of factors always work together to produce its characteristic rhythm: tempo, accents, and the interaction of rhythm with melody and harmony, to name a few. Also, since the subtle rhythmic qualities of every style of music differ from each other, musicians learn to make slight adjustments when performing, in order to accommodate the specific rhythmic demands of a particular style.

Musical Problem

The following three-part rhythms are taken from Appendix B. As a class, clap and count these rhythms. Then, divide into small groups and clap and count them again. It may be helpful to have someone in each group conduct, using the appropriate conducting pattern.

(continued)

Musical Problem

Listen once again to the works you chose for the first musical problem of Chapter 1. This time, try to explain in more musical terms what is taking place rhythmically. Be specific when talking about the pulse, meter, and tempo. Discuss in a general way the interaction of the various rhythmic elements. In one or more paragraphs for each piece, describe your experience of the rhythm. Does this new description show that you now have a better understanding of musical rhythm in general?

Chapter 3

Pitch

The ability to read music from the printed page is not a skill possessed by all musicians. Nor does music have to be written on paper to exist as music. Most folk music traditions of the world are oral, with tunes passing by rote from one performer to another and from one generation to the next. Even the classical music of some cultures, much of it of great complexity, is maintained primarily by an oral tradition. Moreover, some styles of music—for example, jazz or rock in America or the raga tradition in India—require improvising skills such that written arrangements in these styles are little more than skeletons or postcards, reminding us of the actual performance when the "real" music appears.

But, even though some musical traditions can exist without a highly organized notational system, the art music of the past 500 years in Europe and America cannot. In order to play the music of Bach, or Chopin, or Gershwin, for example, we need a precise set of plans—a sort of blueprint or map. There are, of course, obvious advantages in being able to write down your musical ideas. First, the ideas can be preserved exactly—they will not be forgotten or altered unconsciously. Second, complicated musical structures can be built in a standard manner easily understood by all. Third, the music can be accurately and efficiently transmitted to other musicians, both immediately and hundreds of years later. In addition, we can assume that it will always sound the same. This is no small accomplishment, when you think about it.

Consider the great piano pieces and symphonies of the past. Could they ever have been performed in the first place, much less saved for centuries, without a system of notation? What about the music played by the Swing Era bands of Count Basie or Duke Ellington? Although there was a great deal of solo improvising, the arrangements themselves were tightly organized and carefully written out.

As you continue the process of learning to read musical notation, remember that you are, in essence, learning a new language—the language of music. This language will allow you to communicate with other musicians, both those of today and those of the past.

Musical Problem

Listen to a recording of a short orchestral work by a Classical composer like Mozart or Haydn. As you listen, consider that this music was written more than 150 years ago. The reason it can still be performed today is because the notational system conveys information to contemporary performers that allows them to re-create the music accurately. As a class, discuss the kinds of musical information a notational system for this style of music would need to contain. You may wish to look at a score, either during or after the discussion.

In contrast, most rock music of today is not notated. Although the arrangements are played virtually the same way each time, they are seldom written on paper and read during the performance in the manner of classical music. As a class, listen to a current rock piece and discuss what kinds of information a notational system for this style of music would need, so that someone who has never heard this music could play it in a recognizable way a century and a half from now.

Enharmonic Pitches

The fact that F sharp and G flat, or C sharp and D flat, are the same note on the keyboard may be momentarily confusing. When two different letter names identify the same pitch, we call them **enharmonic pitches**. The term means that the two pitches, while written differently, actually sound the same tone. At this point, the best way of dealing with enharmonic pitches is to remember that sharped notes sound above the pitches they relate to, while flatted notes sound below. The reason for this duality in labeling will become clear when we discuss scales in a later chapter.

Every pitch can be raised (sharped) or lowered (flatted). Since there is no black key between E and F or B and C, however, it is necessary to have white key enharmonic sharps and flats. We identify the pitch *E sharp* as the key directly above E, which is white and also called *F*. In the same way, *C flat* is the key directly below C, which is white and also called *B*.

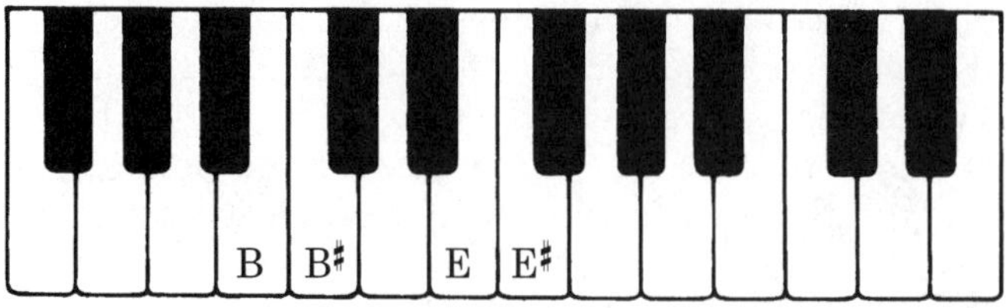

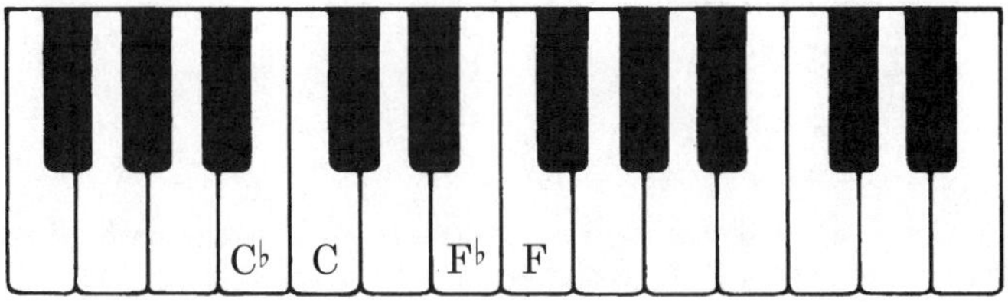

EXERCISE 3•1

Locate the specified pitches on the following keyboards, and write each pitch in the correct place. If the pitch is a white key, write it directly on the keyboard. If it is a black key, use the answer line given above the keyboard. Then practice finding and playing each of the pitches at the piano.

1. F sharp
   D flat
   A sharp
   E flat
   F flat

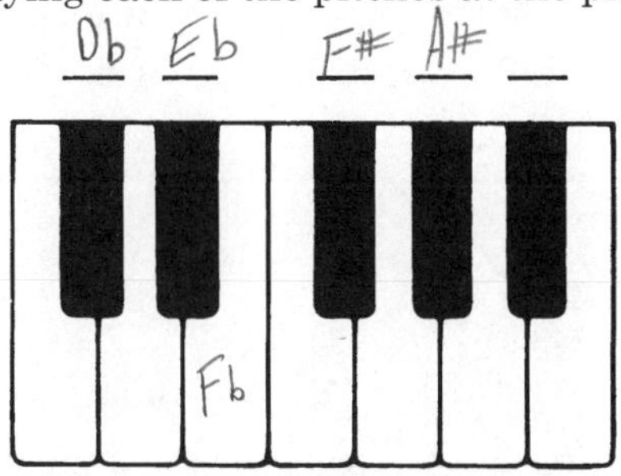

2. G flat
   B flat
   A flat
   C sharp

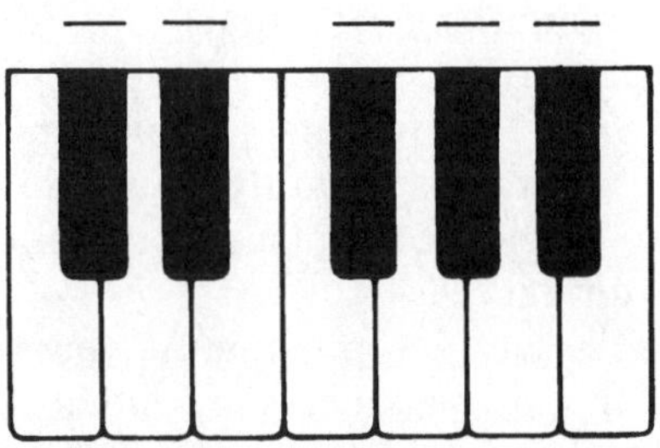

3. G sharp
   D sharp
   F sharp
   A sharp
   E sharp

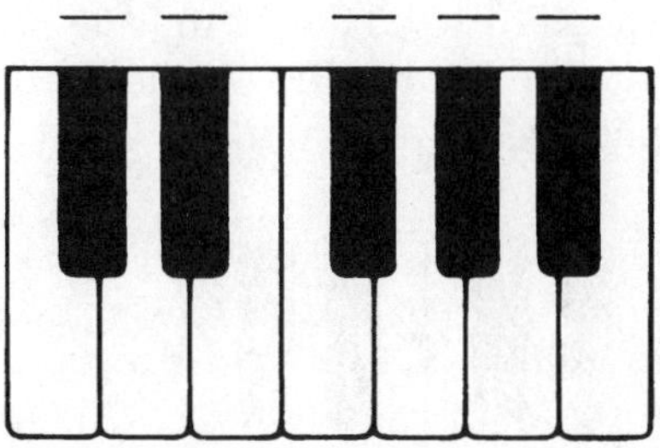

Accidentals

In written music, the following signs, called **accidentals,** are used to alter the pitch of a note chromatically:

♯	**sharp**	raises the pitch to the next adjacent note (i.e., a half step)
♭	**flat**	lowers pitch by a half step
𝄪	**double sharp**	raises pitch by two half steps (one whole step)
𝄫	**double flat**	lowers pitch by two half steps (one whole step)
♮	**natural**	cancels a sharp, double sharp, flat, or double flat

When pitches are written as words, the accidentals follow the note (as when spoken); for example C♯ is read C sharp. When pitches are notated on a staff, however, all accidentals are placed to the left of the pitches they affect and on the same line or space as the note.

When writing an accidental before a note on the staff it is important to remember that the placement of that accidental must be exact. If the note is centered on a space, then the accidental before it must also be centered in the *same* apace. This is also true for a note located on a line—the accidental before it must be centered on the *same* line. This precision in placement is necessary because musicians read the note and the accidental as a single unit. If you are careless and place the accidental in the wrong place, you will be sending contradictory information to the performer.

Double sharps and double flats can be confusing. As you know, the sharp sign raises a pitch by a half step. In most instances, this means that a pitch will be raised from a white key to a black key—for example, F to F♯, C to C♯. Since a double sharp raises a pitch *two* half steps, or one whole step, this means that quite often the resulting pitch is a white key. Thus, F to F𝄪 appears on the keyboard as F to G. In the same way, E to E𝄫 appears on the keyboard as E to D. (Remember, F𝄪 and G are enharmonic; so are E𝄫 and D.)

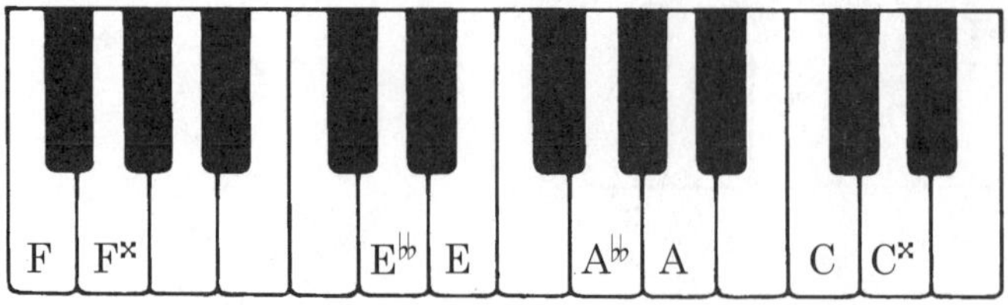

You may be wondering why we can't simply ignore double sharps and double flats. In fact, these signs seldom appear in music, but when they do they have a specific function, which we shall discuss in Chapter 8. For now, pay special attention to the double sharps and double flats in the following exercise.

EXERCISE 3•2

Locate the indicated pitches on the following keyboards by drawing a line from the written pitch to the key it represents. Then, play each of the pitches on the piano.

1.

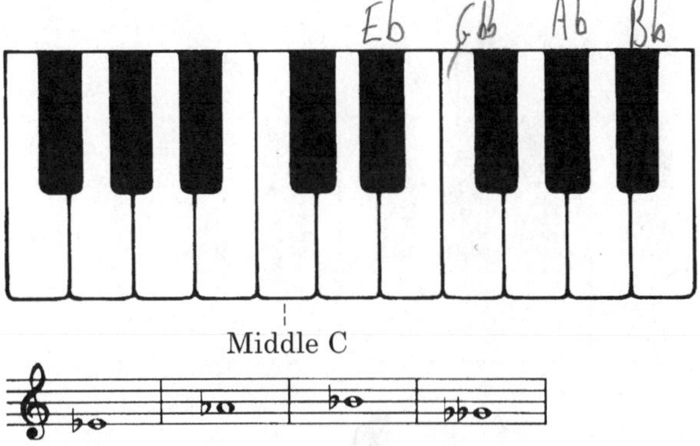

2.

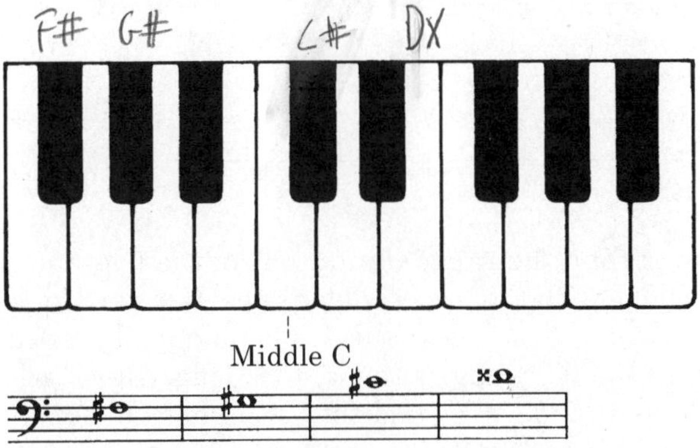

3.

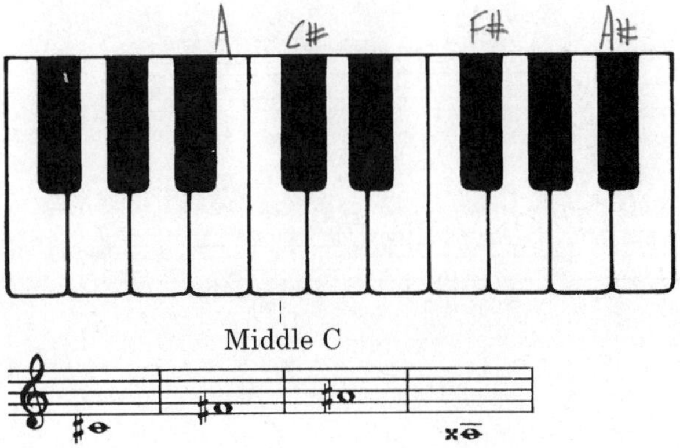

4.

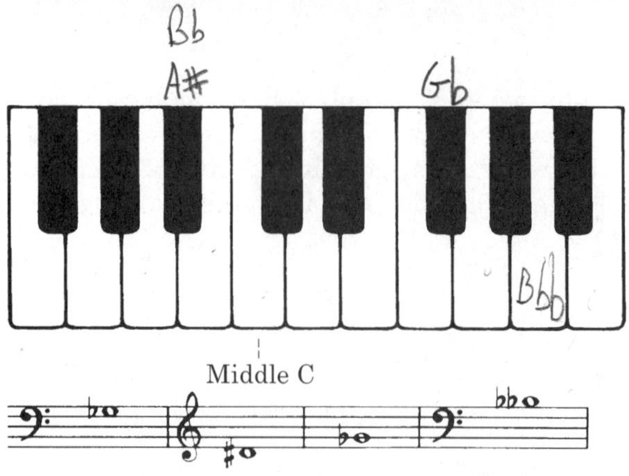

5.

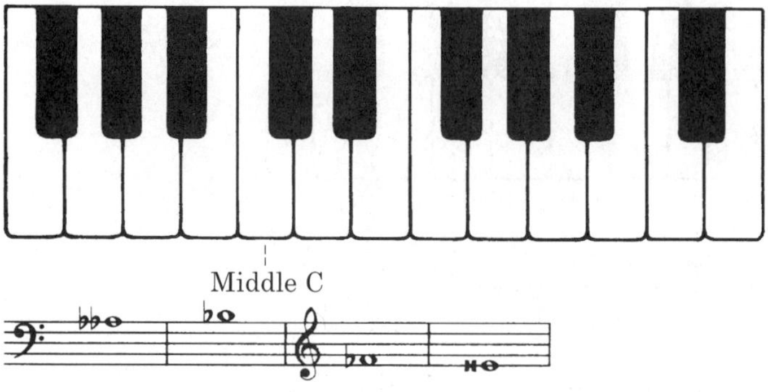

Ledger Lines

Often, pitches higher or lower than the range limitations of the five-line staff need to be indicated. This is done with the use of ledger lines. **Ledger lines** are short, individual lines added above or below the staff, having the effect of extending the staff. Notice (in the following example) that ledger lines are the same distance apart as the lines of the staff and that the ledger lines for one note do *not* connect to the ledger lines for another note.

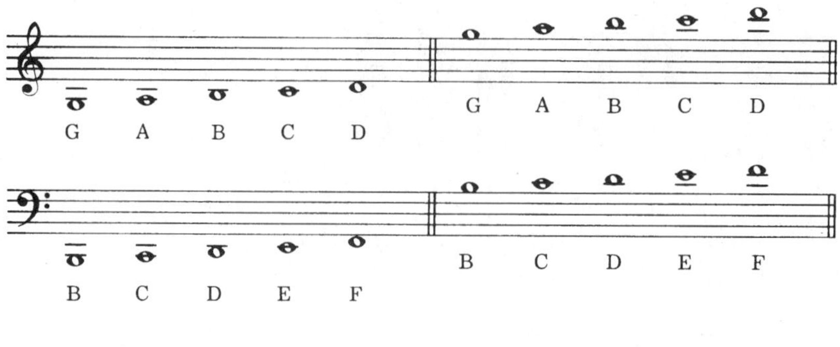

It is not necessary to enclose a pitch with ledger lines.

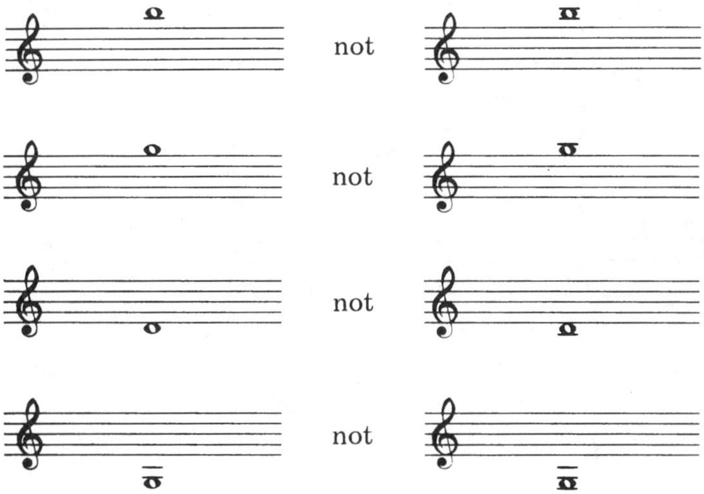

EXERCISE 3•3

Identify the following pitches by letter name.

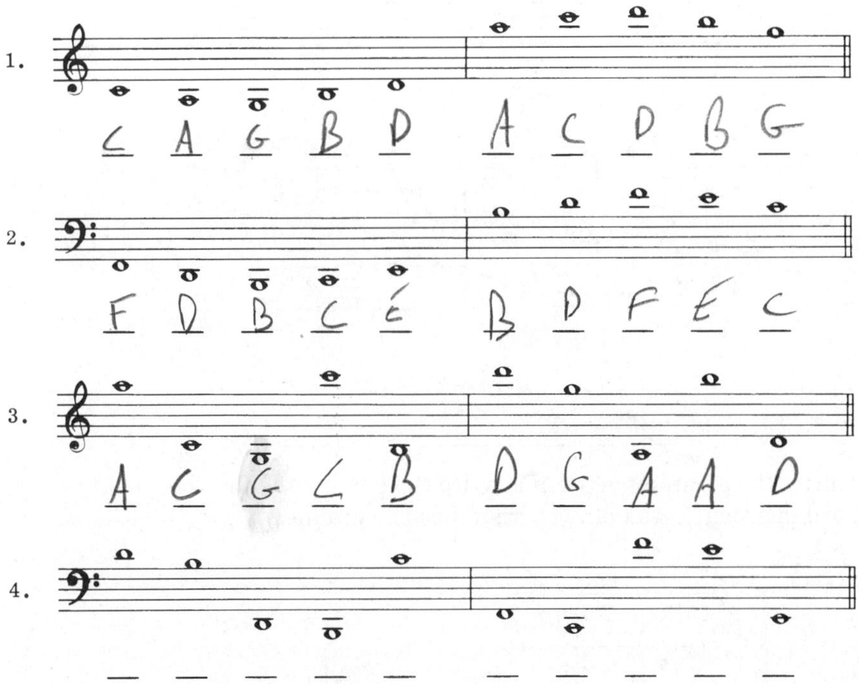

The use of ledger lines within the great staff can be momentarily confusing. In the following example, both notes in each vertically aligned pair represent the same pitch. This notational overlap within the great staff is useful because it allows pitches to be clearly grouped with the musical line to which they belong.

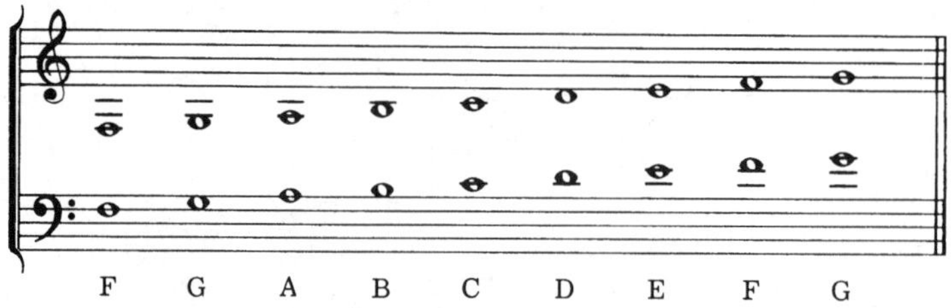

In the following piano music example, the left hand plays pitches located above middle C. To avoid confusion, however, these pitches are written with ledger lines in the bass clef.

Mozart: Sonata in B♭ Major, K. 570, III

EXERCISE 3•4

First identify the given pitch; then rewrite the same pitch, but in the other clef. A keyboard is provided to help you visualize the pitches.

EXAMPLE:

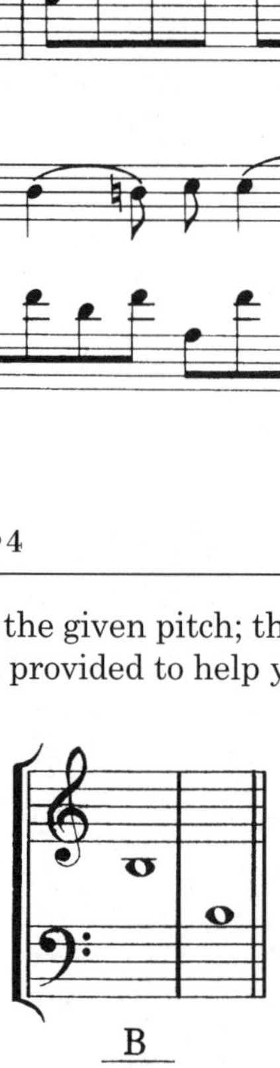

1.

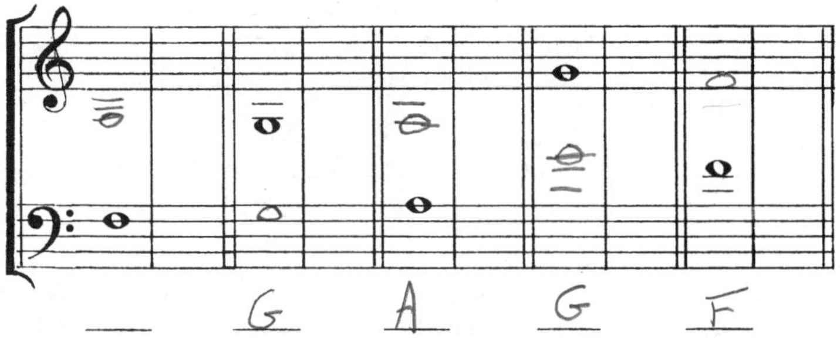

2.

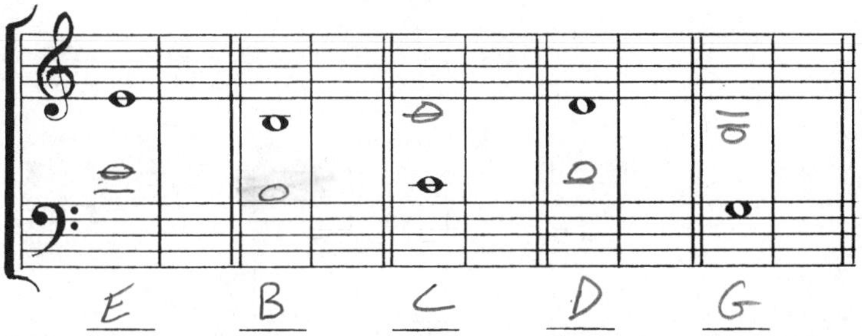

3.

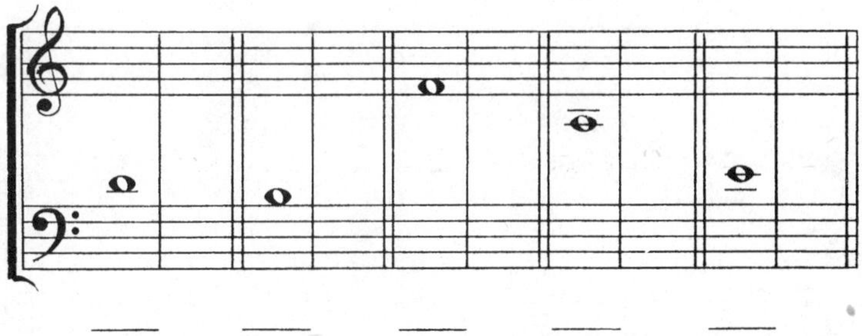

4.

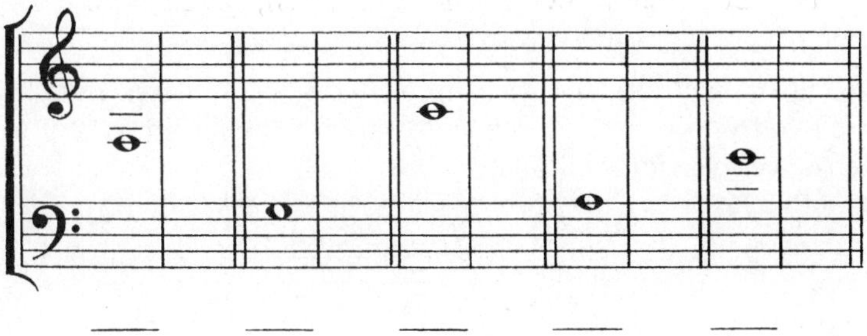

The Octave Sign

Musicians are most comfortable reading music that is written on the staff or close to it. The excessive use of ledger lines makes music difficult to read and should be avoided. The **octave sign,** *8va*----¬ or *8*----¬, is another notational device, in addition to the C clef, that helps overcome this problem.

An octave is the distance between any note and the next note of the same name, either higher or lower. The octave sign *above* a group of notes, then, indicates that the notes under the sign are to be played one octave *higher* than written.

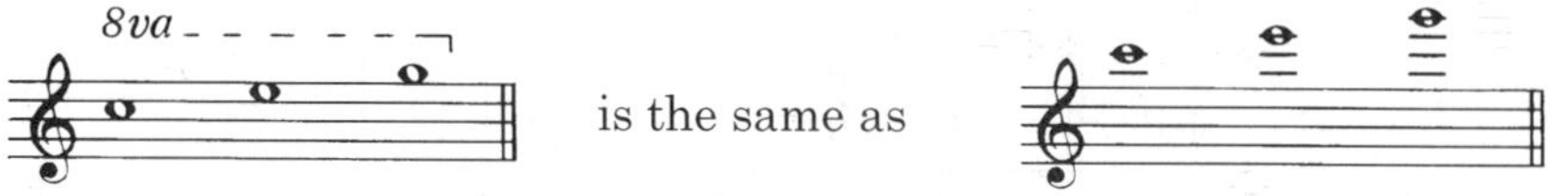

The following example shows how the octave sign can be used to keep the ascending-scale passage on or close to the staff.

Kuhlau: Rondo from Sonatina, Op. 20, No. 1

When the octave sign appears *below* a group of notes, it indicates that those notes are to be played one octave *lower* than written. Sometimes the word *bassa* is added to the octave sign.

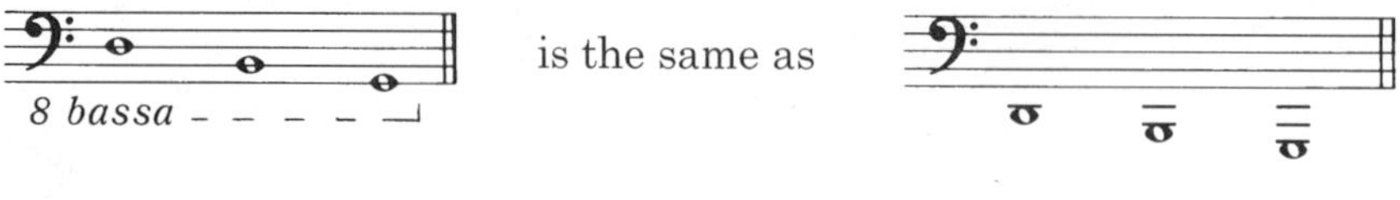

The following example, by Debussy, uses octave signs above and below pitches in order to explore the extremes of the piano range.

Debussy: "Brouillards" from Preludes, Book II

EXERCISE 3•5

Name the pitches given below. Then rewrite the passages using the octave sign to avoid the use of ledger lines.

1.

2.

3.

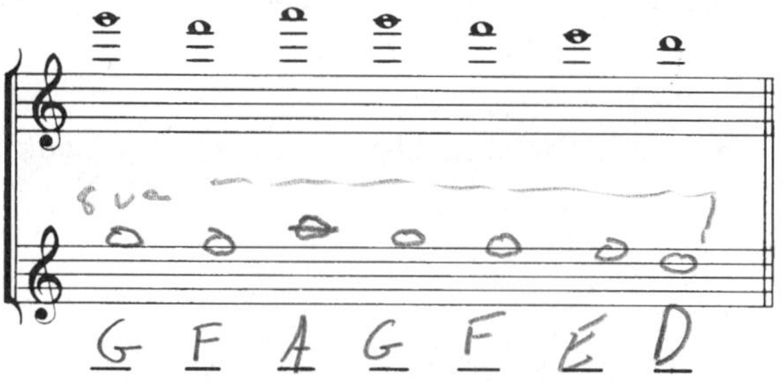

4.

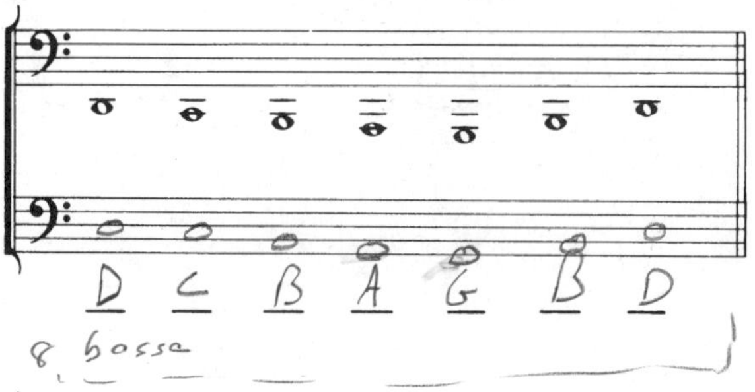

5.

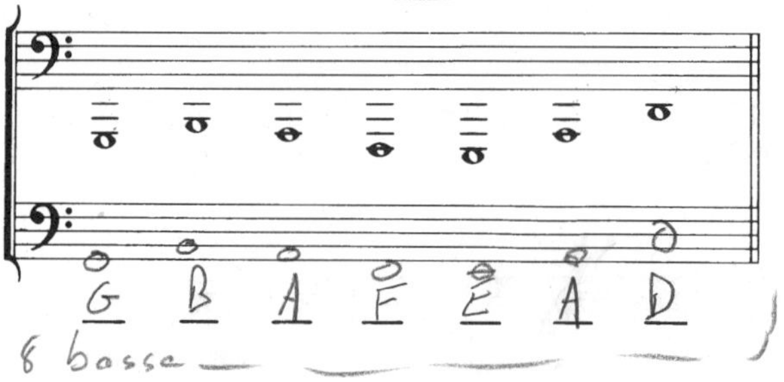

Octave Identification

It is often useful to be able to refer to a pitch in a particular octave. To identify each octave separately, a special system is used. Unfortunately, more than one system is being used today. The one given below is for the piano, and refers to middle C as C4. If you own a synthesizer or electronic keyboard, however, your manual may refer to middle C as C3. This is confusing, but it happens because most electronic keyboards don't have all eighty-eight keys, and middle C on them is the third, not the fourth, C from the left.

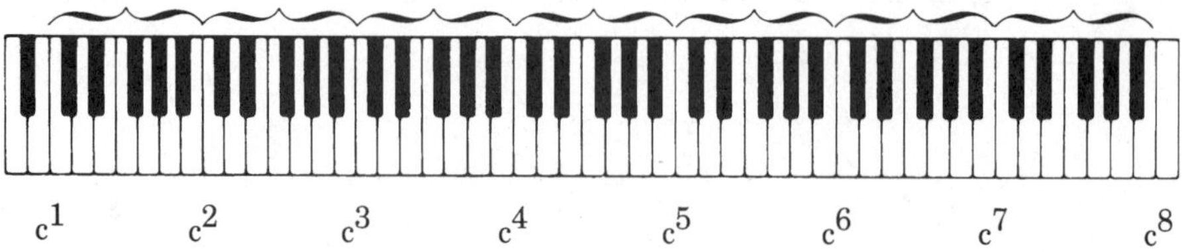

We will use the system that spans the entire piano keyboard. Here, the octave beginning on middle C is labeled as follows:

c^4 b^4

Any pitch within this range can be identified by a lowercase letter with superscript numeral 4.

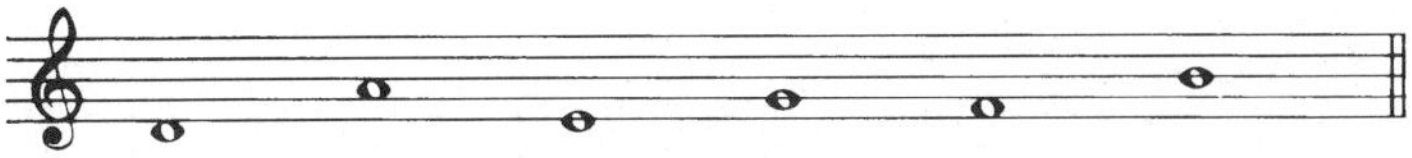

d^4 a^4 e^4 g^4 f^4 b^4

The following illustration shows how the octaves above middle C are identified.

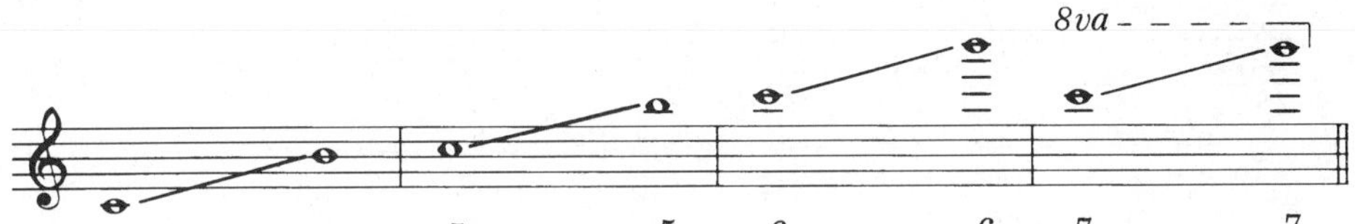

c^4 b^4 c^5 b^5 c^6 b^6 c^7 b^7

Any pitch within these ranges can be identified by a lowercase letter and the appropriate superscript.

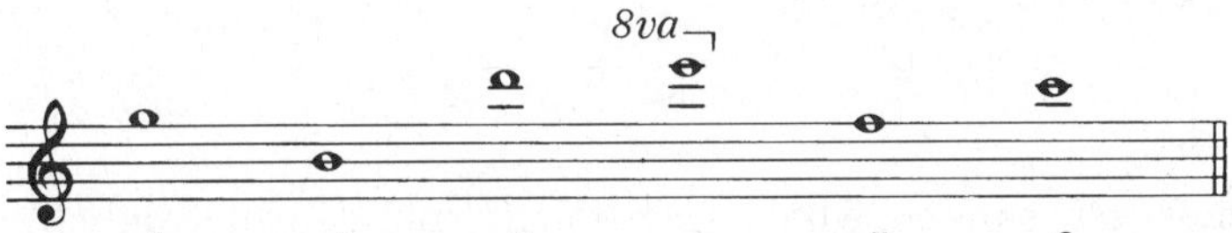

g^5 b^4 d^6 e^7 f^5 c^6

EXERCISE 3•6

Give the correct name and octave identification for the following pitches.

1. 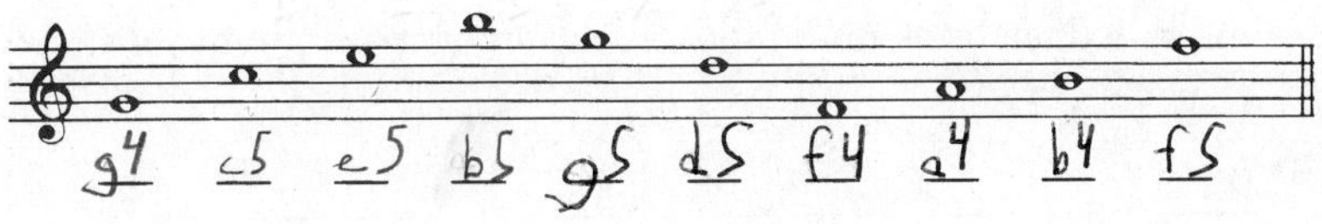

2.

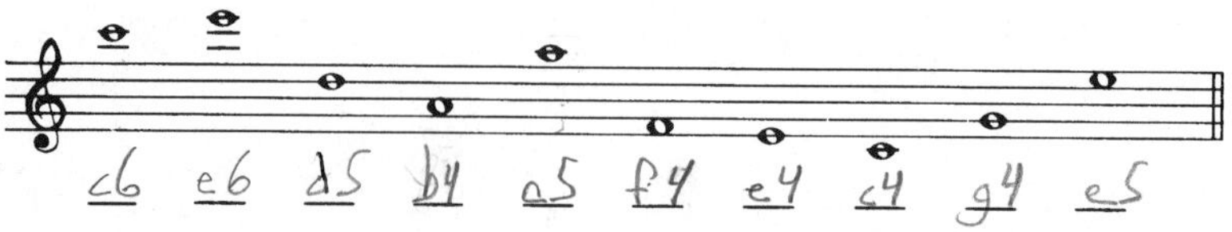

3.

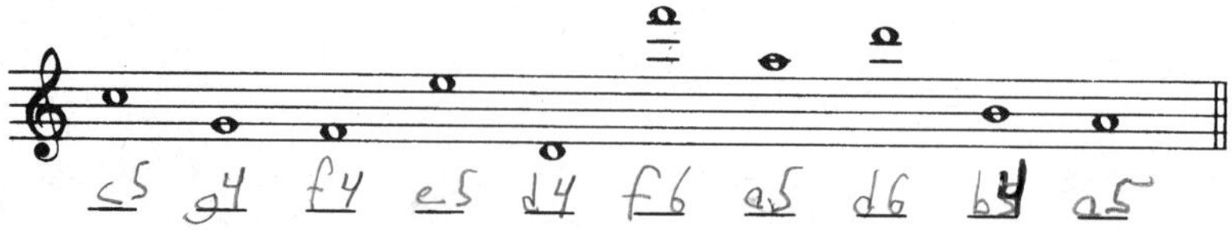

4.

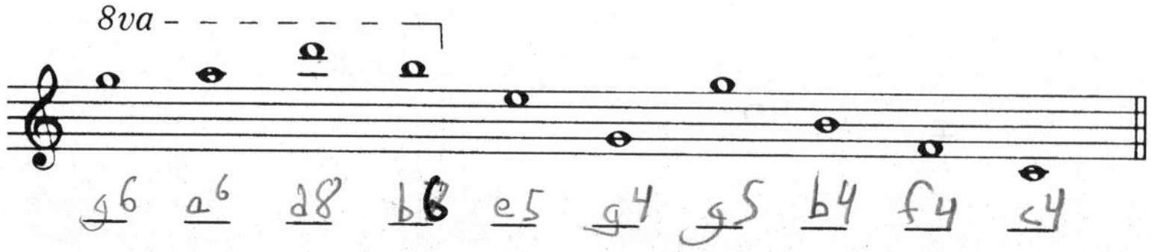

5.

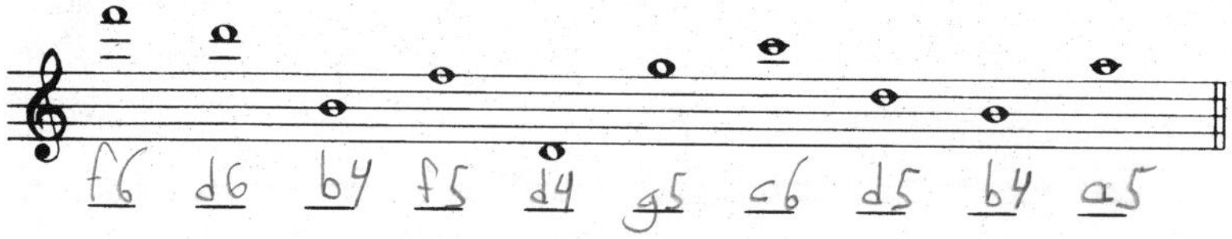

The octaves below middle C are labeled with descending numerals in a similar way.

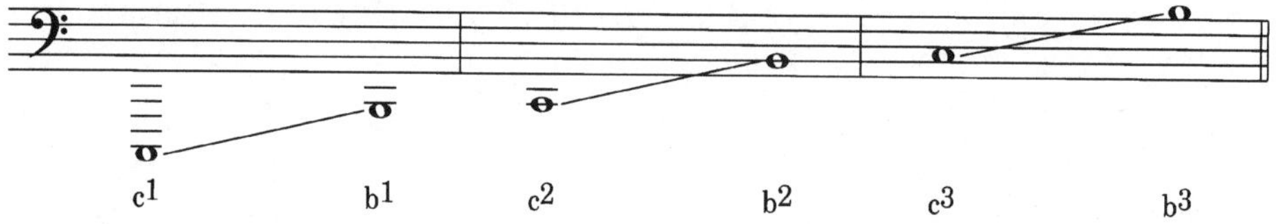

The lowest three pitches on the piano, which are below c1, are identified only by their name.

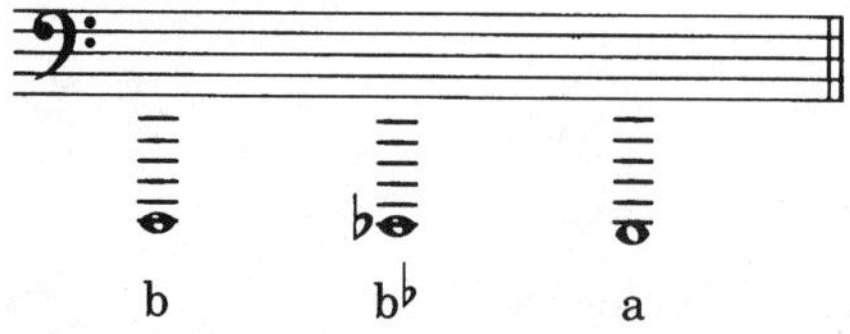

Notice how so many ledger lines make identification of these pitches difficult.

EXERCISE 3•7

Give the correct octave identification for the following pitches in the bass clef.

1. 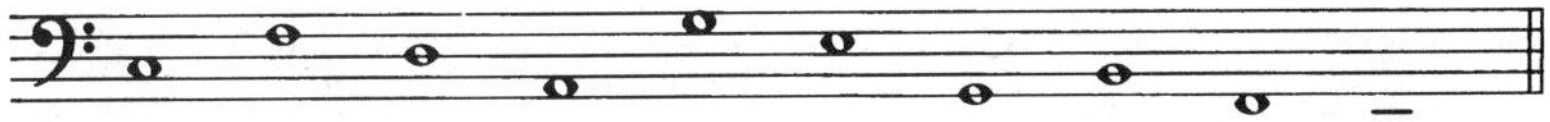

2. 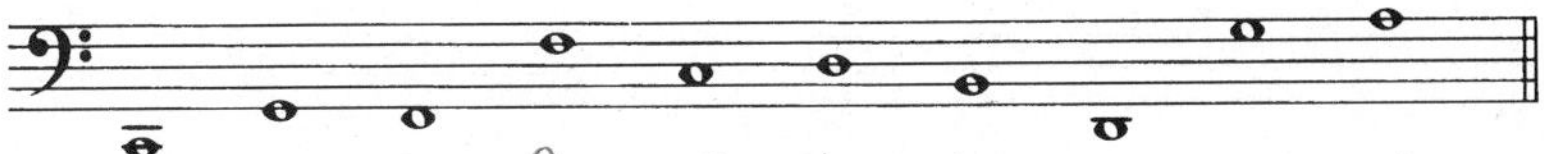

3. 

4. 

5. 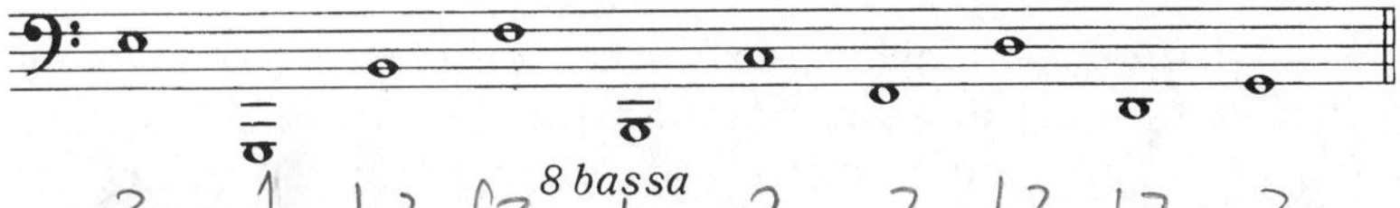

EXERCISE 3•8

Write each indicated pitch in the correct octave. The octave sign may be used where necessary.

1. 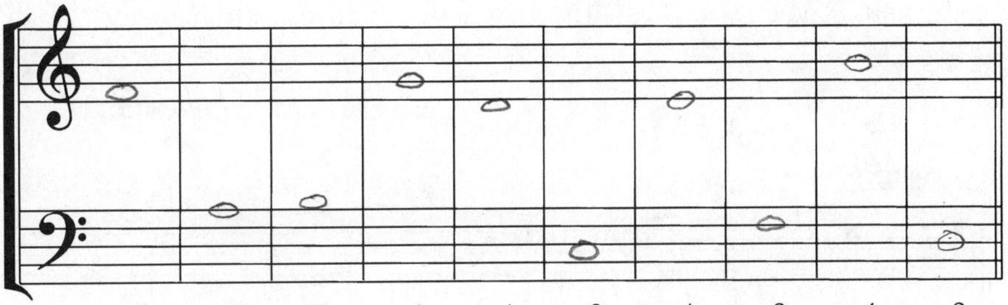

f^4 a^3 b^3 g^4 d^4 c^3 e^4 f^3 b^4 d^3

2.

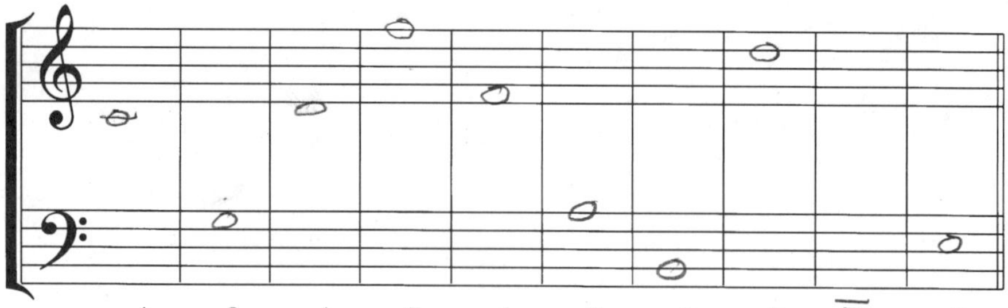

c^4 g^3 d^4 f^5 g^4 a^3 b^2 d^5 a^1 e^3

3.

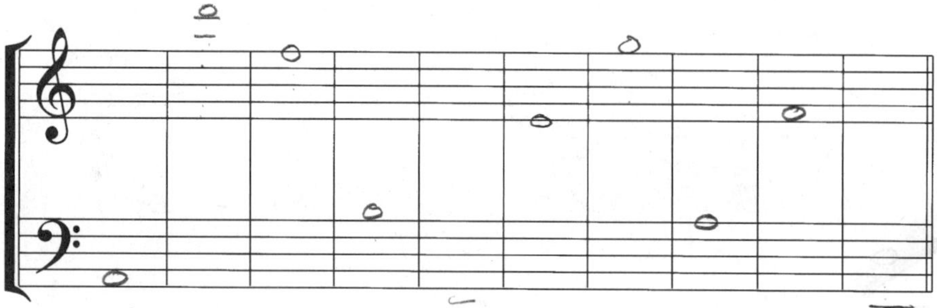

a^2 d^6 f^5 b^3 c^1 e^4 g^5 a^3 f^4 d^2

How to Read a Musical Map

Many pieces of written music, when performed, are played straight through. That is, you begin at the top and play to the end, in the same way as you would read a newspaper column, or a paragraph on a page. But not all pieces are this straightforward. Some contain notational shortcuts—space-saving devices indicated by a variety of symbols and abbreviations. If you understand the code (recognize the symbols and abbreviations), then reading the musical map is easy. But if you don't you can become hopelessly confused.

Let's begin by looking at a piece of piano music by Muzio Clementi, a composer who lived about the same time as Beethoven. This sonatina may, at first, appear to be thirty-eight measures long, but that is not the case. In fact, when performed correctly it actually consists of seventy-six measures. Clementi is able, in performance, to double the amount of music contained on the printed page by using the device of repetition, a device he uses not once, but twice.

Clementi, ***Sonatina,*** **Op. 36, No. 1**

Clementi's first repetition occurs at the end of measure 15. The double bar with two dots before it is a repeat sign that should be familiar to you from your work in Chapter 1. It indicates that the first fifteen measures are to be repeated before continuing. The second repeat occurs in measure 38, at the very end. Here, as before, a repeat sign sends us back into the piece. This time, however, we do not go back to the beginning, but only back to measure 16, where a repeat sign (with the two dots now to the right of the double bar), brackets the 23 measures Clementi wants repeated.

anacrusis ↓ the pick-up note

Now, let's look at "Siciliana," from Robert Schumann's *Album for the Young.*

Schumann: "Siciliana" from *Album for the Young*

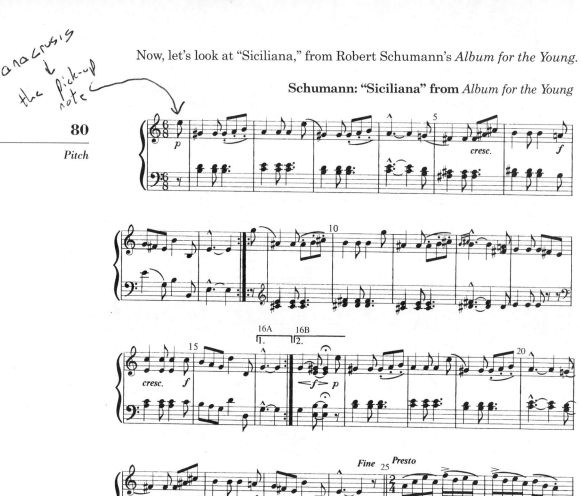

Da capo al fine senza repetizione

This example, which represents a more complicated musical map, contains three different kinds of repetition. The first kind occurs at the end of measure 8, and is similar to the ones we saw in the Clementi sonatina. The second device, however, is new. It occurs at measure 16 and is called the *1st and 2nd endings*. This device is in some ways similar to the repeat sign for the first eight measures. Notice that the double bar and the two dots in measures 8 and 16 indicate that the musical material between measures 9 and 16 is to be repeated. In this case, however, there are two *different* final measures. The first time the passage is performed, the first ending is played, but on the repetition, only the second ending is used. That is, measures 9–15 are played, measure 16A is omitted, and measure 16B is played in its place.

The third device is even more complicated. Notice the Italian phrase *Da capo al fine senza repetizione* below measures 35 and 36. This phrase indicates that the performer is to return to the beginning of the piece (*da capo* = the head, the beginning) and play to the end (*fine* = the end) without repeating either measures 1–8 or 9–16 (*senza repetizone* = without repetition). The actual end of the piece, therefore, is at measure 25, not at measure 36 as it may have appeared originally.

These devices may at first seem to be extremely confusing ways to organize a score, but if you perform very much music, you will quickly grow used to them. In fact, this example contains all of the commonly used devices except one: *Dal segno al fine*. This phrase, which is similar to *Da capo al fine*, is used when the composer wishes to return to the middle of the piece rather than to the very beginning. In this case the symbol 𝄋 is placed at the point where the repetition is to begin, and the performer is expected to return to the sign (*Dal segno*) and play to the end (*al fine*).

Not all pieces of music utilize devices of repetition, and even those that do can vary in slightly different ways. But if you study the following chart carefully, you should be able to find your way through almost any piece of music without too much difficulty.

Device of Repetition	*Abbreviation*	*Meaning*
Repeat signs		Perform the measures located within these signs twice.
1st and 2nd endings		Perform the indicated measures twice—the first time using the first ending, the second time using only the second ending.
Da capo al fine	*D.C. al fine*	Return to the beginning and play to the indicated end.
Dal segno al fine	*D.S. al fine*	Return to the sign and play to the indicated end.

Musical Problem

Ask several members of the class who perform to locate one or more scores that use various devices of repetition. As a group, discuss these pieces. Can you identify the devices and what they mean? Can you work your way through the score successfully?

Focus

Pitch identification is a major component of musical notation. So far you have been introduced to and given practical experience with pitch notation in the treble and bass clefs, as well as on the great staff. It is important that you become familiar with pitch notation as quickly as possible, since the rest of the book is based on the information contained in this chapter. One of the easiest ways of falling behind in the study of music fundamentals is by being uncertain of and too slow at pitch identification.

Musical sound has four characteristics—duration, pitch, timbre, and volume. While this book concentrates on developing your skills with duration and pitch, timbre and volume should not be ignored altogether. At this point, you may wish to look at Appendix G, "A Discussion of Dynamics," and Appendix H, "An Introduction to Timbre." Later, your teacher may ask you to study these sections in more detail. For now, keep in mind that being musical involves more than just playing the right notes in the correct rhythms.

Major Scales

All of the world's music is made using some kind of musical scale. A **scale** is a group of pitches—usually from five to eight—that are most often arranged in ascending or descending patterns of whole steps and half steps (explained later on). The scale is a fundamental building block of music, much as the skeleton is the foundation of our bodies. The fact that music of one culture often sounds strange to people of another culture is largely due to an unfamiliarity with the scales upon which this "strange"-sounding music is built.

A great variety of scales are used throughout the world today. Most of them date from antiquity, and we don't really know how they came into being. Some of them use intervals smaller than the half step; others have gaps in them that are larger than a whole step. These scales have in common the ability to define and color music in a fundamental way.

The music familiar in the West today is based almost entirely on two scales. These are the **major scale** and the **minor scale,** and both of them are built out of whole steps and half steps. The music written with these two scales is called **tonal music** and includes such widely divergent styles as the music of Bach, Miles Davis, and Madonna, as well as the music we hear most frequently on television and at the movies.

It would be a mistake to assume that because major and minor scales are the most familiar to us, all the other scales are unimportant. As you will see in Chapter 9, some of these other scales have appeared repeatedly within Western tonal music. Keep in mind, too, that much of the world's music is still written in scales other than the major and minor.

Intervals

Before beginning our discussion of scales, we must first learn about two musical intervals—the half step and the whole step. The musical distance between two pitches, whether sounded or written on the staff, is called an **Interval.**

Half Steps

The smallest interval on the piano is a **half step**. This is the distance from any key to the key immediately above or below it. The following example shows the three situations in which half steps can occur: (1) between a white key and a black key, (2) between a black key and a white key, and (3) between a white key and a white key. Notice that the third possibility, between a white key and a white key, appears in only two places in each octave—between E and F and between B and C. As you look at this example, remember that an interval is the distance *between* two notes.

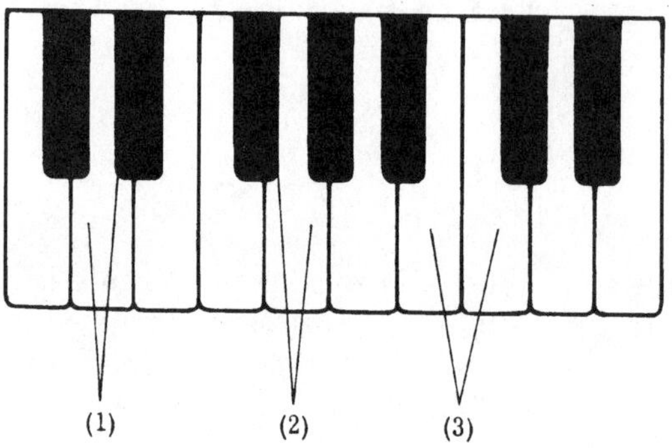

Half steps are either diatonic or chromatic. A **diatonic half step** consists of two pitches with *adjacent* letter names and staff locations. The following are all examples of diatonic half steps:

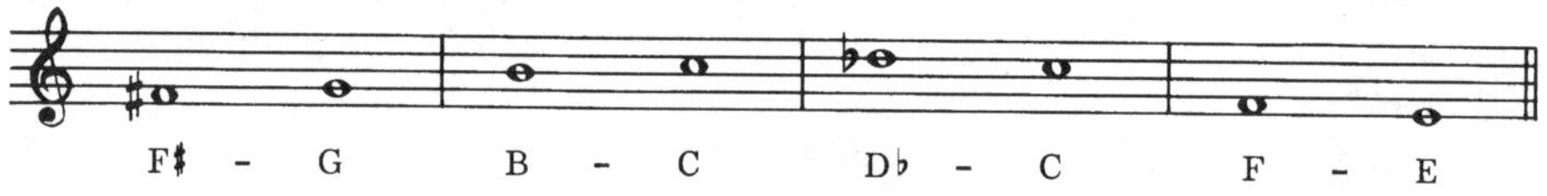

A **chromatic half step** employs two pitches of the *same* letter name and staff location, such as the following:

The significance of this distinction will become clear in later chapters, when we discuss minor scales and modes.

Whole Steps

A **whole step** consists of two half steps. On the keyboard, there will be one key between the two pitches that are a whole step apart. Whole steps can appear (1) between a white key and a white key, (2) between a black key and a black key, and (3) between a white key and a black key. In each instance, the whole step has one pitch in between.

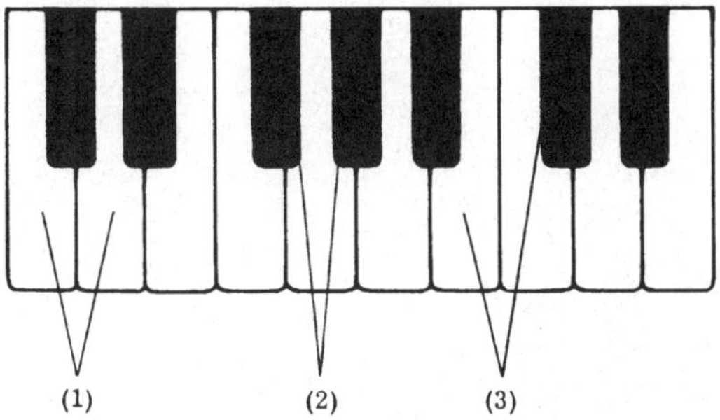

Whole steps *usually* involve pitches of adjacent letter names, as in the following cases:

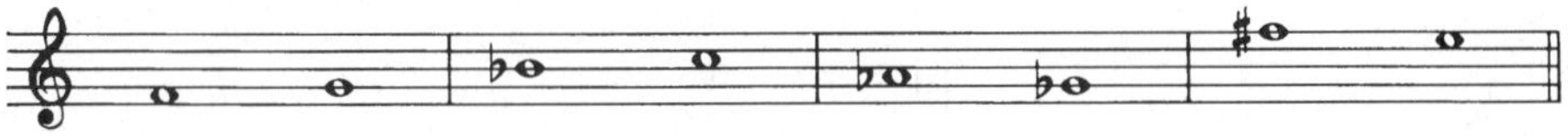

F - G   B♭ - C   A♭ - G♭   F♯ - E

EXERCISE 4•1

On the following keyboards, identify each indicated interval as either a whole step or a half step. Use the letters *W* or *H* to indicate the interval and write them in the space provided.

1.

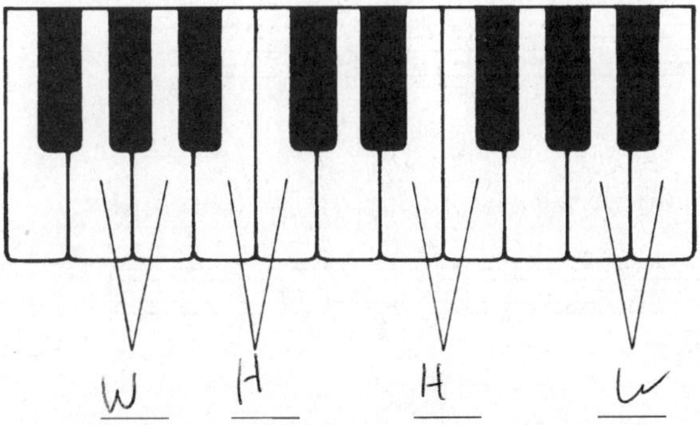

2.

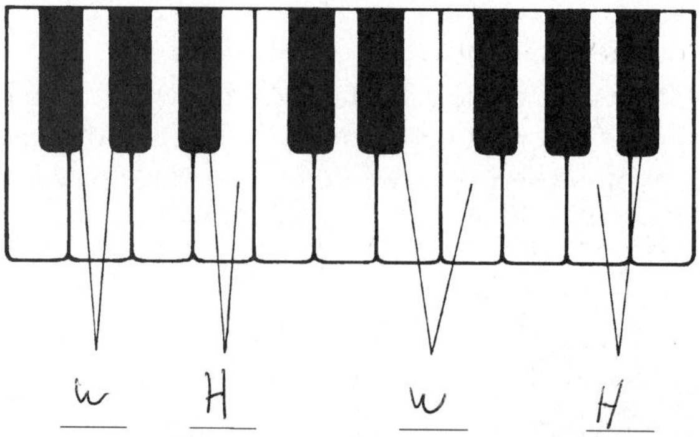

3.

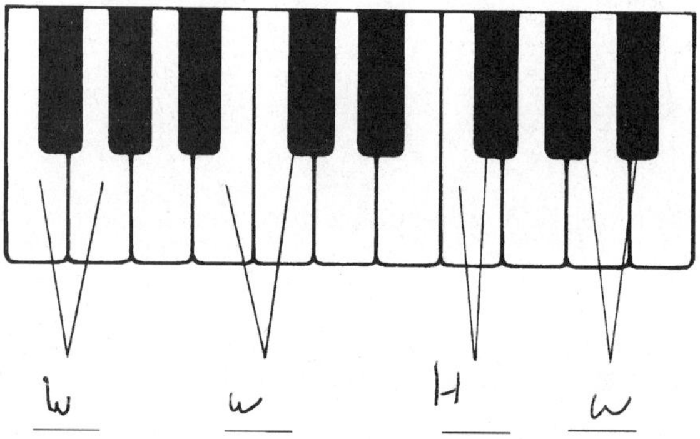

Scales as Interval Patterns

Western music divides the octave into twelve equal half steps. A scale formed by dividing the octave in this way is called a **chromatic scale**.

Ascending chromatic scale (usually written with sharps):

Descending chromatic scale (usually written with flats):

Notice that these are all the notes on the keyboard—black and white—within one octave.

Because the chromatic scale consists entirely of half steps, it seldom functions in itself as a musical scale. Rather, it is the source material from which a huge variety of other scales are drawn. Many scales combine whole steps and half steps, and some scales use one or more intervals larger than the whole step. This variation in interval size gives each scale, and the resultant music in that scale, a particular color, quality, or ambience. The unique interval patterns of a scale are transferred to the melody and the harmony of music written in that scale. The major scale and the natural minor scale (which will be more fully discussed later) are both seven-note scales having five whole steps and two half steps, yet they sound strikingly unlike each other because the pattern of whole steps and half steps is different. The concept of a scale as an interval pattern that controls the interval patterns of melody and harmony is fundamental to the understanding of tonal music.

EXERCISE 4•2

Write one-octave chromatic scales beginning on the pitches indicated. Remember to use sharps for the ascending scale and flats for the descending scale. Remember also to keep the notated pitch sequences B–C and E–F intact, since the interval between them is already a half step.

Ascending Scales

1. 

2. 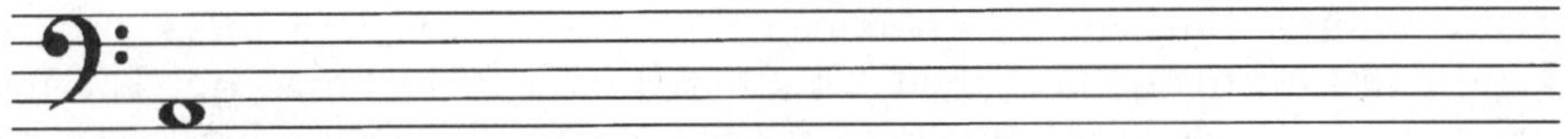

Descending Scales

3. 

4. 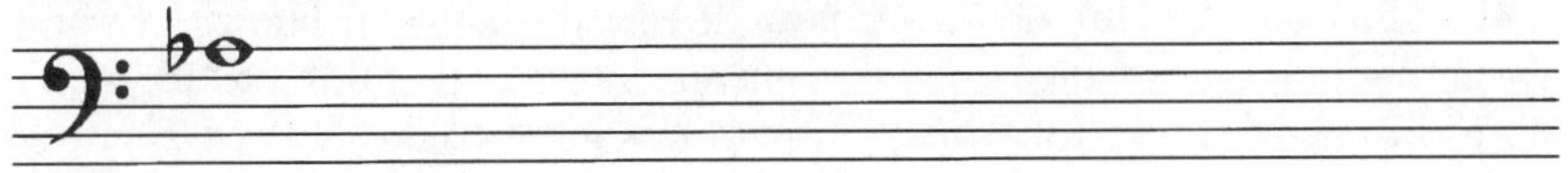

Elements of the Major Scale

The major scale is an interval pattern of five whole steps and two diatonic half steps. The half steps always occur between the third and fourth tones and the seventh and first tones of the scale. On the keyboard, the major scale falls on all white keys when it begins on the pitch C.

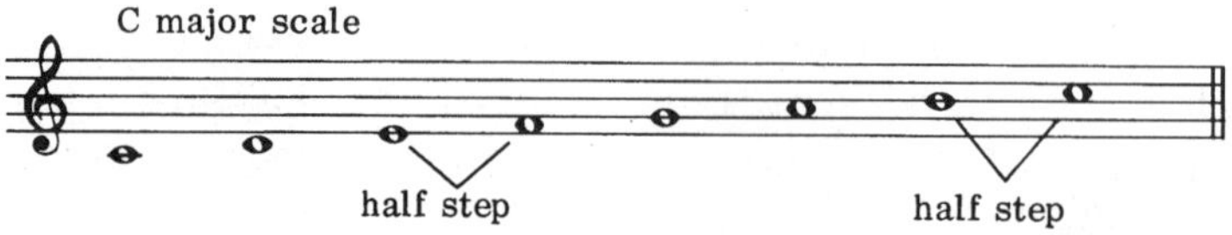

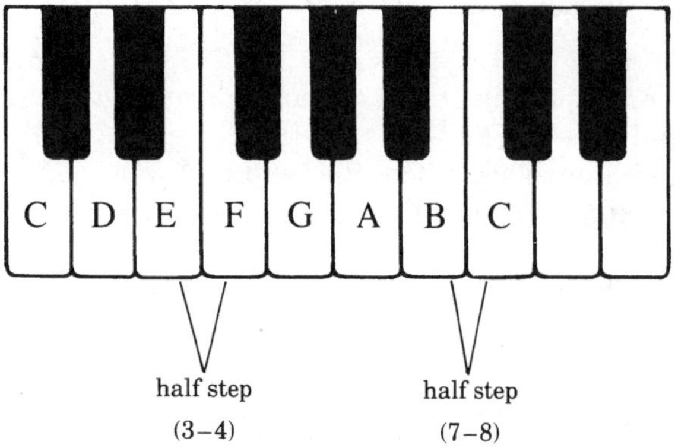

This pattern of whole steps and half steps gives the major scale its characteristic quality. The half step between the seventh and first tones creates a strong pull toward the first tone. This first tone is called a **tonic**. The tonic, sometimes also called the home note, is the pitch to which the other tones of the scale seem to be related. As you sing or play a major scale, notice how the tonic becomes the focus for a group of seemingly related pitches, similar to a center of gravity.

Musical Problem

As a group, make a list of five melodies that most class members know well. These can be themes from your favorite television shows or songs from the movies, as well as melodies from classical, popular, or folk music. Two things are important in making your choices. The first is to choose only songs in major keys (your teacher will help you if necessary). The second is to choose melodies that the class knows well and can sing.

1. ______________________________

2. ______________________________

3. ______________________________

4. ______________________________

5. ______________________________

As a group, sing the melodies you have chosen and identify the tonic of each by sound. Notice how often and in what places the tonic occurs. Are these places restful or active?

After you have sung each melody and located the tonic, sing a major scale beginning on the tonic of that melody. Do you notice the relationship between the scale and the melody?

The pattern of whole steps and half steps that produces a major scale can be moved to any other beginning pitch and, if the pattern is kept intact, will form a different major scale. In all, there are fifteen different major scales—seven that use flatted notes, seven that use sharped notes, and one natural scale. In the G major scale, for instance, an F♯ is needed to produce the whole step between the sixth and seventh degrees and the half step between the seventh and first degrees:

G major scale

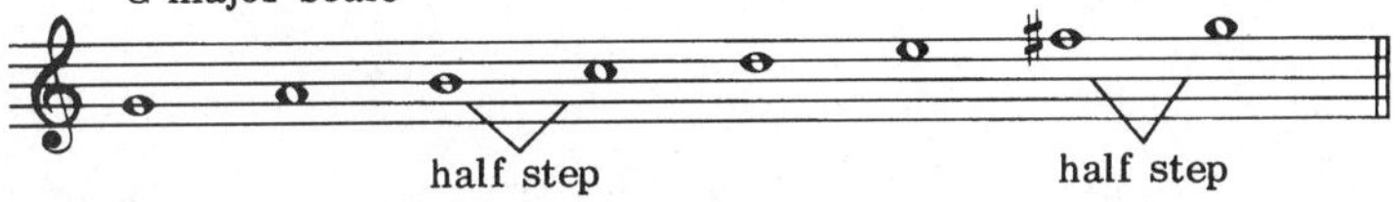

Similarly, the major scale beginning on A requires three sharps (F♯, C♯, G♯) to produce the correct pattern:

A major scale

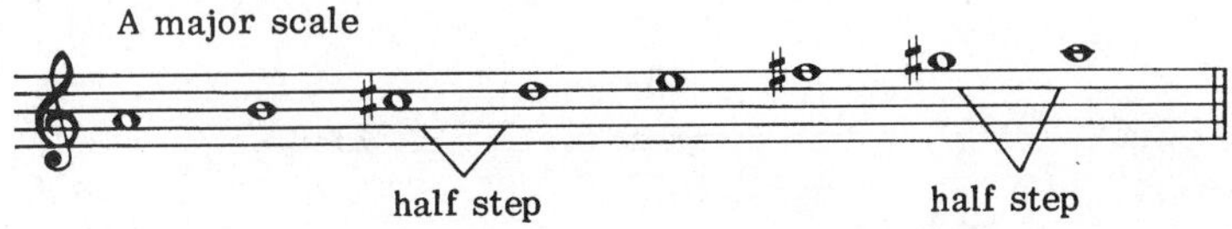

In the following example, five flats are required to produce the correct pattern of whole steps and half steps.

D♭ major scale

As you practice writing scales, remember that as long as you reproduce the pattern of whole steps and half steps exactly, the result will be a major scale, regardless of the pitch you begin on. Remember, also, that major scales are alphabetical sequences of pitches. All major and minor scales use only diatonic, not chromatic, half steps.

EXERCISE 4•3

Write ascending and descending major scales, in both treble clef and bass clef, from each starting pitch. When writing major scales, there should be only one pitch of each letter name. For example, it is incorrect to have both G♭ and G♮ in the same scale. The correct sequence is F♯–G. (The sequence of scales in this exercise is arranged so that each succeeding scale requires only one additional sharp.)

When you have written the scales, check that the half steps occur between the third and fourth degrees and between the seventh and first degrees. Indicate the half steps for each scale. A keyboard is given to help you visualize the whole steps and half steps.

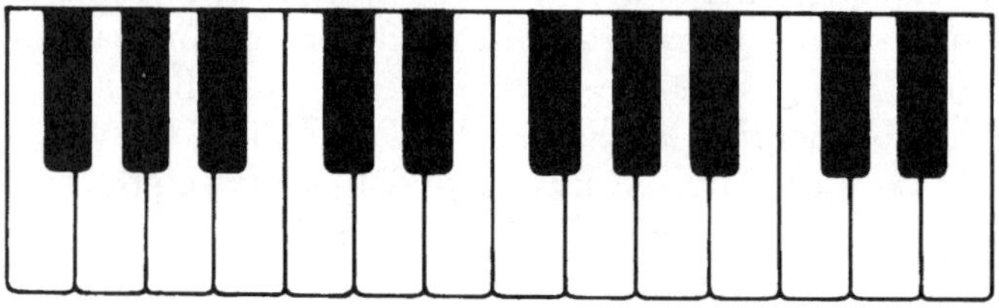

EXAMPLE:

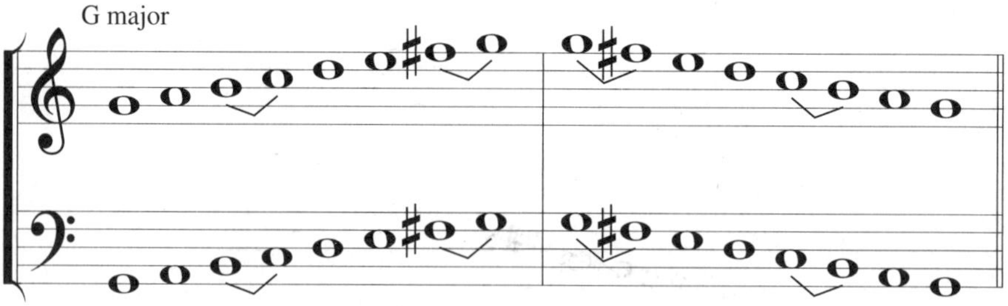

1.

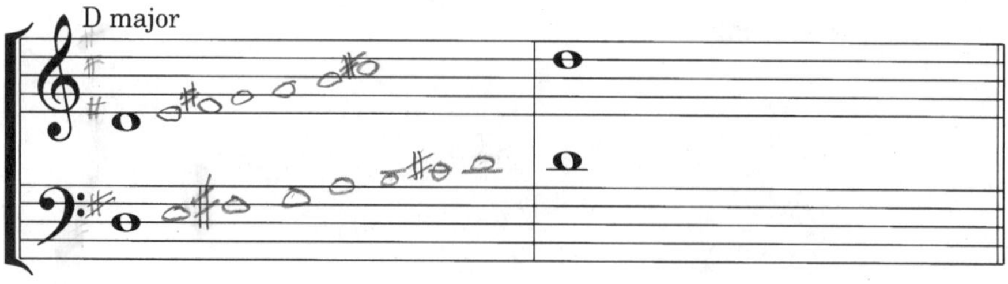

FCG

2.

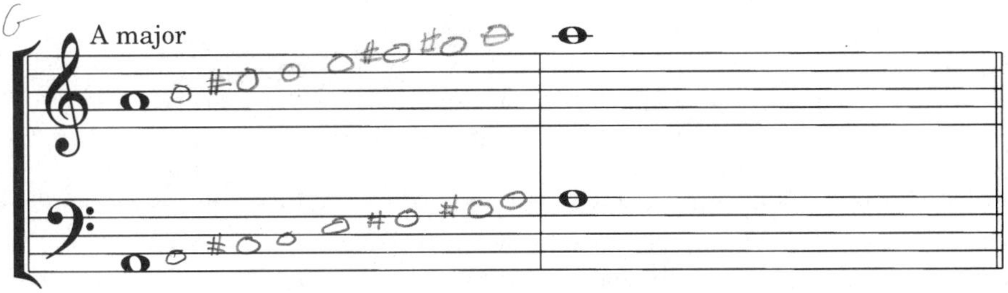

FCG

FCGD

3.

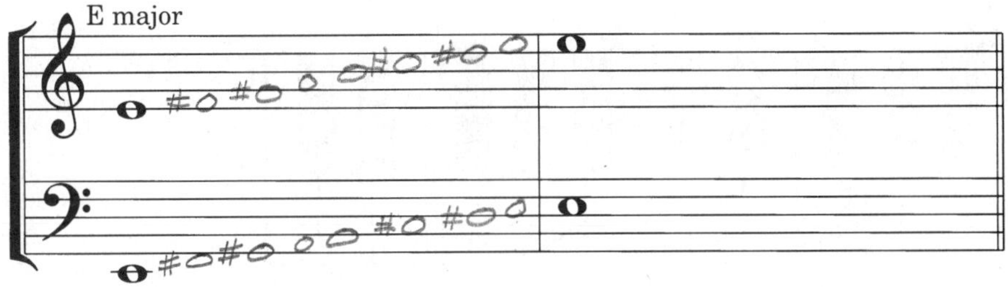

FCGDA

4.

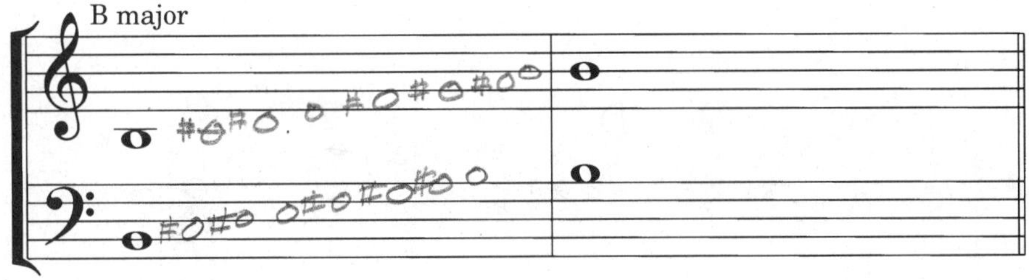

FCGDAE

5.

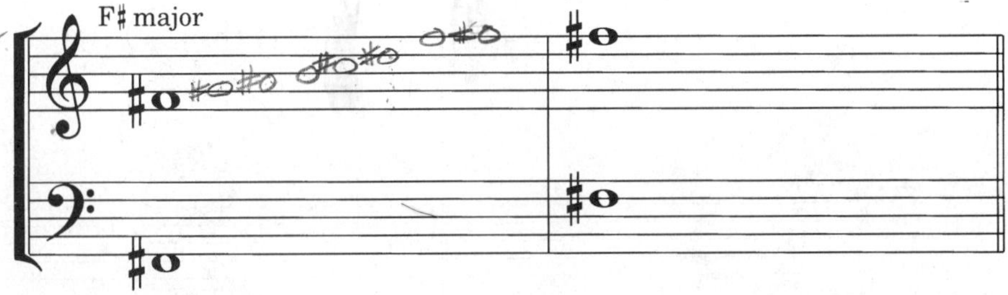

6.

FCGDAEB

EXERCISE 4•4

Write ascending and descending major scales from each starting pitch. (The sequence of scales in this exercise is arranged so that each succeeding scale requires one additional flat.)

When you have written the scales, check that the half steps occur between the third and fourth degrees and between the seventh and first degrees. Indicate the half steps for each scale. A keyboard is given to help you visualize the intervals.

EXAMPLE:

F major

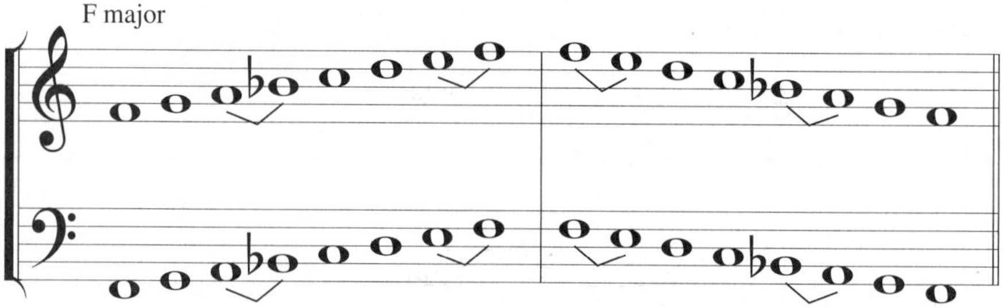

B♭ major

1. 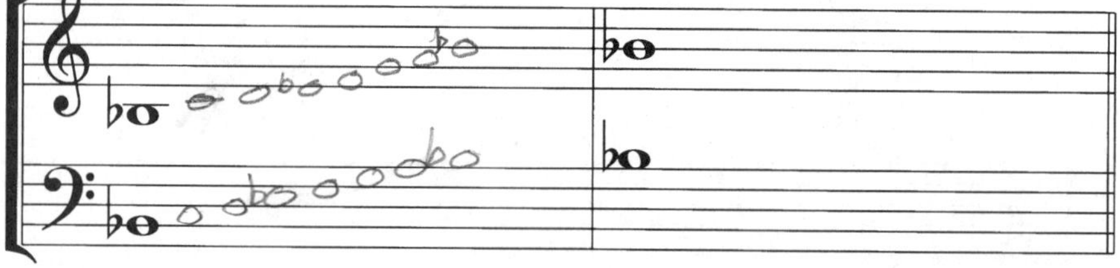

E♭ major

2. 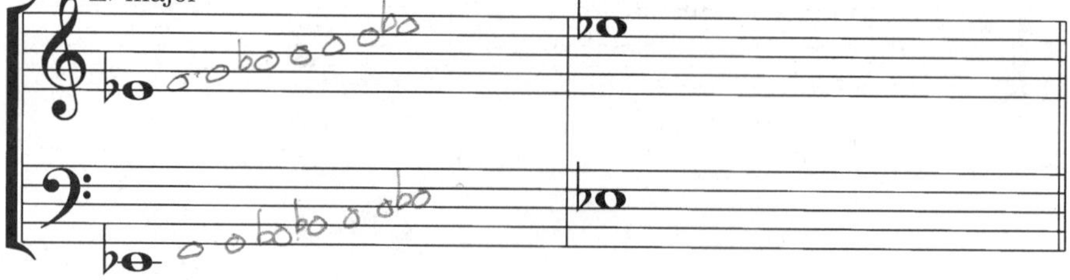

3.

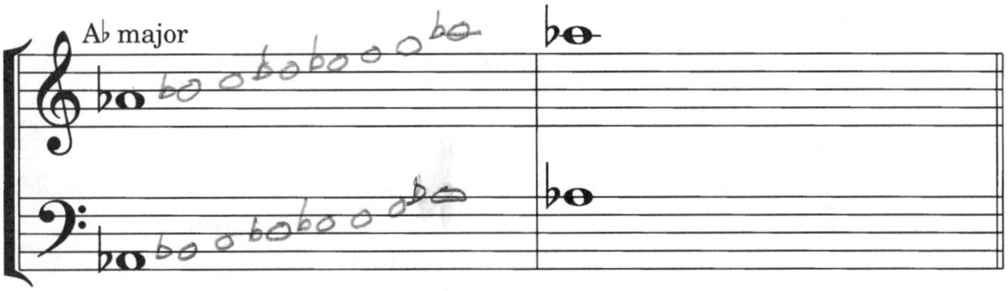

4.

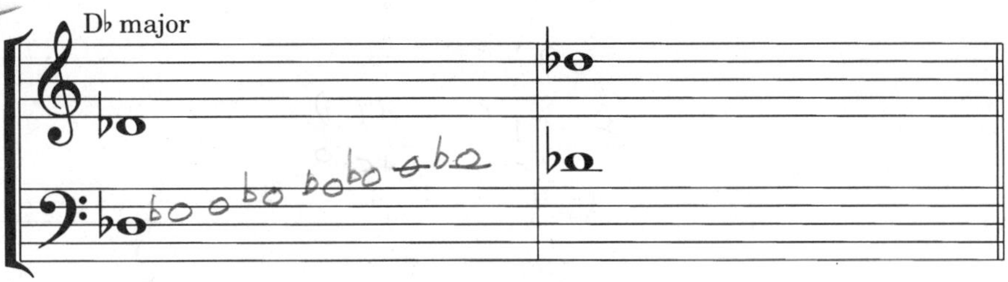

5.

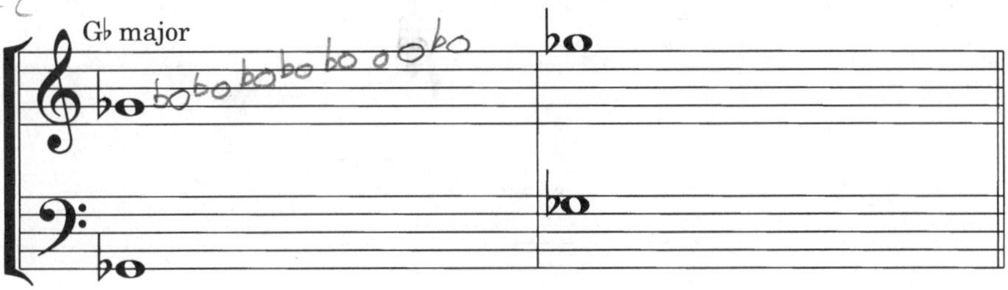

6.

EXERCISE 4•5

Write ascending major scales starting from the given tonic pitches. These are the same scales as in Exercises 4-2 and 4-3, but here they are in no particular order. Remember to use only one pitch of each letter name. When you have written each scale, write the names of the third and fourth scale degrees and the seventh and first degrees in the chart. Are both intervals half steps?

EXAMPLE:

Half Steps

b–c; f♯–g
3–4 7–1

a–b♭; e–f
3–4 7–1

1. 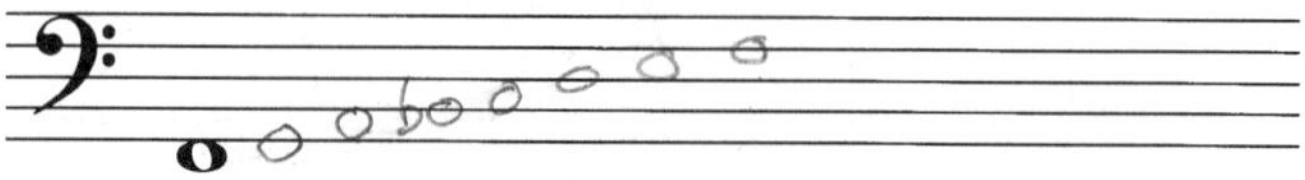

____; ____ 2. 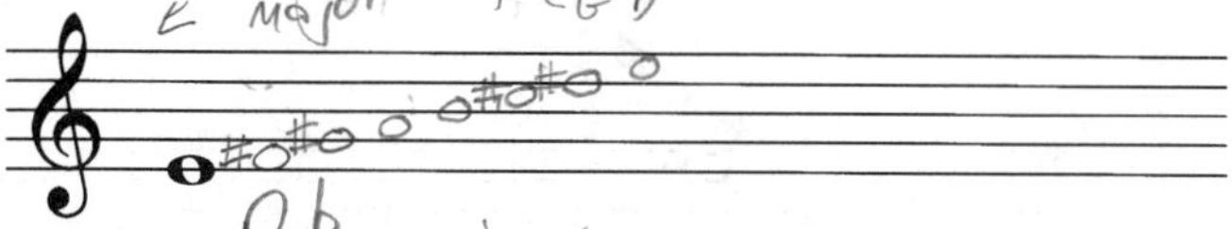

____; ____ 3. 

____; ____ 4. 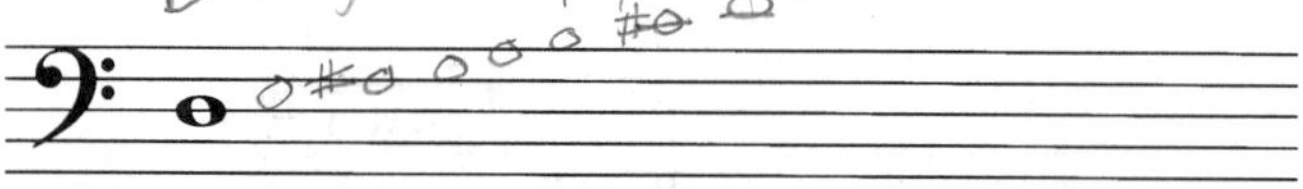

____; ____ 5. 

____; ____ 6. 

____; ____ 7. 

____; ____ 8. 

____; ____ 9. 

______; ______ 10.

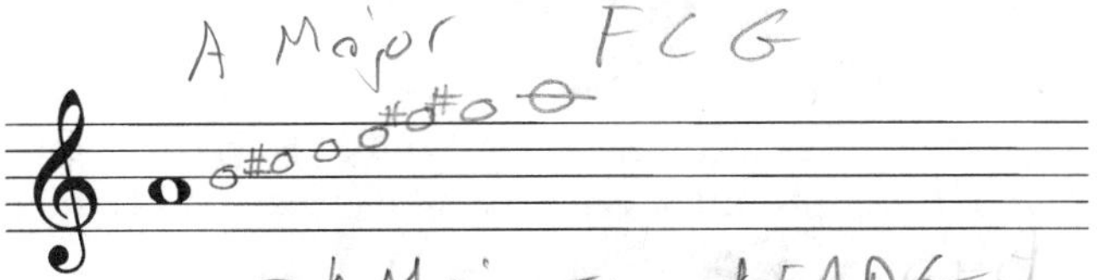

______; ______ 11.

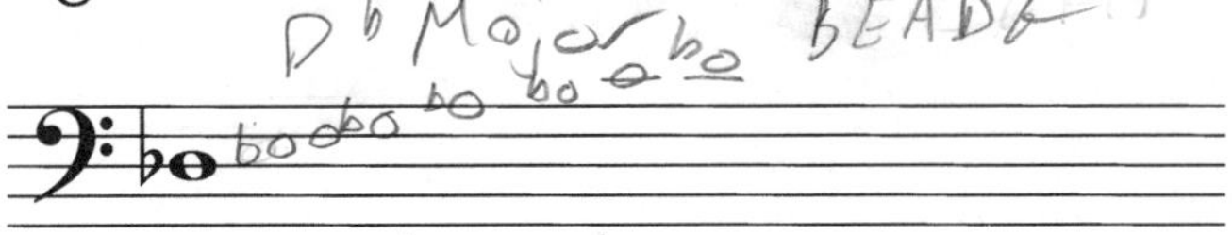

______; ______ 12.

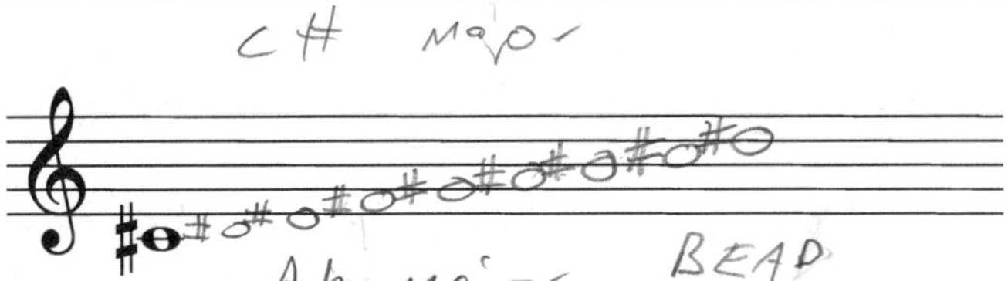

______; ______ 13.

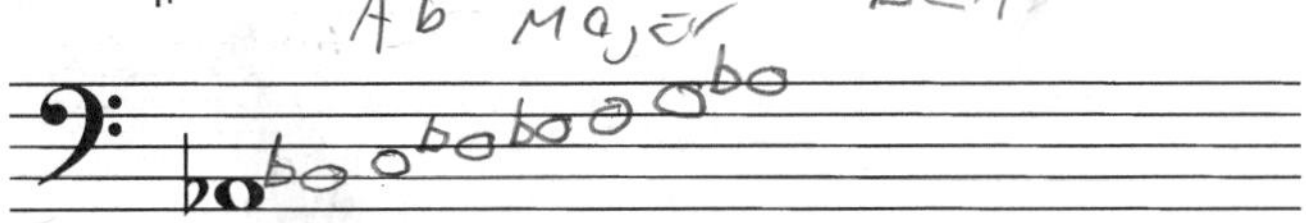

Musical Problem

The keyboard can be a valuable aid in helping you understand scale construction. The whole-step and half-step patterns and the scales that these patterns form can be visualized and recalled more easily when practiced on the keyboard.

Practice playing and singing one-octave, ascending major scales starting from the following pitches. It is not necessary to use the proper scale fingering at this time; however, you should not use just one finger. A good rule is to avoid using a thumb on a black key. (If you prefer to learn the correct fingerings now, they are given in Appendix E.)

1. G major
2. D major
3. G♭ major
4. C♯ major
5. E♭ major
6. B♭ major
7. D♭ major
8. F major
9. B major
10. A major

EXERCISE 4•6

Starting from the given tonic pitches, write major scales in descending form. This exercise is essentially the same as Exercise 4-4, except it is in reverse—that is, you must start on the eighth scale degree and work down—7, 6, 5, 4, 3, 2—to the first degree. Remember to use only one pitch of each letter name.

Remember also that the pitches of a scale remain the same whether the scale is in ascending or descending form. When you have written each scale, write the names of the first and seventh scale degrees and the fourth and third degrees. Are both intervals half steps?

100

Major Scales

EXAMPLE:

Half Steps

f–e / 1–7; b♭–a / 4–3

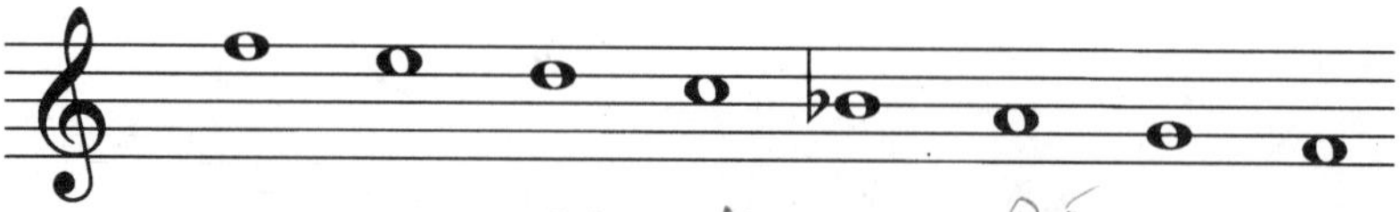

______; ______ 1.

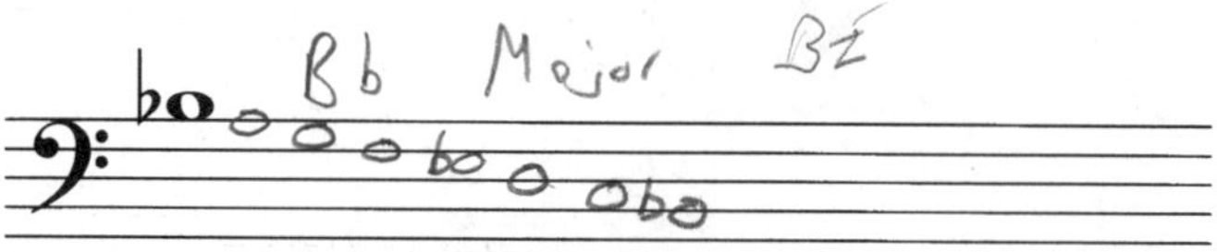

______; ______ 2.

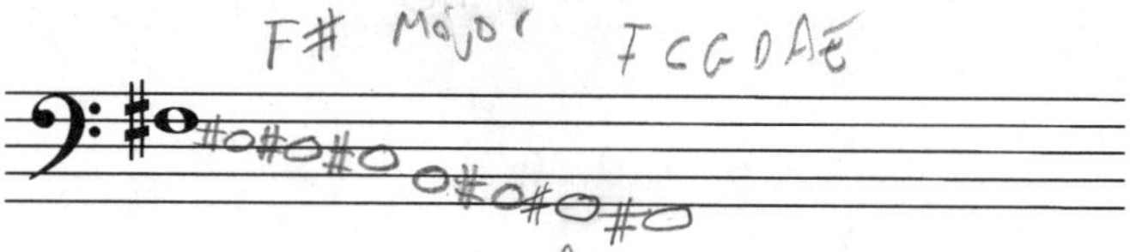

______; ______ 3.

______; ______ 4.

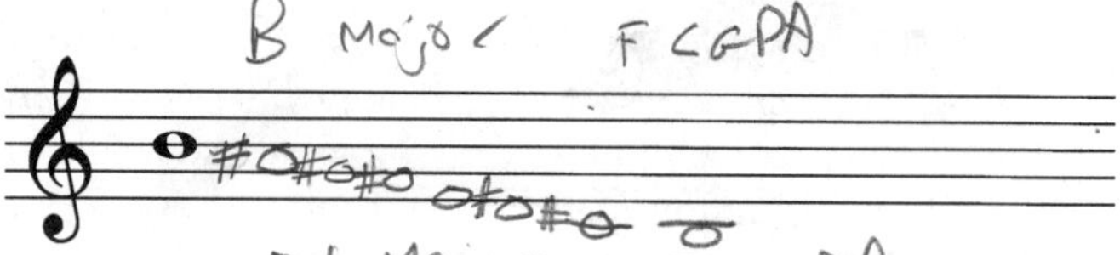

______; ______ 5.

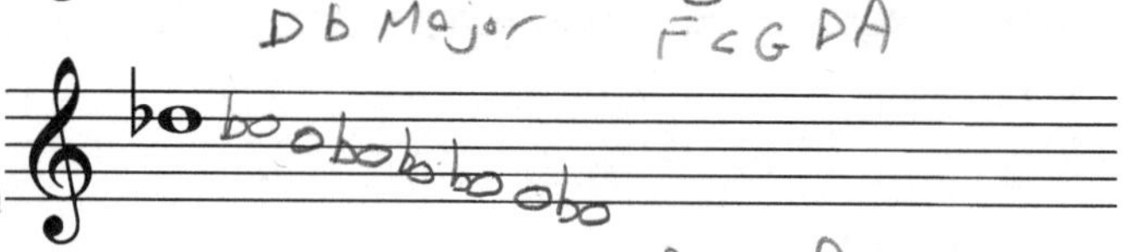

______; ______ 6.

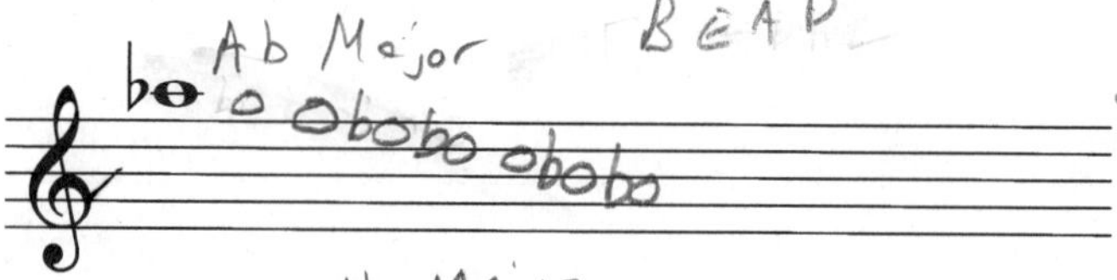

______; ______ 7.

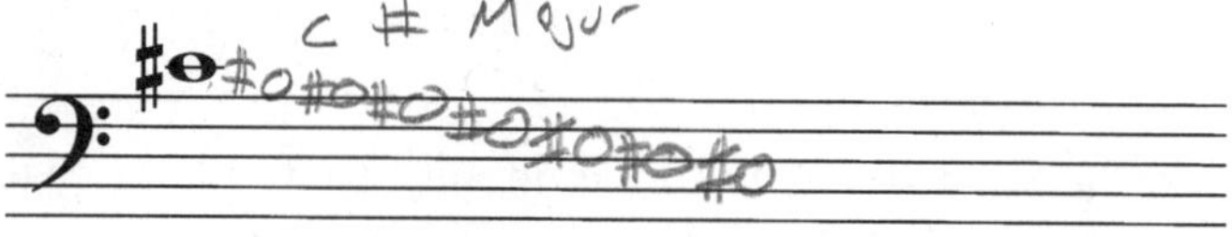

______; ______ 8.

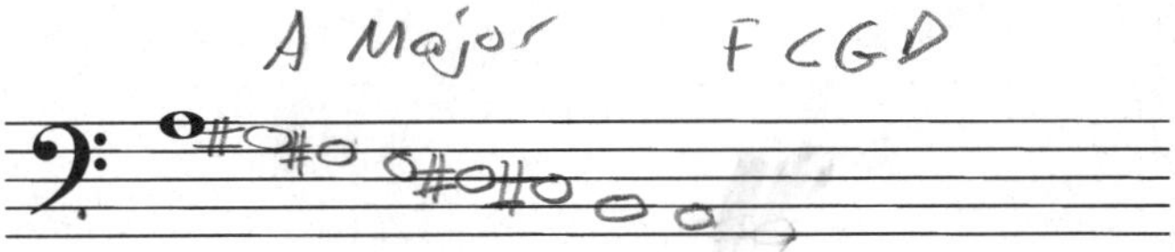

______; ______ 9.

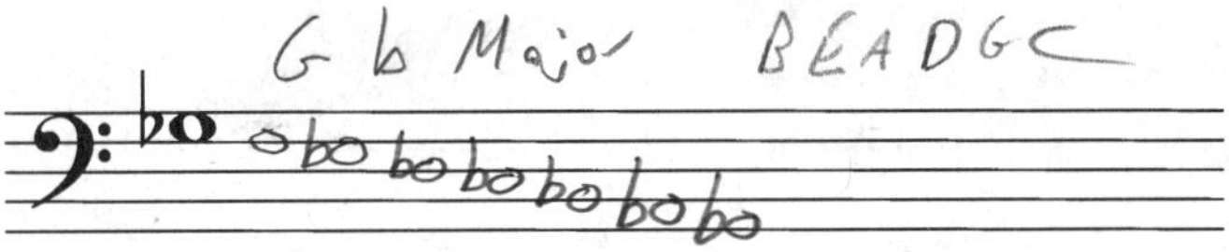

______; ______ 10.

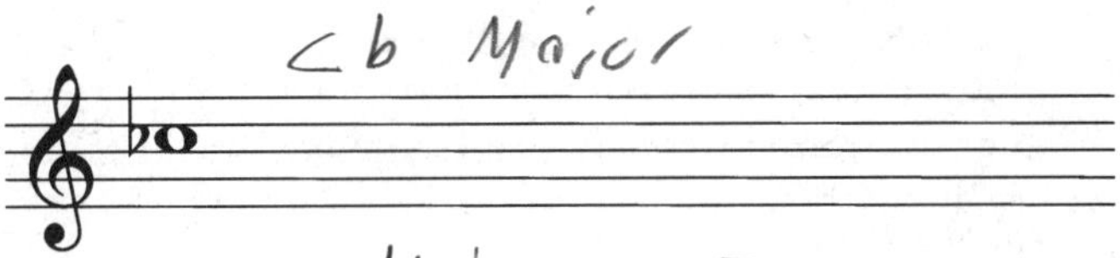

______; ______ 11.

______; ______ 12.

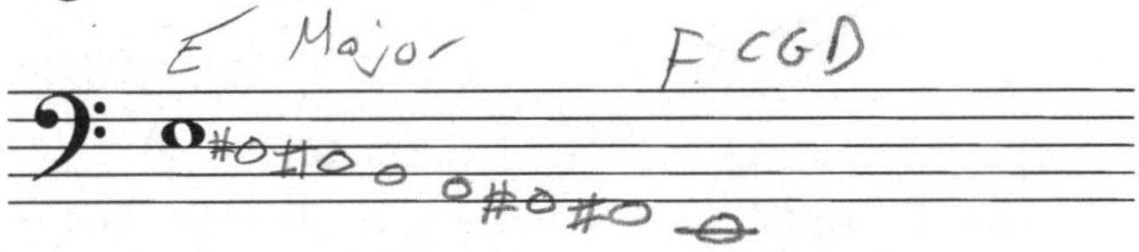

______; ______ 13.

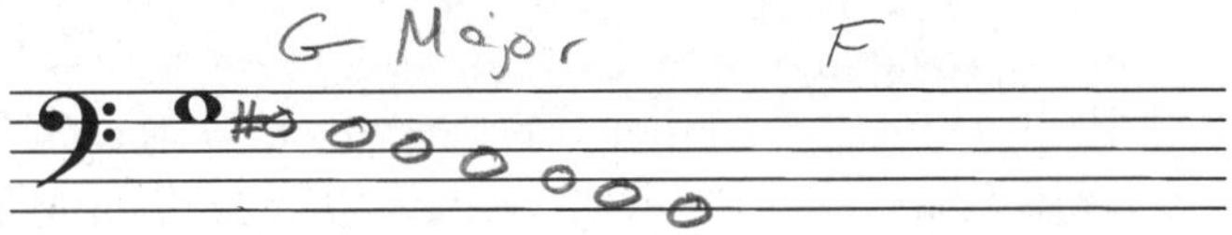

Musical Problem

Practice playing and singing one-octave, descending major scales from each of the following pitches. It is not necessary to pay attention to the correct fingerings at this time, but they are given in Appendix E if you wish to use them.

1. F major	8. G♭ major
2. G major	9. C♯ major
3. D major	10. F♯ major
4. B major	11. D♭ major
5. A major	12. E♭ major
6. E major	13. A♭ major
7. C major	14. B♭ major

Musical Problem

The ability to sing melodies at sight is a valuable tool for both the professional musician and the serious amateur. A number of methods exist that help develop this ability. Probably the most common system is called **movable *do*,** which assigns a specific syllable to each pitch of the scale. In this system, the tonic of a scale is always *do*. Study the following illustration and practice singing the major scale, both ascending and descending, using the syllables. Then, practice singing the exercises that follow the illustration. These exercises may seem difficult at first, but stick with them—they are intended to help you become familiar with the syllables in various combinations.

C major scale

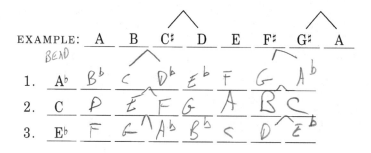

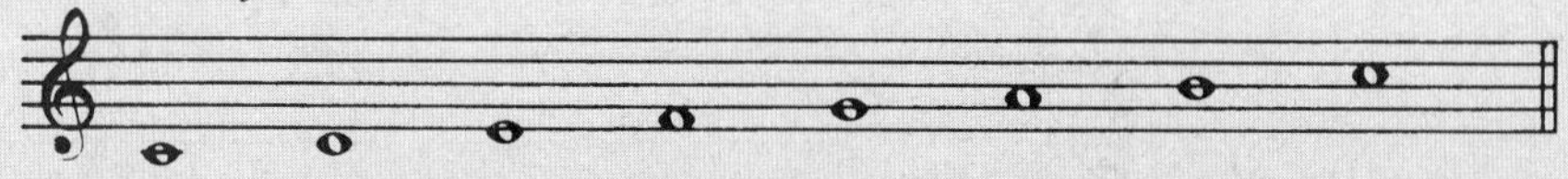

1. do re mi, re mi fa, mi fa sol, fa sol la, sol la ti, la ti do, ti do re do;
   do ti la, ti la sol, la sol fa, sol fa mi, fa mi re, mi re do, re do ti do

2. do mi, re fa, mi sol, fa la, sol ti, la do, ti re do;
   do la, ti sol, la fa, sol mi, fa re, mi do, re ti do

Although movable *do* is perhaps the most commonly used system, it is not the only one in use. Consequently, your teacher may prefer that you use an alternative system, such as substituting the numbers 1 to 7 for the scale degrees, or using the actual pitch names.

EXERCISE 4•7

Spell the following ascending major scales using letter names and any necessary accidentals. Mark the position of half steps as shown in the example. Practice spelling major scales, beginning on any pitch.

EXAMPLE: A B C♯ D E F♯ G♯ A

BEAD

1. A♭ B♭ C D♭ E♭ F G A♭
2. C D E F G A B C
3. E♭ F G A♭ B♭ C D E♭

BEA

4. D E F♯ G A B C♯ D
5. F G♯ A♯ B C♯ D♯ E♯ F♯
6. C♯ D♯ E♯ F♯ G♯ A♯ B♯ C♯
7. B C♯ D♯ E F♯ G♯ A♯ B
8. C♭ D♭ E♭ F♭ G♭ A♭ B♭ C♭
9. B♭ C D E♭ F G A B♭
10. G A B C D E F♯ G
11. D♭ E♭ F G♭ A♭ B♭ C D♭
12. G♭ A♭ B♭ C♭ D♭ E♭ F G♭
13. F♯ G♯ A♯ B C♯ D♯ E♯ F♯
14. E F♯ G♯ A B C♯ D♯ E

Musical Problem

Sing each of the following melodies, using a neutral syllable like *la*, the letter names of the pitches, or the scale-degree numbers. Locate the tonic by sound. Then write the sight-singing syllables below each note. Finally, notate the major scale on which each melody is built.

"Michael, Row the Boat Ashore"

1.

Scale

(continued)

"Barbara Allen"

2.

Scale

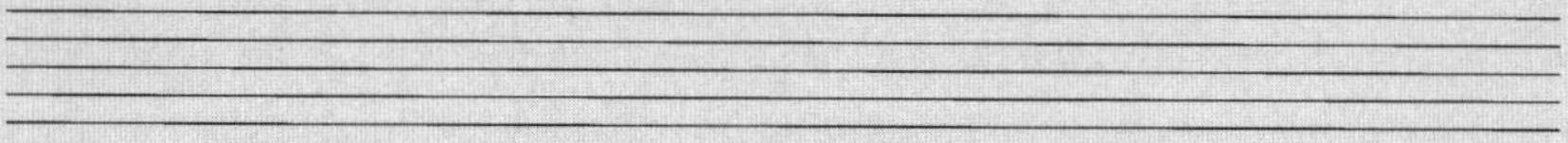

"Sur le Pont d'Avignon"

3.

Scale

Mozart, "Ein kleine Nachtmusik"

4.

"America"

5.

Naming Scale Degrees

Each scale degree has a specific name. The scale degrees, in ascending order, are: **tonic**, **supertonic**, **mediant**, **subdominant**, **dominant**, **submediant,** **leading tone,** and **tonic.** These scale-degree names always remain the same regardless of the octave in which the pitch of that name appears.

C major scale

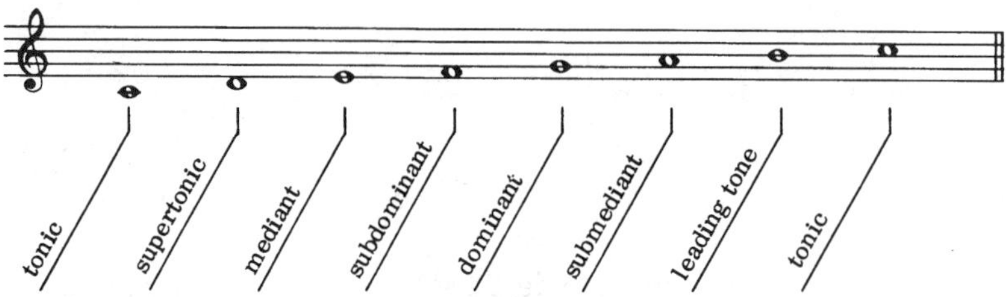

At first, these names might appear arbitrary. If, however, you consider the tonic as the tonal center of gravity, then the names logically describe the relationship between the scale degrees. Notice how the tonic becomes the central pitch when the scale degrees are arranged in the following way:

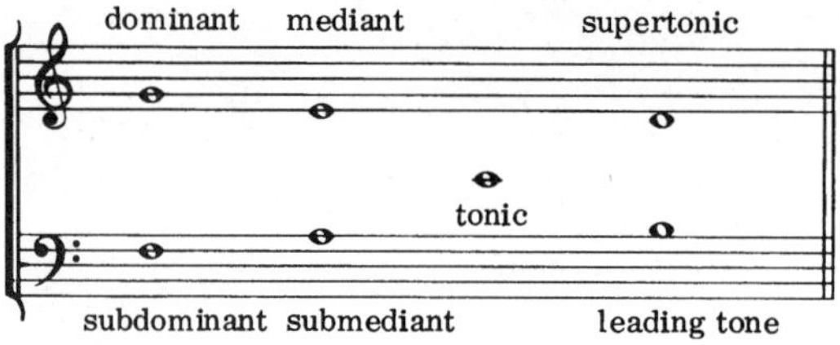

EXERCISE 4•8

Name the following scale degrees.

1. third degree mediant
2. fifth degree dominant
3. sixth degree submediant
4. first degree tonic
5. seventh degree leading tone
6. second degree supertonic
7. fourth degree subdominant

It may seem momentarily confusing to you that the individual pitches of a scale may be referred to in more than one way. Perhaps the following chart will be helpful in clearing up the confusion. The pitch names on the far left are an ascending C major scale; the terms to the right indicate three different ways each particular scale degree can be referred to or labeled. Although the third option (numbers) has not been previously discussed in this book (the concept is easily understood), it is used frequently in written analytical discussions of music, and all musicians should become familiar with it.

C	do	tonic	$\hat{1}$
D	re	supertonic	$\hat{2}$
E	mi	mediant	$\hat{3}$
F	fa	subdominant	$\hat{4}$

G	sol	dominant	$\hat{5}$
A	la	submediant	$\hat{6}$
B	ti	leading tone	$\hat{7}$

F C G D A E B

~~B E A D G C F~~

. F G A

EXERCISE 4•9

Identify by letter name the following scale degrees.

1. mediant of the F major scale *A*
2. supertonic of the D major scale *E*
3. subdominant of the B♭ major scale *E♭*
4. leading tone of the G major scale *F♯*
5. mediant of the D♭ major scale *F*
6. subdominant of the A♭ major scale *D♭*
7. mediant of the C major scale *E*
8. submediant of the D major scale *B*
9. supertonic of the F major scale *G*
10. subdominant of the C♯ major scale *F♯*
11. mediant of the B major scale *D♯*
12. submediant of the C♭ major scale *A♭*

Musical Problem

Instrumentalists should be able to play one- and two-octave major scales, both ascending and descending. If you cannot do this, you should begin at once to develop this facility. Improving your ability to play scales will be of immediate benefit, since many of the patterns of tonal music are directly related to the scales on which they are based. To begin, practice the easier scales slowly and evenly, concentrating on accuracy and quality of tone. After you have mastered these, move on to more difficult scales.

EXERCISE 4•10

Complete the following:

1. F♯ is the mediant of the _____*D*_____ major scale.
2. C is the submediant of the _____*E♭*_____ major scale.
3. E♭ is the subdominant of the _____*B♭*_____ major scale.
4. D is the mediant of the _____*B♭*_____ major scale.

5. A is the leading tone of the _______ major scale.
6. B♭ is the subdominant of the _______ major scale.
7. F♯ is the dominant of the _______ major scale.
8. E is the subdominant of the _______ major scale.
9. G is the mediant of the _______ major scale.
10. D is the submediant of the _______ major scale.
11. C is the leading tone of the _______ major scale.
12. F is the dominant of the _______ major scale.

Musical Problem

Sing in your mind any of the following melodies that you know. Put a check mark by the ones that are based on a major scale. Then, as a class, sing aloud all the melodies you can. If you don't know a particular melody, listen as it is sung and decide if it is in a major key.

1. "The Simpsons" TV show theme _____
2. "Titanic" theme _____
3. "South Park" TV show theme _____
4. "Star Wars" theme _____
5. "2001" theme _____
6. "Moon River" _____

Ear Training

All musicians need to *hear* music as completely as they can. This involves listening not to the emotional content but to the actual mechanics of the music. Identifying the instruments that are playing, distinguishing the number of lines or voices in a work, and accurately notating rhythms that you hear are all part of developing your ear. But most people, when they think of training themselves to hear better, think first of pitch and pitch discrimination.

Some people have excellent ears. That is, they have an astonishing ability to make extremely fine aural discriminations. Some people can even name pitches as they hear them played or sung. This ability is called **perfect pitch,** and the people who have it were born with it. Although there are degrees of ability within perfect pitch—some people can name all the pitches in a cluster of notes played on the piano, others can only name the notes when played individually—this ability cannot be learned.

A similar ability can, however, be developed with practice. This ability is called **relative pitch.** Relative pitch involves learning the sounds of the various intervals and applying this knowledge when listening and performing. People with highly developed relative pitch can also name notes that they hear, if they are given a beginning pitch. If you improvise or play jazz, rock, or pop music by ear, you may already have good relative pitch. But it can be made even better with practice. If you want to play by ear, or write music, or just better understand the music you like to listen to, remember that these abilities can be developed and expanded with practice.

Ear training is the term musicians give to the process of developing their ability to hear better. We have already done some of this in the Musical Problems of this book, and we will do more from time to time. If this is a skill that you feel you need to develop, keep in mind that progress may be slow at first, and success may, as with most skills, seem to come in plateaus. Keep in mind too that everyone begins at a different level of ability. You should not be discouraged by other people's abilities. If you work consistently, you will see your own abilities grow and develop.

Musical Problem

Your teacher or another member of the class will play a major scale. Then he or she will play one pitch that will be either the tonic or the dominant from that scale. In the spaces below, indicate which pitch is being played.

1. ____________ 5. ____________
2. ____________ 6. ____________
3. ____________ 7. ____________
4. ____________ 8. ____________

Now try the same thing using three pitches—tonic, dominant, and submediant.

1. ____________ 5. ____________
2. ____________ 6. ____________
3. ____________ 7. ____________
4. ____________ 8. ____________

Finally, see if you can identify one of four different pitches—tonic, dominant, submediant, or subdominant.

1. ____________ 5. ____________
2. ____________ 6. ____________
3. ____________ 7. ____________
4. ____________ 8. ____________

Focus

The major scale is known to all of us. Most people over the age of ten can sing a major scale, complete with the correct syllables. In fact, this very familiarity may be a problem for beginning music students. We tend to think of the major scale as quite simple—a stepping-stone to more interesting musical matters.

You should not allow yourself to become complacent about scales, however. A thorough knowledge of scales is basic to understanding and performing music. The major scale seems familiar because so many of the melodies and so much of the harmony you have heard throughout your life are based on it. To deal *theoretically* with music based on major scales, you must both understand the major scale as an interval pattern and acquire skill and facility in writing, playing, and singing this common pattern.

Musical Problem

Below are several melodies in major keys from Appendix D. Practice singing these melodies, but on *la* and with moveable *do.* Once you are familiar with the melodies, practice conducting them as you sing. It would also be helpful to practice playing them at the keyboard.

1.

2.

3.

4.

5.
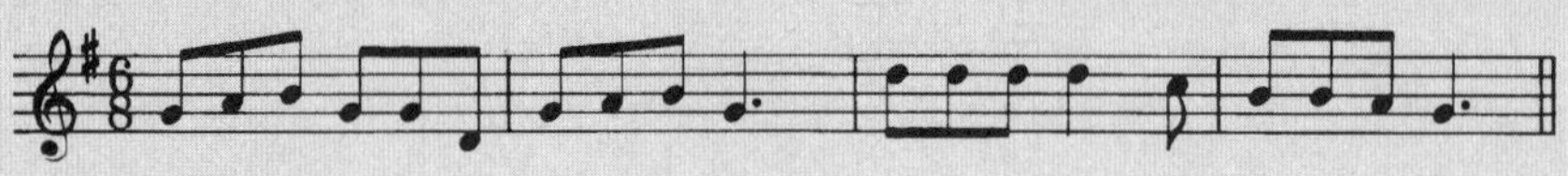

Chapter 5

Major Key Signatures

The Key Signature

In the previous chapter, you were asked to use individual accidentals when writing scales. This practice is useful in learning scale construction, but it makes performing, particularly sight-reading, extremely complicated. Consider the difficulty reading a piece of music in a key in which every pitch has a sharp sign, as in the following example.

Bach: "Preludio III" from *Well-Tempered Clavier,* Book I
(key of C♯ major written without key signature)

Since every scale has the same consistent interval structure, a musical shorthand has been developed to indicate, just once for an entire composition, the pitches requiring accidentals. It is called the **key signature**. The key signature is a grouping, at the beginning of each staff, of all the accidentals found in the scale on which the piece is based. The following illustration shows how a key signature would be used with the previous example.

Bach: "Preludio III" from *Well-Tempered Clavier,* Book I (with key signature)

An important point to remember is that an accidental appearing in the key signature applies to that note in all octaves. For instance, an F♯ in the key signature indicates that all Fs encountered in the piece are to be played or sung as F♯s. A similar rule holds for chromatic alterations *within* a measure. That is, once an accidental is introduced in a measure, it remains in force for the entire measure unless canceled by a natural sign.

Sharp Keys

The number and placement of sharps and flats in a key signature is not arbitrary; there is a definite order, an order that makes key signatures easy to read and remember. The following shows the order for the sharp major keys. Study it carefully and learn it.

Key Signatures: Sharp Major Keys

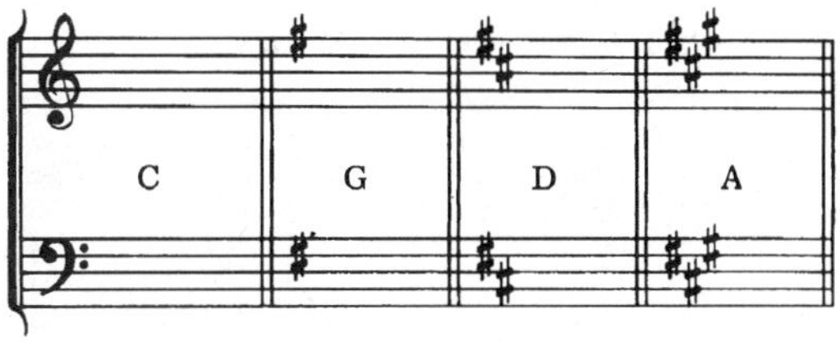

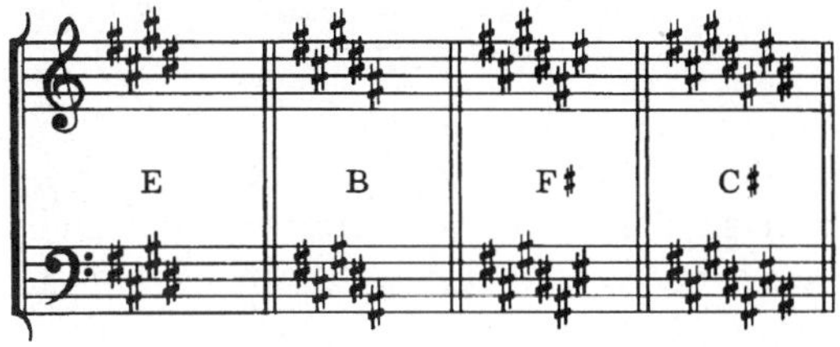

Notice the invariable pattern for sharp key signatures: If there is only one sharp, that sharp is always F♯; if two sharps, they are always F♯ and C♯, and so on. The complete order of sharps is F♯–C♯–G♯–D♯–A♯–E♯–B♯. You should learn both the order and the location of the sharps in both the treble and bass clefs. Fortunately, once you've learned them, you know them; they never change.

EXERCISE 5•1

On the stave below, copy the pattern of sharps for the sharp major keys. Make sure that the sharps are clearly centered, either on a line or in a space. Also make sure that you are placing each of them in the right octave.

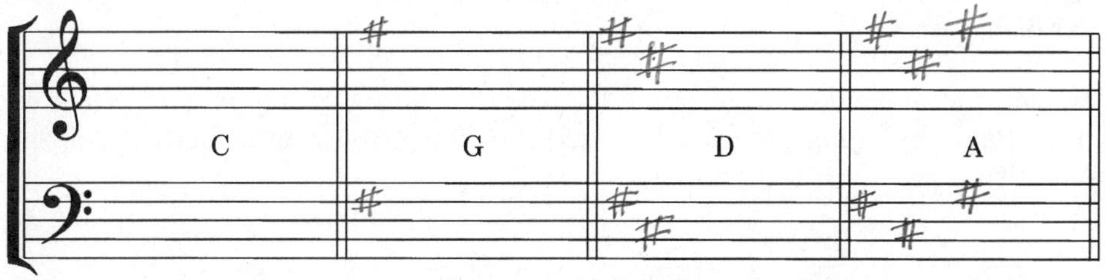

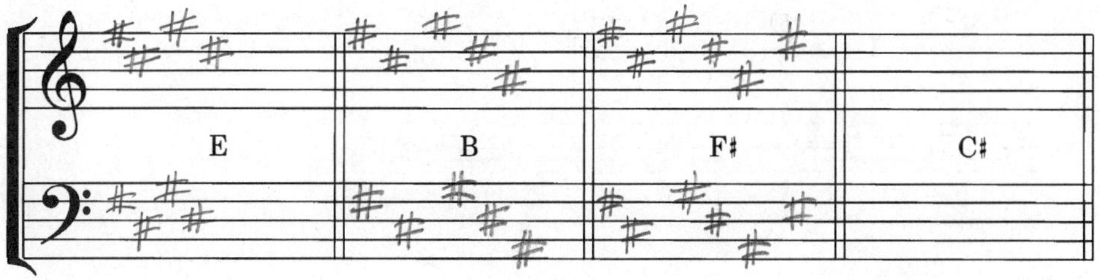

In identifying major key signatures that use sharps, the key is always the pitch a half step above the last sharp indicated in the signature. This is because the last added sharp is always the *leading tone* of that key.

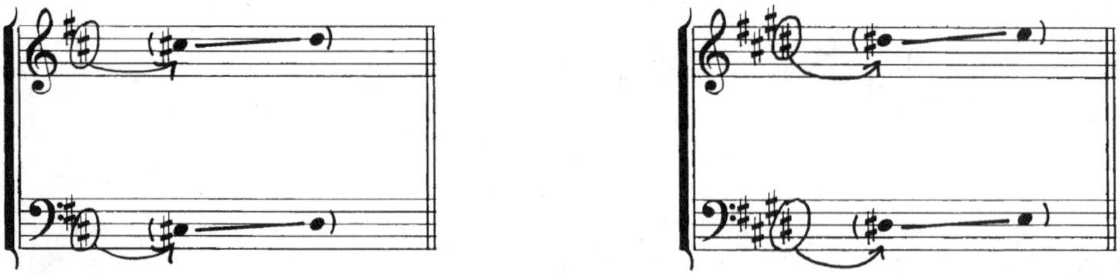

This method of identifying sharp keys is useful, but you should also memorize the number of sharps associated with each major key—information that is given in the following chart. Study the chart carefully until you can identify the sharp key signatures using either method.

Major Key	*Number of Sharps*
C	0
G	1
D	2
A	3
E	4
B	5
F♯	6
C♯	7

EXERCISE 5•2

Identify the major key represented by each of the following sharp key signatures. Begin by drawing a circle around the sharp that represents the leading tone of that key.

1.

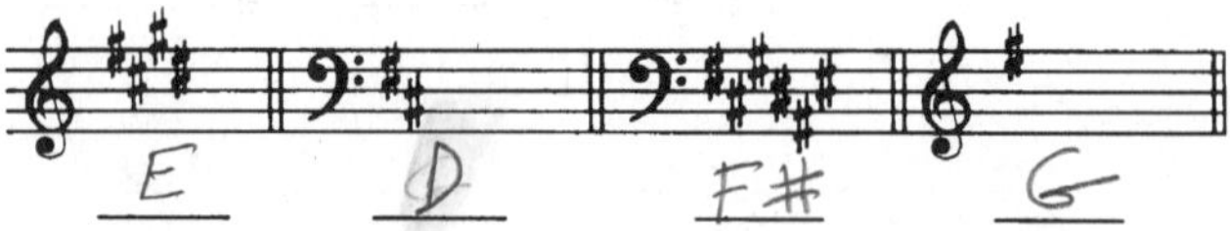

2.

3. 

4. 

Flat Keys

The order of flats in major key signatures is as follows:

Key Signatures: Flat Major Keys

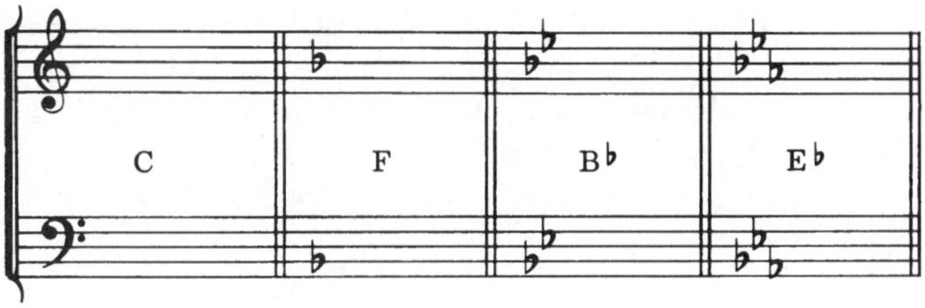

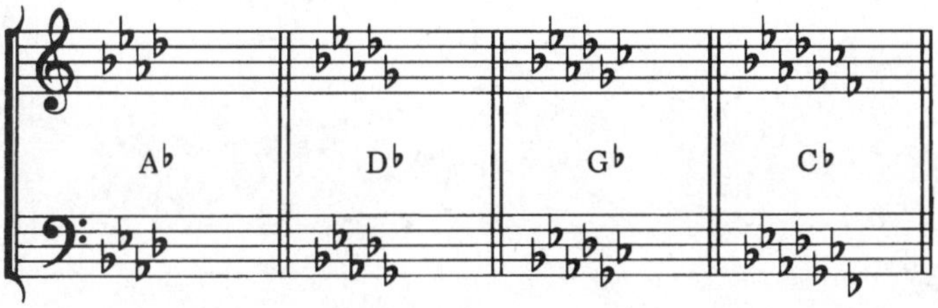

Flat key signatures, like sharp key signatures, have a consistent order and location on the staff. Notice that the last added flat is always the subdominant of that key. The complete order of flats is B♭–E♭–A♭–D♭–G♭–C♭–F♭. Both the order and the location of the flats should be learned for both the treble and bass clefs.

EXERCISE 5•3

On the staves provided, copy the pattern of flats for the flat major keys. Make certain that the flats are clearly centered on a line or in a space, and that they are in the correct octave.

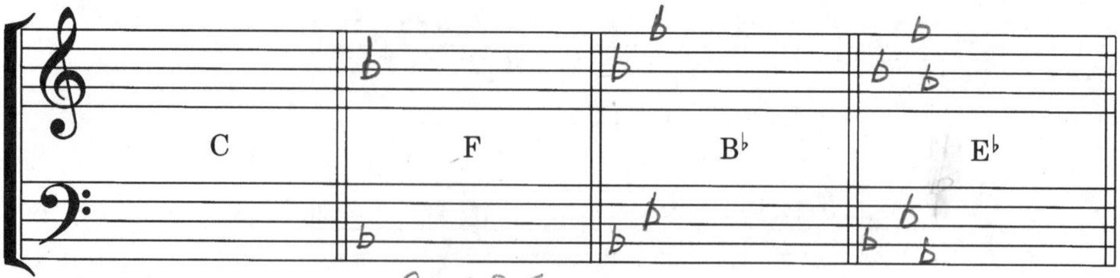

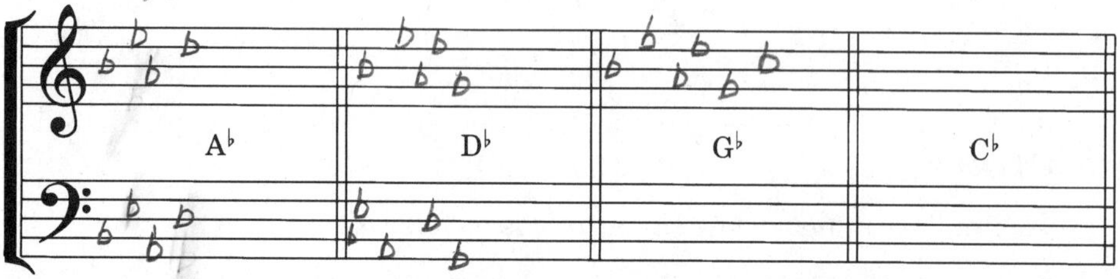

The name of the key is the same as the next to last flat. (Obviously, this does not apply to the key of F major, since F major has only one flat.) As with sharp key signatures, this method of identification should merely supplement the information contained in the following chart.

Major Key	*Number of Flats*
C	0
F	1
B♭	2
E♭	3
A♭	4
D♭	5
G♭	6
C♭	7

EXERCISE 5•4

Identify the major key represented by each of the following flat key signatures.

1. 

2. 

3. 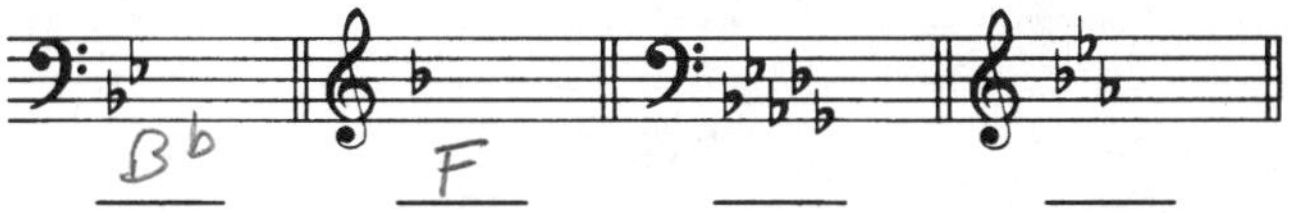

4. 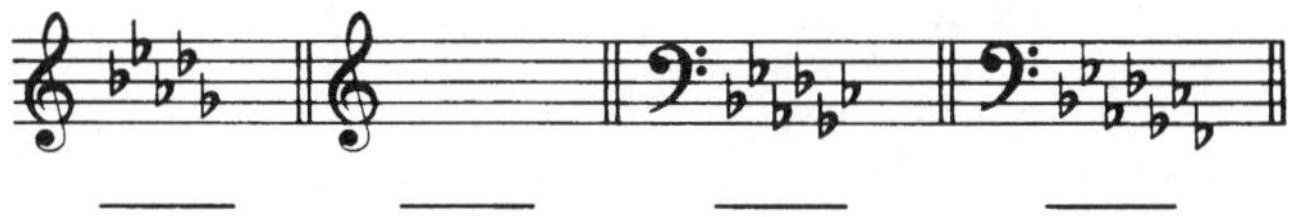

BEAD GCF
FCGDAEB

EXERCISE 5•5

Write out the indicated major key signatures, using either sharps or flats as required. A helpful mnemonic device for keeping all the sharps and flats in order in your mind is to remember that the order of flats—B–E–A–D–G–C–F—is the reverse of the order of sharps—F–C–G–D–A–E–B.

1. 

A major

2. 

E major

3. 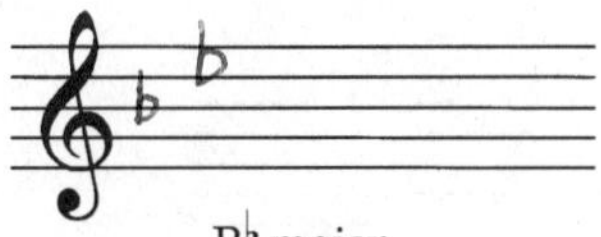

B♭ major

4. 

D♭ major

5. 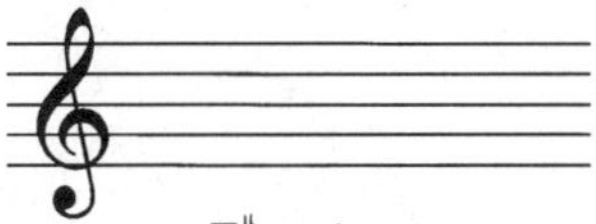

F♯ major

6. 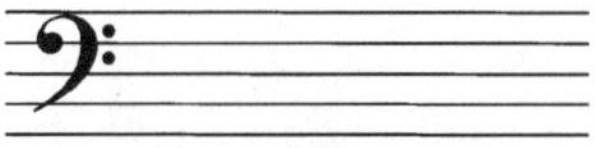

A♭ major

7. 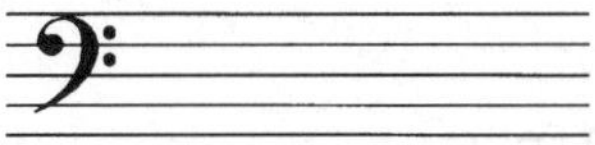

F major

8. 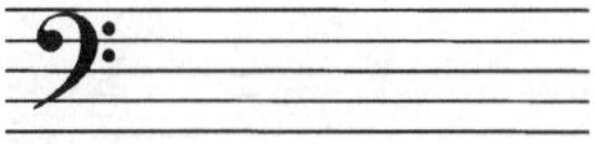

C♯ major

FCGDAEB
BEADGCF

9. 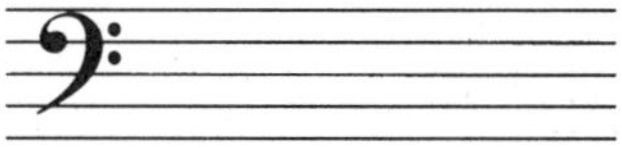

D major

10. 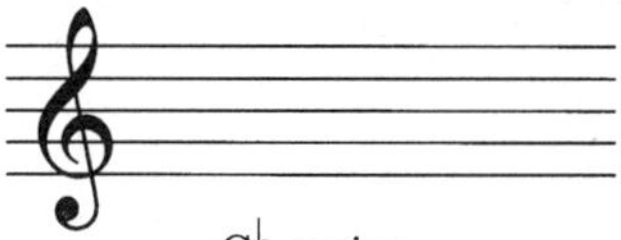

G♭ major

11. 

E♭ major

12. 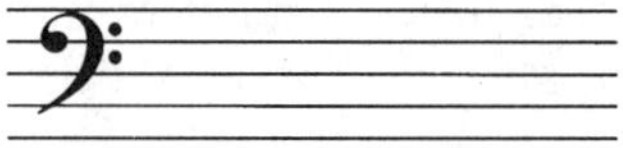

B major

13. 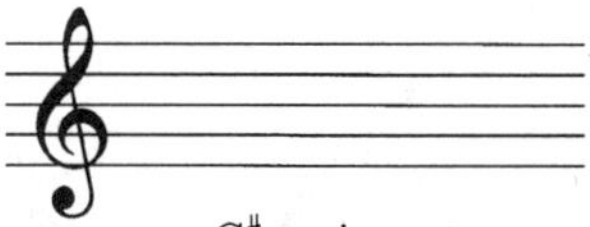

C♯ major

14. 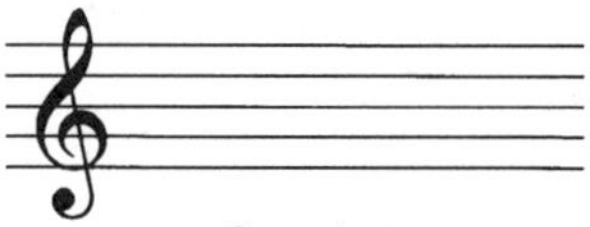

G major

15. 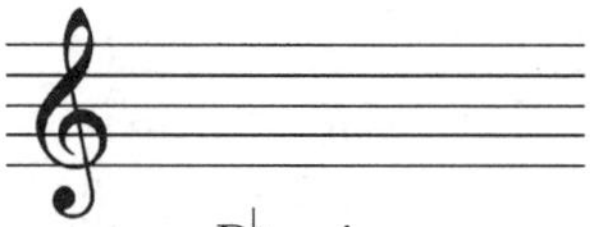

D♭ major

16. 

G♭ major

17. 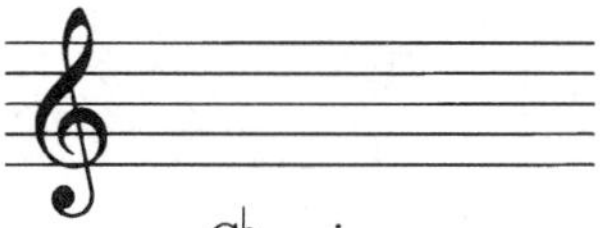

C♭ major

18. 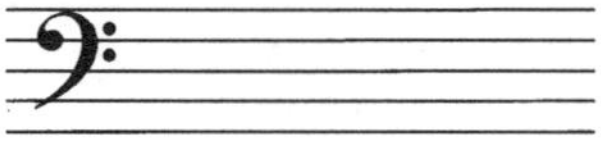

G major

19. 

A♭ major

20. 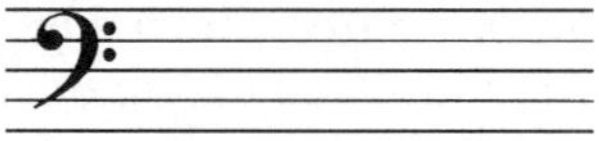

B♭ major

21. 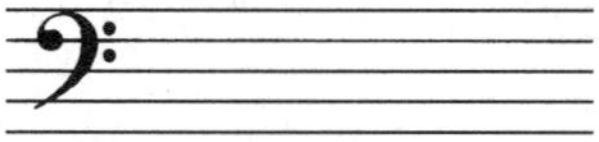

A major

22. 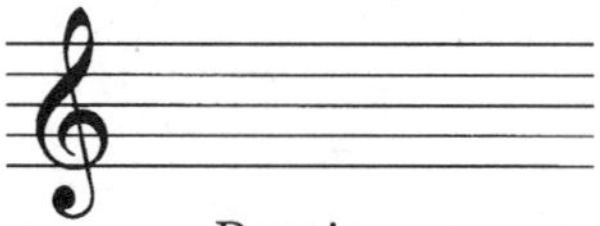

D major

23. 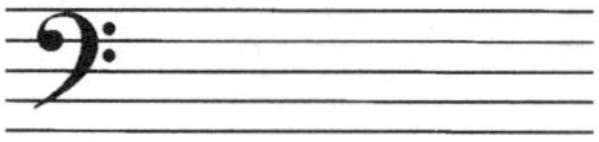

F♯ major

24. 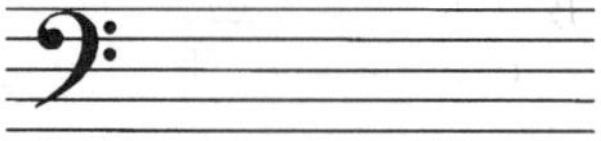

C♭ major

25. 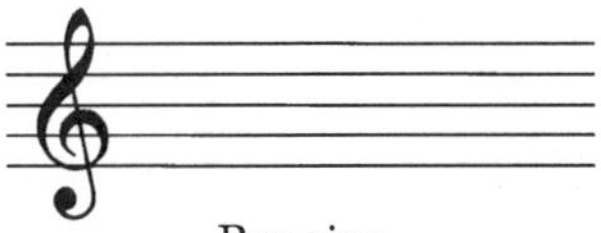

B major

27. 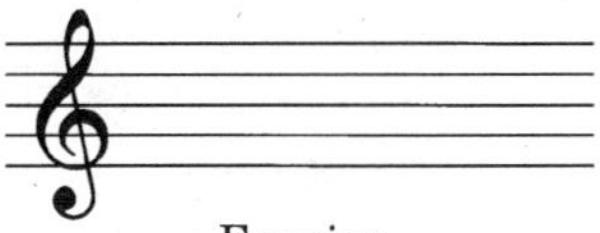

F major

26. 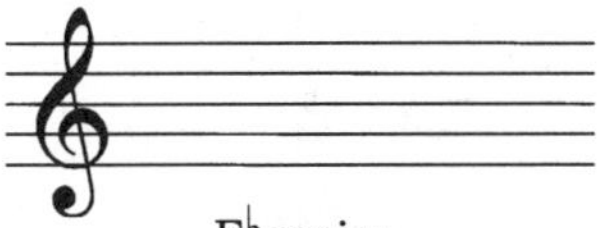

E♭ major

28. 

E major

Enharmonic Keys

You may have noticed that three of the sharp major scales (B, F♯, and C♯) are enharmonic with three of the flat major scales (C♭, G♭, and D♭). Thus, although they are written differently, they sound the same.

B (5 ♯s) sounds like C♭ (7 ♭s)

F♯ (6 ♯s) sounds like G♭ (6 ♭s)

C♯ (7 ♯s) sounds like D♭ 5 ♭s)

In actual practice, the key of B major is found more frequently than the key of C♭ major; the keys of F♯ major and G♭ major occur with about equal frequency; and the key of D♭ major appears more often than does the key of C♯ major.

The Circle of Fifths: Major Keys

The interval of the perfect fifth—an interval of seven half steps that we will study in the next chapter—turns out to be important in understanding a special relationship among major key signatures. If the major key signatures are arranged in order of increasing number of sharps, they progress, one to the next, by a perfect fifth. Thus, C major has no sharps (or flats), G major (a perfect fifth higher) has one sharp, D major (a perfect fifth above G) has two sharps, and so on. In the flat keys, the progression by perfect fifths works in reverse order, by the number of flats. (The circle of fifths for minor keys is discussed in Chapter 7.)

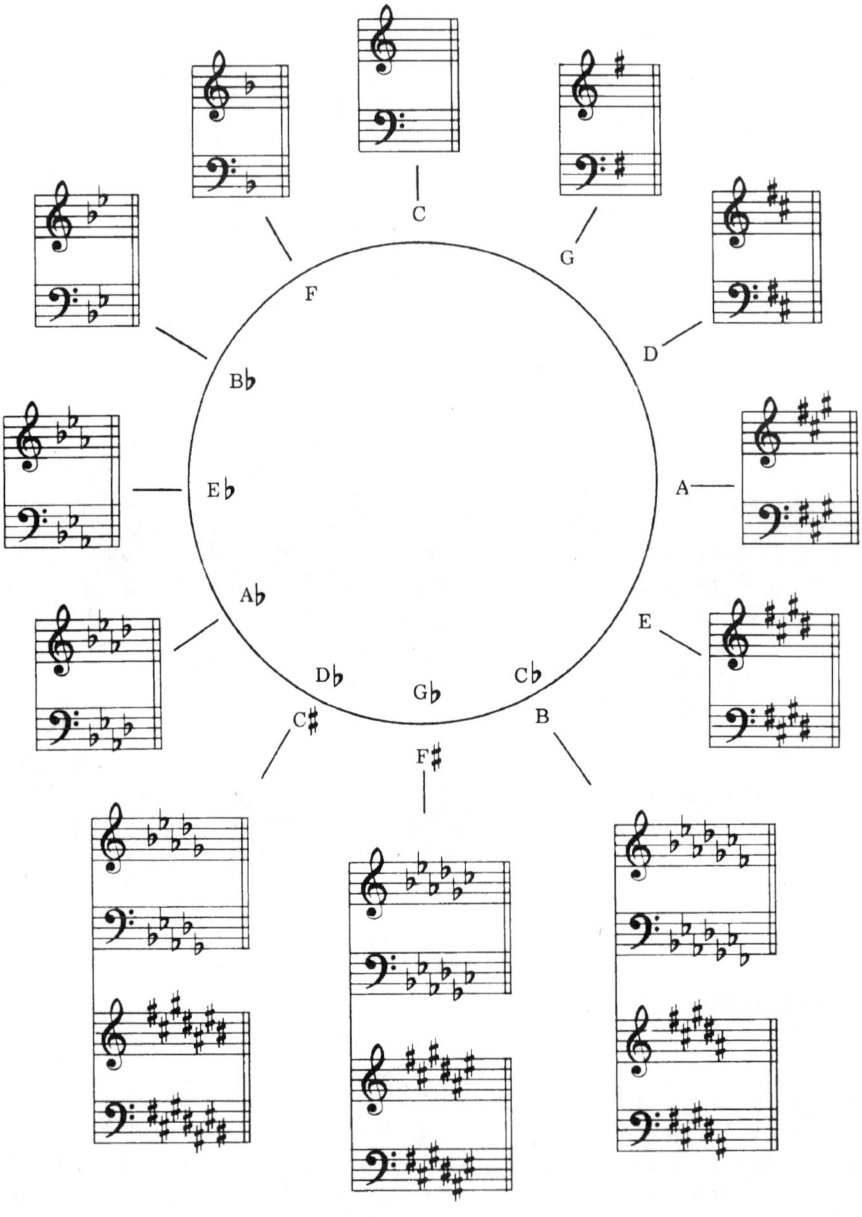

EXERCISE 5•6

Identify the correct major key, based on the number of sharps or flats indicated.

1. three sharps ____________
2. six sharps ____________
3. one sharp ____________
4. four sharps ____________
5. three flats ____________
6. six flats ____________

7. two sharps ____________
8. two flats ____________
9. seven flats ____________
10. one flat ____________
11. five sharps ____________
12. five flats ____________
13. four flats ____________
14. seven sharps ____________

Focus

If you play an instrument, you have undoubtedly had the experience of playing a wrong note when you momentarily forgot the key signature. At such a time, you might have felt that key signatures are a nuisance, that music would be easier to play without them. But this is *not* the case, for without key signatures most music would be sprinkled with an incredible number of accidentals. The resulting clutter would make music more difficult to read and perform. Key signatures are often perplexing at the beginning, but they are quickly mastered with the necessary drill. Once you are comfortable with the shorthand of key signatures, it will be impossible to imagine written tonal music without them.

6 Chapter

Intervals

Why do we have to study intervals? Most people think that learning intervals is the most complicated and the most tedious part of learning music, requiring, as they do, a lot of necessary practice and memorization. So, must we really understand intervals in order to understand tonal music? These are good questions, but look at it this way: **Intervals** measure musical distances. How could you be a musician without knowing how to do that? Think of your work with intervals as learning the basic language skills of tonal music. It's a step you can't afford to slight. Intervals are fundamental.

Here is something else to consider. Perhaps you or someone you know studies piano or synthesizer. If so, the chances are good that you or they spent a lot of time playing scales. But too often, beginning students play scales mechanically, without much appreciation for why it's an important thing to do. Scale practice isn't just something music teachers inflict on their students to develop technique. Scales contain the fundamental patterns on which tonal music is built. By practicing these patterns—in the form of scales—the performer becomes musically acquainted with material that will appear repeatedly in the music itself.

But what, exactly, are these patterns contained in scales? They are *interval patterns.* The interval patterns of scales become the interval patterns of melody and harmony. What we hear and define as music is actually combinations of interval patterns. The interval, therefore, is one of *the* basic units of tonal music. In this chapter, we will learn a way to recognize and identify intervals that will also be used in future chapters concerned with triads and harmony. So remember, not only do you not want to skip this, the knowledge will be of little use to you if it is only half learned. Make sure you understand intervals thoroughly before moving on.

Interval Identification

As we learned earlier, an interval is the musical distance between two pitches. If these two pitches are sounded simultaneously, the interval is called a **harmonic interval**. If the two pitches are sounded in succession, like two tones of a melody, the interval is called a **melodic interval**. In either case, it is the distance between the two pitches that is identified and measured. Two elements are considered in identifying intervals: arithmetic distance and quality.

Arithmetic Distance

The first step in identifying an interval is to determine the **arithmetic distance** it covers. Sometimes this is referred to as "interval size." Determining arithmetic distance is done by counting the letter names of the two pitches whose interval we are trying to determine plus the letter names of all the pitches in between.

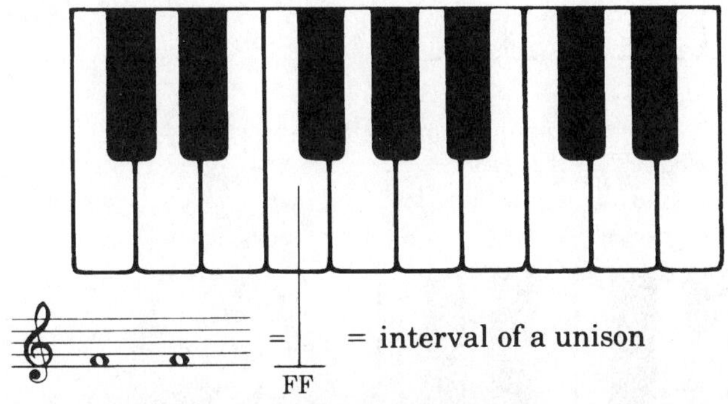

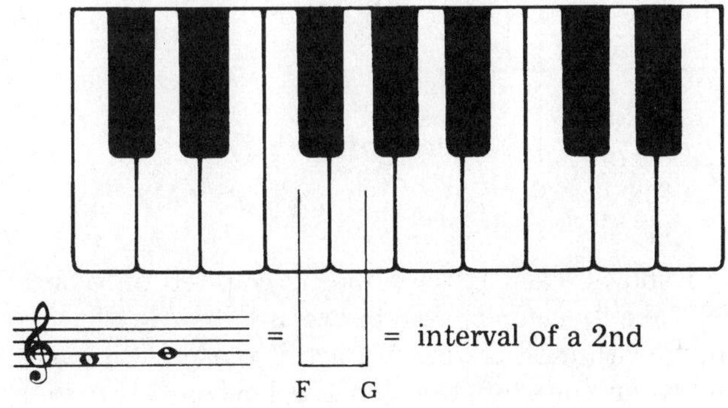

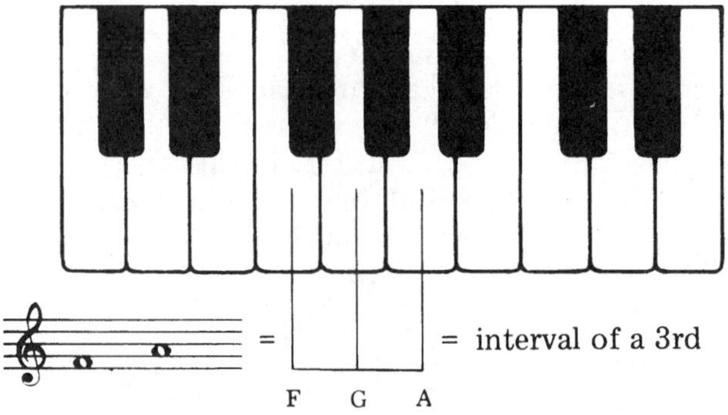

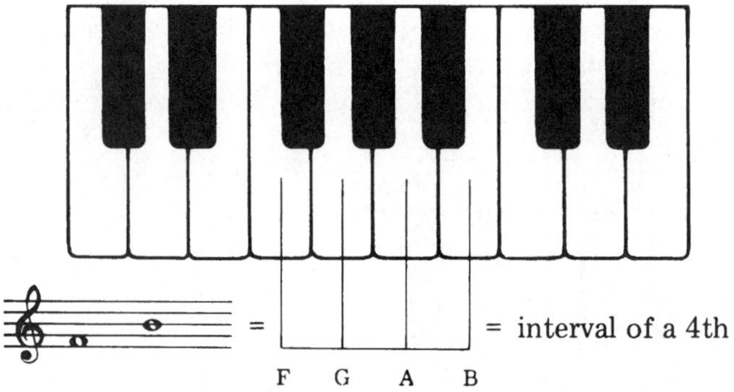

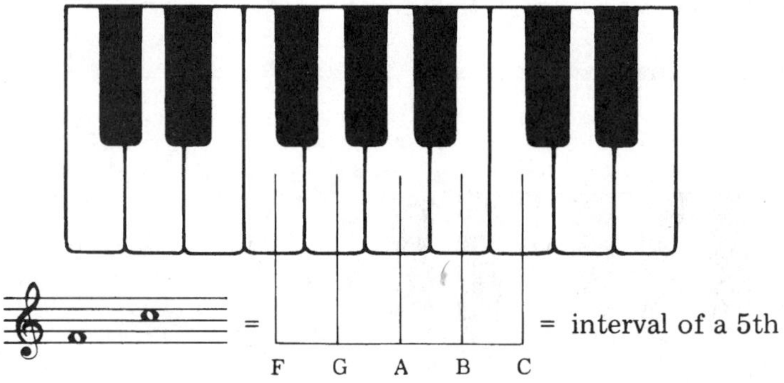

As the preceding illustration shows, each letter name is counted only once. Thus, in the second example, the enharmonic pitch between F and G (F♯ or G♭) was not counted in determining arithmetic distance. For this reason, it is easier to measure arithmetic distance on the staff than on the keyboard. Furthermore, the staff facilitates interval recognition because of the following rules concerning the position of intervals on the staff:

The notes of a *second* always appear on adjacent lines and spaces.

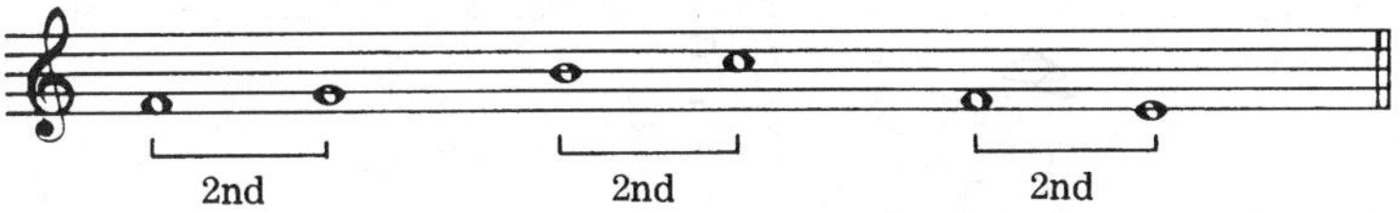

The notes of a *third* always appear on consecutive lines or spaces.

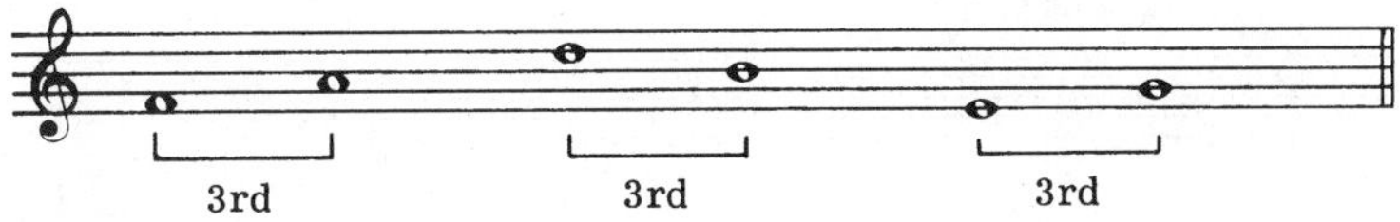

Fourths always have one pitch on a line and the other in a space, with a space and a line between.

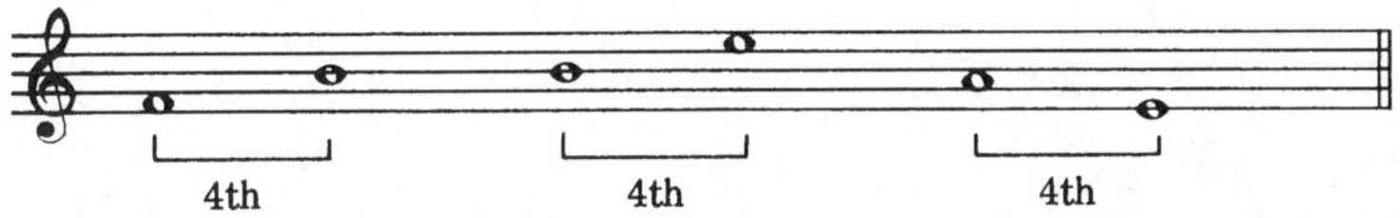

Fifths always have either (1) both pitches on lines, with one line between, or (2) both pitches in spaces, with one space between.

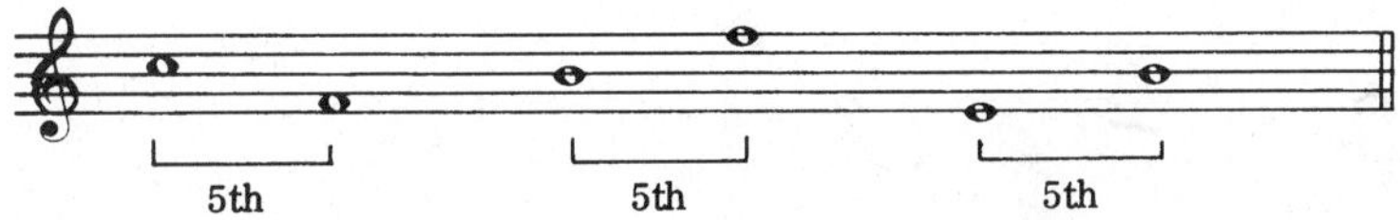

This pattern continues for sixths, sevenths, octaves (the term for the arithmetic distance of an eighth), and so on. As the pitches become farther apart, however, the pattern becomes increasingly difficult to recognize. Until you become familiar with the overall appearance of the wider intervals, it is probably wise to count the lines and spaces between the pitches of the interval.

EXERCISE 6•1

Identify the arithmetic distance of the following melodic intervals.

EXAMPLE:

1. 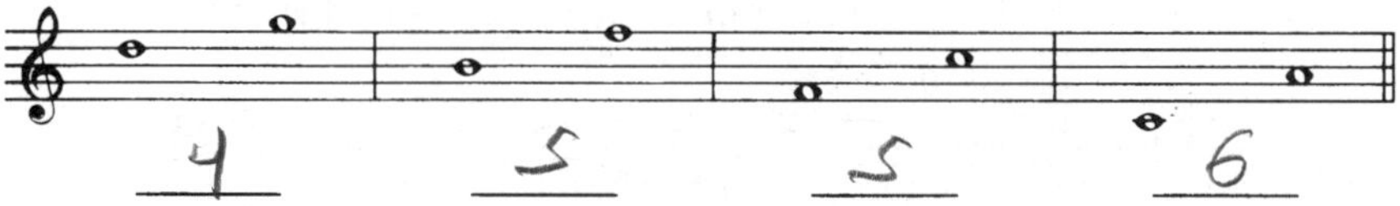

2. 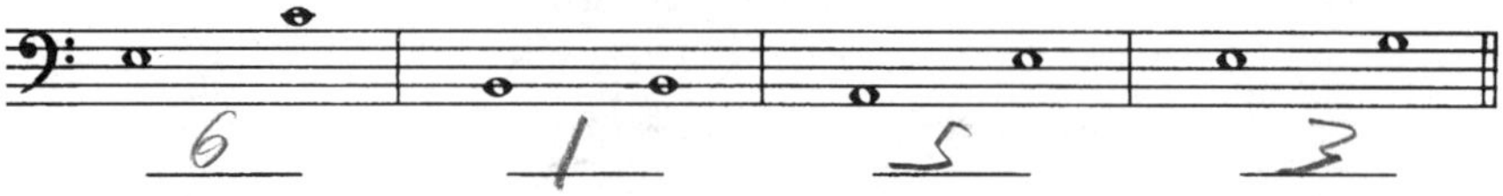

3. 

4. 

5. 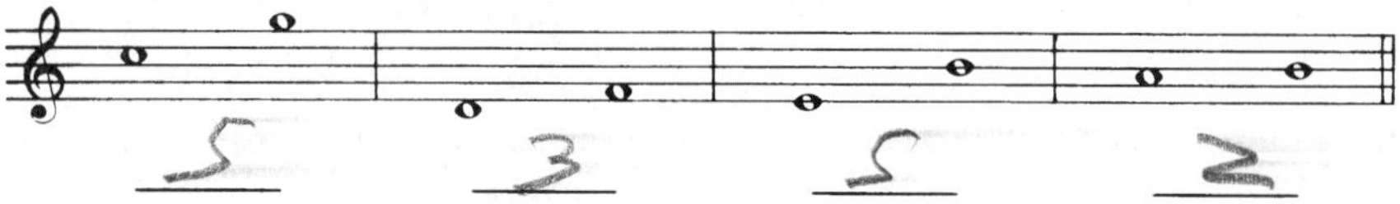

EXERCISE 6•2

Complete the following harmonic intervals by writing in the pitch that is the correct arithmetic distance *above* the given pitch.

EXAMPLE:

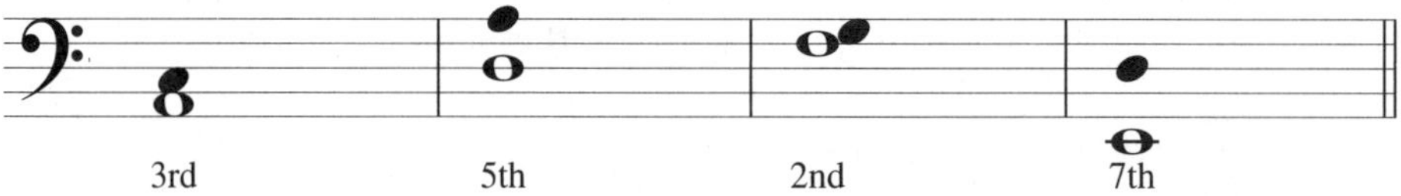

1. 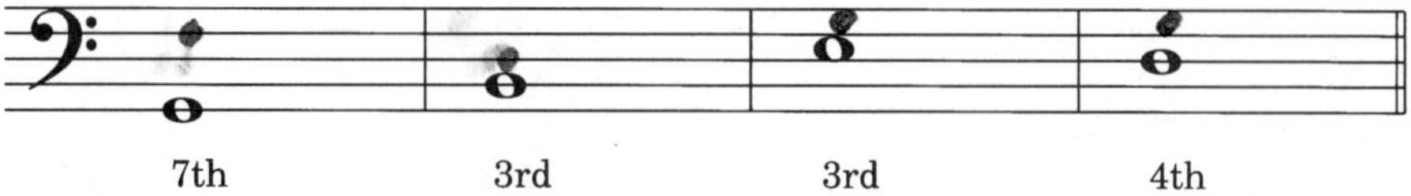

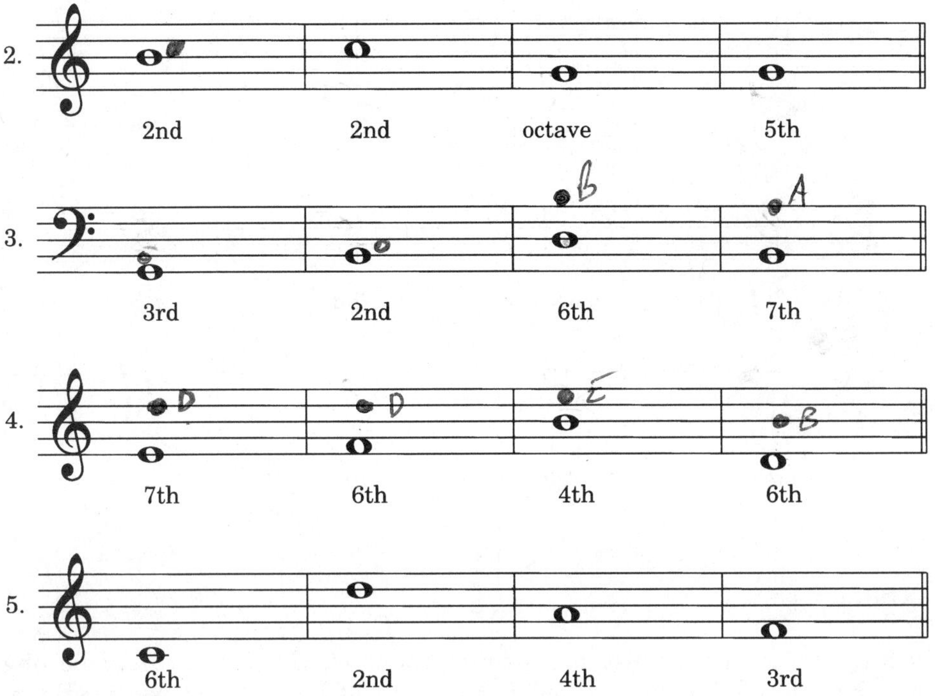

EXERCISE 6•3

Complete the following harmonic intervals by writing in the pitch that is the correct arithmetic distance *below* the given pitch.

EXAMPLE:

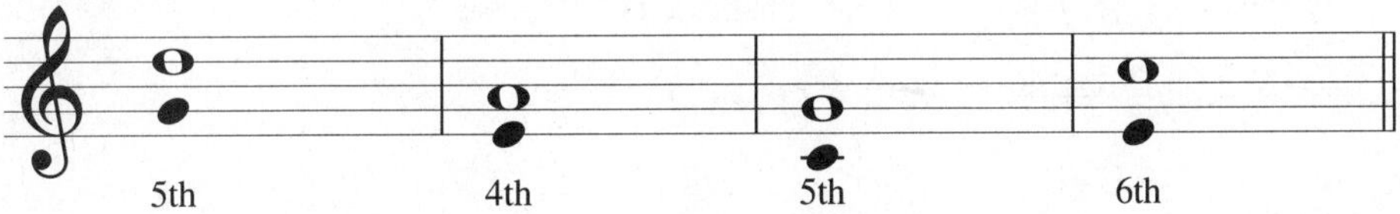

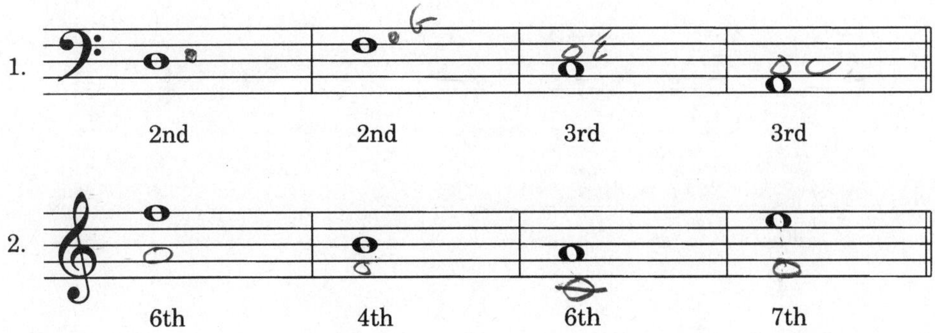

3.

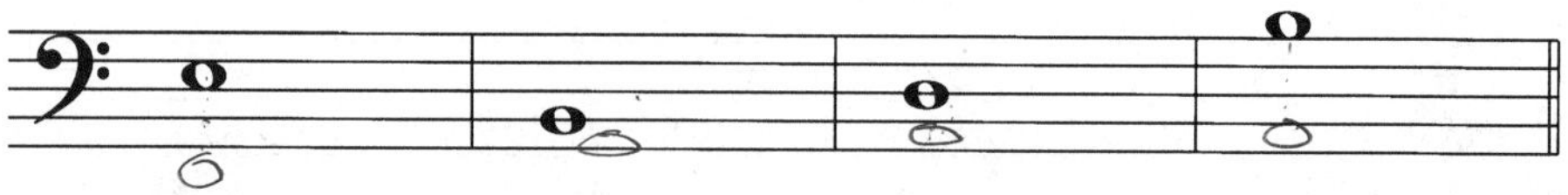

7th 2nd 4th 7th

4.

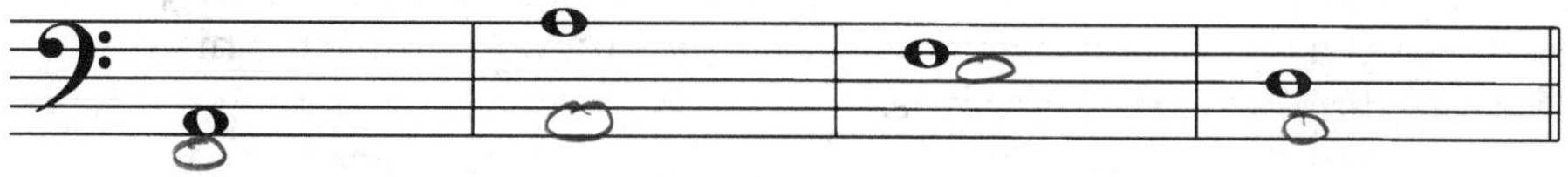

3rd octave 2nd 4th

5.

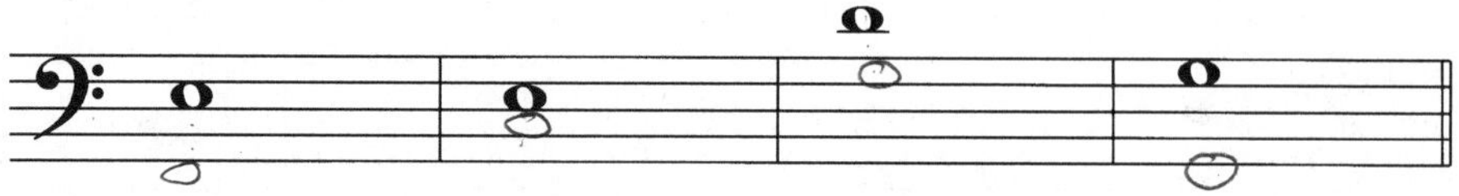

7th 3rd 5th 7th

EXERCISE 6•4

Identify the arithmetic distance between the pitches in each of the following sets. In the first three lines, consider the second pitch to be *above* the first pitch. In lines four, five, and six, consider the second pitch as *below* the first one.

1.	E–F (2)	D–A (5)	G–B (3)	F–E (7)
2.	F–A (3)	F–B (4)	A–B (2)	C–B (7)
3.	G–E (6)	B–E (4)	D–F (3)	A–D (4)
4.	E–A (4)	G–B (5)	F–G (7)	F–A (6)
5.	G–C (5)	G–F (2)	A–D (4)	A–F (3)
6.	E–B (4)	D–B (3)	E–A (5)	G–D (4)

Interval Quality

The second step in recognizing an interval is to identify the sound *quality* or *color* of the interval. The quality or color of an interval is related to the number of half steps contained between the two pitches. In the following example, all four intervals are thirds. But if you play them on a keyboard or sing them, you will find that each has a distinctly different quality or color. This is because they are different kinds of thirds.

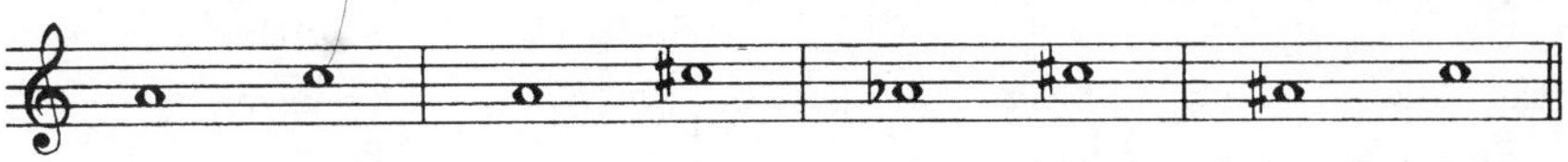

The following terms are used to describe the quality of intervals:

Interval	*Abbreviation*
Perfect	P
Major	M
Minor	m
Augmented	A or +
Diminished	d or °

Determining the quality of an interval may be done in one of two ways. One way is to memorize the number of half steps contained in the various kinds of intervals, and then to use this information when confronted with a new interval. The problem with this method is that it involves both a lot of memorizing and a lot of counting half steps.

The other way to determine interval quality is to remember the types of intervals that occur between the first note of a major scale and each of the other notes in the scale, and then to gauge new intervals against this information.

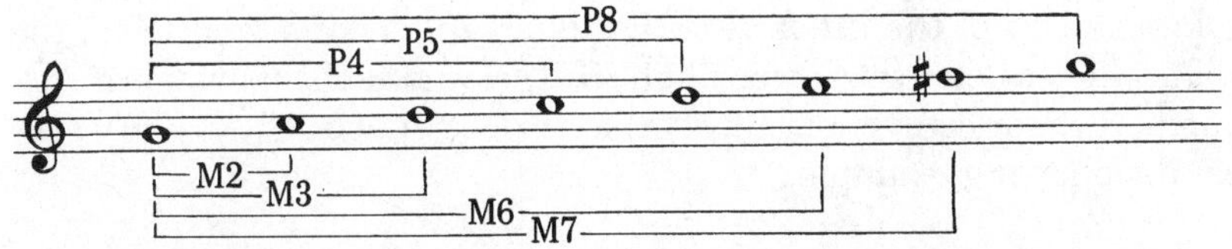

Although both ways of identifying intervals work equally well, the major-scale method (when you know your scales well) is probably faster and more accurate. Counting half steps can involve too much rote learning and is subject to error.

Perfect Intervals

Only four kinds of intervals are called *perfect intervals*: the unison, the fourth, the fifth, and the octave. They are labeled *perfect* because in Medieval and Renaissance music they were considered the only intervals suitable for momentary or permanent stopping places (called cadences) in a piece. The following illustration shows (1) the number of half steps in each type of perfect interval and (2) the standard way of identifying intervals, using letters for quality and numbers for arithmetic distance.

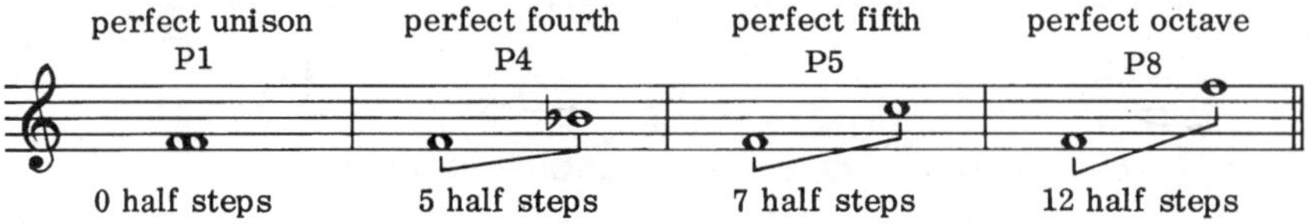

For any particular interval, both the arithmetic distance and the quality must be correct in order for the interval itself to be correct. Remember that the arithmetic distance is the total count of letter names included in the interval, while the quality is determined by counting half steps. In the case of a perfect fifth, for example, the arithmetic distance must be a fifth, and the interval must contain exactly seven half steps.

In a major scale, the quality of the intervals between the tonic and the subdominant, dominant, or octave is always perfect.

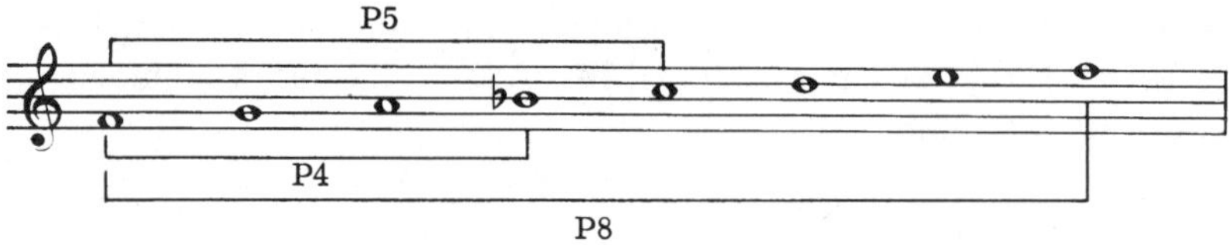

Therefore, you can quickly check the quality of any of these intervals by assuming that the lower pitch of the interval is the tonic, and asking yourself if the upper pitch is in the scale of the lower pitch. If it is, and if the arithmetic distance is a fourth, fifth, or octave, the interval is perfect in quality.

Consider the following example:

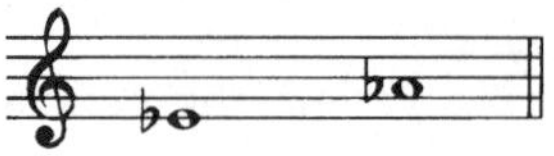

The arithmetic distance is a fourth. To determine the quality, we assume that the E♭ is the tonic of a major scale. Is A♭ in the E♭ major scale? Since the answer is yes, this is a perfect fourth. If the upper pitch were not in the scale, then the quality of the interval would be something other than perfect.

Perfect intervals can also be *augmented* or *diminished.* A perfect interval is made augmented by retaining the arithmetic distance while, at the same time, expanding the interval by a half step.

perfect fourth
P4

5 half steps

augmented fourth
A4

6 half steps

A perfect interval is made diminished by retaining the arithmetic distance and decreasing the interval by a half step.

perfect fifth
P5

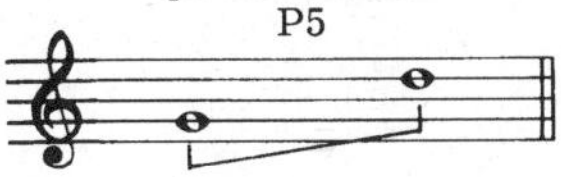

7 half steps

diminished fifth
d5

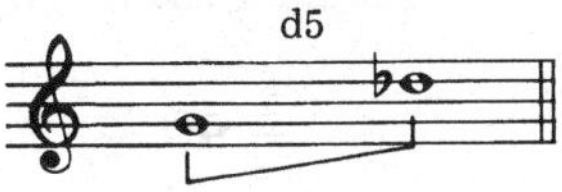

6 half steps

Notice that although the augmented fourth and the diminished fifth both contain six half steps, one is identified as a fourth and the other as a fifth. This is because the arithmetic distance of the two is not the same.

EXERCISE 6•5

In the following harmonic intervals, circle the perfect unisons, fourths, fifths, and octaves. (Refer to the illustration on page 130 if you need to.) Remember to ask yourself if the upper pitch is in the major scale of the lower pitch.

6. 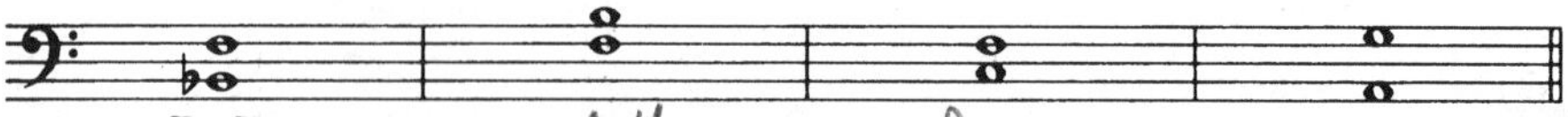

7. 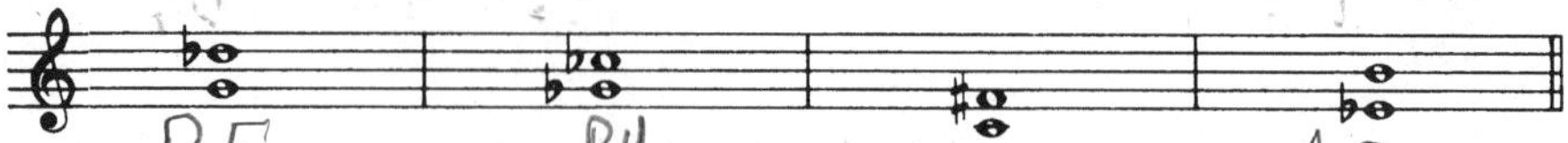

8. 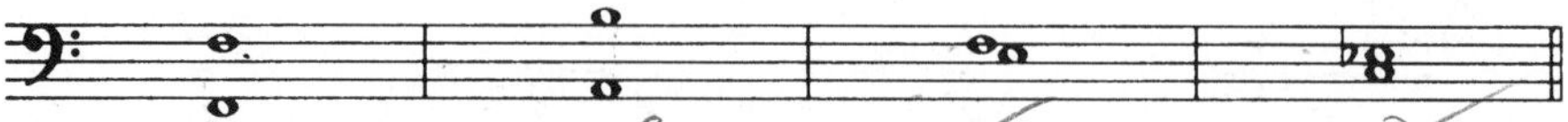

9. 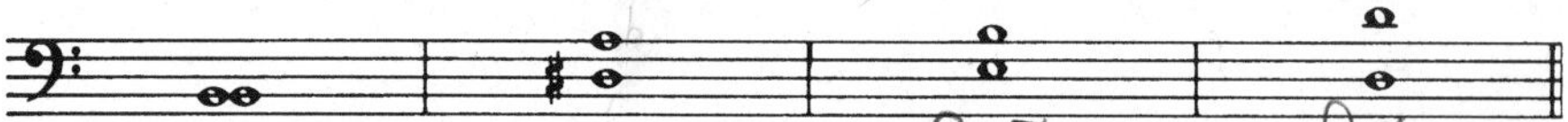

10. 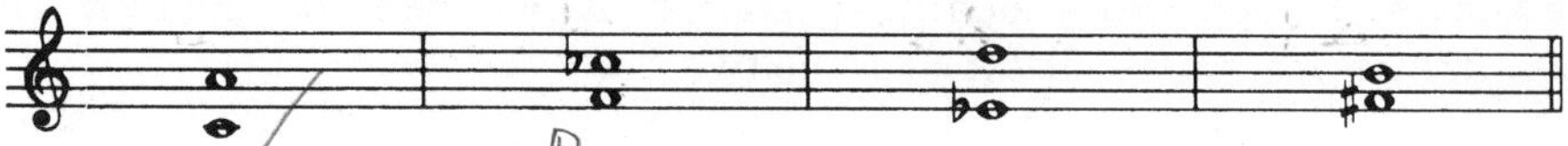

EXERCISE 6•6

Identify each of the following melodic intervals as either a unison, a fourth, a fifth, or an octave, and as either perfect (P), augmented (A), or diminished (d). A keyboard is provided to help you visualize the half steps. Remember that the major scale contains perfect fourths, fifths, and octaves, and that augmented intervals will be a half step larger than these, diminished intervals a half step smaller.

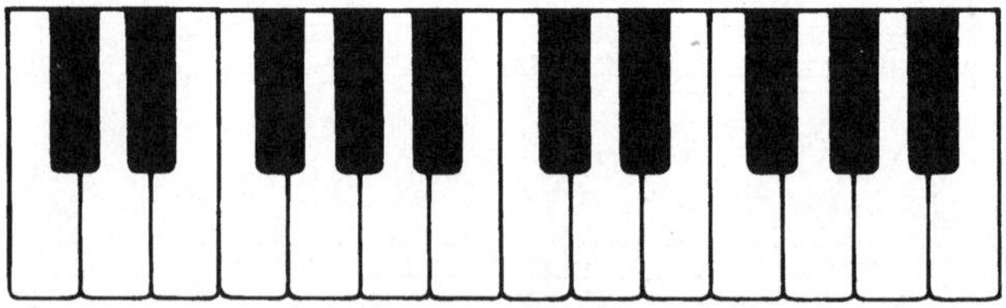

EXAMPLE:

half steps	5	4	1
interval	P4	d4	A1

1.

2.

3.

4.

5.

6.

7.

8.

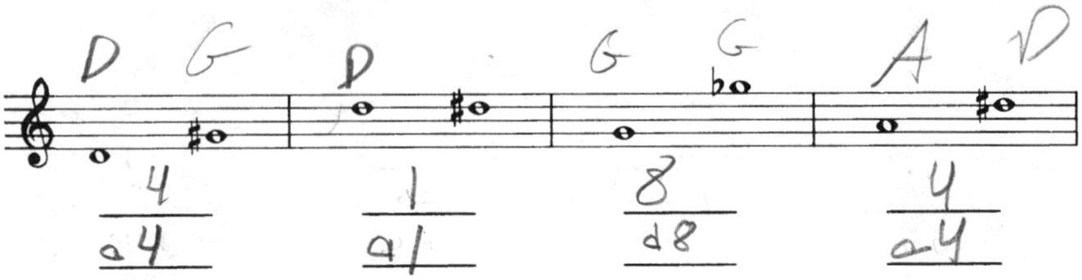

9.

10.

11.

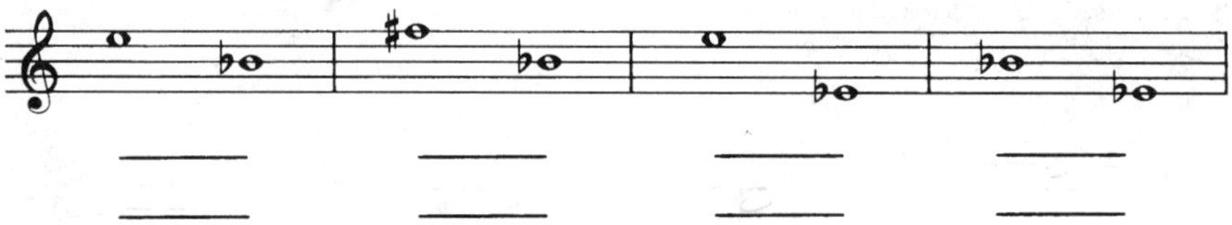

12.

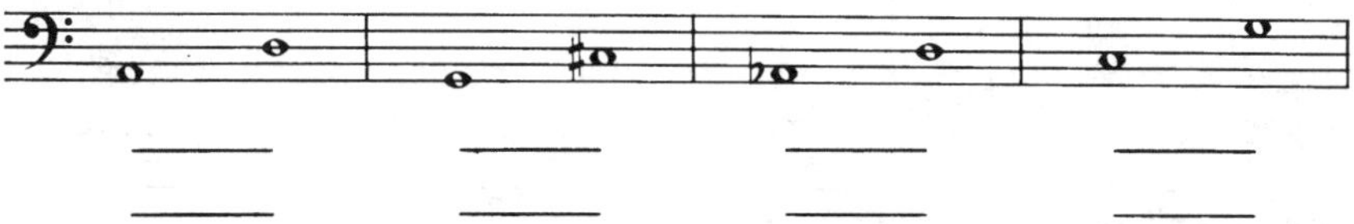

Musical Problem

When you have finished Exercise 6-6, ask someone in class to play some of the lines on an instrument or keyboard. Try to identify the arithmetic distance and the quality of each interval. You may be able to do this all at once, or you may need to identify each element (distance and quality) separately. If you have never tried this, it may seem difficult at first, but it gets easier with practice. Remember that some intervals like d5 and A4 look different but sound the same.

EXERCISE 6•7

Complete each of the indicated intervals by notating the correct *higher* pitch. You may write them as either melodic or harmonic intervals. This exercise deals with unisons, fourths, fifths, and octaves only. Use the keyboard to help you visualize the half steps. Remember to maintain the correct arithmetic distance. Begin by thinking of the major scale for each given pitch; this will give you the perfect interval.

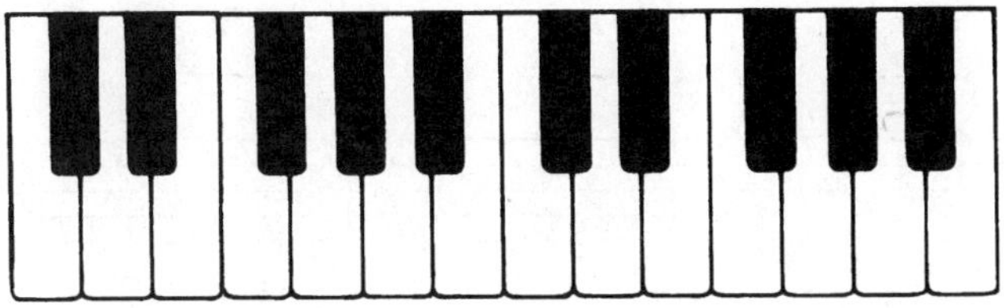

6. 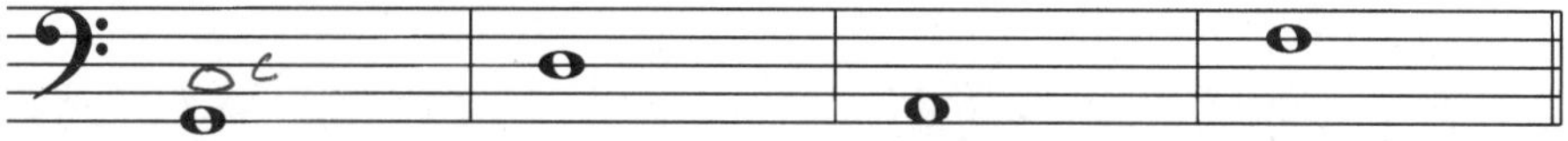

P4 | P4 | d4 | P5

7. 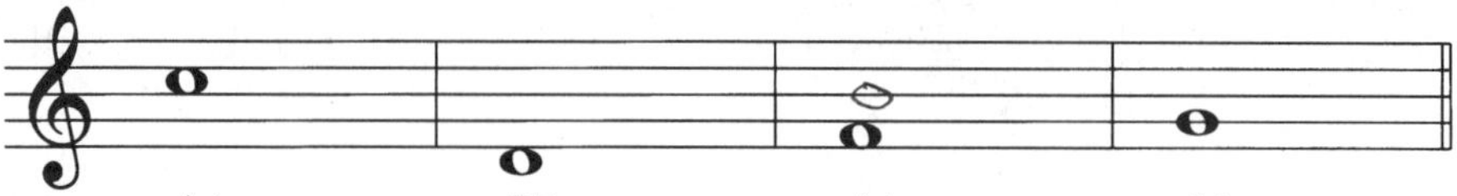

A4 | P5 | A4 | d4

8. 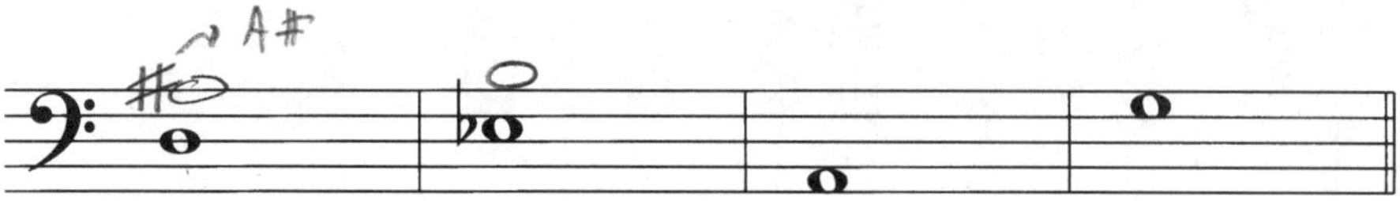

A5 | A5 | d5 | A1

9. 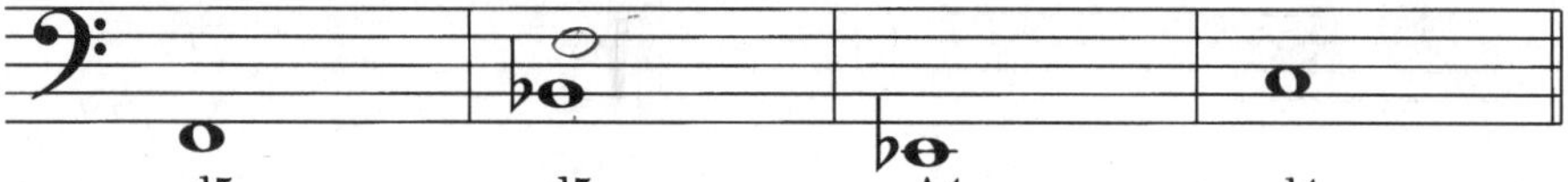

d5 | d5 | A4 | d4

10. 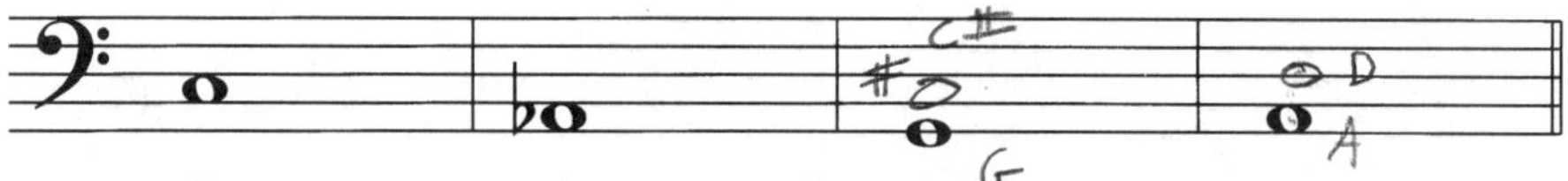

P5 | A4 | A4 | P4

Musical Problem

Locate and identify all the perfect intervals in the following piece.

Estampie (13th-Century Dance)

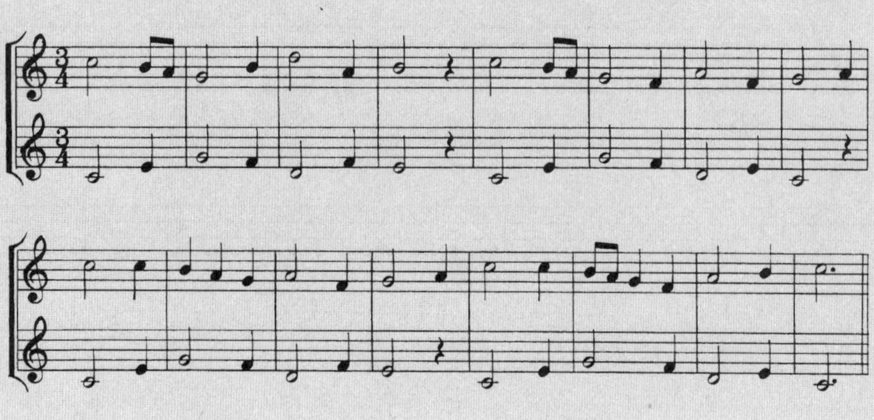

When you have identified the perfect intervals, play the piece, or sing it with the class. Discuss where the perfect intervals occur, and the type of sound they contribute to the piece.

Major and Minor Intervals

While any interval can be augmented or diminished in quality, perfect intervals can never be major or minor in quality. The intervals of major and minor quality are the second, the third, the sixth, and the seventh. The following illustration shows the number of half steps contained in each of the four types of major intervals.

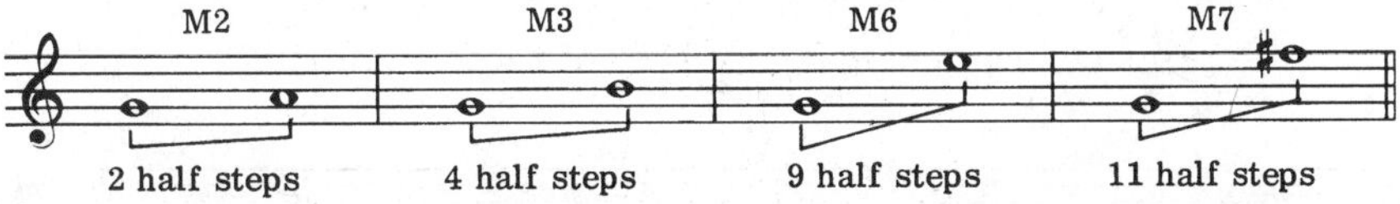

In a major scale, the quality of the intervals between the tonic and the supertonic, mediant, submediant, and leading tone is always major.

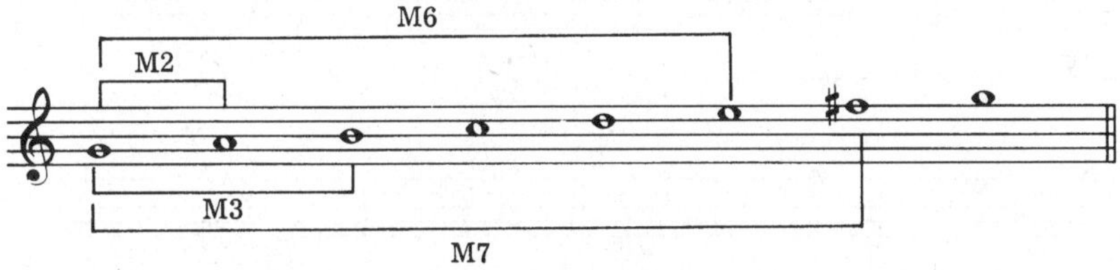

The same procedure for identifying perfect intervals can be applied to seconds, thirds, sixths, and sevenths as well. We simply assume that the lower pitch is the tonic; if the upper pitch is in the major scale of the lower pitch, the interval is major.

Another good way to learn this information is contained in the following chart. It lists the intervals found within a major scale and the number of half steps in each interval. Although you should be familiar with both ways of identifying and writing intervals, you can use whichever way seems easiest to you.

INTERVALS OF THE MAJOR SCALE

Interval	*Number of Half Steps*
Perfect unison	0
Major 2nd	2
Major 3rd	4

Interval	Number of Half Steps
Perfect 4th	5
Perfect 5th	7
Major 6th	9
Major 7th	11
Perfect 8th	12

BEADGCF
FCGDAEB

EXERCISE 6•8

Identify and circle the major seconds, thirds, sixths, and sevenths in the following set of harmonic intervals. Remember to ask yourself if the upper pitch is in the major scale of the lower pitch, or to use the chart of half steps.

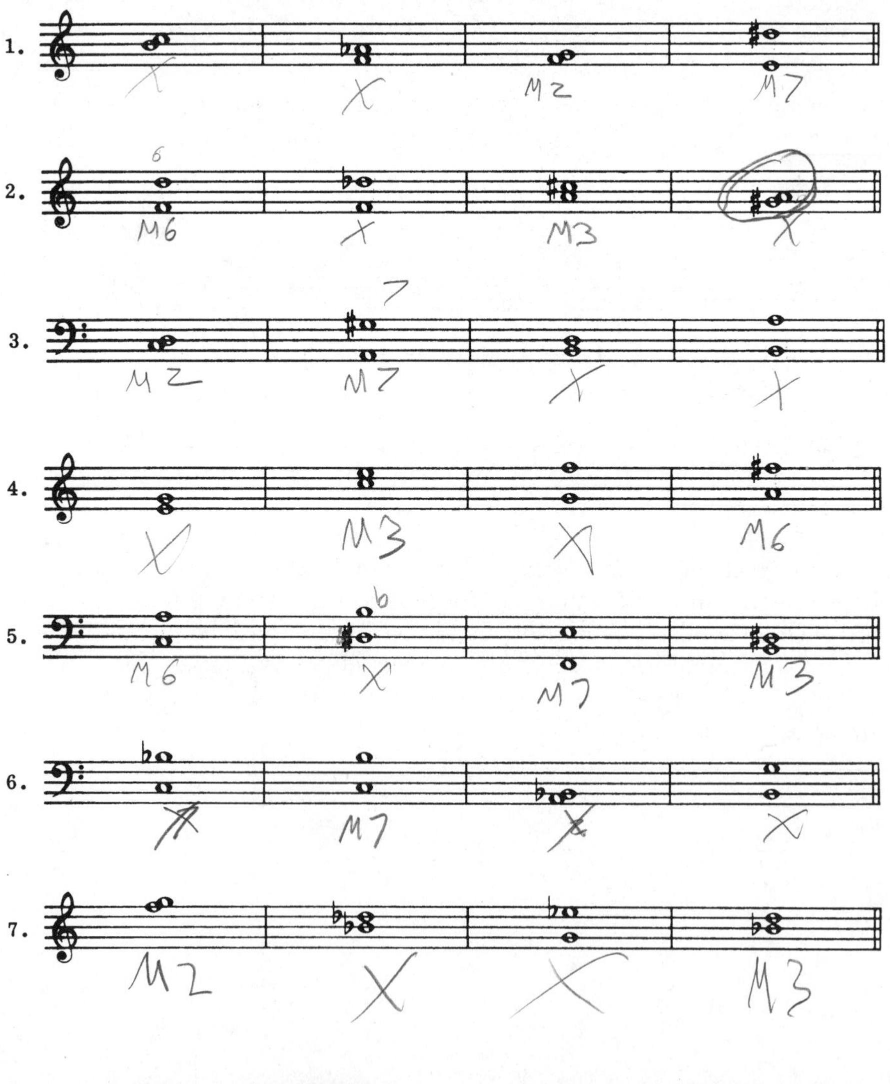

EXERCISE 6•9

Construct the indicated major interval, either harmonic or melodic, by writing the correct *higher* notehead. Begin by thinking of the major scale for each given pitch.

The number of half steps in each of the major intervals should be memorized. It then becomes simple to change the quality of major intervals to minor, augmented, or diminished. For example, a major interval decreased by a half step becomes minor in quality.

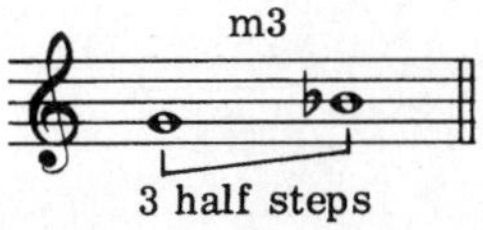

A minor interval further decreased by a half step becomes diminished. A major interval can be diminished by decreasing it a whole step (two half steps) while maintaining the correct arithmetic distance.

A major interval increased by a half step becomes augmented.

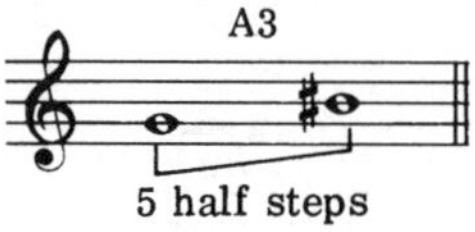

Notice that both the augmented third and the perfect fourth contain five half steps. Even though they have the same sound, they are not written the same because of their different arithmetic distances. The augmented third must *look* like a third, and the perfect fourth must *look* like a fourth.

EXERCISE 6•10

Identify the following melodic intervals as either a second, a third, a sixth, or a seventh, and as either augmented (A), major (M), minor (m), or diminished (d) in quality. (Capital and lowercase Ms can often be confused unless you print them carefully. For this reason, your teacher may prefer that you use MA for major and MI for minor.) Use the keyboard to help visualize the half steps. Remember that the major scale produces major seconds, thirds, sixths, and sevenths above the tonic.

F C G D A E B

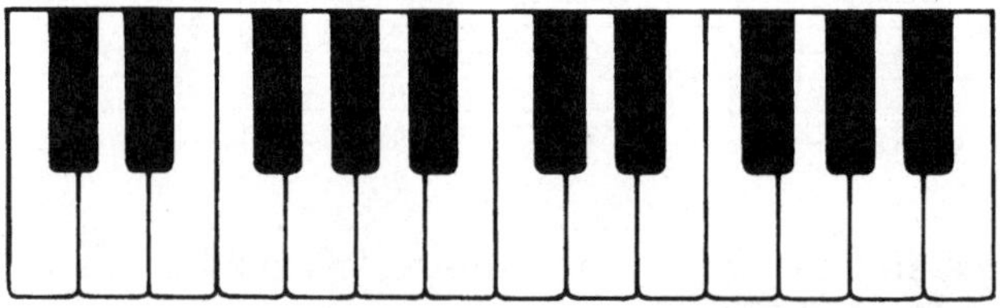

1.
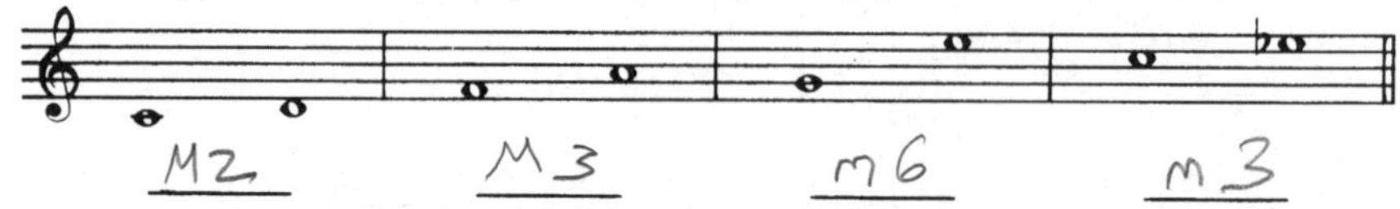

2.
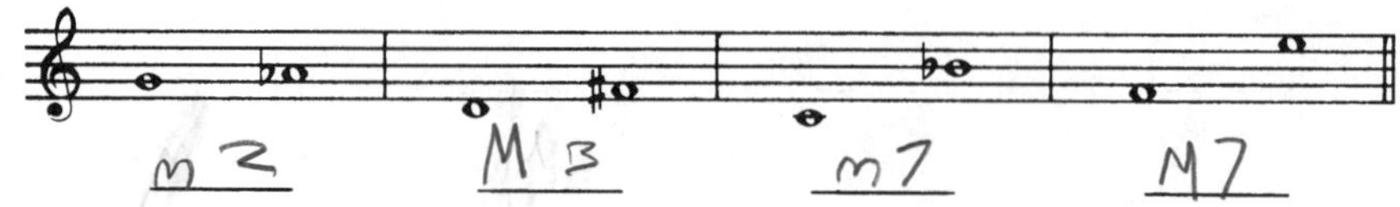

3. 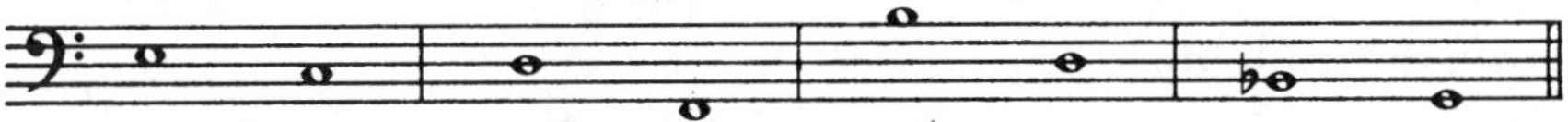

M3 A6 M6 m3

4. 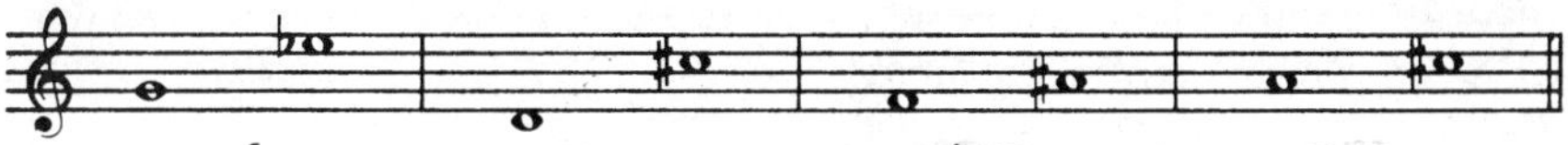

m6 M7 A3 M3

5. 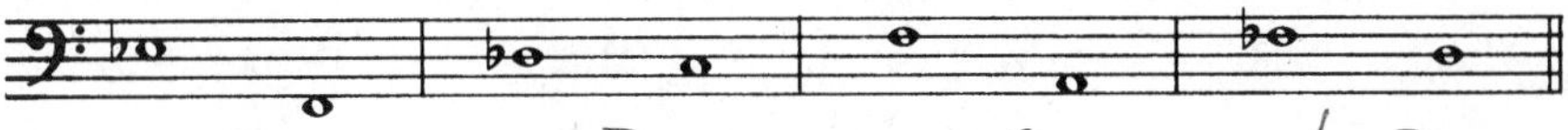

m7 M2 m6 d3

6. 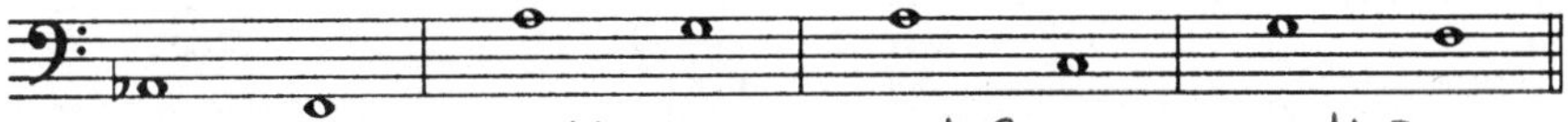

m3 M2 M6 M2

7. 

m2 m6 A3 A3

8. 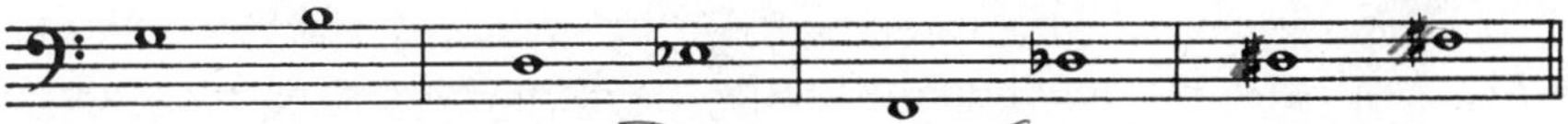

M3 m2 M6 m3

9. 

M2 M6 m7 d3

10. 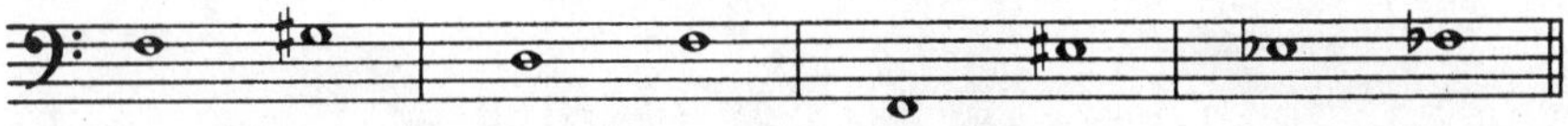

a2 M3 a7 m2

11. 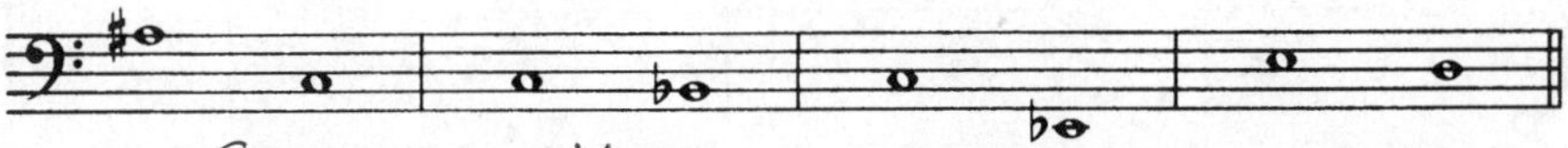

a6 M2 M6 M2

12. 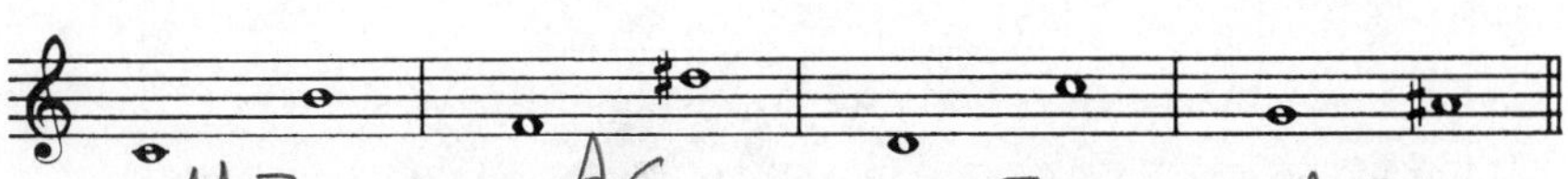

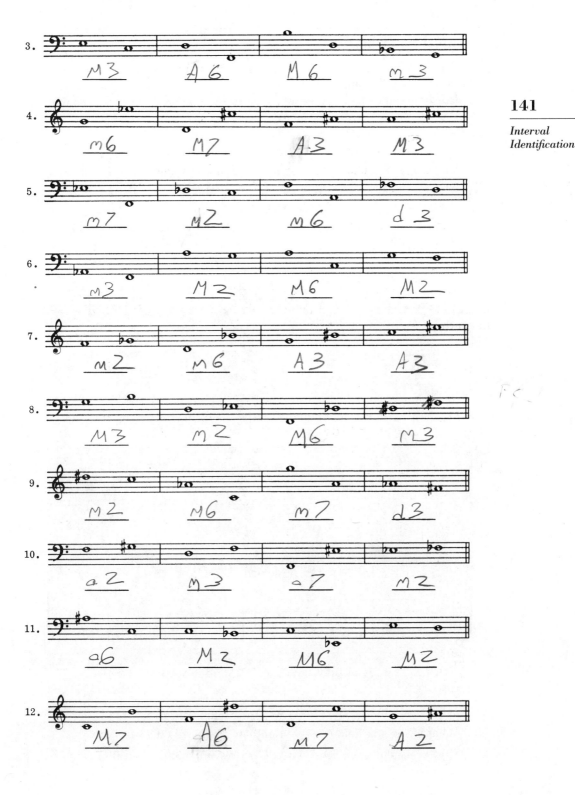

M7 A6 M7 A2

Musical Problem

In the following two excerpts identify the harmonic intervals created between the upper and lower voices. Put your answers in the spaces provided. Remember that the interval changes when one voice moves while the other voice remains stationary.

"Nowel syng we" (Medieval English Carol)

Landini: "Ecco la Primavera"

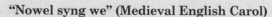

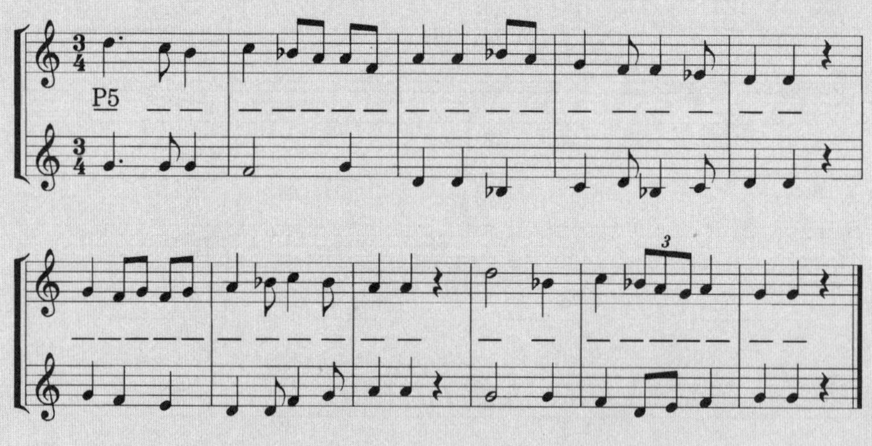

As a class, sing or play each excerpt; then discuss the following questions:

1. What is the largest interval and how frequently does it occur?
2. What is the smallest interval and how frequently does it occur?
3. How are the perfect intervals used? How important are they?

4. Are there any repetitions of interval patterns?
5. Did you have trouble performing the figure  at the end of the Landini excerpt? It is a borrowed division. Do you remember what these are and how they are to be counted? If not, refer back to the "Triplets and Duplets" section of Chapter 2.

Now that you know all the possible intervals within an octave, it may be useful to look at that information in chart form. The following chart gives the sizes of all the intervals in progressive order, along with the number of half steps in each. Notice the relationship between the growing sizes of the intervals and the number of half steps they contain.

INTERVALS WITHIN AN OCTAVE

Interval	*Number of Half Steps*
P1	0
m2	1
M2	2
m3	3
M3	4
P4	5
A4 (d5)	6
P5	7
m6 (A5)	8
M6	9
m7	10
M7	11
P8	12

EXERCISE 6•11

Construct the indicated harmonic or melodic intervals by writing the correct *higher* notehead. This exercise deals only with seconds, thirds, sixths, and sevenths. Remember to keep the correct arithmetic distance. Use the keyboard to visualize the intervals. Begin by thinking of the major scale that starts on each given pitch.

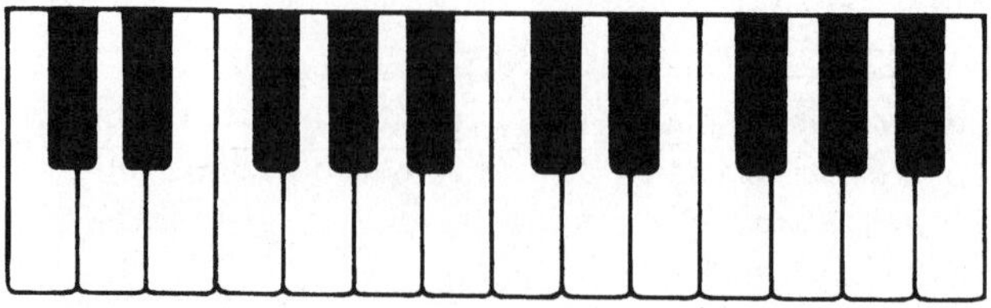

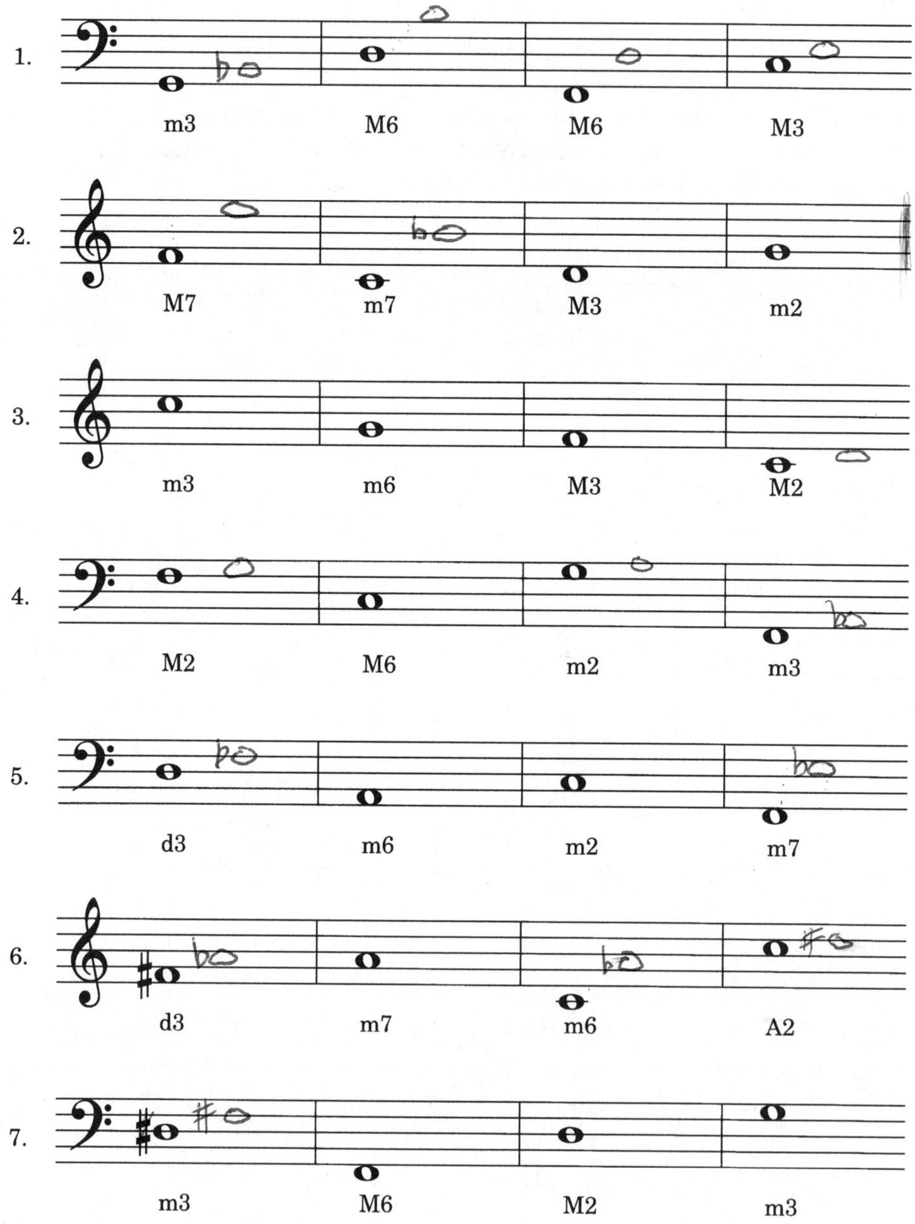
1. m3 M6 M6 M3
2. M7 m7 M3 m2
3. m3 m6 M3 M2
4. M2 M6 m2 m3
5. d3 m6 m2 m7
6. d3 m7 m6 A2
7. m3 M6 M2 m3

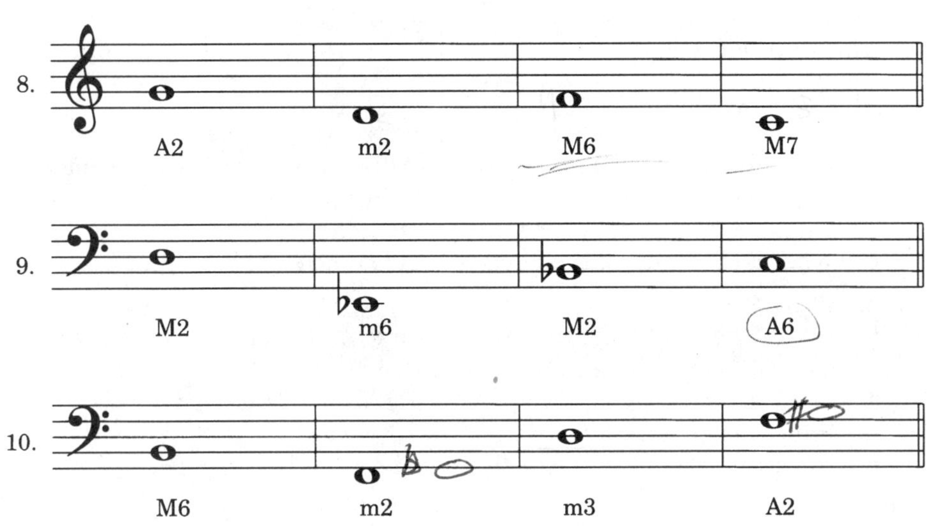

Musical Problem

It is important that you practice singing intervals and playing them at the keyboard. You can do both at once, using a piano or synthesizer to check your singing. Keep in mind that a few minutes' practice each day is far more beneficial than a lengthy practice session only once or twice a week.

You can practice interval skills any number of ways, but keep your exercises simple so that you can build on your successes. Use the following exercises as samples from which to develop your own. Perhaps each member of the class could design one singing exercise and one playing exercise for class use; these could then be shared so that every class member would have a sizable collection of practice exercises.

Sight-Singing Practice

1. Begin by singing *ascending* intervals in the major scale, as follows:

   do re, do mi, do fa, do sol, do la, do ti, do do

   When you can do this comfortably and accurately, try *descending* intervals, beginning an octave above where you began before:

   do ti, do la, do sol, do fa, do mi, do re, do do

2. Another useful ascending-interval exercise:

   do mi sol, re fa la, mi sol ti, fa la do, sol ti re, la do mi, ti re fa, mi

   This can also be done in reverse order, beginning at the top of the scale and working down:

   mi do la, re ti sol, do la fa, ti sol mi, la fa re, sol mi do, fa re ti, do

Both of the above exercises can also be sung using scale-degree numbers. Doing this will give you a slightly different perspective on the major scale and the intervals that it contains.

(continued)

Keyboard Practice

1. a. Play c^4.
   b. Play a pitch a P4 higher. Name this pitch. (Remember that you must always consider the arithmetic distance as well as the number of half steps.)
   c. From the new pitch, play a pitch a m2 lower.
   d. What is the name of the pitch you have reached? ________

2. a. Play $e^{\flat 5}$.
   b. Play a pitch a P5 higher. Name this pitch. (Remember to consider the arithmetic distance.)
   c. From the new pitch, play a pitch a M3 lower. Name this pitch.
   d. From this new pitch, play a pitch a P5 lower.
   e. What is the name of the pitch you are on now? ________

3. a. Play d^2.
   b. Play a pitch a M6 higher.
   c. From the new pitch, play a pitch a m3 higher.
   d. From this new pitch, play a pitch a m7 lower.
   e. What is the name of the pitch you are on now? ________

4. a. Play $f^{\sharp 4}$.
   b. Play a pitch a P4 higher.
   c. From the new pitch, play a pitch a M3 higher.
   d. From this new pitch, play a pitch a P5 lower.
   e. What is the name of the pitch you are on now? ________

5. a. Play a^4.
   b. Play a pitch a M3 higher.
   c. From the new pitch, play a pitch P4 higher.
   d. From this new pitch, play a pitch a M6 higher.
   e. What is the name of the pitch you are on now? ________

6. a. Play g^3.
   b. Play a pitch a m7 lower.
   c. From the new pitch, play a pitch M3 lower.
   d. From this new pitch, play a pitch a P5 higher.
   e. What is the name of the pitch you are on now? ________

7. a. Play $b^{\flat 1}$.
   b. Play a pitch a M6 higher.
   c. From the new pitch, play a pitch a m2 higher.
   d. From this new pitch, play a pitch a P4 higher.
   e. What is the name of the pitch you are on now? ________

8. a. Play $d^{\flat 4}$.
   b. Play a pitch a M3 higher.
   c. From the new pitch, play a pitch a m3 higher.
   d. From this new pitch, play a pitch a A4 higher.
   e. What is the name of the pitch you are on now? ________

Compound Intervals

Intervals that are one octave or smaller in size are called **simple intervals,** while intervals larger than an octave are known as **compound intervals.** The following example illustrates a major ninth, a major tenth, and a perfect eleventh:

Of course, the larger the interval, the more difficult it can be to read and identify correctly. For the purposes of identification it is easier to reduce the compound interval by one octave. Thus, a major ninth becomes a compound major second; a major tenth, a compound major third; and a perfect eleventh, a compound perfect fourth.

becomes

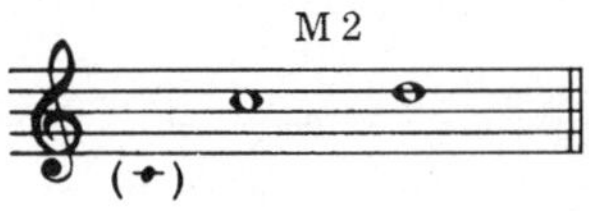

becomes

becomes

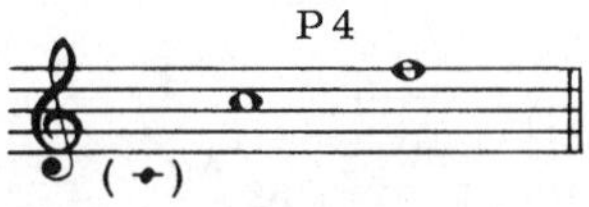

Compound intervals are major, minor, augmented, diminished, or perfect, depending on the quality of the corresponding simple interval. Remember that the quality always stays the same because all you are doing when you reduce a compound interval to a simple interval is subtracting one octave.

EXERCISE 6•12

Identify the following compound harmonic intervals by reducing them by one octave and labeling the simple interval that results:

EXAMPLE:

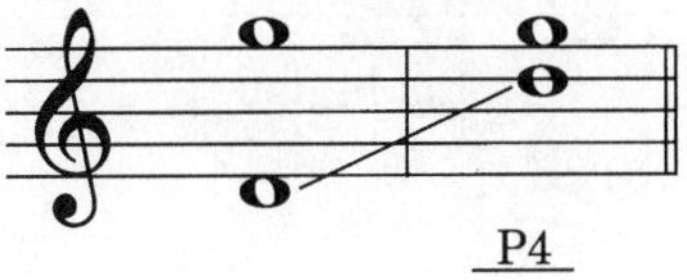

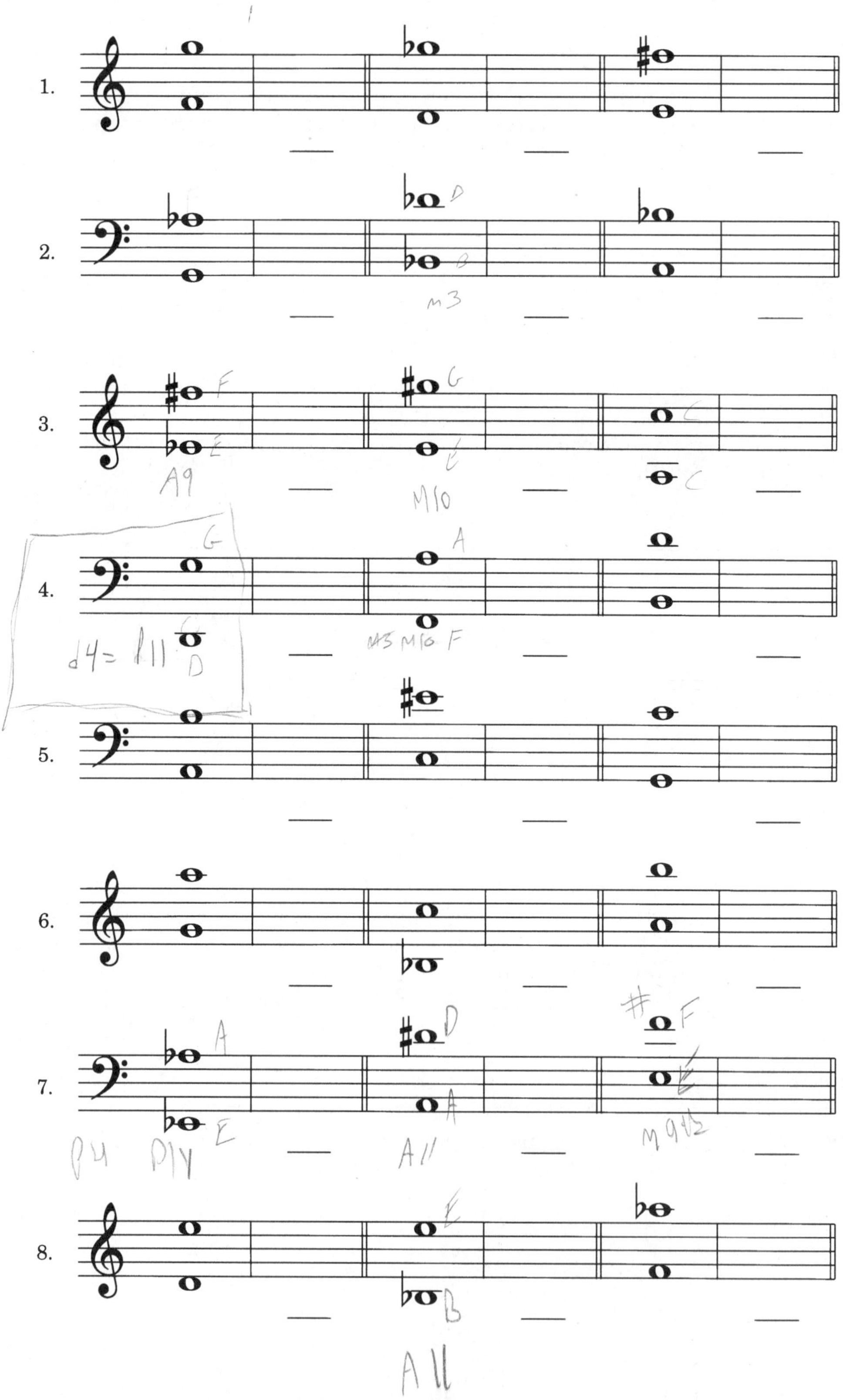
1.
2.
3.
4.
5.
6.
7.
8.

EXERCISE 6•13

Identify the following compound harmonic intervals. Even though you are not asked to reduce each interval by an octave this time, you may find it helpful to do so mentally. Remember also that the quality of the compound interval is the same as the quality of the corresponding simple interval.

1. 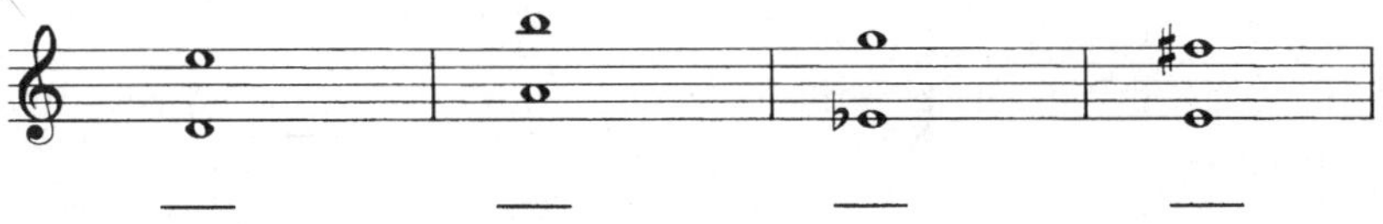

2. 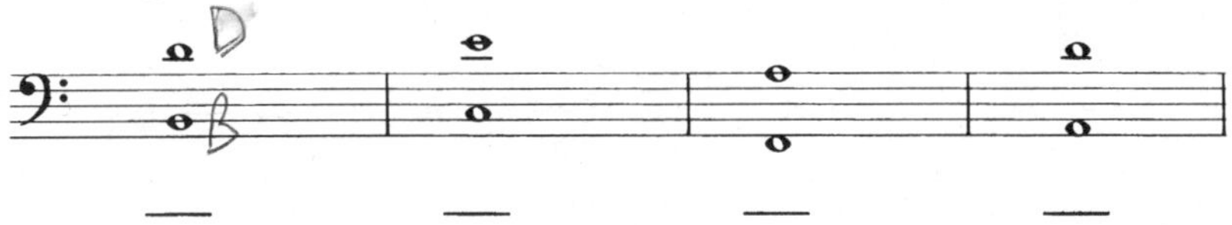

3. 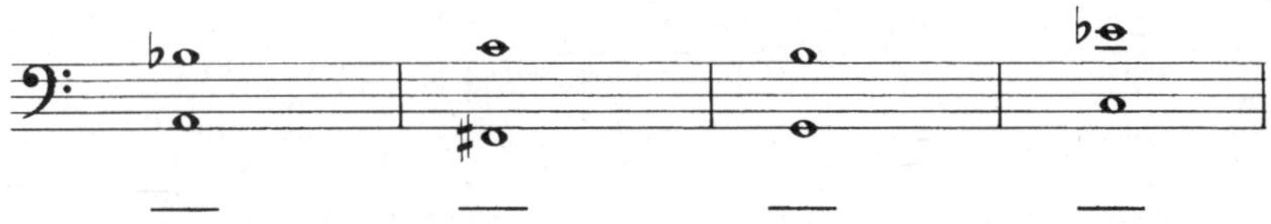

4. 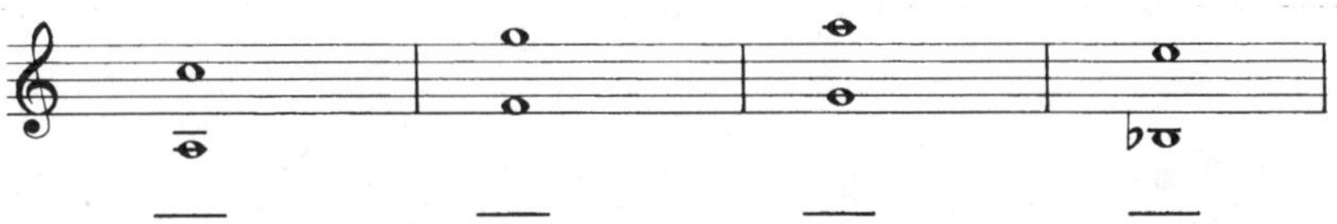

Harmonic Inversion of Intervals

Intervals are inverted harmonically by reversing the pitches from top to bottom. That is, the higher pitch is moved one octave lower so it is below the other pitch. The same interval results if the lower pitch is moved one octave higher. The point to remember when inverting intervals is that one pitch remains stationary and the other moves an octave.

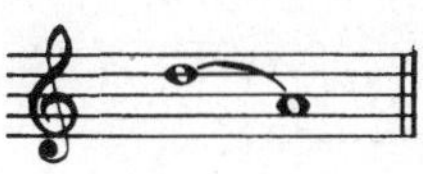 inverts to 

The arithmetic distance always changes when an interval is inverted. A fifth inverts to a fourth, a sixth to a third, and a seventh to a second. Notice that *the sum of the interval plus its inversion always equals nine.*

The quality of inverted intervals changes in the following ways:

Perfect intervals always invert to perfect intervals.

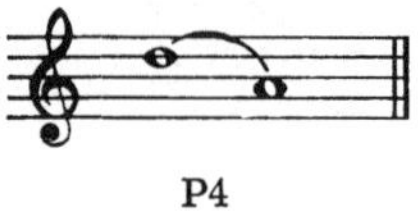
P4

becomes

P5

Major intervals always invert to minor intervals; minor intervals always invert to major intervals.

M6

becomes

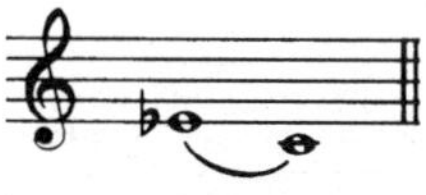
m3

m2

becomes

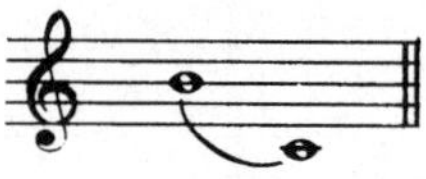
M7

Augmented intervals always invert to diminished intervals; diminished intervals always invert to augmented intervals.

A4

becomes

d5

d5

becomes

A4

Another important point to remember is that inverted intervals can, in some ways, be considered to belong to the same interval family. That is, although the two pitches have changed location, and the interval between them has changed, the pitches themselves have not changed.

EXERCISE 6•14

First label the given melodic interval, then invert it and identify the interval that results. Remember that the sum of any interval plus its inversion always equals nine.

EXAMPLE:

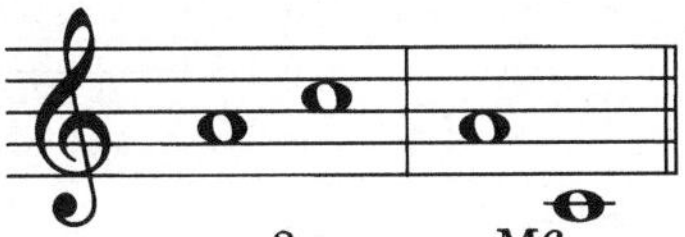

m3 M6

1. 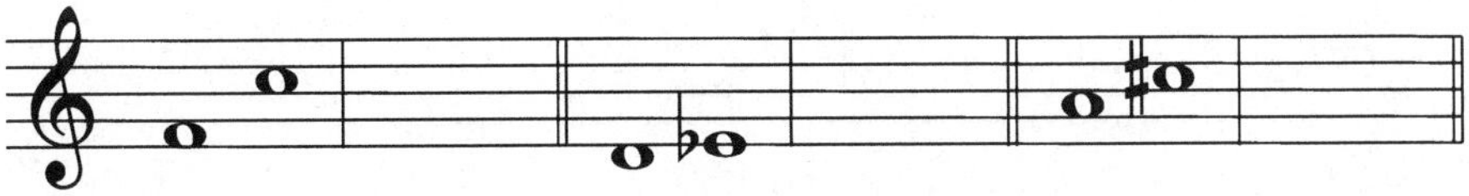

2. 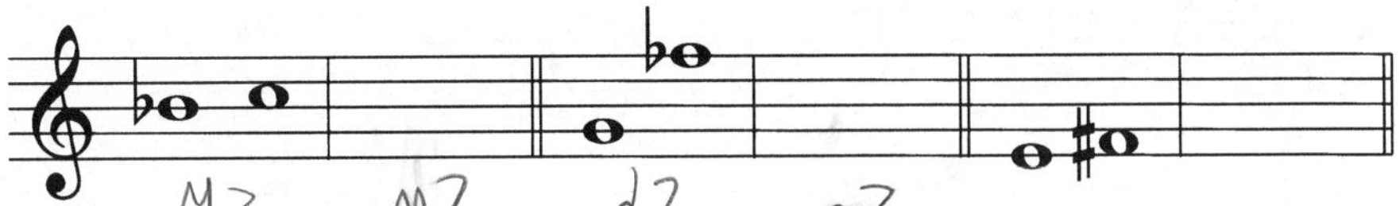

M2 M7 d7 a2

3. 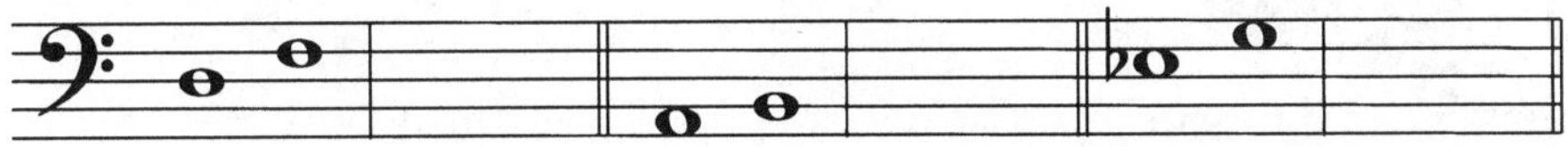

4. 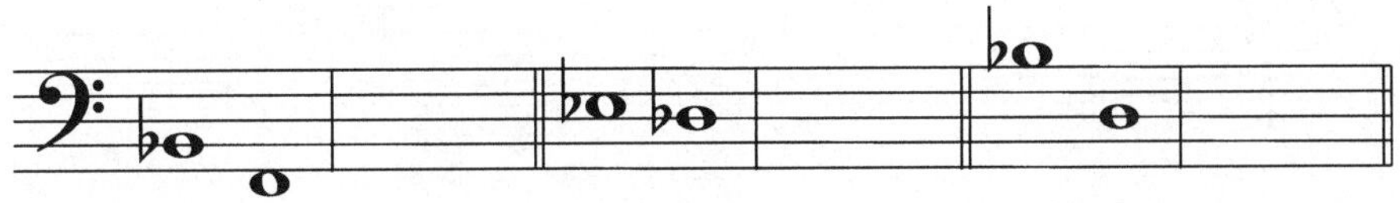

5. 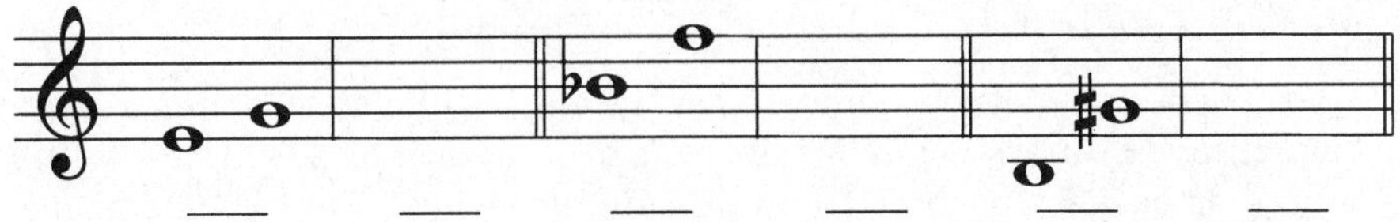

6. 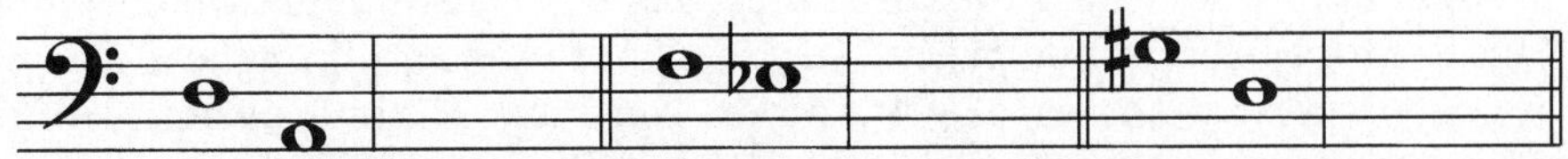

7. 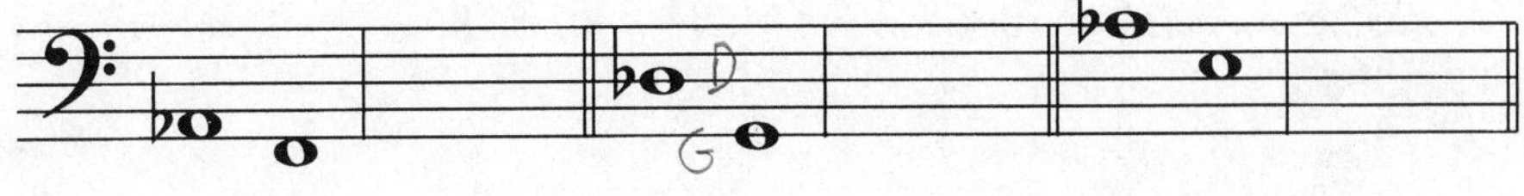

d5
A4

8. 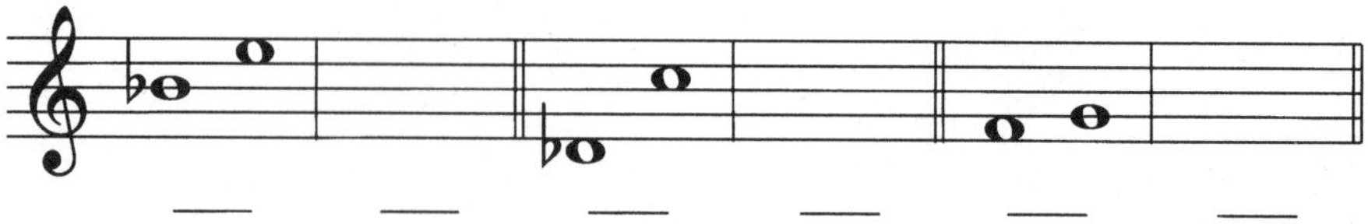

9. 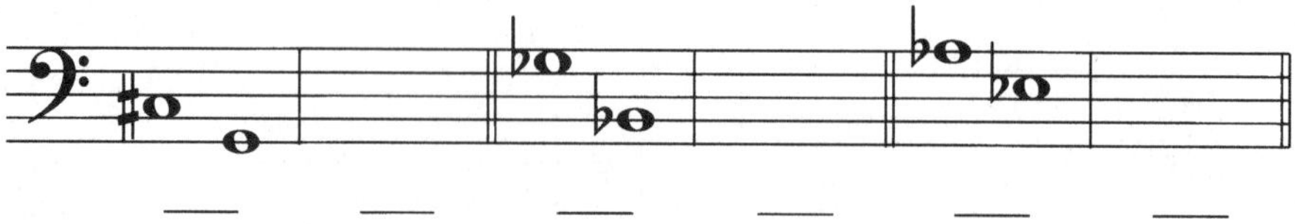

10. 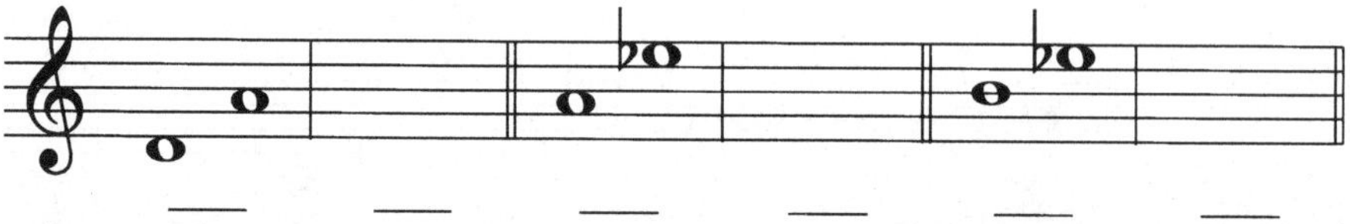

11. 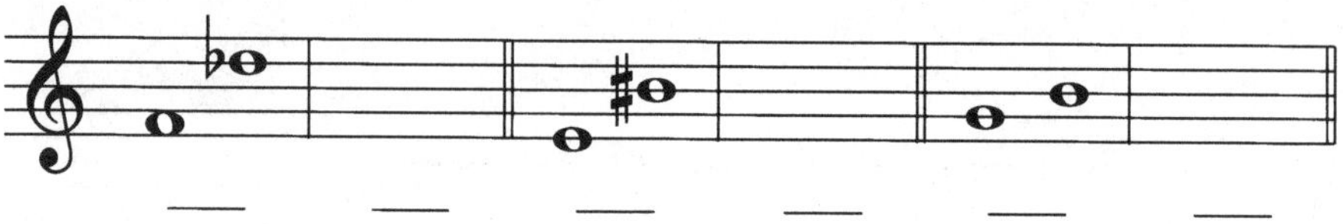

12. 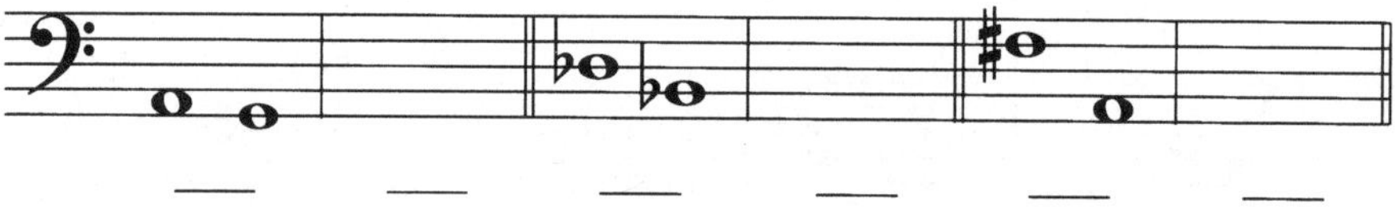

Musical Problem

Your teacher or another student from the class will play various intervals, beginning on different pitches, for you to recognize by ear. These will be played as either harmonic (sounding simultaneously) or melodic (sounding in succession) intervals. The intervals have been grouped in limited combinations according to size and quality in order to make your beginning work easier. As you practice, remember that ear training is a continuous process; it grows easier as you continue. If time permits, your teacher may wish to return to this Musical Problem several times in the future. An alternative to this would be for you and a friend from the class to practice on your own.

Major 2nds and Major 3rds only

1. ________	4. ________	7. ________
2. ________	5. ________	8. ________
3. ________	6. ________	9. ________

Major 3rds and Perfect 5ths

1. ______	4. ______	7. ______
2. ______	5. ______	8. ______
3. ______	6. ______	9. ______

Perfect 4ths and Perfect 5ths

1. ______	4. ______	7. ______
2. ______	5. ______	8. ______
3. ______	6. ______	9. ______

Major 2nds, Perfect 4ths, and Major 6ths

1. ______	4. ______	7. ______
2. ______	5. ______	8. ______
3. ______	6. ______	9. ______

All intervals from the major scale, including the Major 7th

1. ______	4. ______	7. ______
2. ______	5. ______	8. ______
3. ______	6. ______	9. ______

Focus

In this chapter, we have concentrated on identifying and writing intervals. This work can, at times, seem mathematical and tedious if done in a purely mechanical way. It can also seem time-consuming and difficult. But it is absolutely necessary for you to be both familiar with and comfortable about intervals. Intervals are a fundamental element of music; interval patterns are the building blocks of tonal music.

Even if the mechanics of writing and recognizing intervals becomes drudgery, keep in mind that acquiring these skills is essential in advancing your understanding of tonal music. In the same way that musicians practice scales to acquaint themselves with scale patterns, they work with intervals to become familiar with interval patterns. Perhaps the following musical problem will help us understand that melodies are patterns of intervals.

Musical Problem

In your mind, sing the beginning of any of the following songs that you know. Beside the name of each, write the interval that occurs between the first and second notes of the song. This may seem difficult at first, but two

(continued)

hints may help: (1) Only the intervals found in a major scale are used—P1, M2, M3, P4, P5, M6, M7, P8. (2) Songs that don't begin on the tonic quite often begin on the dominant. If you continue to have trouble, try singing up or down the scale from the tonic to the other note.

1. "The Simpsons" TV show theme _____
2. "Titanic" theme _____
3. "South Park" TV show theme _____
4. "Star Wars" theme _____
5. "2001" theme _____
6. "Moon River" _____

Both scales have one and the same accidental—B♭. In fact, if you begin on the sixth degree of *any* major scale and follow its note pattern for one octave, the result will always be a new, natural minor scale. Here's another example:

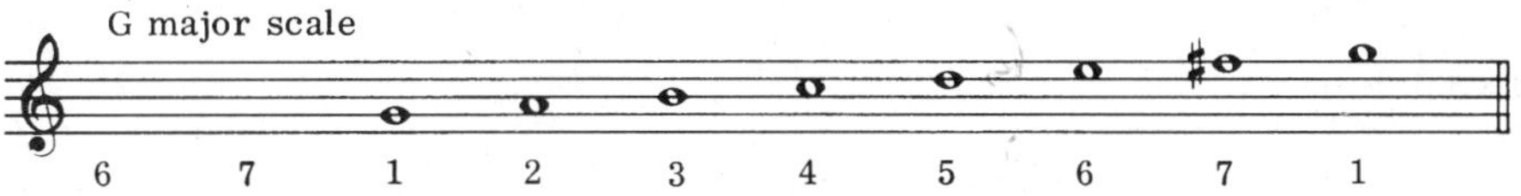

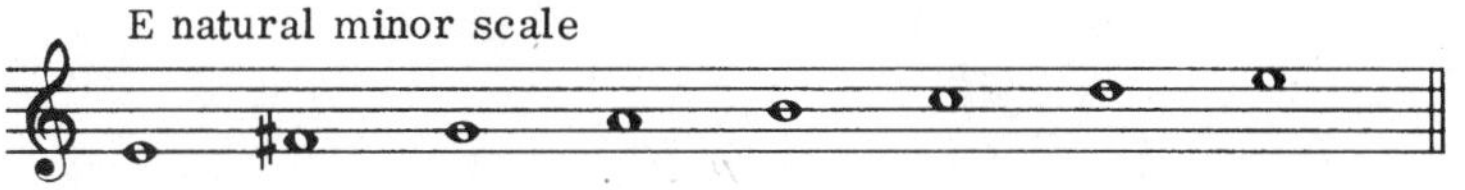

This relationship, which is constant for all of the major keys, means that there are pairs of keys—one major, one minor—related by the same pitch content, hence by the same key signature. Such keys are called **related keys.** The term *relative minor* refers to the minor key or scale that is related to a particular major scale by having the same key signature. The term *relative major* refers to the major key or scale with the same key signature as a particular minor scale.

The relative minor-major relationship may be remembered in two ways: (1) The relative minor scale always begins on the sixth degree of the major scale. (2) The relative minor scale always begins three half steps (a minor third) below its related major scale. Most students find the second way easier. Either way, remember that related scales always have the *same* key signature but *different* tonics.

EXERCISE 7•1

Identify the relative minor key for the following major keys.

1. E major	C#	8. A♭ major	F
2. D major	B	9. C major	A
3. G♭ major	Eb	10. B major	G#
4. F major	D	11. F♯ major	D#
5. C♯ major	A#	12. D♭ major	Bb
6. G major	E	13. E♭ major	C
7. A major	F#	14. B♭ major	G

EXERCISE 7•2

Identify the major key and the relative minor key that have the given number of sharps or flats.

	Major	*Relative Minor*
1. two flats	B♭	G
2. two sharps	D	B
3. three sharps	A	F♯
4. four flats	A♭	F
5. seven sharps	C♯	A♯
6. five flats	D♭	B♭
7. six sharps	F♯	D♯
8. three flats	E♭	C
9. one sharp	G	E
10. six flats	G♭	E♭
11. five sharps	B	G♯
12. one flat	F	D
13. four sharps	E	C♯
14. seven flats	C♭	A♭

EXERCISE 7•3

Identify the relative major key for the following minor keys.

1. F♯ minor	A	8. E minor	G
2. D minor	F	9. D♯ minor	F♯
3. A♭ minor	C♭	10. F minor	A♭
4. C♯ minor	E	11. B minor	D
5. A♯ minor	C♯	12. E♭ minor	G♭
6. G minor	B♭	13. C minor	E♭
7. B♭ minor	D♭	14. G♯ minor	B

Parallel Keys

Parallel keys begin on the same pitch (that is, they have the same tonic) but have different key signatures. G major and G minor, for instance, are parallel keys.

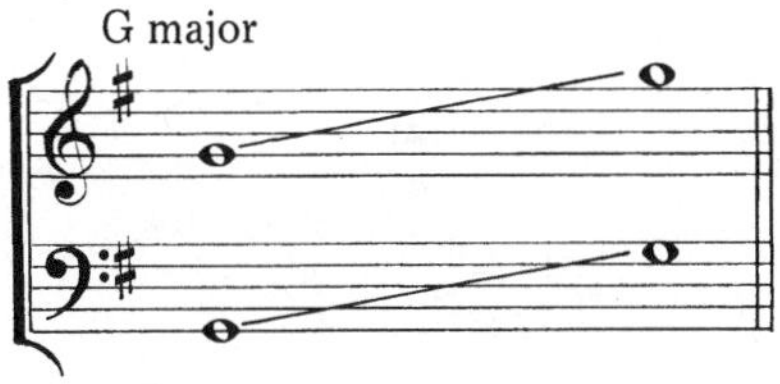

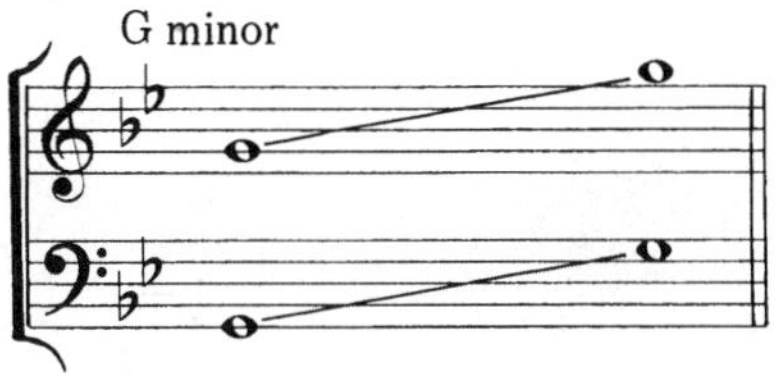

The terms *parallel major* and *parallel minor* are used frequently.

Minor Key Signatures

The minor key signatures, for sharp keys and flat keys, are given below, followed by the number of accidentals associated with each key. Notice that lowercase letters are used to indicate minor keys, which is an acceptable practice. Notice also that the last sharp added to each sharp key is the supertonic, and the last flat added to each flat key is the submediant. As you study these minor key signatures, make a mental association with the relative major for each key.

Key Signatures: Sharp Minor Keys

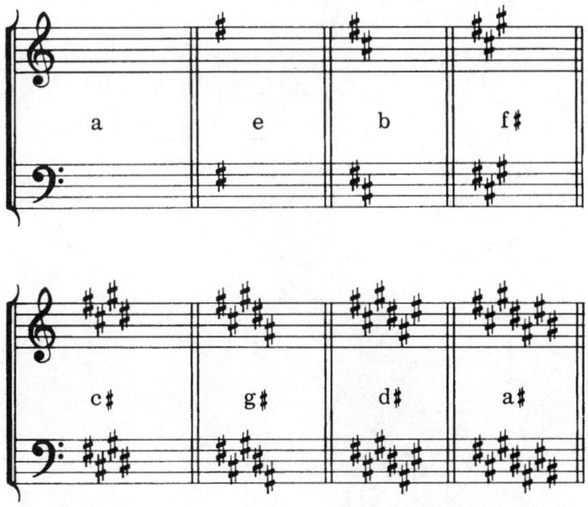

Minor Key	*Number of Sharps*
a	0
e	1
b	2
f♯	3
c♯	4
g♯	5
d♯	6
a♯	7

Key Signatures: Minor Flat Keys

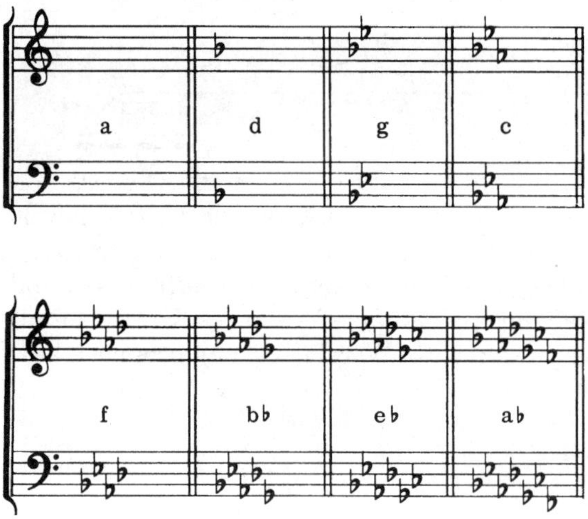

Minor Key	*Number of Flats*
a	0
d	1
g	2
c	3
f	4
b♭	5
e♭	6
a♭	7

As mentioned before, there is more than one version of the minor scale. In fact, there are three: natural minor, harmonic minor, and melodic minor. At this point it is important to remember that the key signature for minor scales supplies the accidentals for the *natural minor* form of the scale only. A piece of music using *harmonic* or *melodic minor* forms of the scale (as most tonal music does) supplies the appropriate accidentals *within the music itself,* directly before the pitches they affect. These extra accidentals never appear in the key signature. The following example is in C minor. The appearance of both B natural and A natural within the excerpt indicates that the melodic minor form is being used at this particular point. The next chapter will explore the three forms of the minor scale in some detail. For now, remember that the minor key signature always indicates the accidentals for the natural minor version of the minor scale.

Scarlatti: Sonata in C Minor

EXERCISE 7•4

Identify the minor keys represented by the following key signatures.

1. 

G   e   g#   B♭

2. 

B♭   F#   F   D#

3. 

D   E♭   A#   A

4. 

C   E   D   C#

5. 

B   C#   a   a♭

6. 

a♭   d#   e♭   c

7. 

a#   b   g#   g

8. 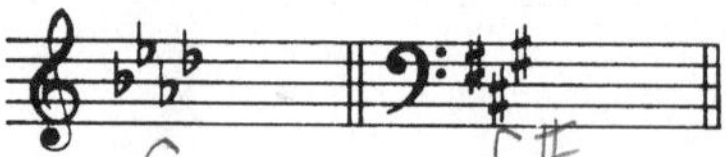

f   f#

Write out the indicated minor key signatures, using sharps or flats as required.

1.

G minor *Bb*

2.

C minor *Eb*

3.

Ab minor *Cb*

4. *FCGDA*

C# minor *E*

5.

A minor

6.

D# minor *F#*

FCC

1 3. 4, 5, 8

7.

Bb minor *Db*

8.

G# minor *B*

9. *BEADGC*

Eb minor *Gb*

10.

A minor

11.

D minor *F#*

12.

A# minor *E#*

FCGDAEB

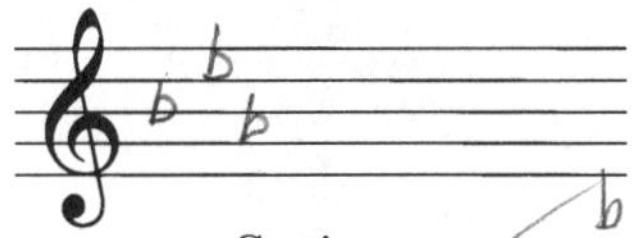

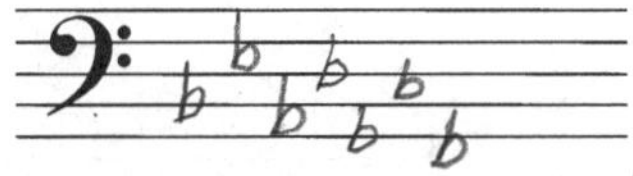

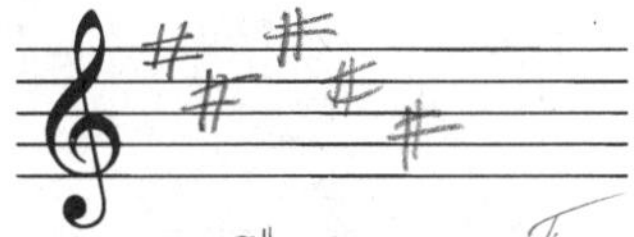

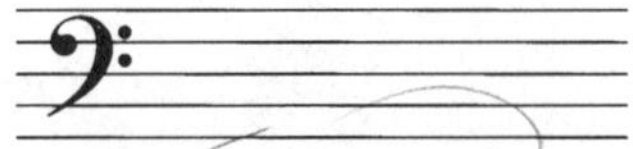

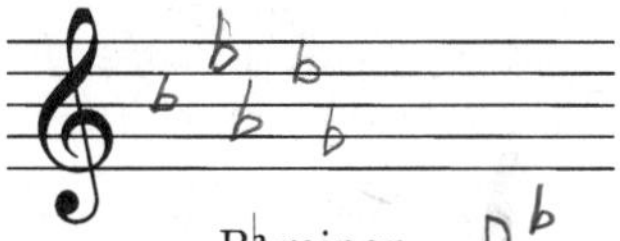

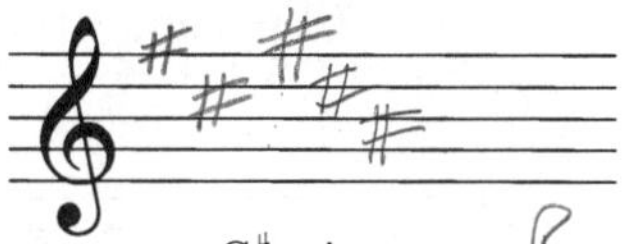

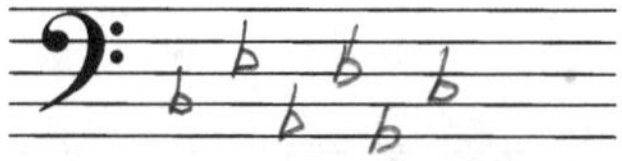

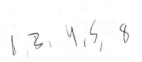

BEAD

BEADGC

13. F minor — Ab

14. G# minor — B · FCGDA

15. F# minor — A · FCC

16. B minor — D

17. D# minor — F#

18. C# minor — E

19. E minor — G

20. Eb minor — Gb

21. F# minor — A · 3 sharps

22. E minor — G · 1 sharp

23. F minor — Ab · 4 flats

24. A# minor — 7 sharps

25. Ab minor — 7 flats

26. B minor — D · 2 sharps

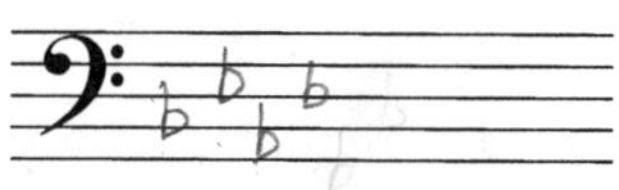

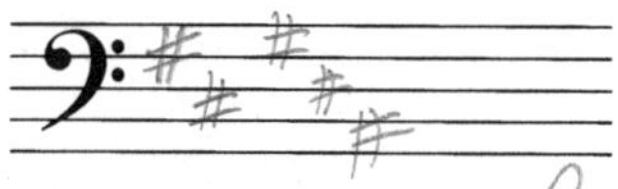

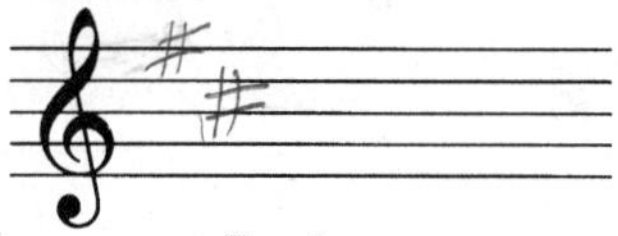

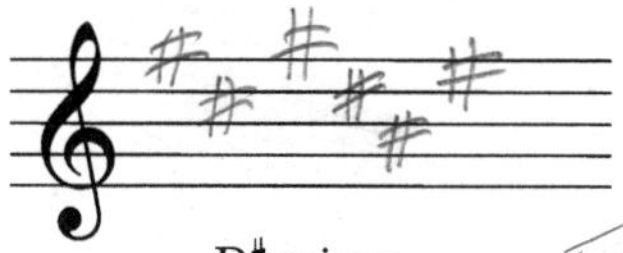

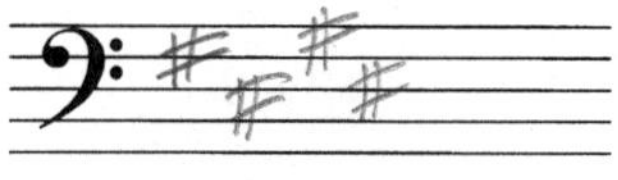

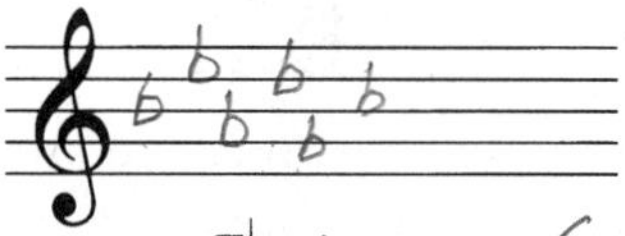

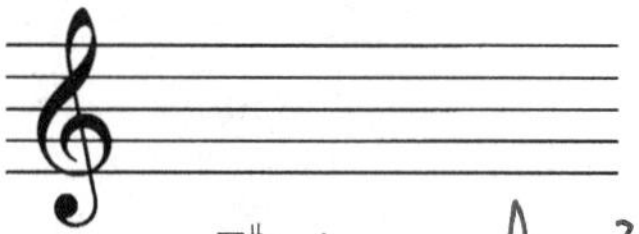

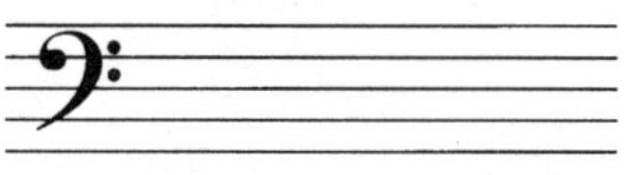

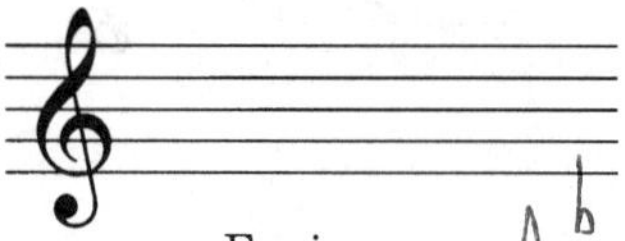

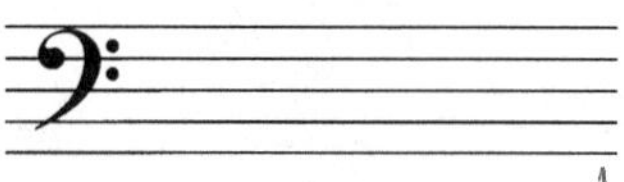

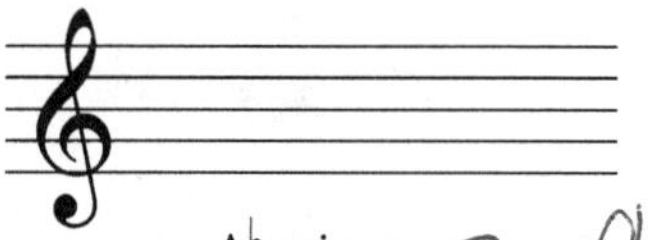

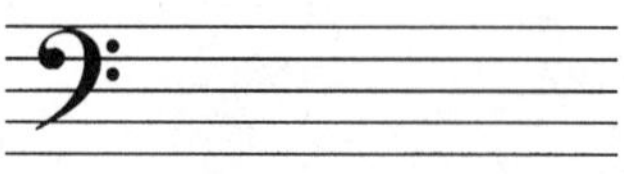

27. C minor *3 flots* Eb

29. Bb minor Db 5 flats

28. D minor *1 flat* F

30. G minor Bb 2 flats

Musical Problem

Have your teacher or another student select and play on the keyboard several of the musical excerpts that are listed below with their location in this book. After listening to each excerpt, decide whether it is in a major key or a minor key.

Composer	Title	Page(s)
1. Bach	Chorale from Cantata No. 180	26
2. Bach	Courante from French Suite No. 2	25
3. Bach	Minuet in G Minor	59
4. Kuhlau	Rondo from Sonatina, Op. 20, No. 1	72
5. Mozart	Sonata in Bb Major, K. 570, III	70
6. Scarlatti	Sonata in C Minor	163
7. Schumann	Choral from *Album for the Young*	246
8. Traditional	"St. James Infirmary"	261

The Circle of Fifths: Minor Keys

For minor keys, as for major keys, a circle of fifths can be constructed. The same perfect fifth relationship between adjacent keys exists, and the enharmonic keys again appear at the bottom of the circle. Notice also that the circle of fifths for major keys can be superimposed over the one for minor keys. This works because of the parallel relationship between major and minor keys

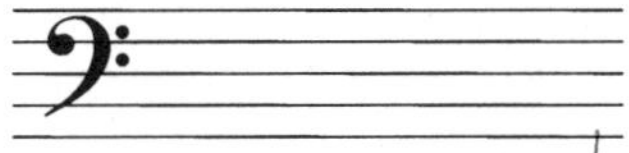

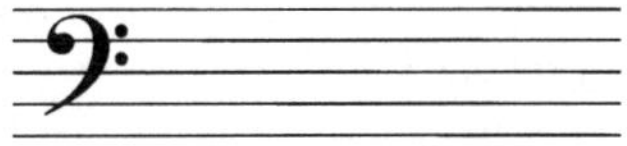

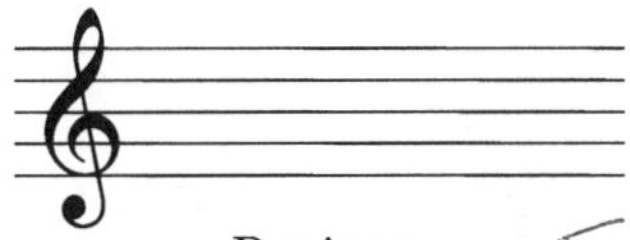

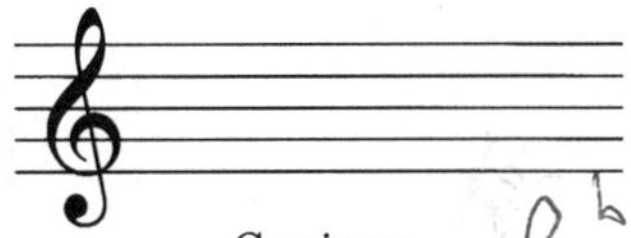

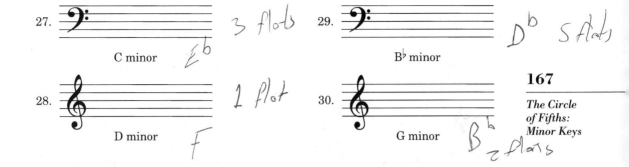

discussed earlier. At this point it might be more useful to you to combine the two in your mind so that you remember one circle of fifths for both major and minor keys.

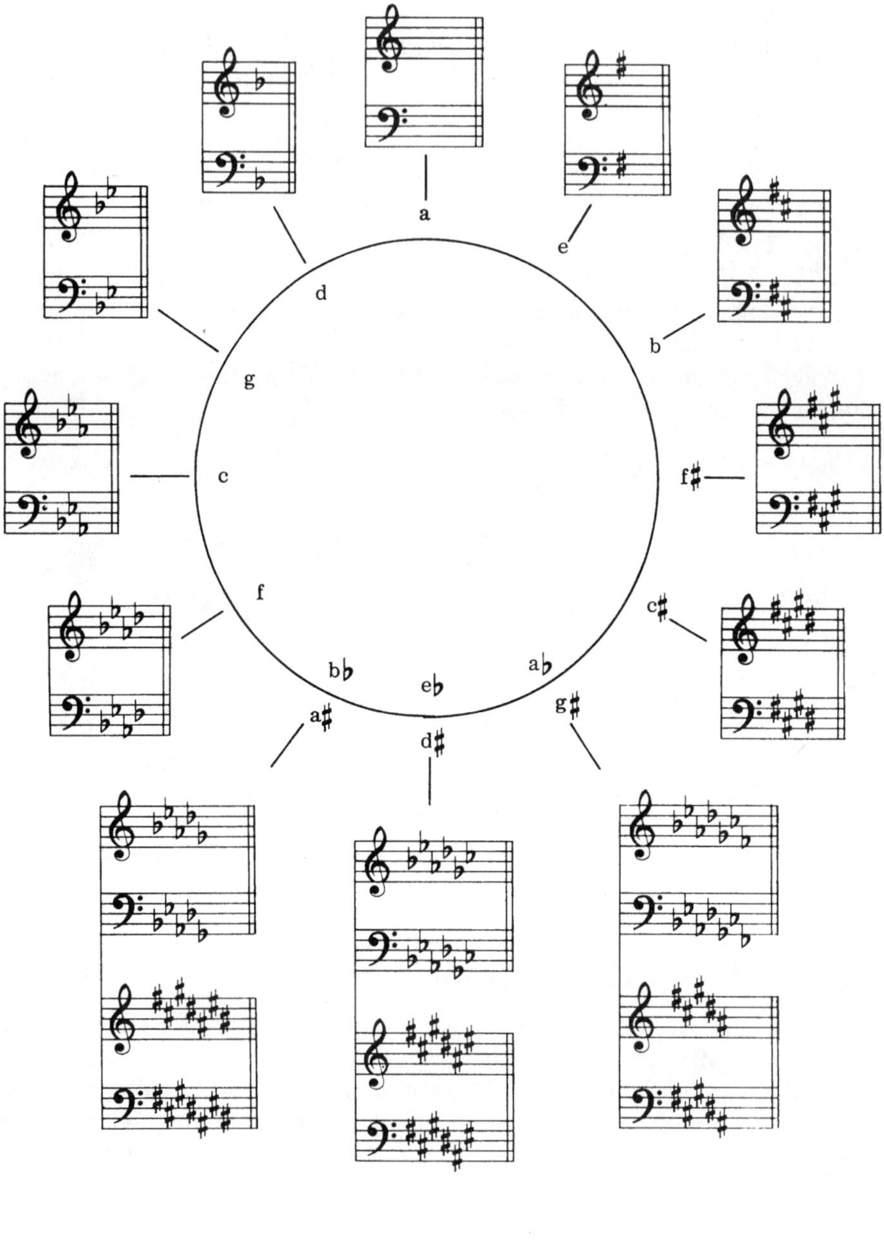

Focus

Almost all beginning musicians have favorite keys. These are usually keys with no sharps or flats, or at most one or two, which seem easier. Sometimes, people study theory or take lessons for years and still find keys with more than four or five sharps or flats too difficult to negotiate successfully. Usually, the problem feeds on itself—some keys are initially easier, therefore we *choose* to work primarily in those keys. But this is a mistake; we don't learn by avoidance.

If you are going to be a good musician, even a good amateur musician, you need to be fluent in all keys—both major and minor. This ability won't come immediately, but it will develop slowly with practice. You can make working with minor scales easier by being certain that you understand the minor key signatures and how they relate to the major keys. If you need additional practice at recognizing or writing minor key signatures, do that now, before you begin the next chapter. You will find Chapter 8 much easier to understand once you are comfortable with the minor key signatures.

8 *Chapter*

Minor Scales

Like the major scales, there are a total of fifteen tonic notes for the relative minor scales. But unlike major scales, each minor scale has three different versions, or forms. These are called *natural* minor, *harmonic* minor, and *melodic* minor.

G natural minor

G harmonic minor

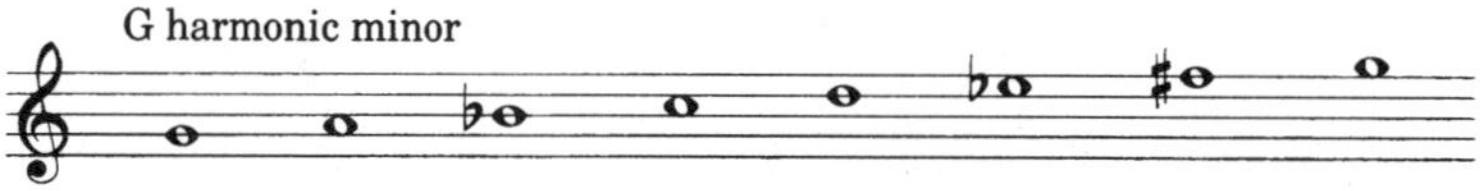

G melodic minor

This can be confusing at first, because of the large number of slightly different minor scales it creates. But if you stay focused on the idea that it is all one scale, keep the concept of relative major/relative minor in mind, and remember the minor key signatures you learned in the previous chapter, you'll go a long way toward making this confusion disappear.

Why are there three different versions of the minor scale? This is a complicated question that has never been completely answered. Some say that the various forms of the minor scale evolved slowly, over a considerable period of time. Others say they grew to serve new melodic and harmonic interests. Still others say the alterations to natural minor are pitches borrowed from the parallel major scale. While there is some truth to all these answers, the one that is most pertinent to our work is this: Even though it's all one scale, each version of that scale has a unique harmonic or melodic advantage that makes it more or less useful for various musical situations. As you study this chapter, remember that each version of the minor scale has a separate pattern of whole steps and half steps that gives the resultant melody and harmony their characteristic sound. Also keep in mind that, even though we will be studying each version individually, most music is seldom written strictly in "melodic" or "harmonic" minor. Composers often change scale forms within a piece, depending on the musical situation.

Musical Problem

The following excerpts are from two folk songs. You may already know one or both of them. The first one is in the key of D major, the second is in D minor. Ask someone to play both examples in class. Remember that the difference in sound or feeling that you hear between major keys and minor keys is a result of two different interval patterns of whole steps and half steps.

"Molly Malone"

(continued)

"Joshua Fit the Battle of Jericho"

Musical Problem

If one key signature can represent two different keys, how can we tell which key a piece is in? This question can give students a great deal of unnecessary trouble. The fact is that the key signature alone does not give the answer; it gives two possibilities—the key is either major or minor. To be certain of the correct key, you must look within the music itself. The following suggestions should help.

1. Check the last note of the piece. The final note is almost certain to be the tonic.
2. Scan the piece for accidentals. Since many pieces in a minor key use more than one version of the minor scale, and since the key signature indicates only the natural minor version, any additional accidentals within the piece indicate a minor tonality (raised sevenths mean harmonic minor, raised sixths and sevenths/lowered sixths and sevenths mean melodic minor.)

Obtain a book of piano or vocal selections, and practice identifying the key of each piece by checking for the tonic and for accidentals. After practicing this method for a while, you should be able to determine the key of a new piece with little difficulty.

Natural Minor Scale

Like the major scale, the **natural minor scale** contains five whole steps and two half steps. The half steps, however, do not occur in the same place. This reordering of the interval pattern gives the natural minor scale its unique quality.

In the natural minor scale, the two half steps occur between the second and third degrees and the fifth and sixth degrees. The following illustration shows a natural minor scale beginning on the pitch A.

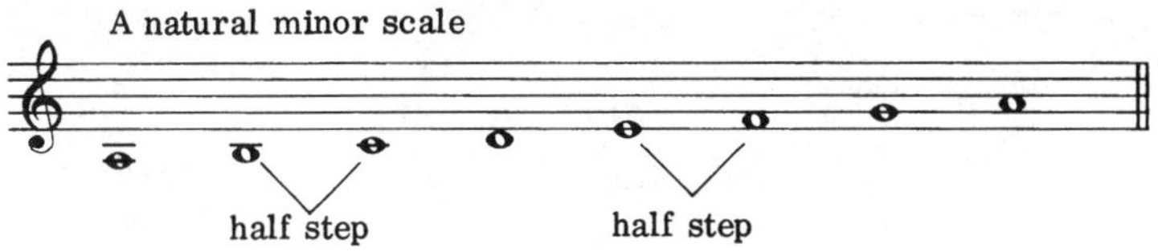

Notice that the natural minor scale beginning on A has no sharps or flats—that is, on the keyboard the pattern falls on all white keys.

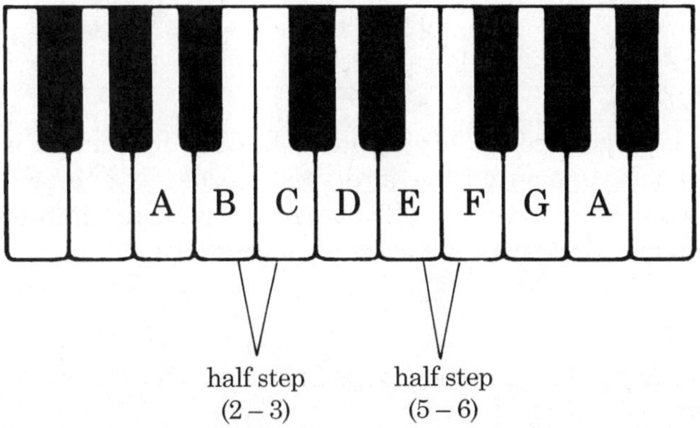

When the natural minor scale begins on any pitch other than A, one or more accidentals will be required to keep the interval pattern intact.

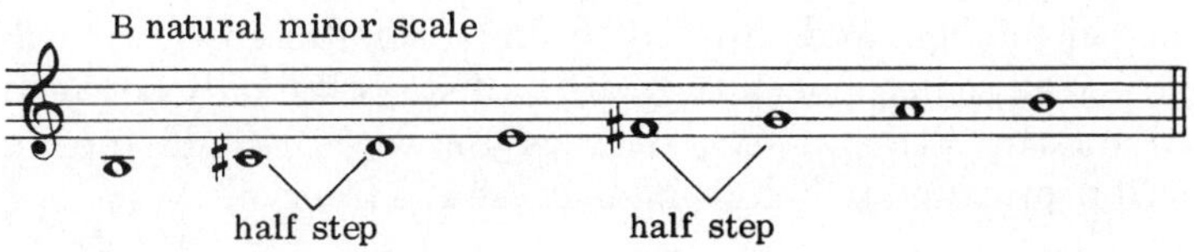

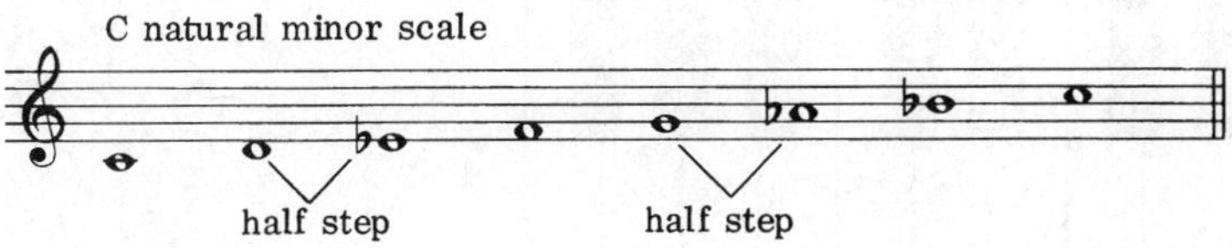

It may be useful to compare the intervals of the natural minor scale with those of the major scale. The following chart lists the intervals found within both scales and the number of half steps in each interval. In particular, compare the intervals of the third, sixth, and seventh between the two scales. It is these minor intervals above the tonic of the natural minor scale that contribute to the "minor" sound of the scale.

INTERVALS OF THE NATURAL MINOR AND MAJOR SCALES

Natural Minor		*Major*	
Interval	*Number of Half Steps*	*Interval*	*Number of Half Steps*
Perfect unison	0	Perfect unison	0
Major 2nd	2	Major 2nd	2
Minor 3rd	3	Major 3rd	4
Perfect 4th	5	Perfect 4th	5
Perfect 5th	7	Perfect 5th	7
Minor 6th	8	Major 6th	9
Minor 7th	10	Major 7th	11
Perfect 8th	12	Perfect 8th	12

Remember, however, that trying to count large intervals with half steps is always subject to error. When dealing with large intervals, it is better, and generally more accurate, to use harmonic inversion. If you need to, refer to Chapter 6 to refresh your memory about the harmonic inversion of intervals.

EXERCISE 8•1

From each starting pitch, write ascending and descending natural minor scales in both treble clef and bass clef. The scales in this exercise are grouped in perfect fifths so that each successive scale requires one additional sharp. The new sharp is always the supertonic of that scale.

Remember that, like the major scale, the minor scale is composed of an alphabetical sequence of pitches, and thus no chromatic half steps are used. When you have written the scales, check that the half steps fall only between the second and third and the fifth and sixth degrees. Indicate the half steps in each scale. A keyboard is provided to help you visualize the intervals.

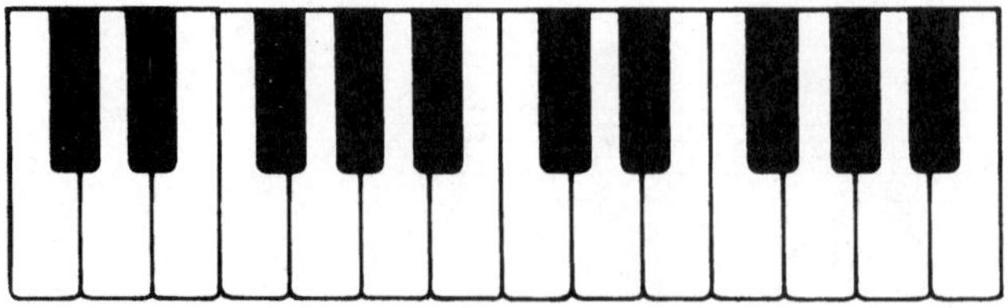

Natural Minor Scale

EXAMPLE:

E natural minor

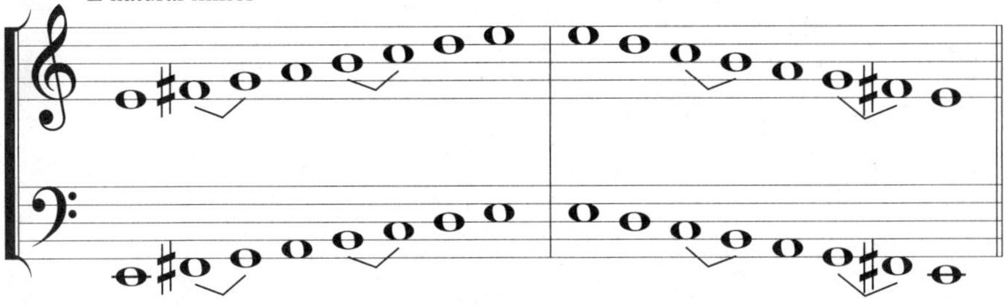

B natural minor

1. 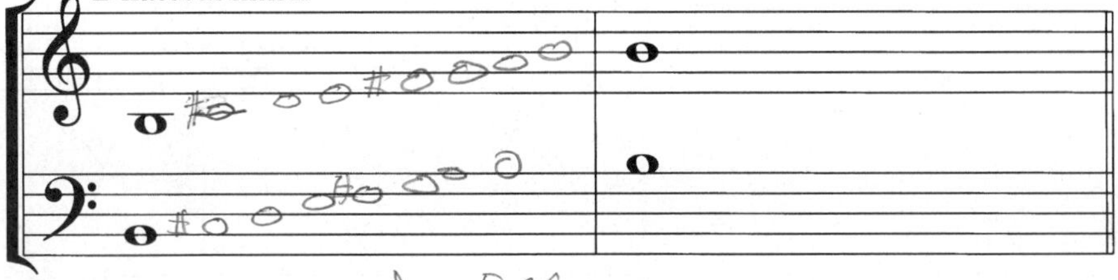

F♯ natural minor

2. 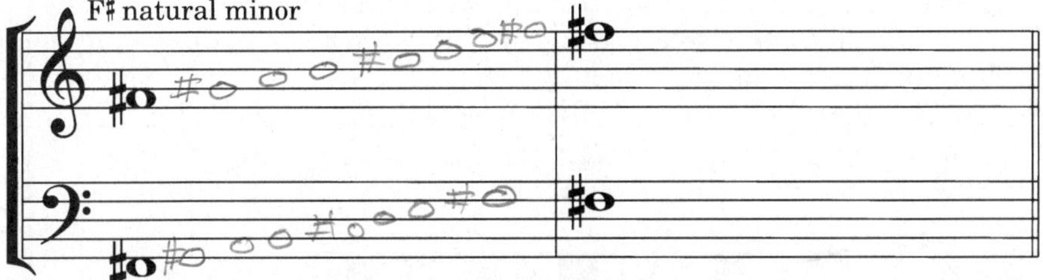

C♯ natural minor

3. 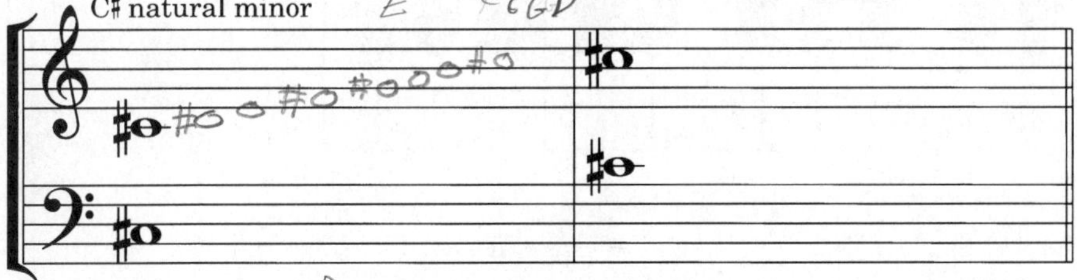

G♯ natural minor

4. 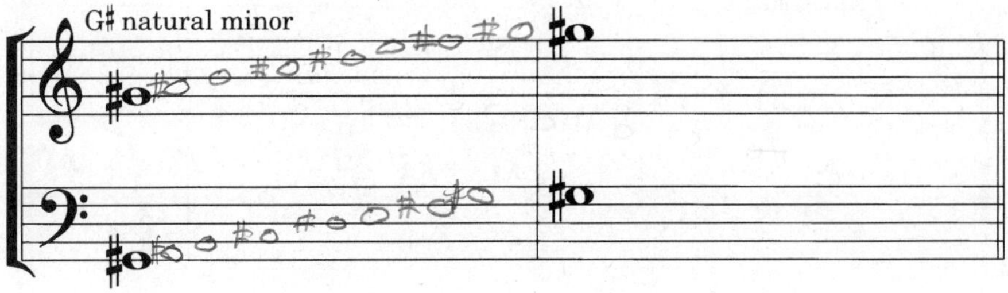

5.

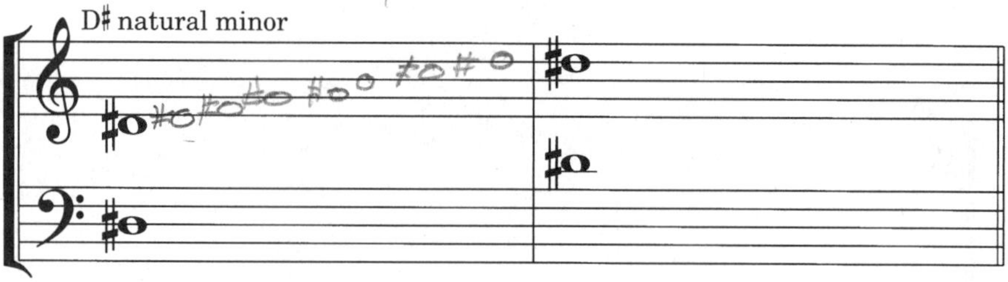

6.

EXERCISE 8•2

Write ascending and descending natural minor scales from each starting pitch. (The scales in this exercise are grouped so that each succeeding scale requires one additional flat—the submediant of that scale.) When you have written the scales, check that the half steps fall only between the second and third and the fifth and sixth degrees. Indicate the half steps in each scale. A keyboard is provided to help you visualize the intervals.

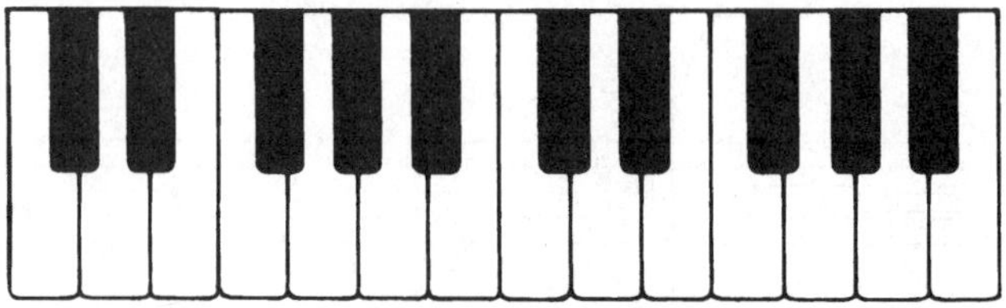

EXAMPLE:

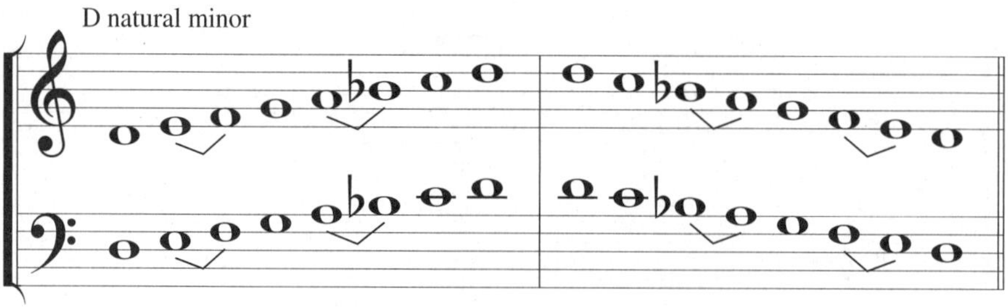

1. G natural minor

2. C natural minor

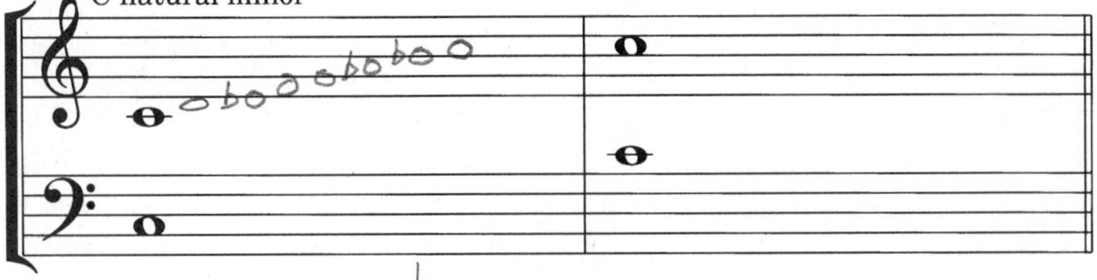

3. F natural minor

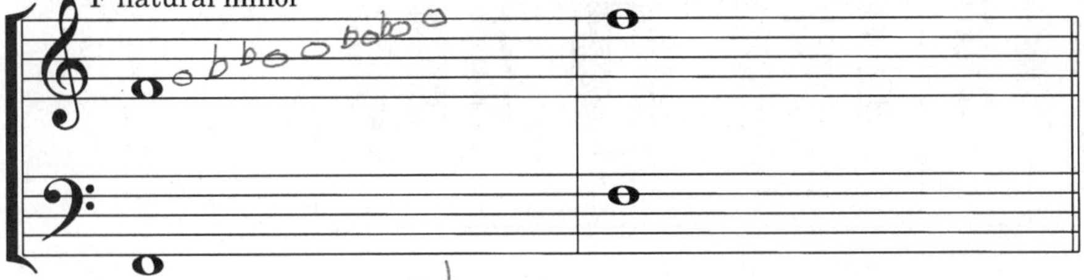

4. B♭ natural minor

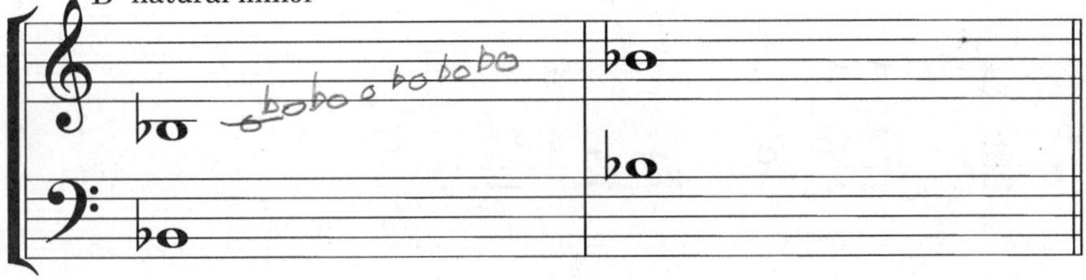

5. E♭ natural minor

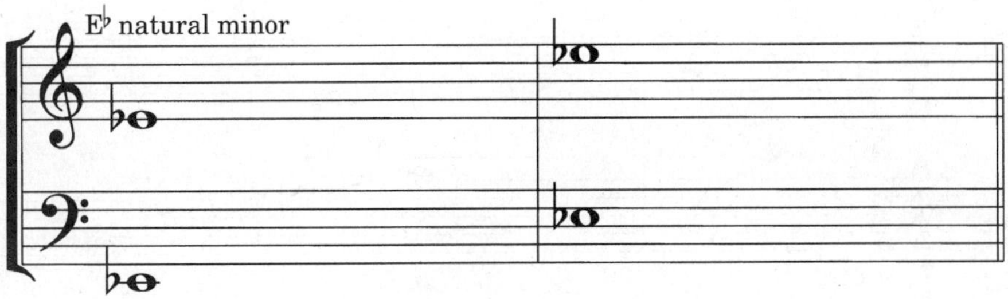

6. 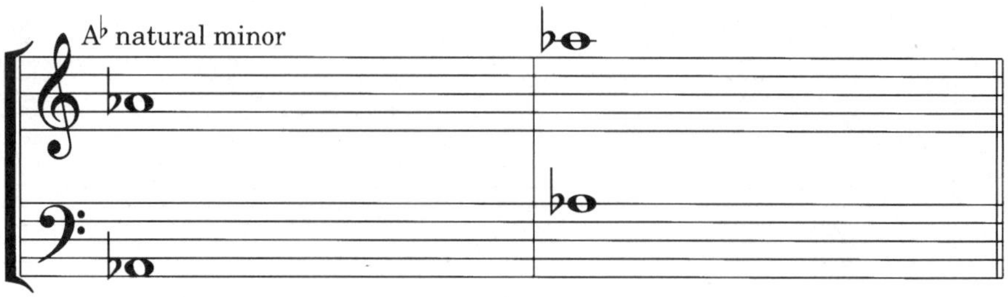

EXERCISE 8•3

Write ascending natural minor scales beginning with the given tonic pitches. This exercise and the one following use the same scales you wrote in the previous two exercises, but now they are out of sequence. A keyboard is provided to help you visualize the intervals.

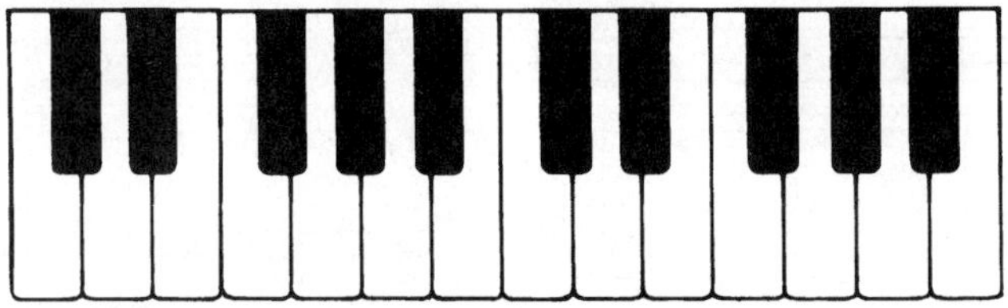

1. 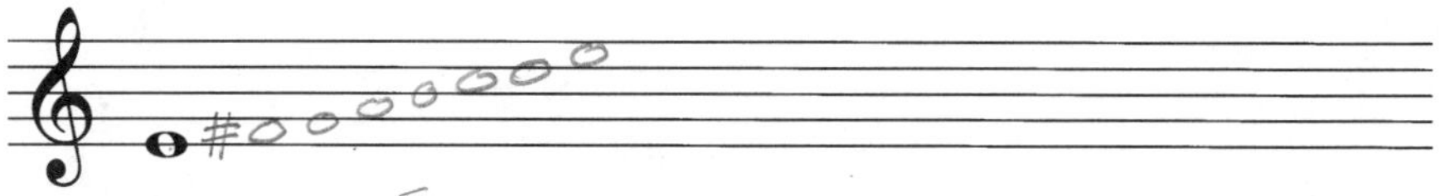

2. 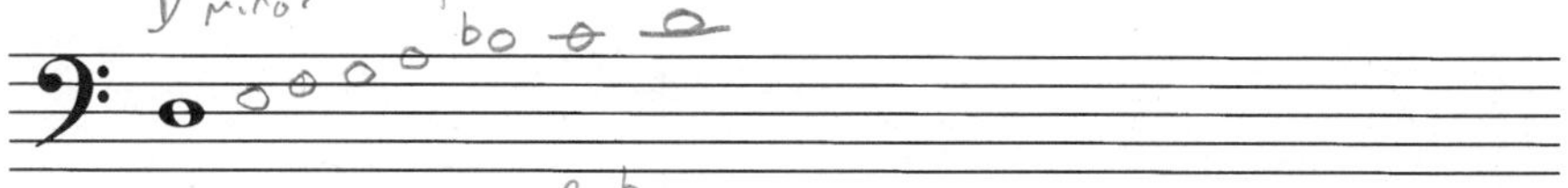

3. 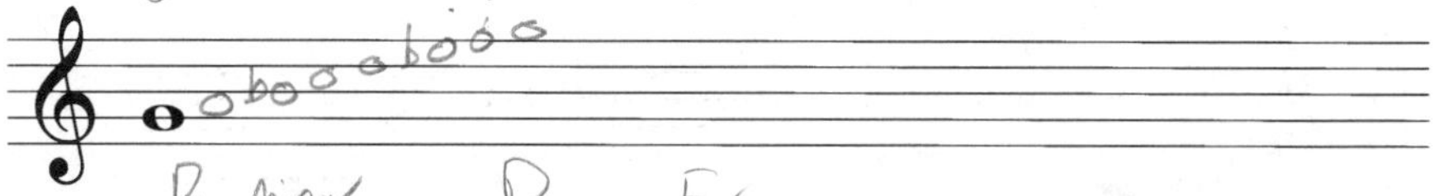

4. 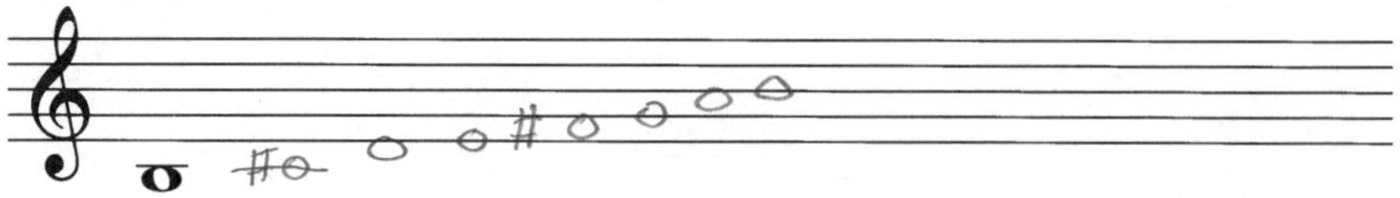

5. 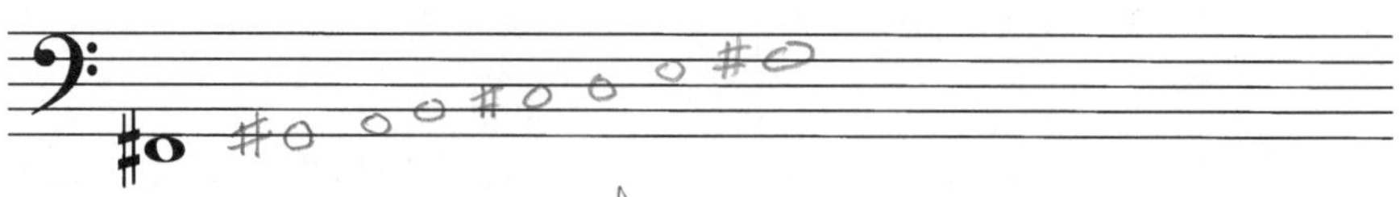

6.

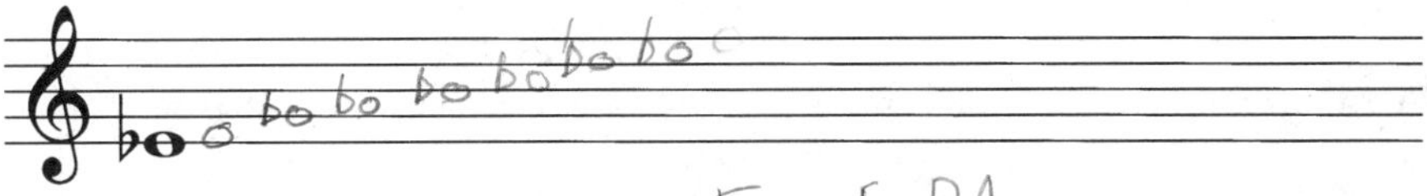

7.

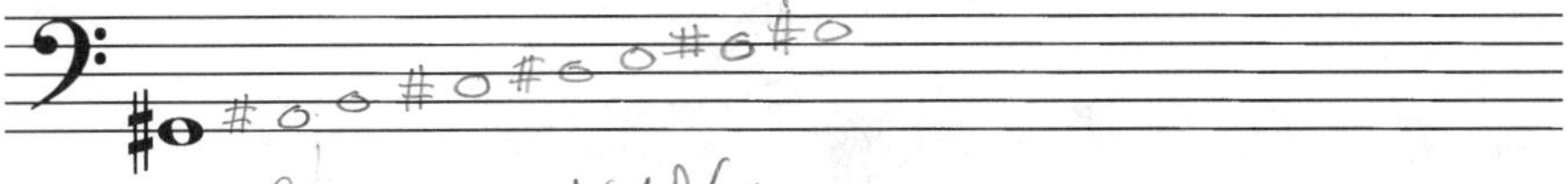

8.

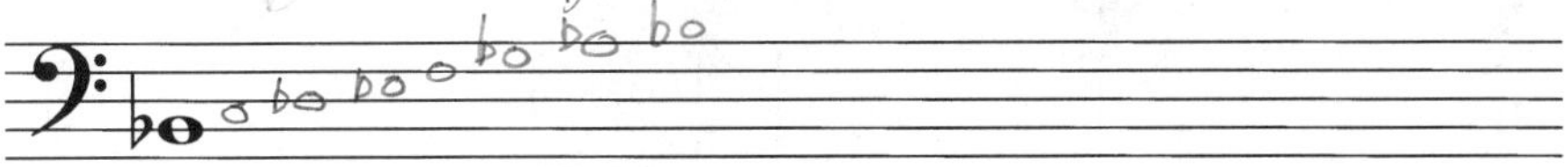

9.

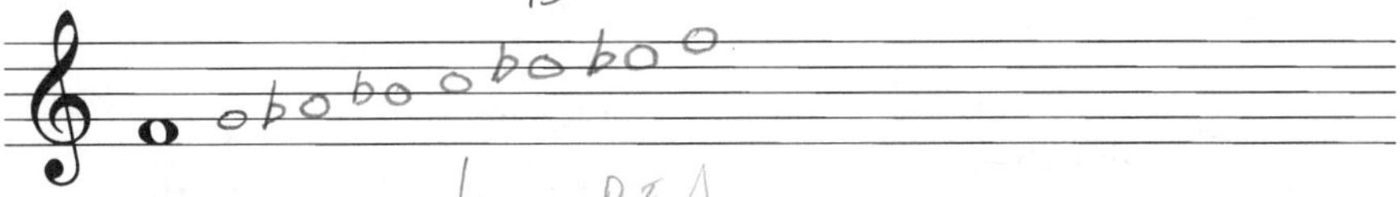

10.

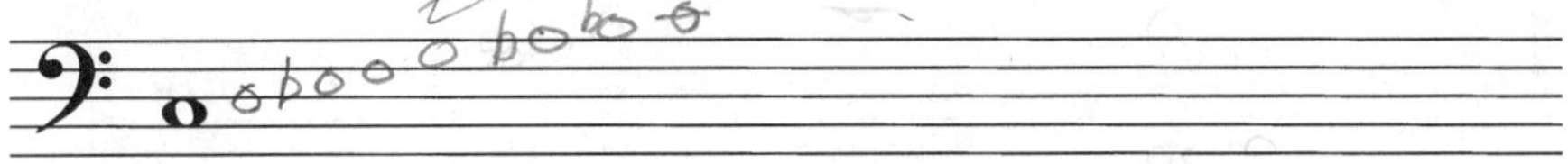

11.

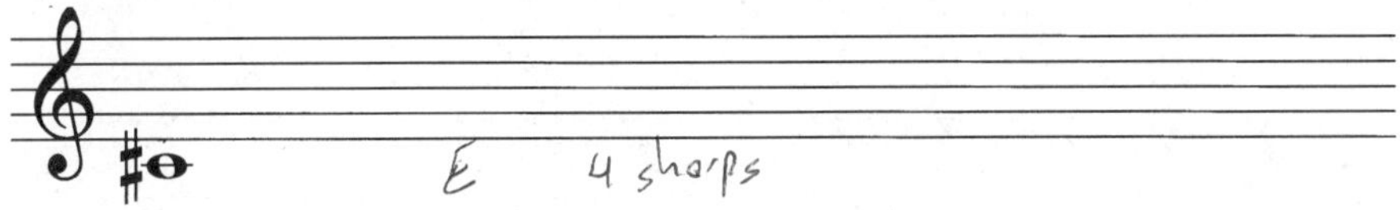

12.

13.

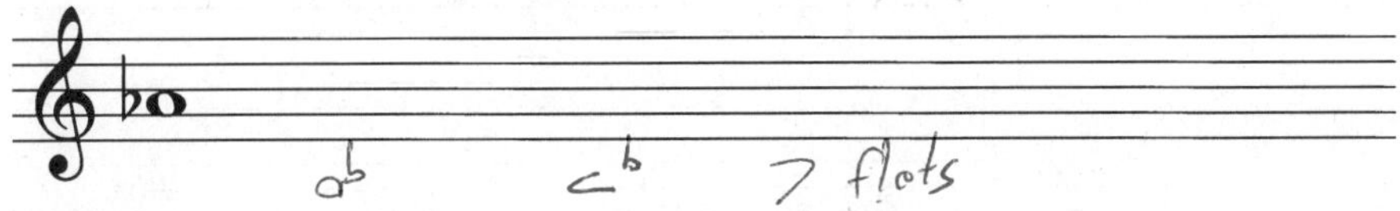

14.

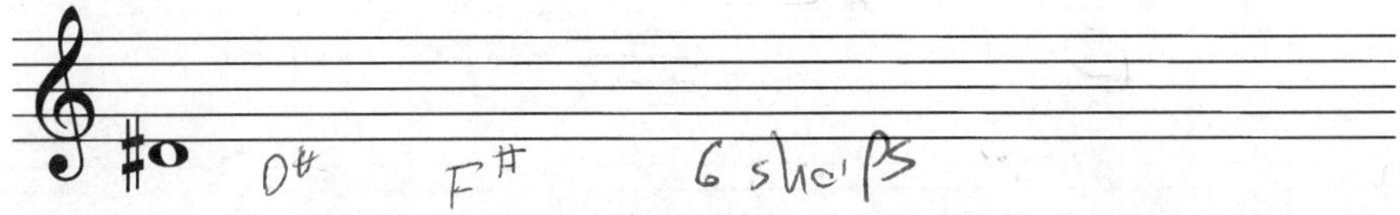

15.

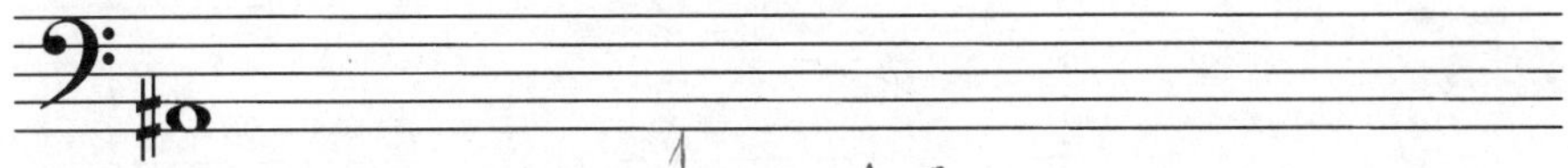

EXERCISE 8•4

Write natural minor scales in descending form, beginning with the given tonic pitches. Indicate the half steps in each scale. Remember that the pitches of a descending scale are in reverse order, i.e., 8-7-6-5-4-3-2-1. A keyboard is provided to help you visualize the intervals.

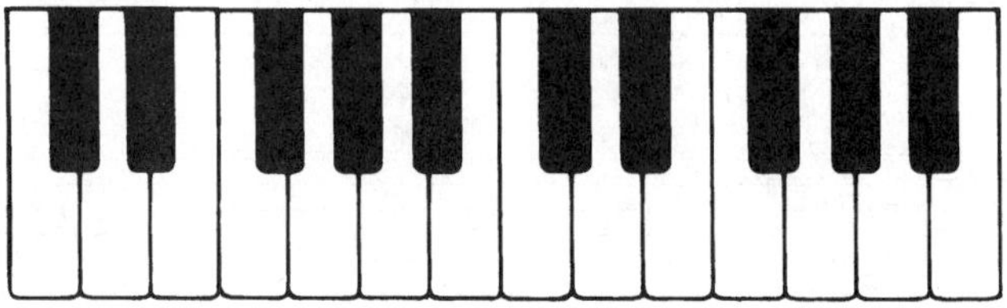

1. 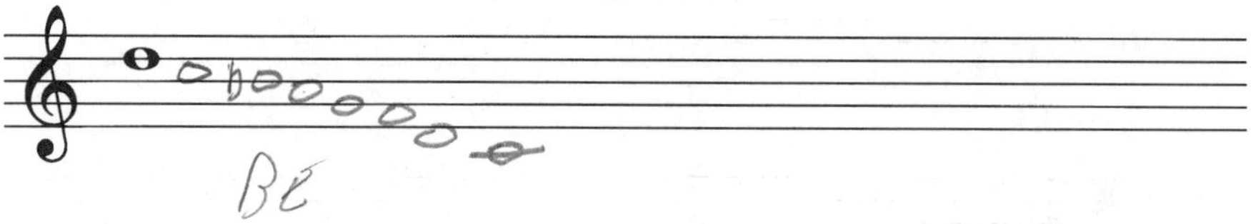

2. 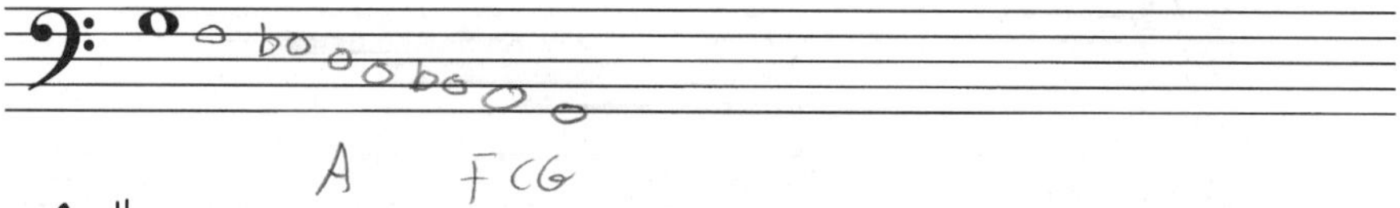

3. 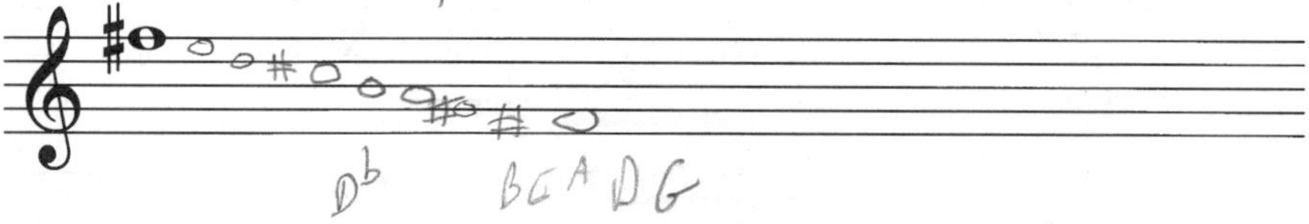

4. 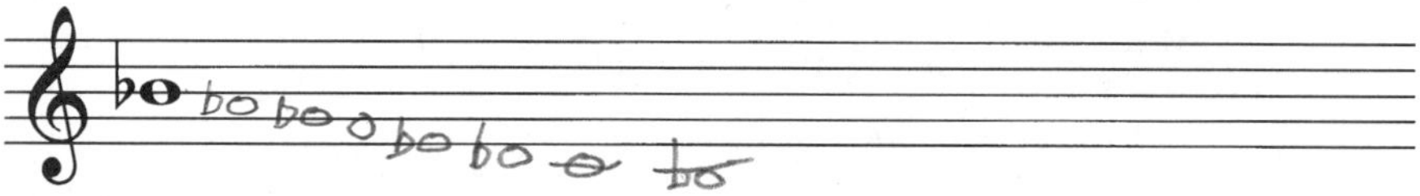

5. 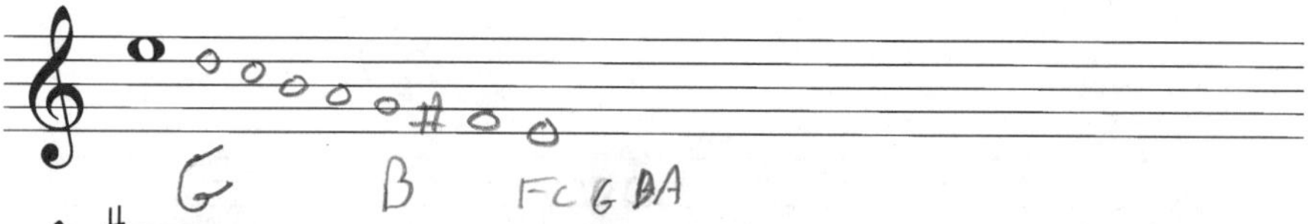

6. 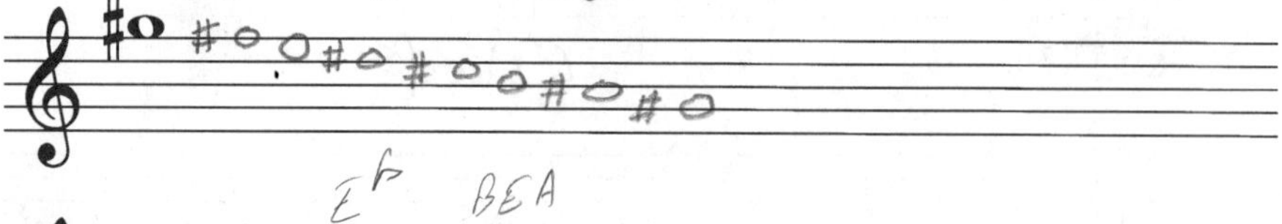

7. 

8. 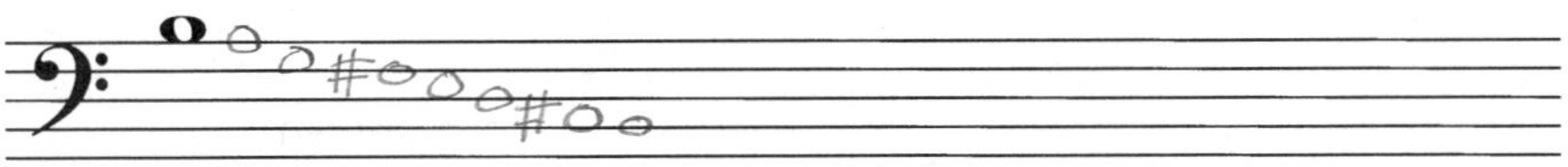

9. 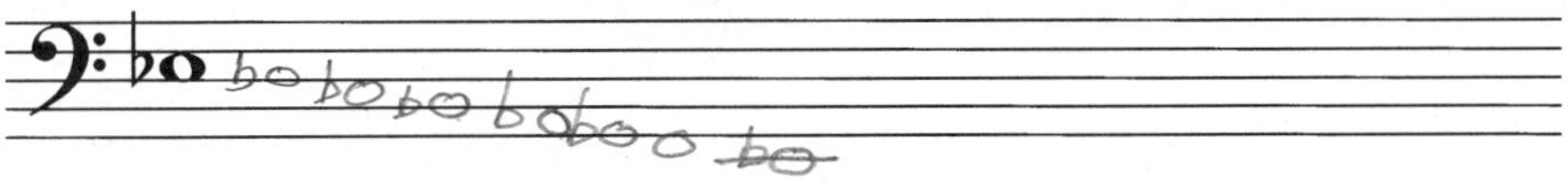

10. 

11. 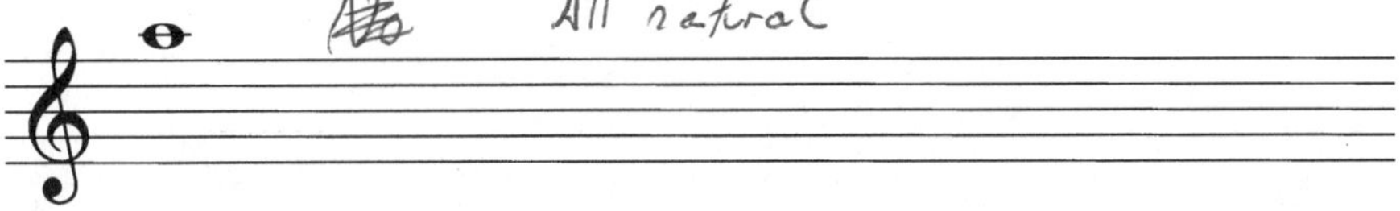

12. 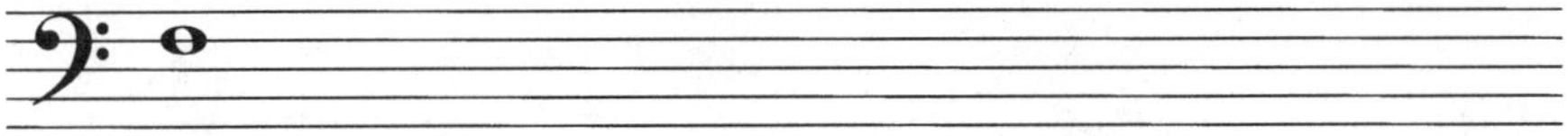

13. 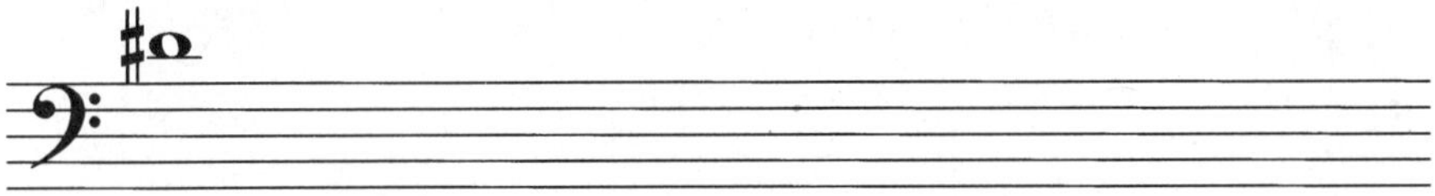

14. 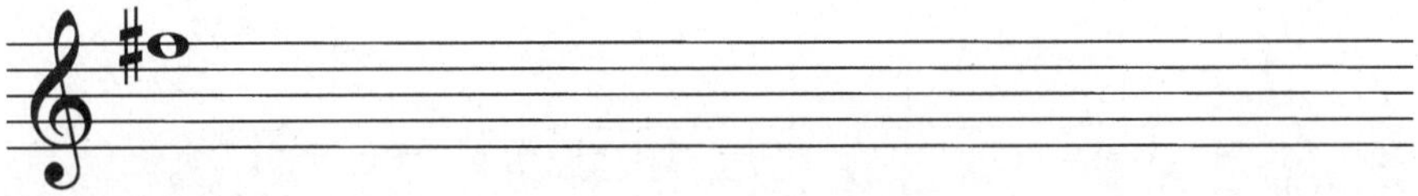

15. 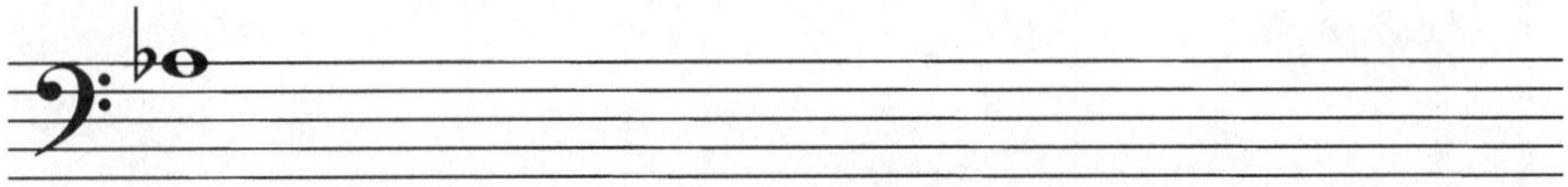

Musical Problem

The American folk song "Erie Canal" is in the key of D natural minor. In the space provided, rewrite this folk song in the key of D major. Then, sing or play both versions in class and discuss the differences between the two types of scales.

(continued)

"Erie Canal"

EXERCISE 8•5

Spell the indicated natural minor scales using letter names and any necessary accidentals. Indicate where the half steps occur in each scale.

EXAMPLE: G A B♭ C D E♭ F G (half steps marked between A–B♭ and D–E♭)

1. D
2. F
3. E
4. C♯
5. B♭
6. A
7. G♯
8. E♭
9. B
10. C
11. A♯
12. F♯
13. A♭
14. D♯

Harmonic Minor Scale

Sing or play a natural minor scale. Then, sing or play a major scale. Do you notice a difference in the interval between the seventh and first degrees of the two scales? The seventh degree of the natural minor scale is not a half step below the tonic; it is a whole step away, and in this position is called a **subtonic** instead of a leading tone.

When the seventh degree of a scale is a whole step below the tonic, a somewhat ambiguous-sounding scale is created. Because of the whole step, the tonic does not seem to offer as strong a center of gravity as it does in the major scale. This weakening of the tonic's attraction is particularly striking in the harmony derived from the natural minor scale. This effect can be demonstrated by having someone in class play the following two versions of the opening measures of a "Praeludium" from *The Little Piano Book for Wilhelm Friedemann Bach* by J. S. Bach. The first version is based on the natural minor scale:

The second version is based on another form of minor scale known as the **harmonic minor scale:**

Notice how much stronger the harmony seems when chords are built from the harmonic minor version of the minor scale.

The difference between the natural minor scale and the harmonic minor is that the harmonic minor version *borrows* the leading tone of the parallel major scale (a pitch a half step below the tonic) to replace its own subtonic (a pitch a whole step below). In technical terms, the subtonic of the natural minor scale is raised a chromatic half step, thereby creating a real leading tone. This was done by composers in order to create a stronger harmony, that is, a greater feeling of harmonic motion between chords.

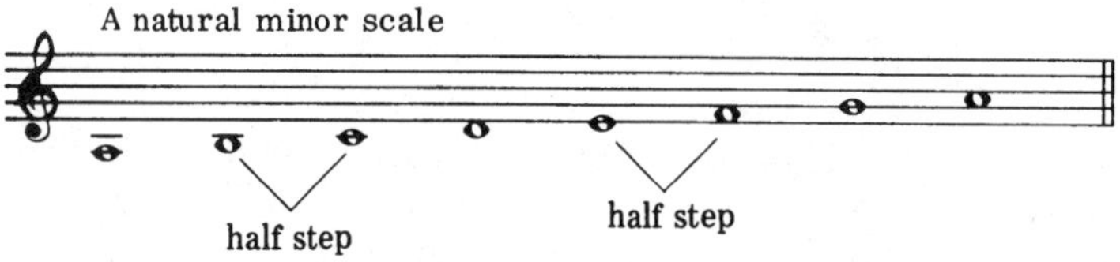

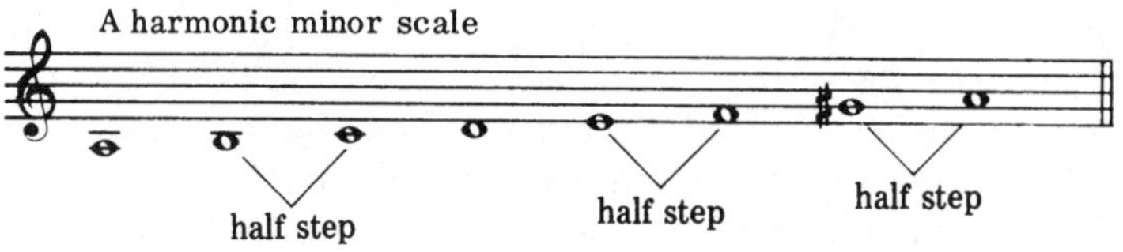

When the seventh degree is raised to create a leading tone, the resulting harmonic minor version of the scale has *three* half steps—between the second and third, fifth and sixth, and seventh and first degrees. To raise the seventh degree and still maintain the practice of having only one pitch of each letter name requires occasional double sharps. Remember: The double sharp sign raises the pitch of a note by two half steps.

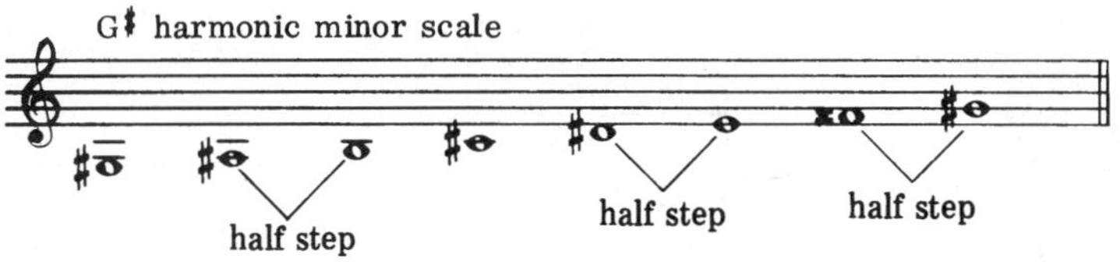

EXERCISE 8•6

Write the following harmonic minor scales, in ascending and descending forms, in both treble clef and bass clef. A simple way to begin is to write a natural minor scale and then borrow the leading tone from the parallel major. This, of course, is the same as raising the seventh degree of the natural minor scale by a half step. (Try to learn to think both ways; don't rely on either method exclusively.) To check your work, make sure that each scale has three half steps, and then mark them. This exercise deals with sharp scales only. If you have any difficulty, use the keyboard to visualize the scale.

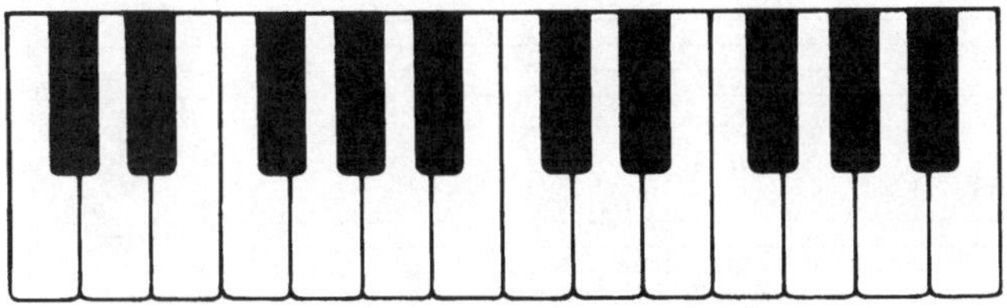

EXAMPLE:

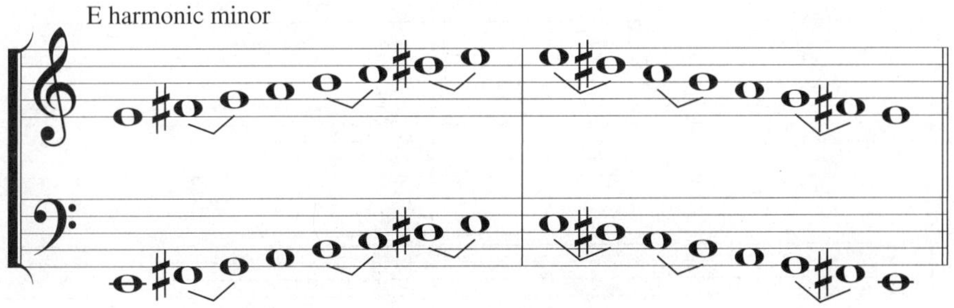

1.

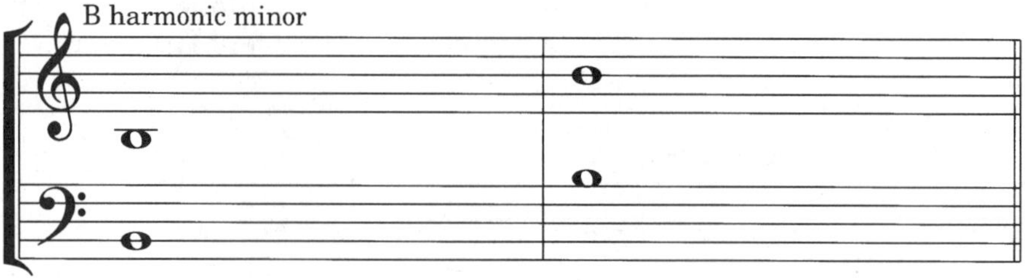
B harmonic minor

2.

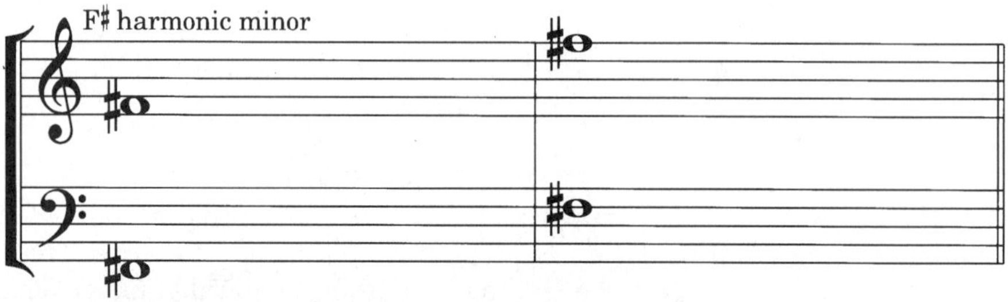
F♯ harmonic minor

3.

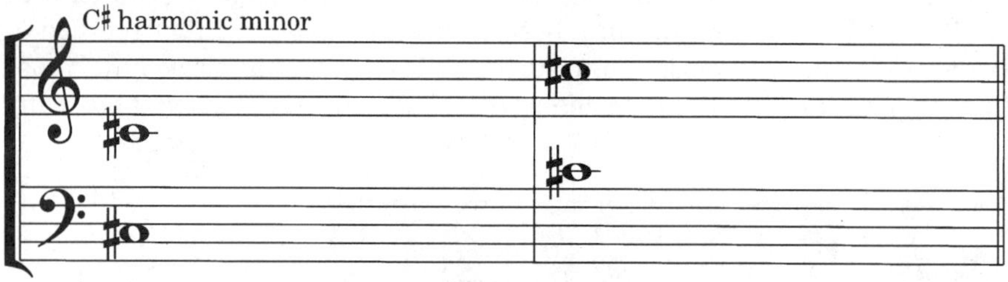
C♯ harmonic minor

4.

G♯ harmonic minor

5.

D♯ harmonic minor

6. 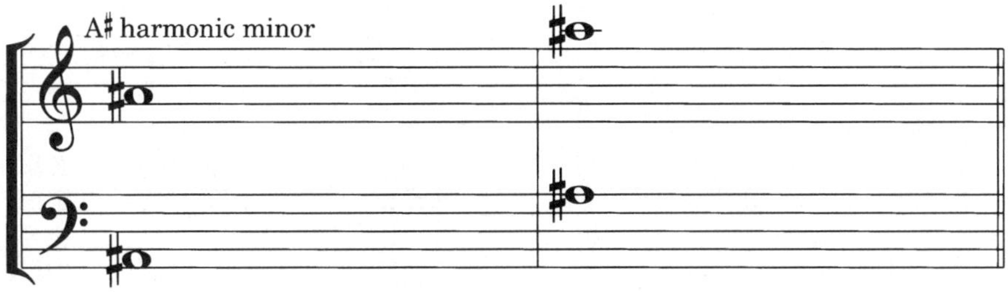

EXERCISE 8•7

Write the following minor scale in the harmonic minor form, in both ascending and descending patterns, using both treble clef and bass clef. Even though this exercise deals with flat scales only, you will occasionally need to use a sharp sign in order to raise the seventh scale degree to the proper pitch. When you finish, check that each scale has three half steps, and mark them. Use the keyboard to help you visualize the scale.

EXAMPLE:

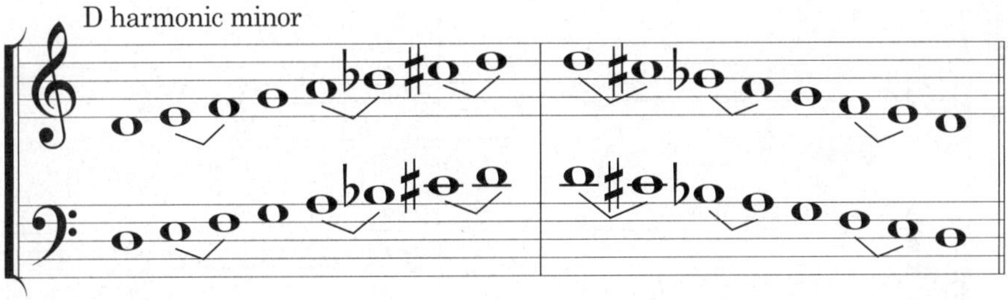

1. 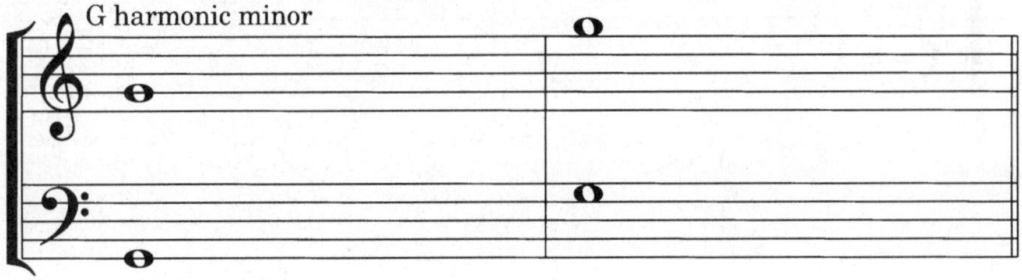

2. C harmonic minor

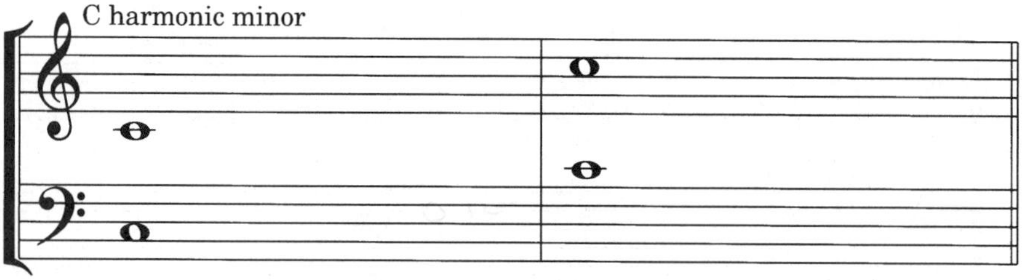

3. F harmonic minor

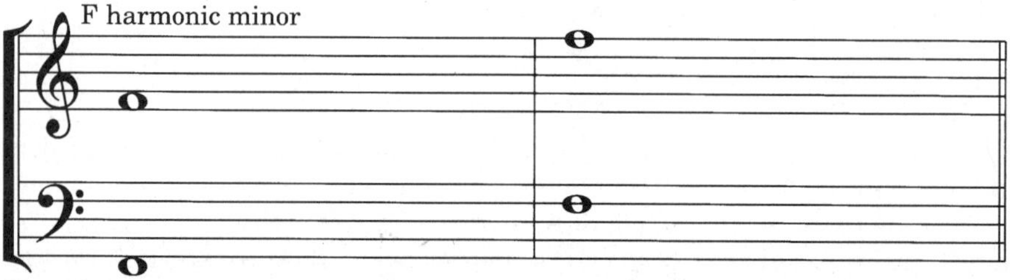

4. B♭ harmonic minor

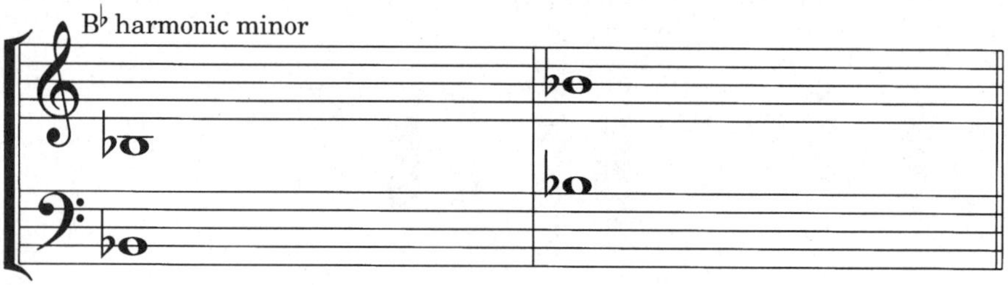

5. E♭ harmonic minor

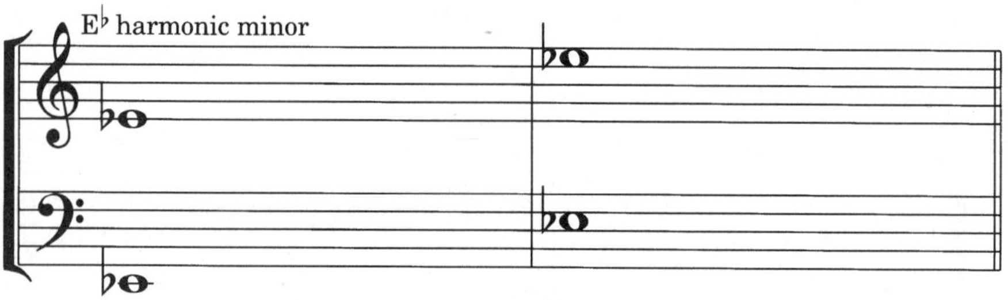

6. A♭ harmonic minor

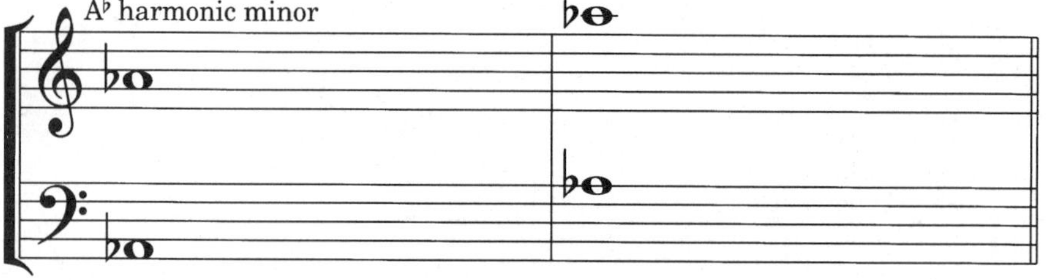

EXERCISE 8•8

Write the following harmonic minor scales in ascending form. This exercise and the one following use the same scales as in the previous two exercises, but now out of sequence. Use the keyboard to help visualize the scale.

1.
2.
3.
4.
5.
6.
7.

8. 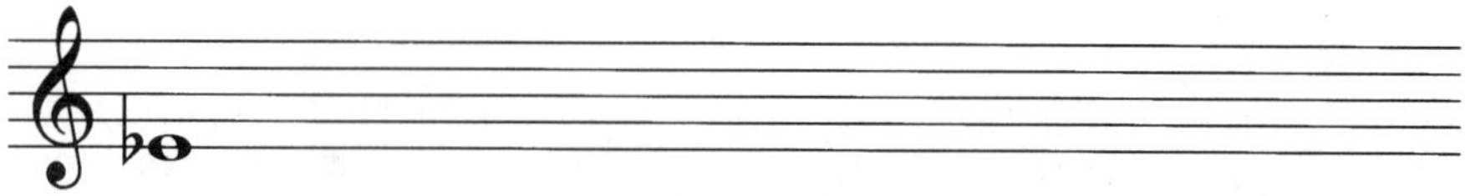

9. 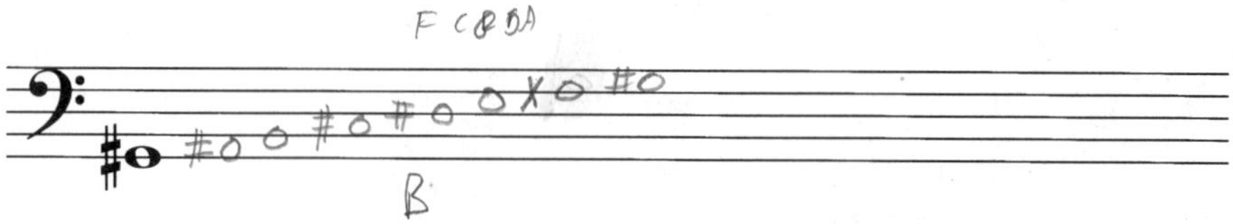

10. 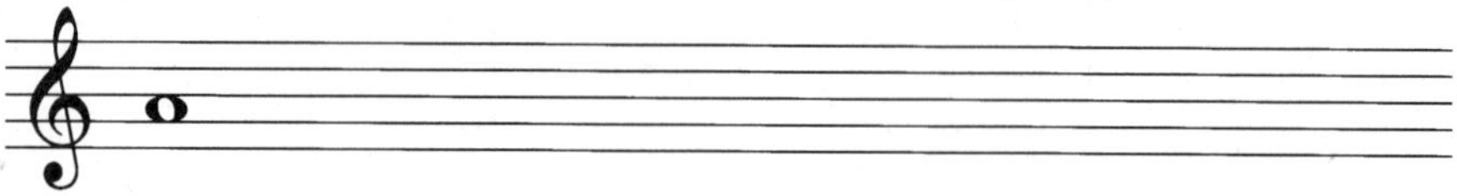

11. 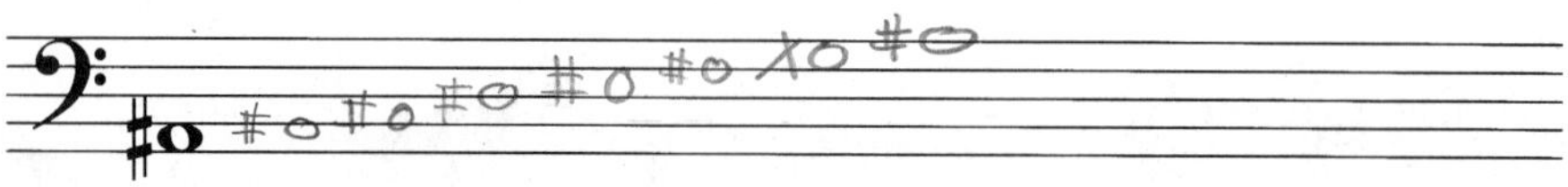

12. 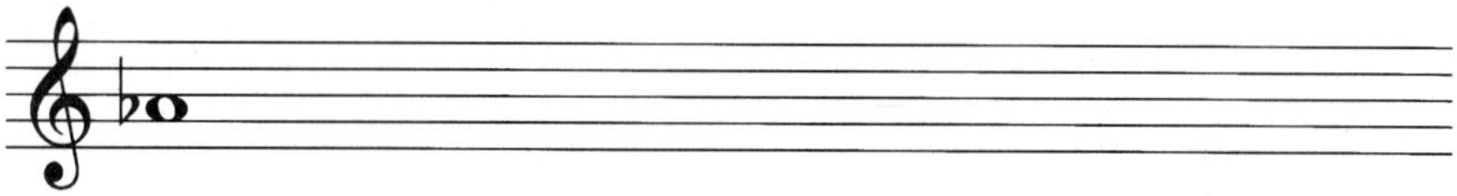

13. 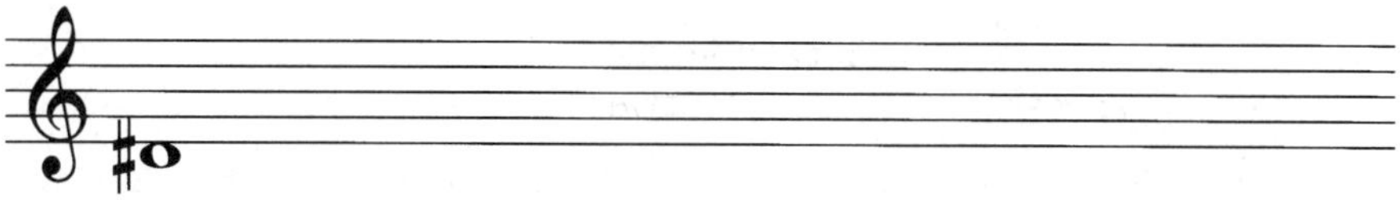

14. 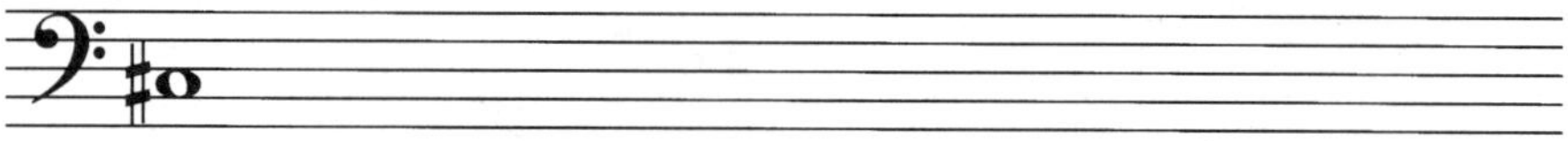

15. 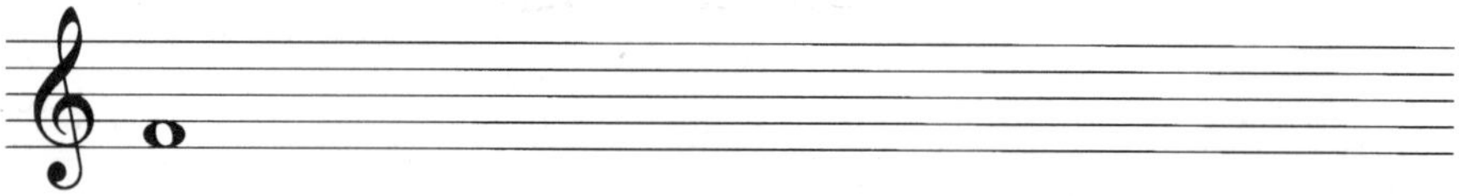

EXERCISE 8•9

Spell the indicated harmonic minor scales using letter names and any necessary accidentals. For each scale, indicate where the half steps fall.

1. G A B♭ C D E♭ F♯ G
2. B C♯ D E F♯ G A♯ B
3. F♯ G♯ A B C♯ D E♯ F♯

4. E F♯ G A B C D♯ E
5. F
6. C♯
7. A♭
8. D♯
9. E♭
10. A
11. G♯ A♯ B C♯ D♯ E F𝄪 G♯
12. C
13. A♯
14. B♭
15. D E F G A B♭ C♯ D

Musical Problem

Rewrite the following melody by transposing it from the original key (G major) to the key of G harmonic minor. Then, sing or play both versions in class. Discuss the differences between the major and harmonic minor versions.

"The Wabash Cannon Ball"

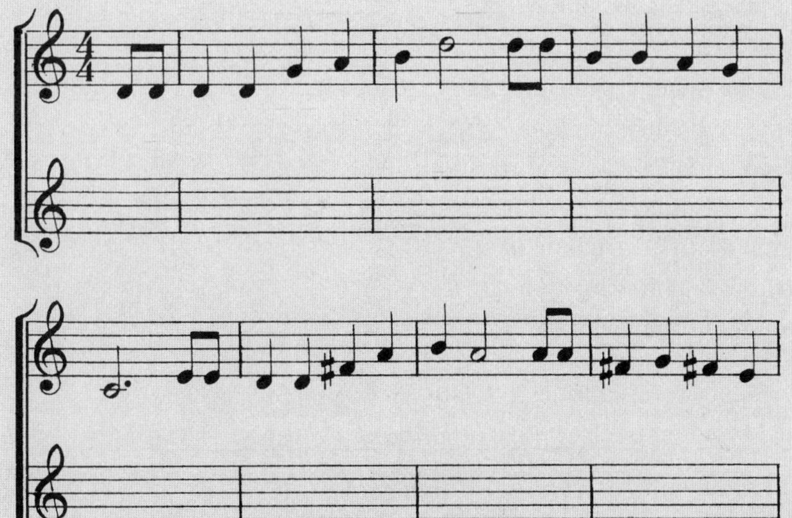

(continued)

EXERCISE 8•10

Identify by letter name the following scale degrees.

1. supertonic of C harmonic minor ______
2. dominant of B♭ harmonic minor ______
3. leading tone of G harmonic minor ______
4. mediant of A harmonic minor ______
5. subdominant of B harmonic minor ______
6. tonic of E♭ harmonic minor ______
7. mediant of C♯ harmonic minor ______
8. submediant of D harmonic minor ______
9. supertonic of B harmonic minor ______
10. subdominant of C♯ harmonic minor ______
11. mediant of B♭ harmonic minor ______
12. submediant of C harmonic minor ______

EXERCISE 8•11

Complete the following:

1. G is the dominant of the ______ harmonic minor scale.
2. B♭ is the mediant of the ______ harmonic minor scale.

3. F is the submediant of the __A__ harmonic minor scale.
4. G♯ is the leading tone of the __A__ harmonic minor scale.
5. A is the leading tone of the __B♭__ harmonic minor scale.
6. C is the mediant of the __A__ harmonic minor scale.
7. E is the leading tone of the __F__ harmonic minor scale.
8. G is the subdominant of the __D__ harmonic minor scale.
9. F is the dominant of the __B♭__ harmonic minor scale.
10. C♯ is the leading tone of the ______ harmonic minor scale.
11. A is the dominant of the __D__ harmonic minor scale.
12. E is the supertonic of the __D__ harmonic minor scale.

Melodic Minor Scale

While the harmonic minor version of the minor scale strengthens the harmony, it also creates a melodic problem. Have you been puzzled by the interval between the sixth and seventh degrees of the harmonic minor scale?

A harmonic minor scale

This interval, created by borrowing the leading tone from the parallel major, is an augmented second (three half steps). The augmented second is often difficult to sing or play in tune. This is because although when written it looks like a second, it has the same number of half steps as a minor third and thus *sounds* wider than it *looks* on the staff.

The **melodic minor** version of the minor scale developed, in part, as a means of avoiding this augmented second. It is the only version of the minor scale that has one interval pattern when ascending and another when descending.

A melodic minor scale

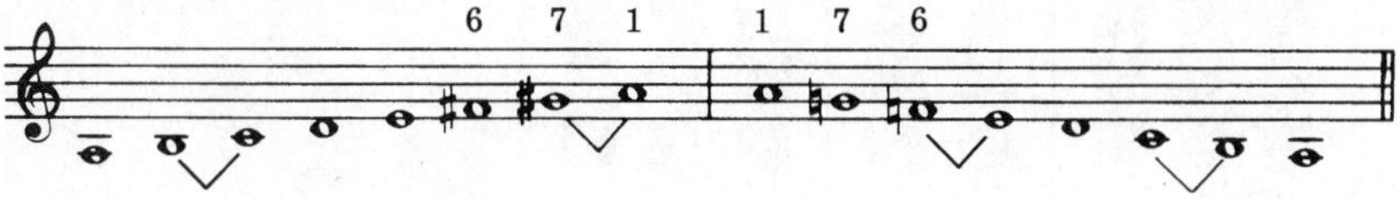

In the ascending form of the melodic minor scale, both the sixth and seventh degrees are borrowed from the parallel major. Technically, the seventh degree, as in the harmonic minor version, is raised to create a half-step relationship between the seventh degree and the tonic, and the sixth degree is raised to avoid the augmented second. Notice, however, that these alterations create a scale in which only the third degree is different from the major scale.

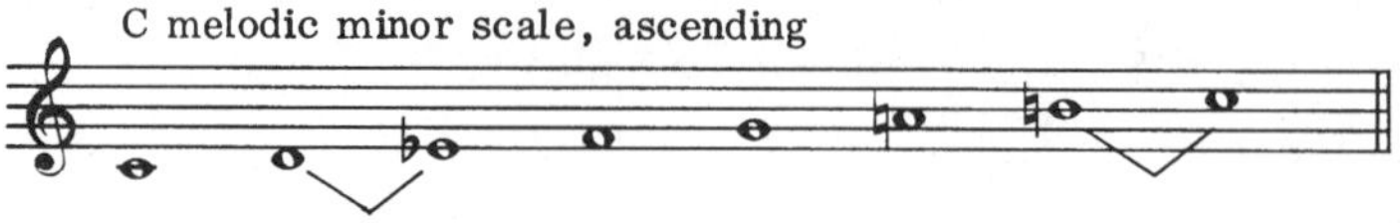

This similarity to the major scale is so noticeable that it almost obscures the minor-sounding quality of this version of the minor scale. Since the leading tone is needed more often in ascending musical passages than in descending ones, the descending version of melodic minor lowers both the seventh and sixth degrees. This alteration, which actually produces a descending natural minor scale, balances the ascending version and helps restore a minor-sounding quality to the scale.

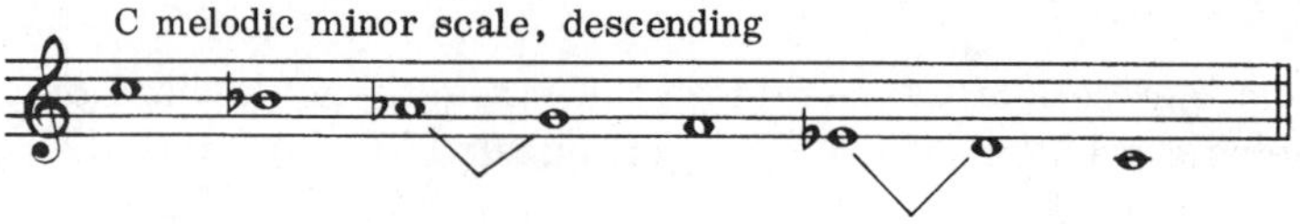

As in the harmonic minor, double sharp signs will occasionally be required to form the melodic minor.

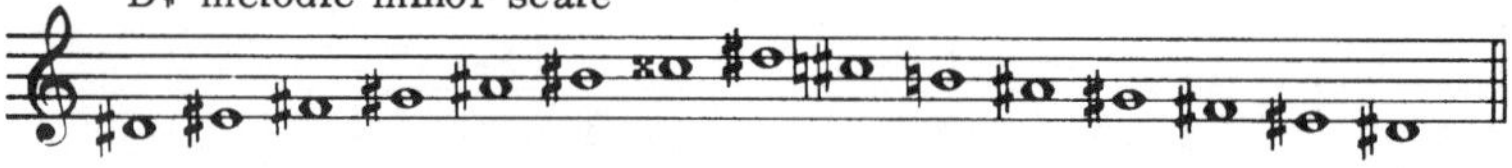

EXERCISE 8•12

Write melodic minor scales, ascending and descending, in both treble clef and bass clef, beginning with the given tonic pitches. (This exercise deals with sharp scales only.) Mark the half steps in each scale. Use the keyboard to visualize the scale.

EXAMPLE:

E melodic minor

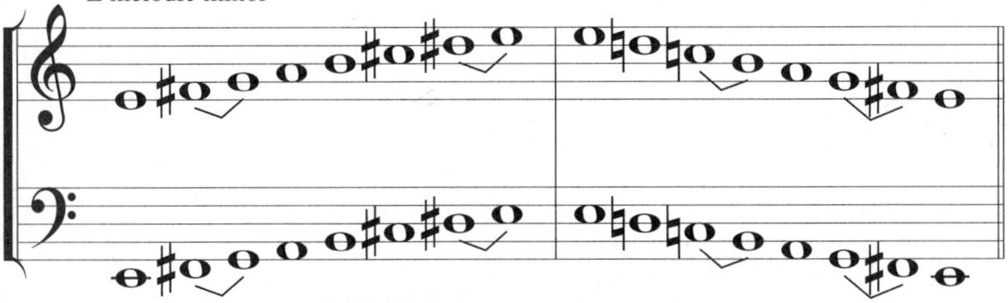

B melodic minor

1. 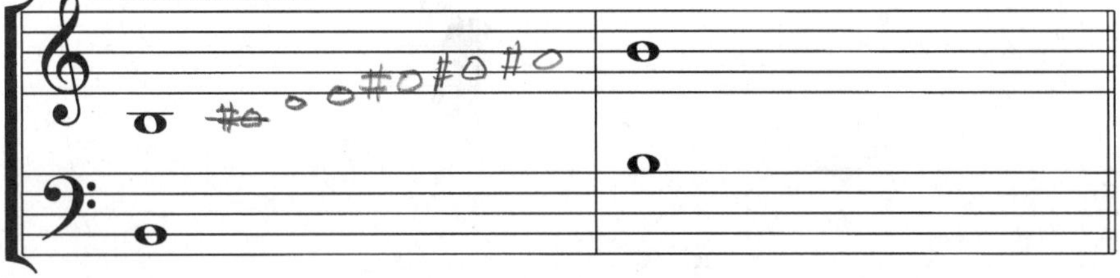

F♯ melodic minor

2. 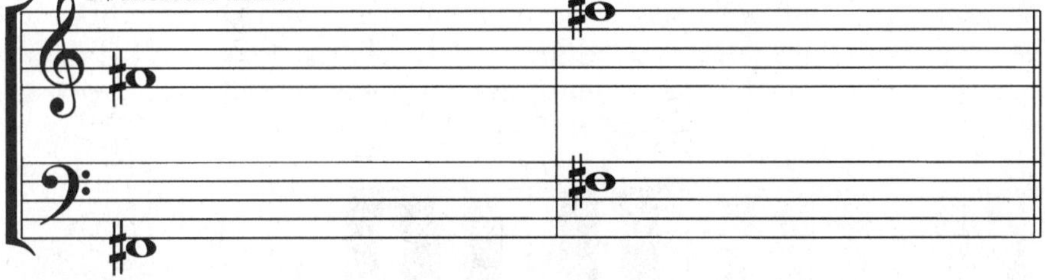

C♯ melodic minor

3. 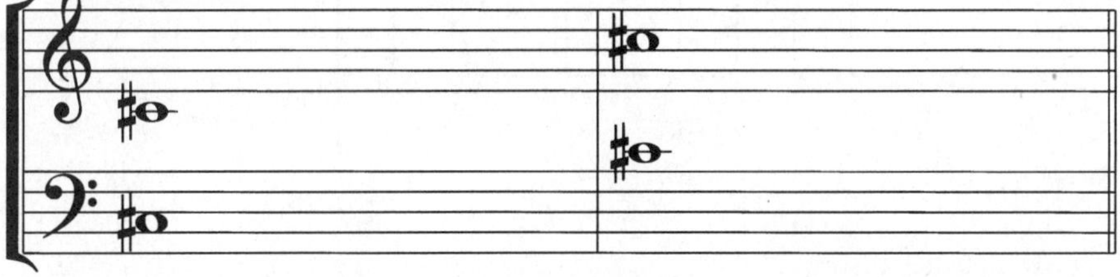

G♯ melodic minor

4. 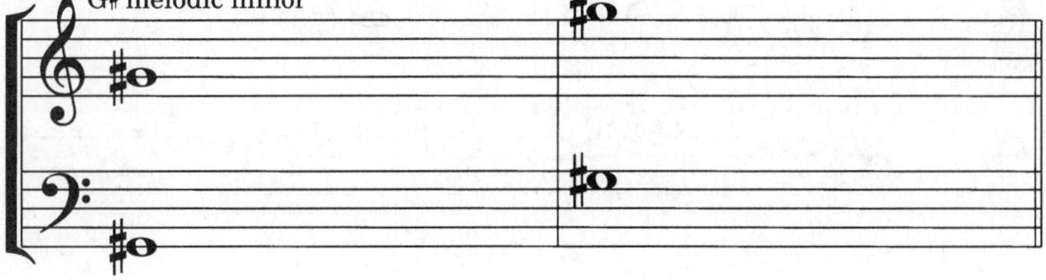

5.

6.

EXERCISE 8•13

Write melodic minor scales, ascending and descending, in both treble clef and bass clef, beginning with the given tonic pitches. Even though this exercise deals only with flat scales, you will need to use sharps occasionally to alter the seventh scale degree. Be sure to mark the half steps in each scale. Use the keyboard to visualize the scale.

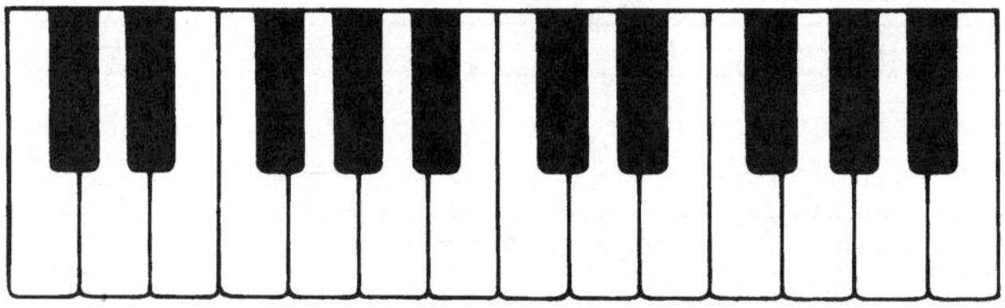

EXAMPLE:

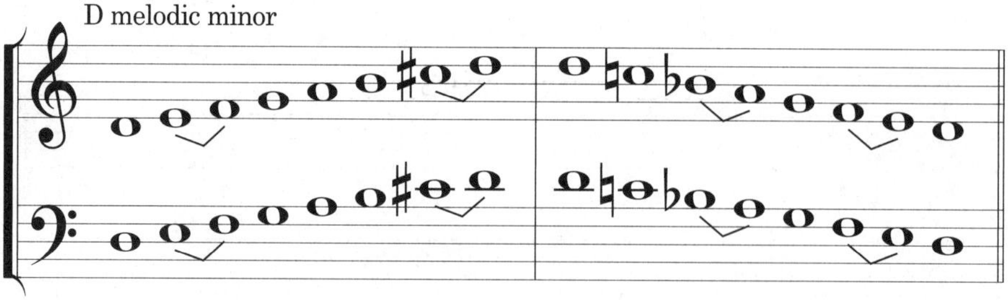

1.
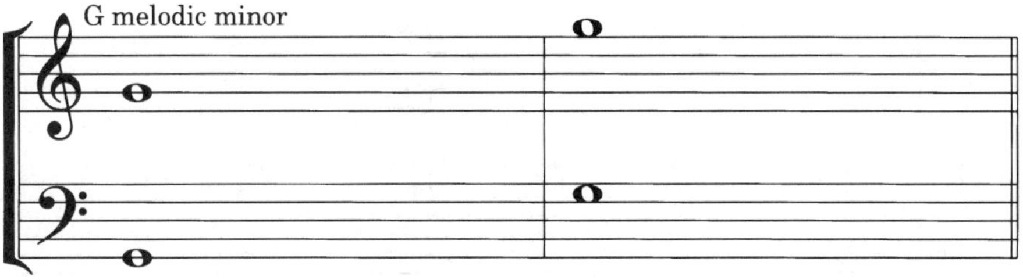
G melodic minor

2.
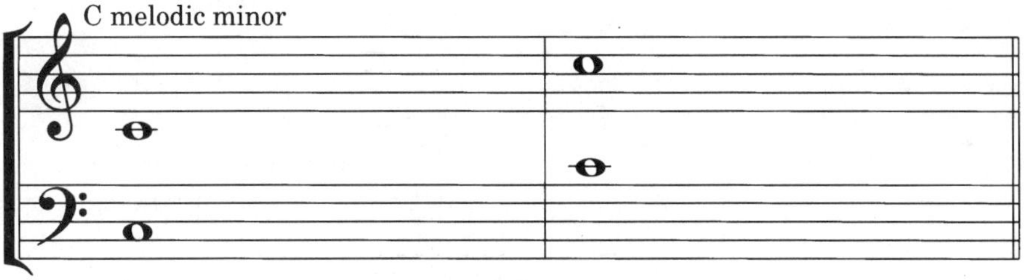
C melodic minor

3.
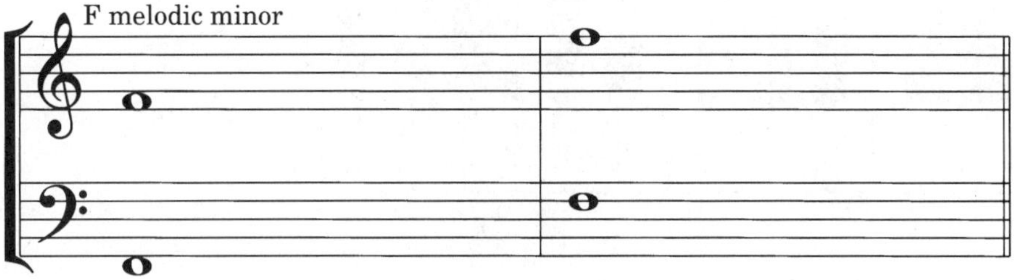
F melodic minor

4.
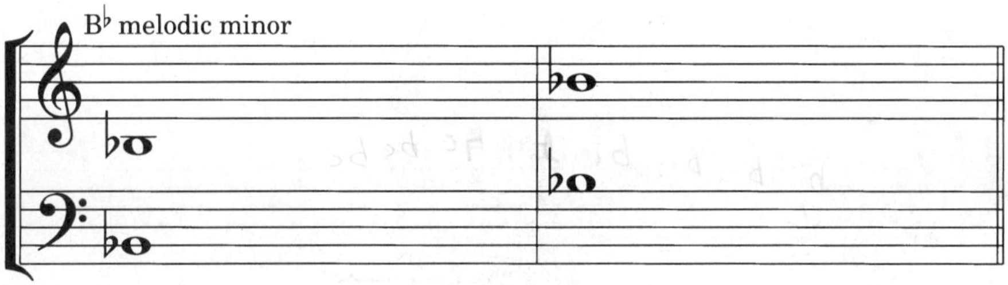
B♭ melodic minor

5.
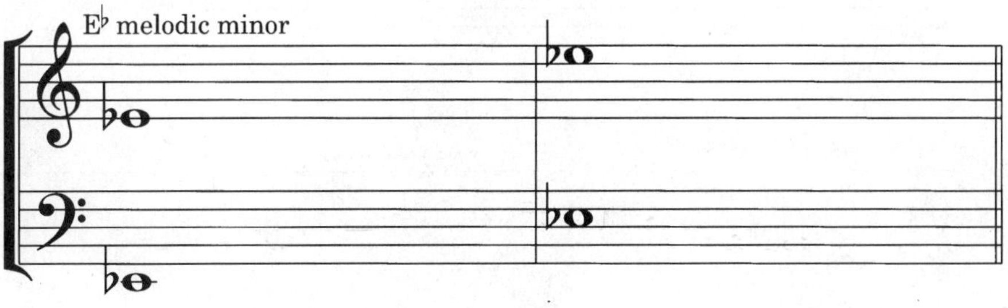
E♭ melodic minor

6. 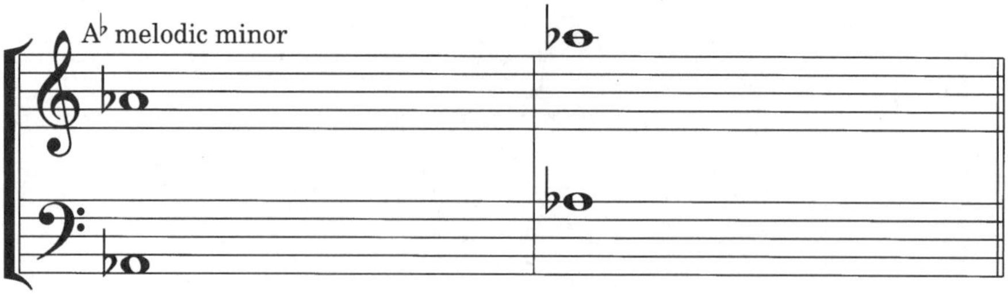

EXERCISE 8•14

Write melodic minor scales, ascending and descending, beginning with the given tonic pitches. These are the same scales as in the two previous exercises, but now out of sequence. Use the keyboard to visualize each scale.

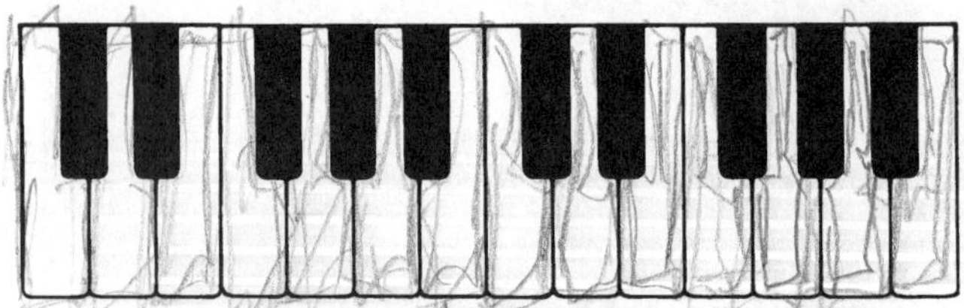

1. 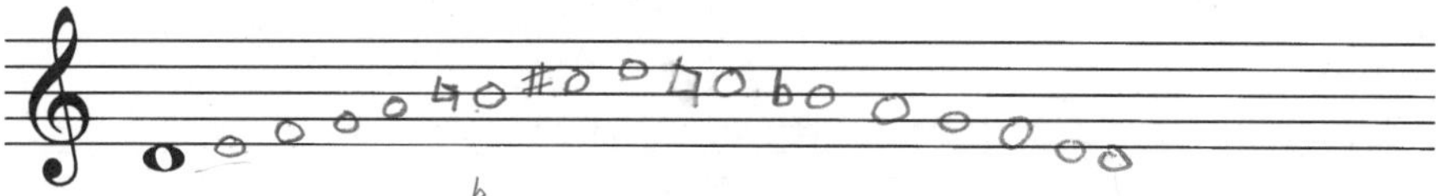

2. 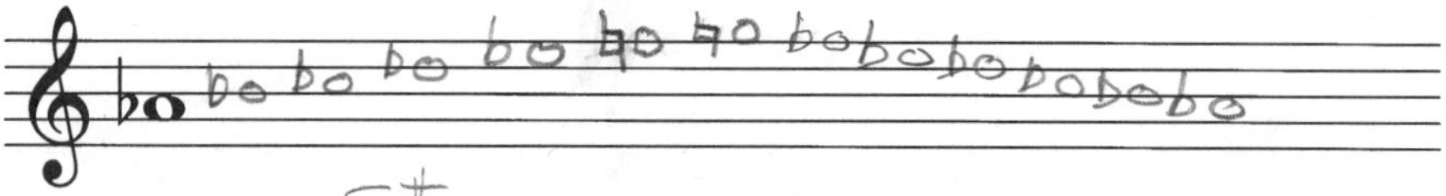

3. 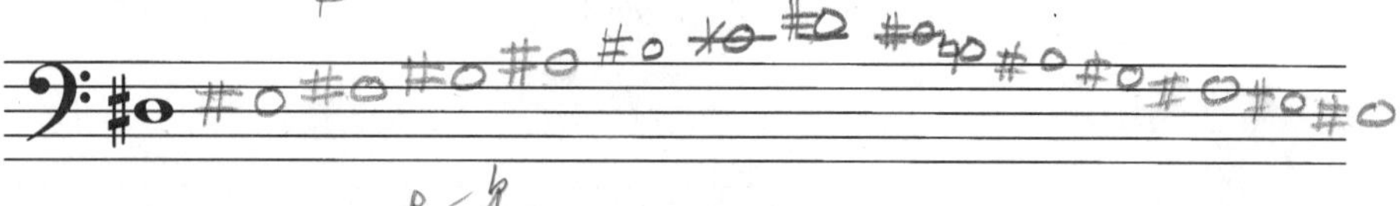

4. 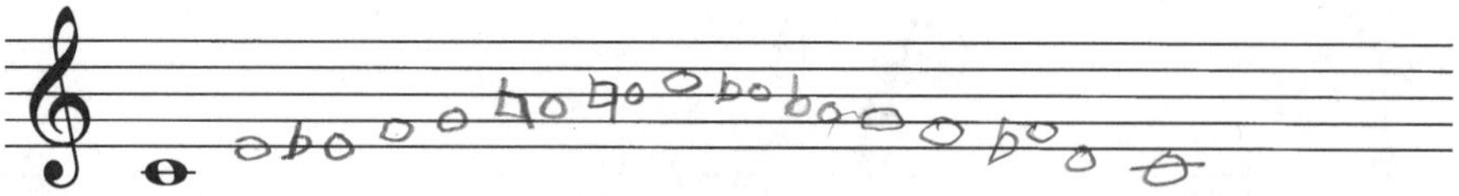

5. 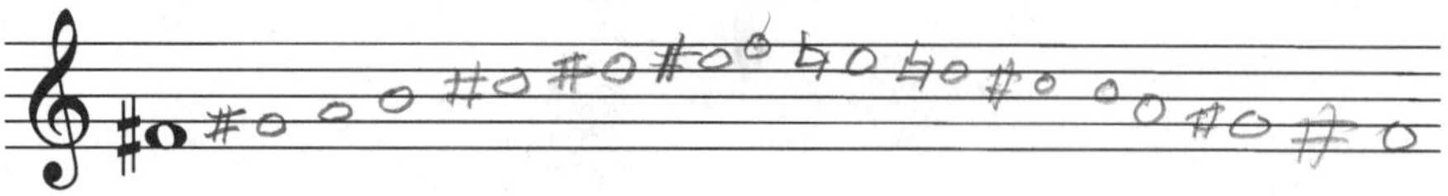

6.
7.
8.
9.
10.
11.
12.
13.
14.
15.

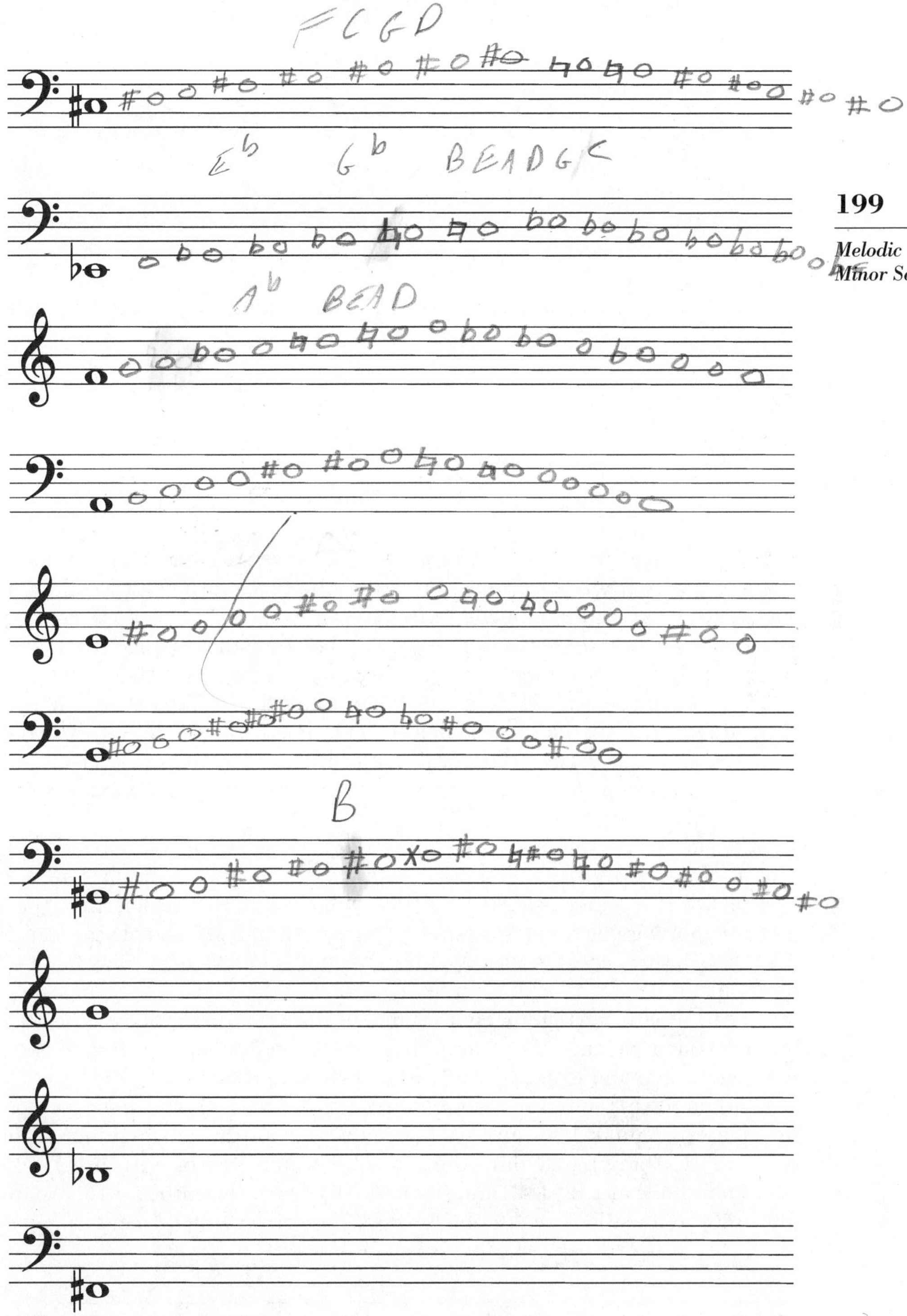

Musical Problem

Ask someone in class who plays an instrument or keyboard to prepare a well-known tune such as "The Star Spangled Banner" or "Three Blind Mice" so that he or she can play it in its original major key as well as in the three forms of the minor scale. As a class discuss the differences between (1) the major and natural minor version and (2) the three forms of the minor versions.

Minor Scales in Musical Situations

So far, this chapter has made it appear that there are three distinct forms of the minor scale, and that composers choose one of them, to the exclusion of the other two, when writing a piece of music in a minor key. Although it is useful to think this way when you are first learning the three forms of the minor scale, this is not what really happens in the music. In actuality, composers view the sixth and seventh degrees of the minor scale as unstable (since these are also the scale degrees borrowed from the parallel major), and they often use all three forms of the scale within the same composition. This is why it is more accurate to say that the three forms of the minor scale are not really three different scales, but rather represent three different solutions, or possible approaches, to various harmonic and melodic problems within a composition written in a minor key.

Consider for a moment the names *harmonic minor* and *melodic minor.* These names give us a clue as to why and how composers might use various versions of the minor scale within the same piece. Remember that the harmonic minor version creates a real leading tone a half step below the tonic, and that this, in turn, creates slightly different chords and stronger harmonies. The harmonic minor form of the minor scale, therefore, is used by composers primarily to create particular chords and harmonic progressions. The melodic minor version, on the other hand, deals with the difficult interval of the augmented second, and is used mainly in melodic situations.

Although this may seem confusing at first, particularly when you look at new pieces in minor keys and try to decide which forms of the minor scale are being used at any particular point, it will become clearer with practice. Just keep in mind that the sixth and seventh degrees of the minor scale are unstable, and you must look *inside* the music to be certain which form is being used.

Sight-Singing of Minor Scales

There are conflicting opinions about the correct method of sight-singing minor scales. One school argues that the syllables of the major scale from *la* to *la* should be used to show the inherent relationship between the major scale and the minor scale. The other school argues that retaining the sound of the tonic with the syllable *do* is more important. According to this view, all scales should be started on *do* and the remaining syllables altered when necessary:

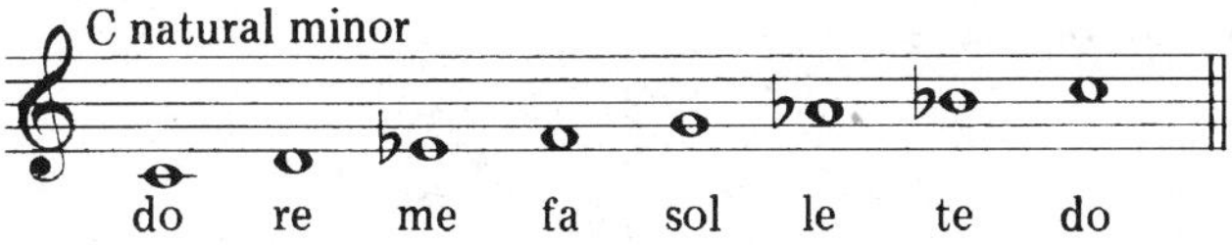

As you can see in this example for natural minor, the syllable for the third scale degree is *me,* rather than *mi,* because the third degree is lowered. Also, the syllables for pitches 6 and 7 are *le* and *te,* rather than *la* and *ti,* because the sixth and seventh scale degrees are lowered. Similar alterations in syllables are necessary for the harmonic and melodic versions of the minor scale.

Musical Problem

The two methods of sight-singing minor scales are given below for each of the three kinds of minor scales. Sing the scales both ways, and decide for yourself which system seems most advantageous. Then, practice that system until you can sing the minor scales easily and accurately.

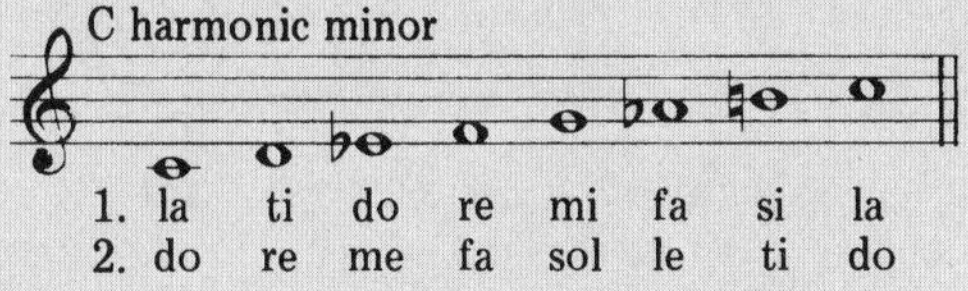

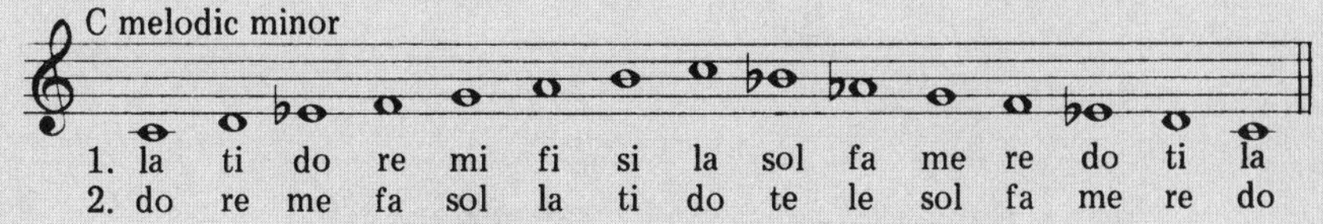

EXERCISE 8•15

Spell the indicated melodic minor scales using letter names and any necessary accidentals. Indicate where the half steps occur.

1. B ________________; ________________
2. E ________________; ________________
3. C♯ ________________; ________________
4. D♯ ________________; ________________
5. A ________________; ________________
6. C ________________; ________________
7. B♭ ________________; ________________
8. D ________________; ________________
9. A♯ ________________; ________________
10. G♯ ________________; ________________
11. E♭ ________________; ________________
12. A♭ ________________; ________________
13. F ________________; ________________
14. F♯ ________________; ________________
15. G ________________; ________________

Musical Problem

Sing or play the following melodies. Locate the tonic for each melody, and identify the principal form of the minor scale on which each melody is based. Then, write the appropriate sight-singing syllables in the spaces provided, and learn to sing one or more of the melodies, using the sight-singing syllables.

"Joshua Fit the Battle of Jericho"

1.

Tonic ______ Form of minor scale ______________

"Johnny Has Gone for a Soldier"

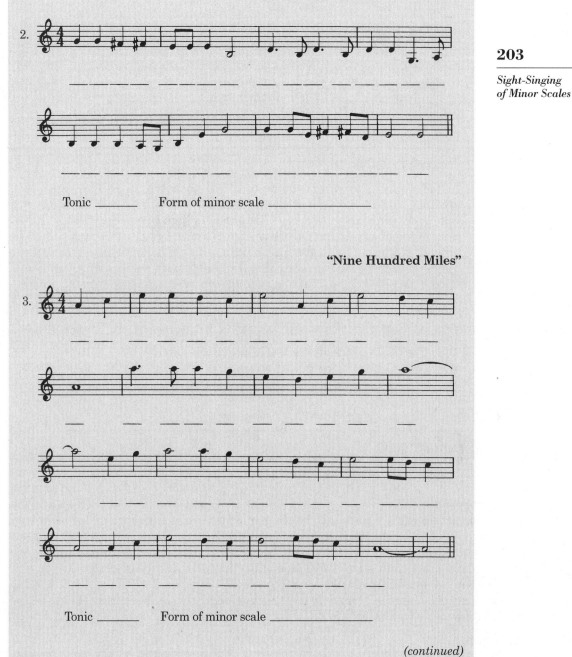

2.

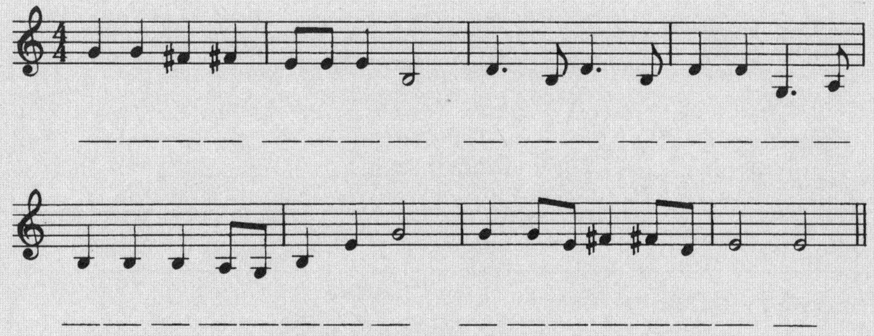

Tonic ______ Form of minor scale ________________

"Nine Hundred Miles"

3.

Tonic ______ Form of minor scale ________________

(continued)

Bach, "Passacaglia," opening measures

4. 

_ _ _ _ _ _ _ _ _ _ _ _ _ _ _ _

Tonic ______ Form of minor scale ______________

Musical Problem

In the previous chapter, you were asked to listen to several musical excerpts located throughout the book to determine by ear whether they were in a major or minor key. The excerpts listed below are those that were in minor keys. Listen to these excerpts once again, this time to determine if they are in natural minor, harmonic minor, melodic minor, or some combination of these versions. This is more difficult to do, and you might make mistakes at first. But keep trying—you will see improvement.

Composer	*Title*	*Page(s)*
1. Bach	Courante from French Suite No. 2	25
2. Scarlatti	Sonata in C Minor	163
3. Traditional	"St. James Infirmary"	261

Focus

The importance of scales cannot be overemphasized. All musicians, from concert pianists to jazz performers, recognize the importance of scales and practice them regularly. For the beginning music student, the first step is to learn the structure of the scales and the ways in which scales influence melody and harmony. The next step is to begin treating scales as the basic musical element they are. If you sing or play an instrument, you should devote some of your daily practice to scale work. It is only through this type of drill that you will become musically familiar with the tonal patterns of the music you wish to play. Practicing scales gives you this familiarity in a way that practicing pieces of music—no matter how difficult—does not.

Musical Problem

As a musician, you should begin to notice the numerous ways in which scale passages appear in tonal music. In addition, you should develop the ability to identify various kinds of scales by their sound. Ask someone who plays piano to select ten scales from Exercises 4-5, 8-3, 8-8, and 8-14 and to play them in a random order. By sound, identify each scale as major, natural minor, harmonic minor, or melodic minor. Repeat the process with different groups of scales until you are consistently successful in identifying them.

Musical Problem

Below are several melodies in minor keys from Appendix D. First, determine the form of the minor scale that each is in. Then, practice singing these melodies, both on *la* and with moveable *do*. Once you are familiar with the melodies, practice conducting them as you sing. It would also be helpful to practice playing them at the keyboard.

1. 

2. 

3. 

4. 

5. 

9 *Chapter*

Other Scales and Modes

Not all the music we hear in our daily lives is based on major and minor scales. While it is true that the major scale and the minor scale have been the primary scales of Western music since the early 1600s, they are only two of the numerous scale forms in use before that time. Thus, much of the Medieval and Renaissance music we hear today is not based on major or minor scales. Even Chopin (1810–1849) employed scale forms other than major and minor, particularly in sections of his mazurkas. And Debussy (1862–1918), who is erroneously thought to have used the whole-tone scale almost exclusively, actually wrote in a wide variety of scales, including the major and minor scales, as well as all the scales discussed in this chapter. Twentieth-century composers have explored many other scales, including the twelve-tone scale and the microtonal scale (which uses intervals smaller than a half step), and it is impossible to listen to American folk music without hearing pentatonic scales and modes.

Most music outside of the Western tradition has never used major or minor scales. This music is not considered tonal. Because of this fact, much of the music of other cultures may sound strange and incomprehensible to us. Some of it, however, has influenced and even infiltrated Western music in unusual ways. And all of it becomes a little more understandable once the scale on which it is based is understood.

In this chapter, we are going to look at three of the most important kinds of non-tonal scales. These scales, which influence and color Western music, both popular and classical, are the pentatonic scale, the church modes, and the whole-tone scale. They are important because the pentatonic scale is the basis for most of the world's folk music; the church modes contain within them the major and minor scales, and also overlap with scales used by many different cultures of the world; and the whole-tone scale, which developed more recently, is used extensively in the Impressionist music of such composers as Debussy and Ravel.

Although the ability to write, sing, and play these nontonal scales is not as essential as your abilities with major and minor scales, some degree of understanding is important. If, because of time constraints, your teacher is unable to cover this chapter in detail, you should at the least read it carefully so as to promote your understanding of these scales and their significance to the music we hear today.

Pentatonic Scales

The **pentatonic scale** is a scale with five tones per octave (Greek *penta* means *five*). It may have been one of the first scales ever used, which might explain why it is the basis for much folk music throughout the world. There are a variety of pentatonic scales, but the best-known version contains no half steps. It also has two intervals greater than a whole step:

Without any half steps, the center of gravity (the tonic) of this pentatonic scale is extremely ambiguous. It may be helpful to think of the above pentatonic scale as a simpler version of the major scale with the half steps removed (scale degrees 4 and 7). This lack of a musical center of gravity is so pronounced that any one of the five pitches of the pentatonic scale can serve as the tonic. You can demonstrate this peculiarity by playing the pentatonic scale pictured above, beginning on each of its five different pitches.

The following version of the pentatonic scale is another one in common use. Notice that in this version the half steps have been eliminated by removing scale degrees 3 and 7 from a major scale.

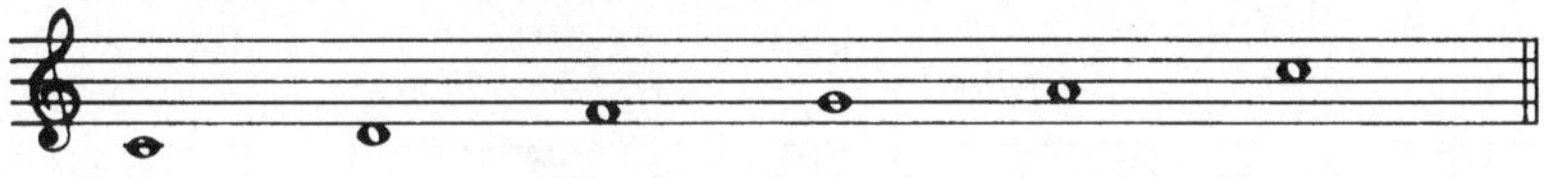

EXERCISE 9•1

Beginning on the indicated pitches, and using the following form as a model, write examples of the pentatonic scale. Check your solutions by singing or playing the scales you have written.

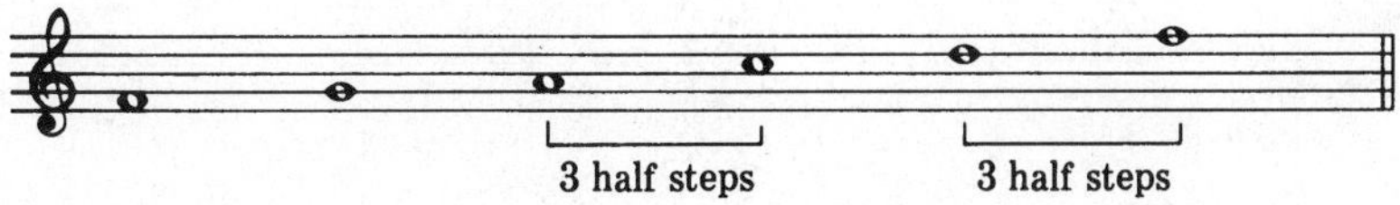

1.
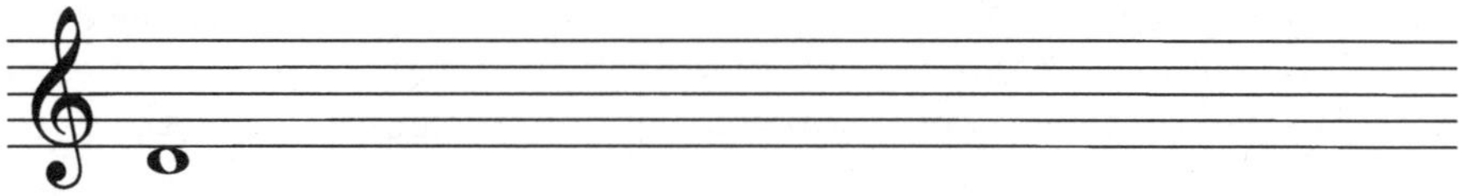

2.
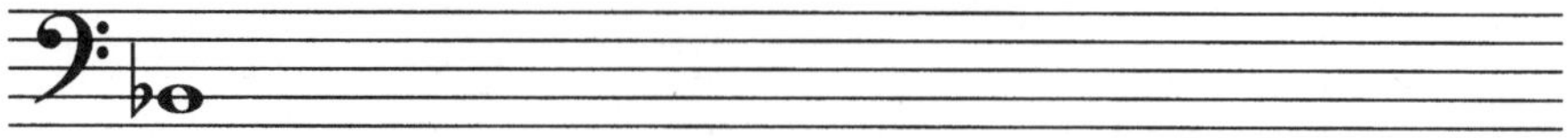

3.
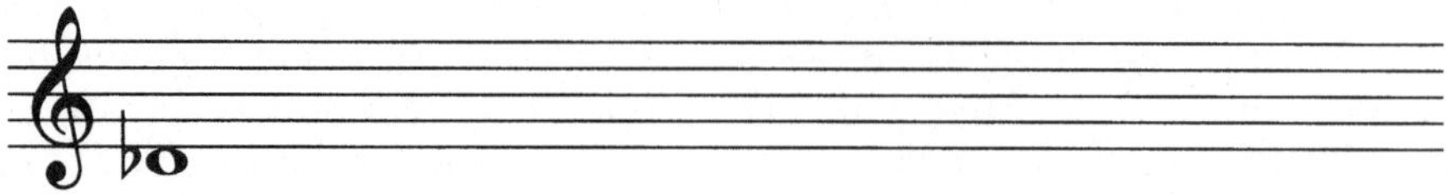

4.
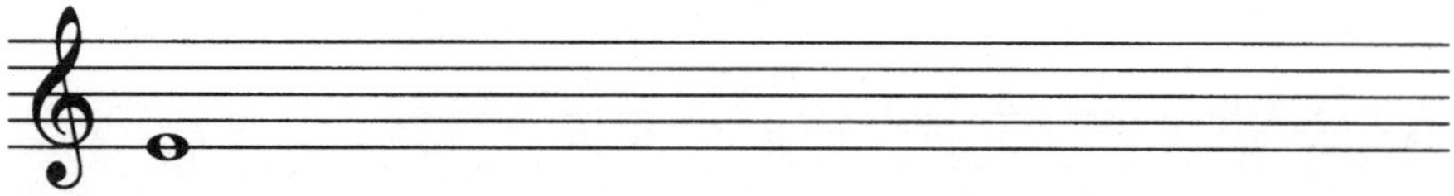

5.
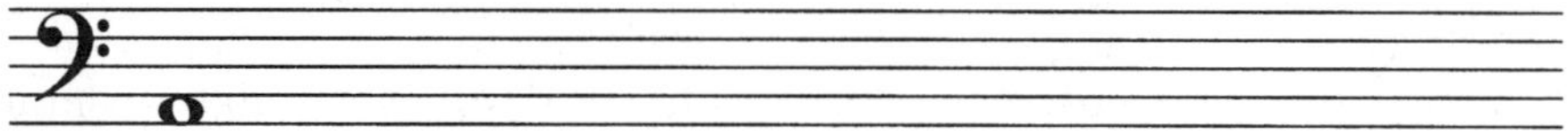

6.
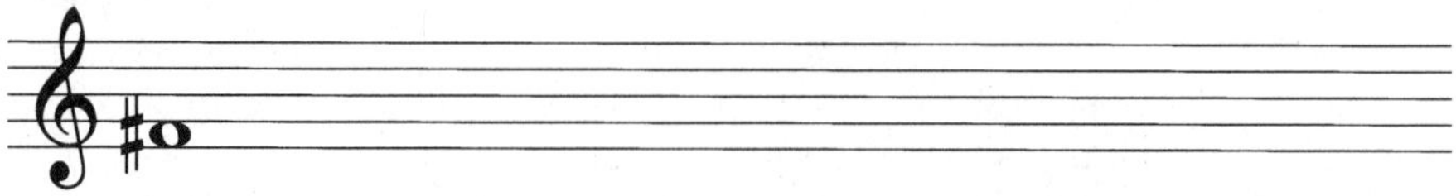

7.
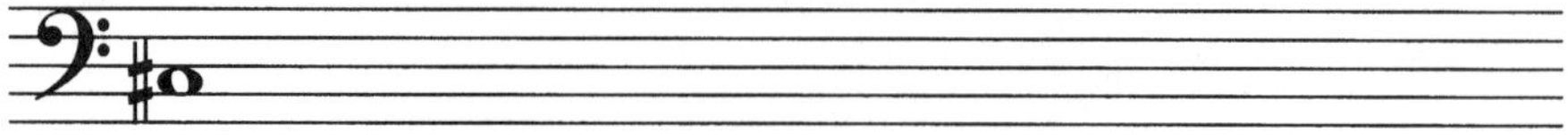

8.
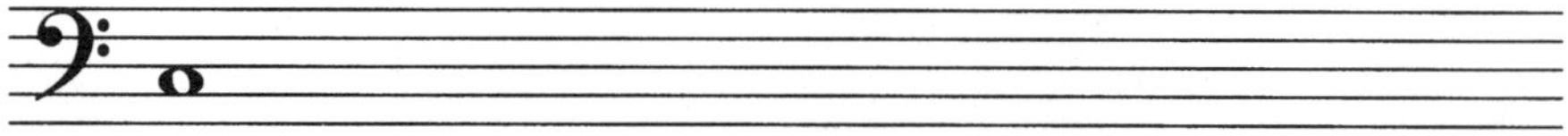

9.
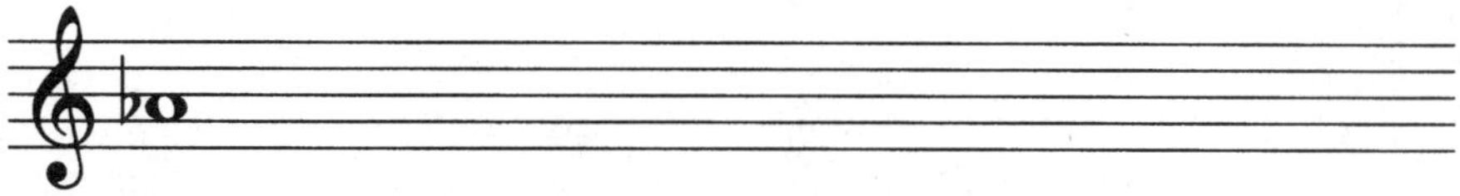

10.
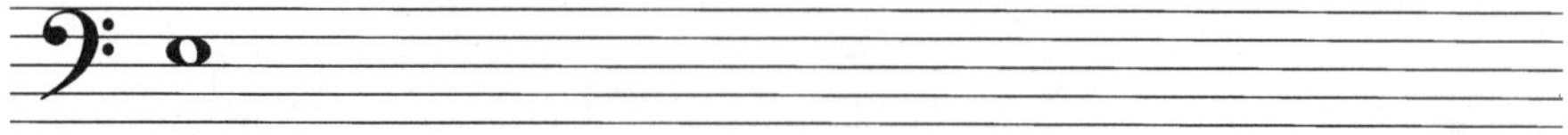

11. 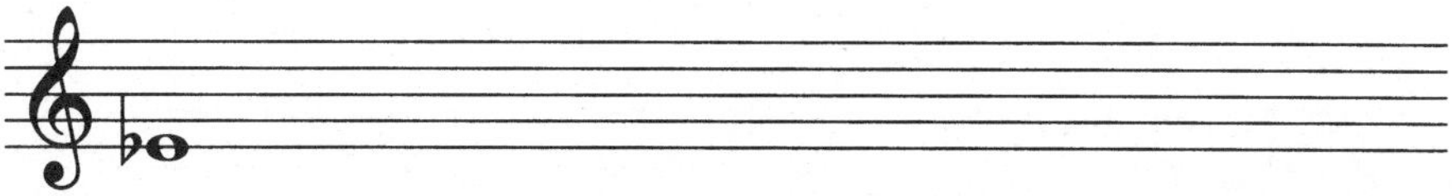

12. 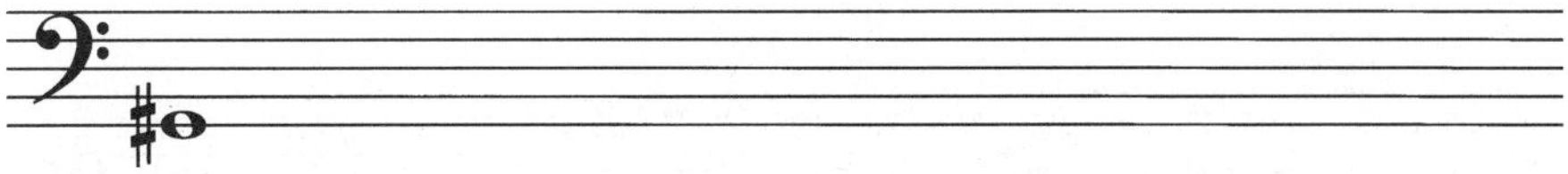

13. 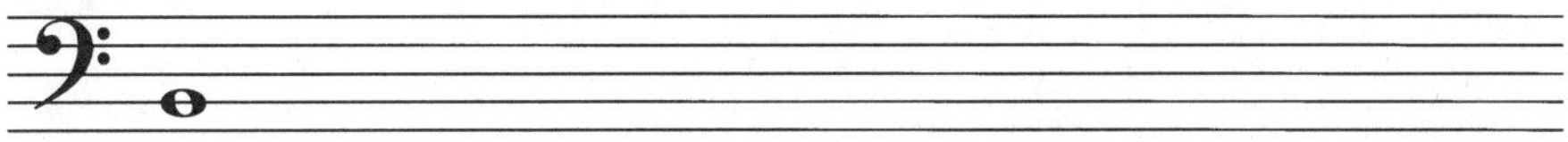

14. 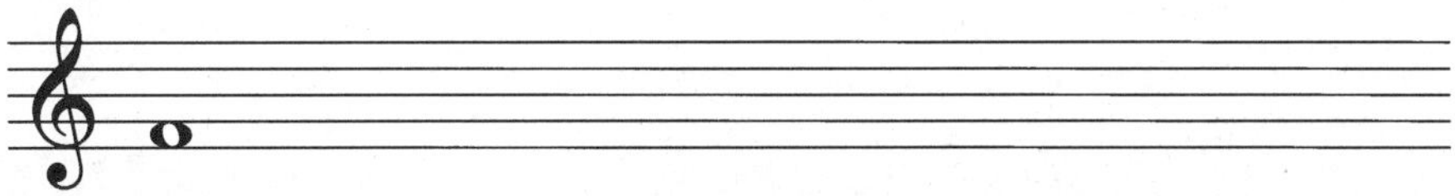

The form of the pentatonic scale in Exercise 9-1 is in wide use, including African, Chinese, Scottish, and Native American music. The following examples are drawn from Western music. Several of them could also be harmonized tonally, that is, with harmonies based on the major scale. This duality produces a most interesting musical combination: The character and ambiguity of the pentatonic scale are preserved in the pentatonic melody, while the harmony and musical center of gravity are tonal.

"Auld Lang Syne"

1. 

"Ol' Texas"

2. 

"Lonesome Valley"

3.

"This Train"

4.

"Tom Dooley"

5.

Rossini: *William Tell*, Overture

Debussy: "Nuages" from *Nocturnes*

Musical Problem

Sing or play the pentatonic melodies of the preceding seven examples. In each, locate and circle the tone that functions as the tonic. Beginning on the tonic, write the pentatonic scale on which each melody is based. Compare the forms of the scales you have written.

1.

2.

3.

4.

(continued)

5.

6.

7.

Modes

The modal system of the Middle Ages developed slowly over a period of several hundred years. By the eleventh century, when the system was complete, it consisted of eight modes or scales. Although each mode is a seven-note scale contained within one octave, just as major and minor scales are, they all sound different from each other because the combination of whole steps and half steps is different for each mode.

These modes, of which the present-day major and natural minor scales are two, were the basis of Western music from the Gregorian chant of the 900s until the early 1600s. They were revived in the twentieth century by composers around the world writing in a wide variety of styles. You are probably far more familiar with these scales than you think you are.

The church modes are all seven-note scales based on patterns of five whole steps and two half steps. Each of the patterns has its own characteristic sound because the placement of the two half steps is different in each mode. Here is a chart showing where the half steps occur in each mode.

Ionian	3–4	7–8
Dorian	2–3	6–7
Phrygian	1–2	5–6
Lydian	4–5	7–8
Mixolydian	3–4	6–7
Aeolian	2–3	5–6
Locrian	1–2	4–5

Notice in the following that the half steps are always from E to F and B to C, but their position in the scale depends on which note is the beginning pitch:

Ionian mode (present-day major scale)

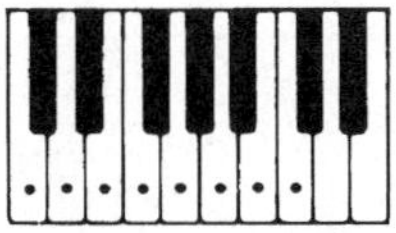

Dorian mode

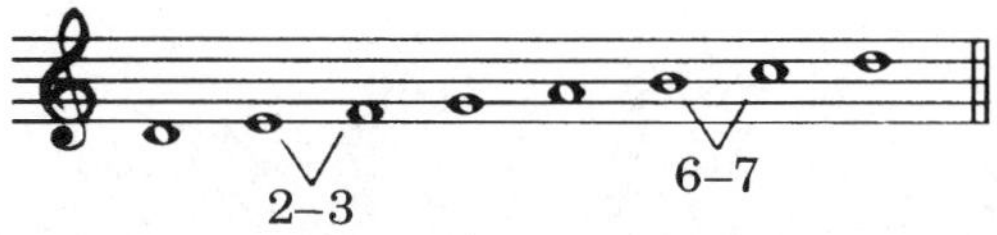

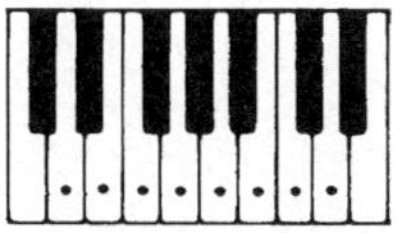

Phrygian mode

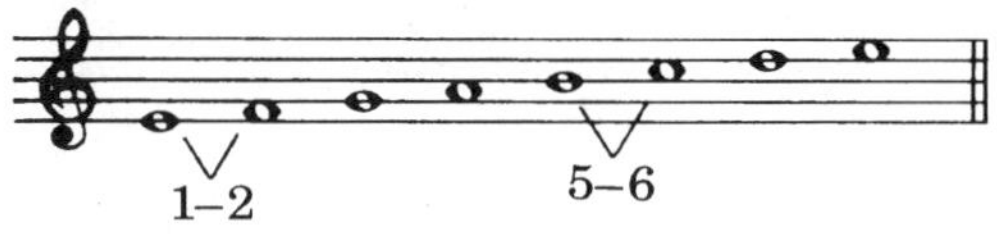

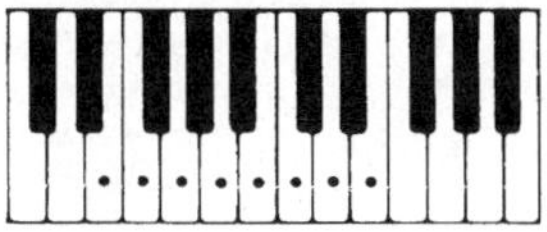

Lydian mode

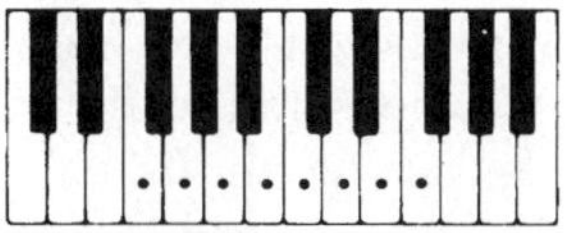

Mixolydian mode

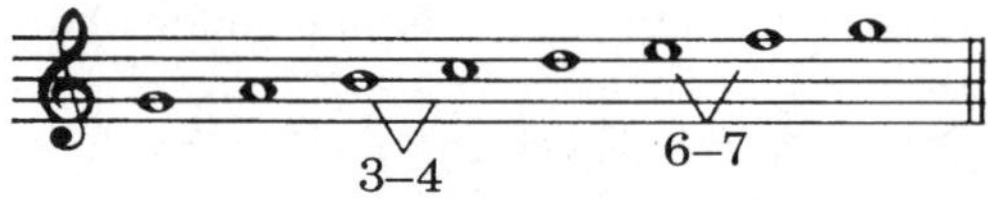

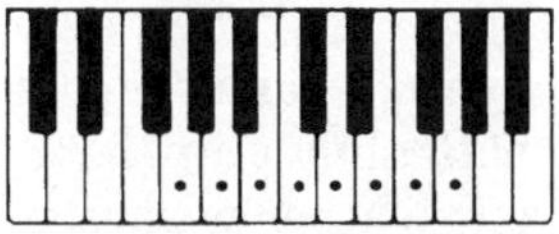

Aeolian mode (present-day natural minor scale)

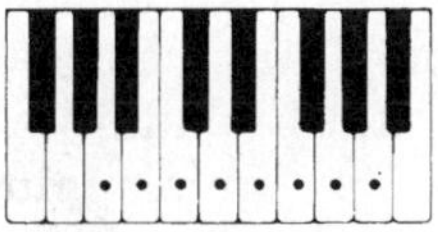

Locrian mode

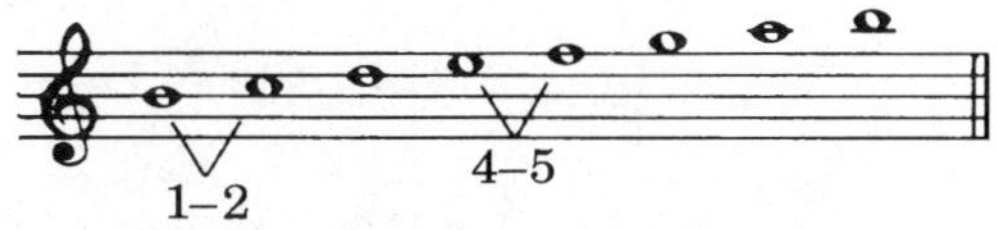

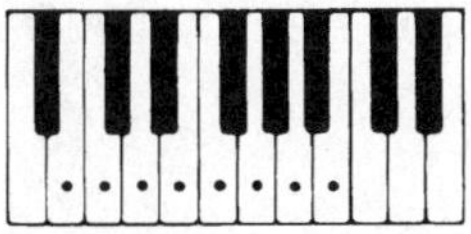

Medieval theorists divided the modes into authentic and plagal modes. Although a discussion of this concept is beyond the scope of this book, the distinction had to do with whether the *finalis,* or tonic as we would call it, was positioned at the beginning of the scale, i.e., the first note, or in the middle. The modes we are studying are all authentic modes because the *finalis* is always the first note of the mode.

Musical Problem

Why were there so many different modes in use, all at the same time, from the 900s to the 1600s? The answer lies in the belief of ancient theorists and philosophers that each of the different modes altered listeners' emotions, and ultimately their personalities, in some fundamental and lasting way. According to this belief, you could be changed as a person based on the music to which you listened.

As a class, discuss whether we still believe that listening to various kinds of music can affect our personalities. You may want to include in your discussion such styles as military march music, religious music, heavy metal, and rap. If there is time, you may also want to consider the impact of using music to sell products.

Transposing the Modes

For a while, the modes were not transposed when they were used musically. That is, composers always used "d" as the *finalis* when they wrote in Dorian mode, "e" as the *finalis* for Phrygian mode, and so on. Gregorian chant, for example, only allowed the use of one accidental, the flat sign, and it was only used to alter one pitch: "b." But slowly, composers began moving the modes to other beginning pitches, mostly to adjust singing ranges to more practical levels. The result has been that, in the music of today, each of the modes can appear with almost any note as the *finalis*.

If your teacher wishes you to learn how to transpose the modes, you will find some material for practice in Appendix H. It may be sufficient at this point, however, to know that the modes exist in transposed form, and that their characteristic sound stays intact as long as their interval pattern stays the same, no matter what the beginning pitch.

Whether you are planning to learn to transpose the modes or not, look at the following selection of modal melodies that span ten centuries (the tenth to the twentieth). Those that use a key signature are transposed, but you should still be able to identify the *finalis* of each.

Gregorian Chant

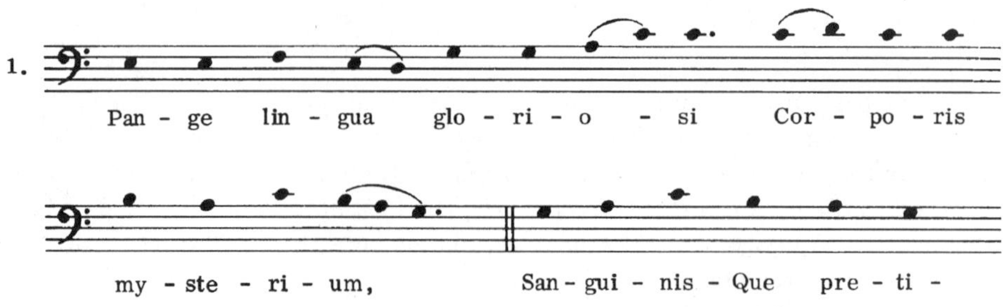

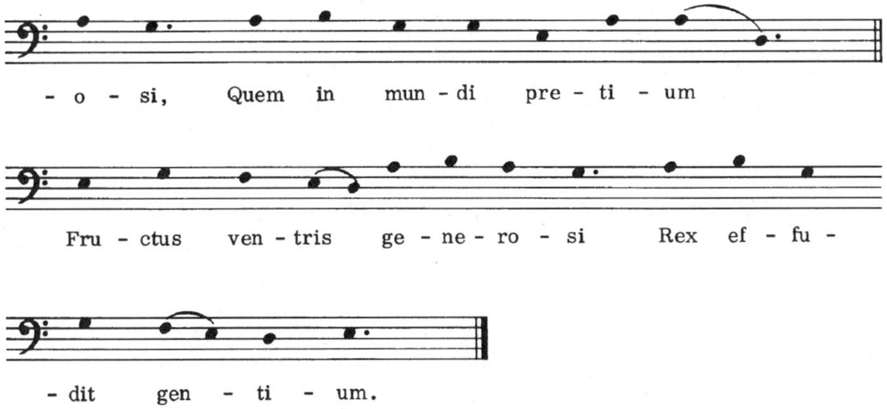
- o - si, Quem in mun - di pre - ti - um
Fru - ctus ven - tris ge - ne - ro - si Rex ef - fu -
- dit gen - ti - um.

"Henry Martin"

2.

Chopin: Mazurka in F Major, Op. 68, No. 3

3.

Poco piu vivo
p

"The Drunken Sailor"

4.

Berlioz: *Symphonie fantastique*

5.

"Old Joe Clark"

6.

Debussy: "L'Isle Joyeuse"

7.

Musical Problem

Sing or play each of the seven modal melodies previously given. For each, locate and circle the tone that acts as the *finalis,* or modal center of gravity. Beginning on this tone, write the pitches (in the form of a scale) on which each melody is based. Be sure to use the actual pitches found in each piece, rather than relying solely on the key signature.

1.

(continued)

2.

3.

4.

5.

6.

7.

Musical Problem

Modal scales are found so frequently in today's music that it is imperative to learn how to sing them. Singing the modes is not difficult if you remember to relate them to the major and minor scales.

Study the following modal scales and practice singing them. You may wish to test yourself at the piano as you learn. When you can sing the scales accurately, practice singing with syllables the folk songs "Old Joe Clark," "The Drunken Sailor," and "Henry Martin," which appear earlier in this chapter.

Dorian mode (natural minor with a raised sixth)

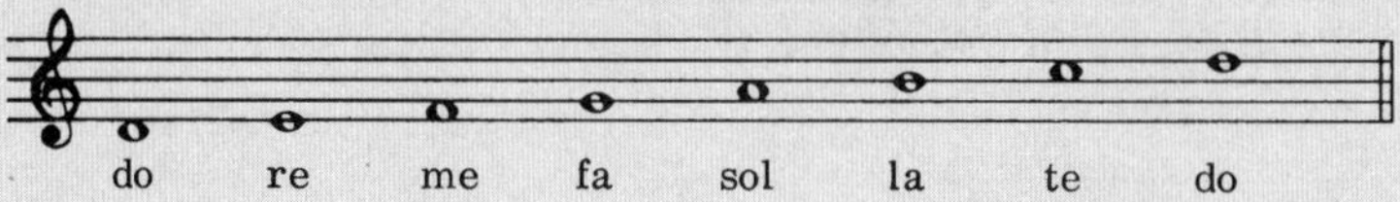

Phrygian mode (natural minor with a lowered second)

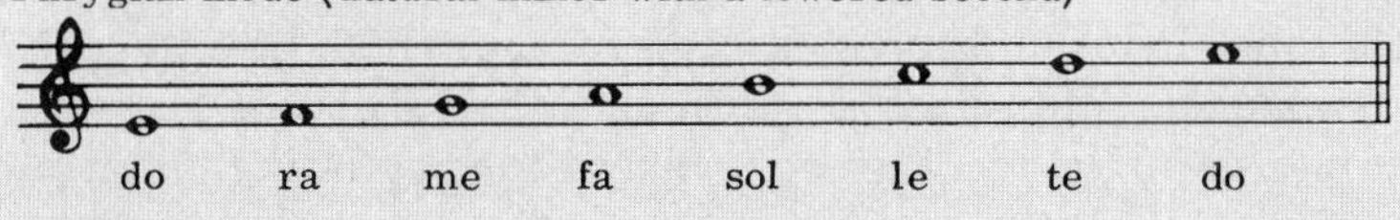

Lydian mode (major with a raised fourth)

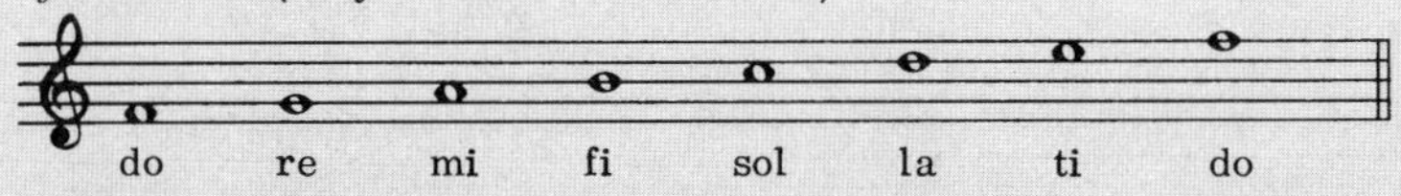

Mixolydian mode (major with a lowered seventh)

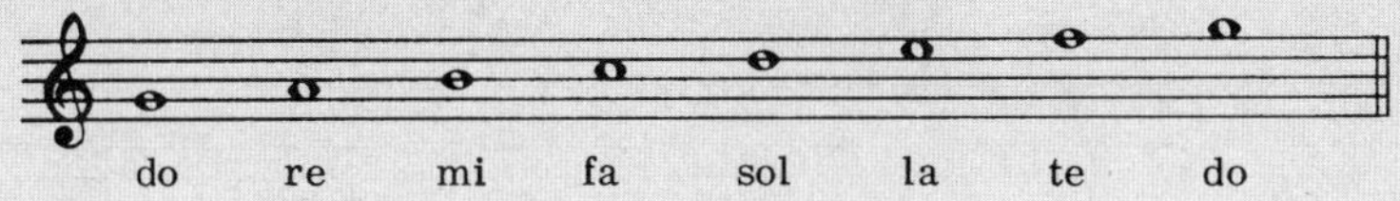

The Whole-Tone Scale

The **whole-tone scale** is a scale of six pitches per octave, each of them a whole step apart. Since this scale contains only one kind of interval—the whole step—it is extremely ambiguous and, like the chromatic scale, lacks the feeling of a center of gravity. Centers of gravity can be established in whole-tone and chromatic melodies, however, by such devices as repeating certain pitches more frequently than others, or repeating accent patterns or harmonic backgrounds. Another peculiarity of the whole-tone scale is that it does not contain the intervals of a perfect fourth or a perfect fifth. Since these intervals are considered essential to tonal music, their absence makes whole-tone music feel unsettled.

Whole - tone scale

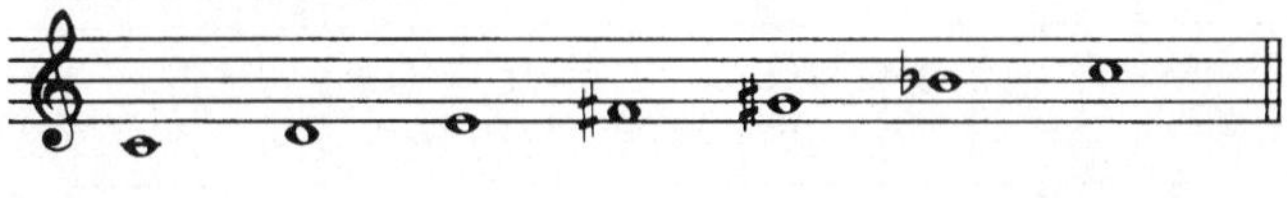

Only two versions of the whole-tone scale exist, the one in the preceding example and the one following.

Whole - tone scale

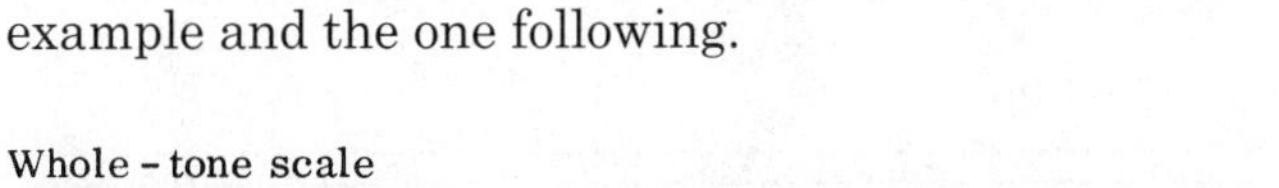

Any other whole-tone scale is simply a reordering of the pitches in one of these two versions. The lack of the half-step interval allows any note within these two scale forms to function equally well as a tonic.

EXERCISE 9•2

Construct whole-tone scales on the given beginning pitches. Use the preceding examples as models. Write each scale so as to avoid double accidentals. Remember that in order to end on the octave above the beginning pitch, one of the whole steps must be notated as a diminished third.

1. 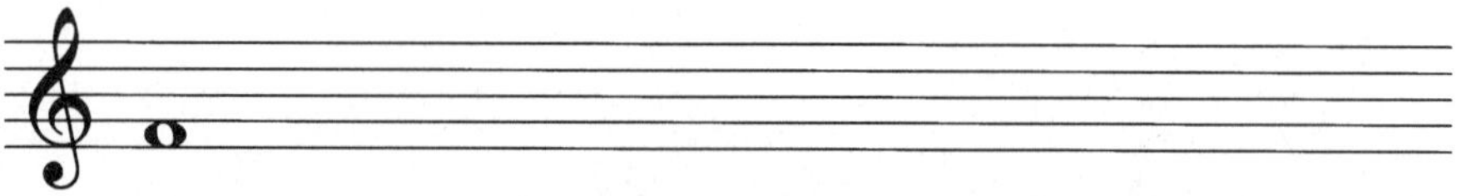

2. 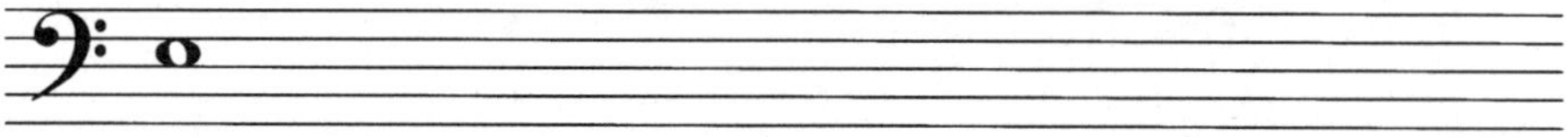

3. 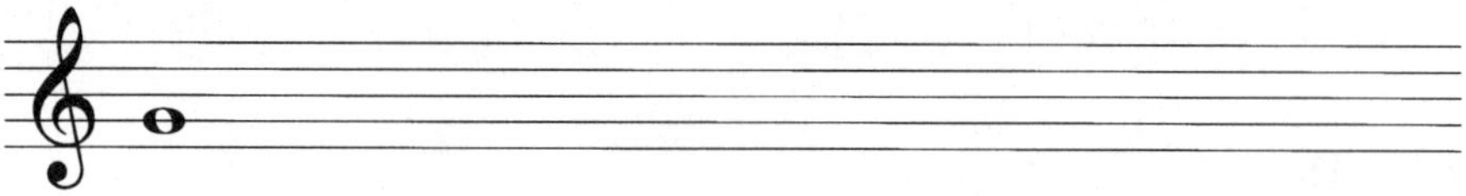

4. 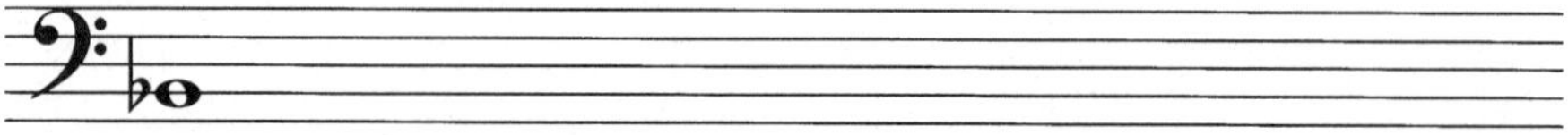

5. 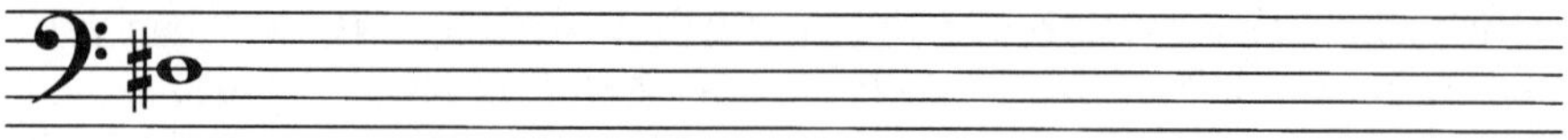

6. 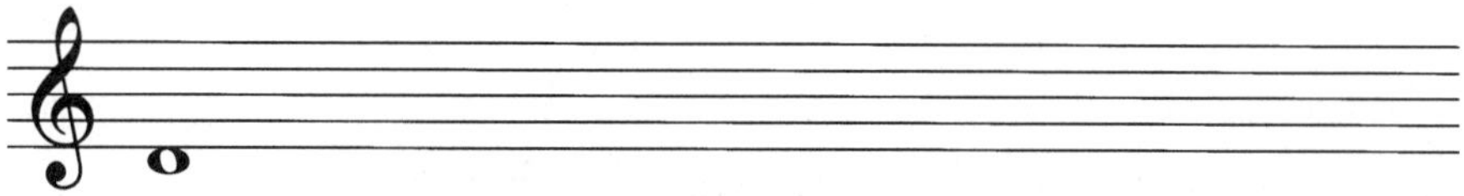

7. 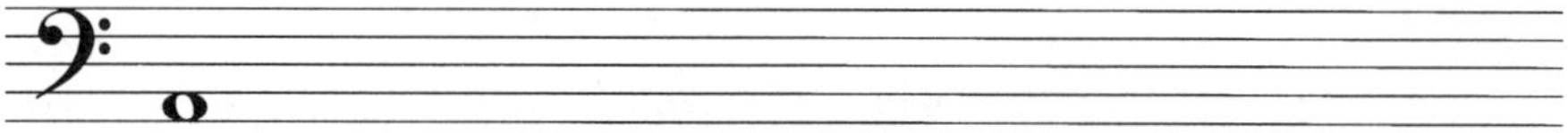

8. 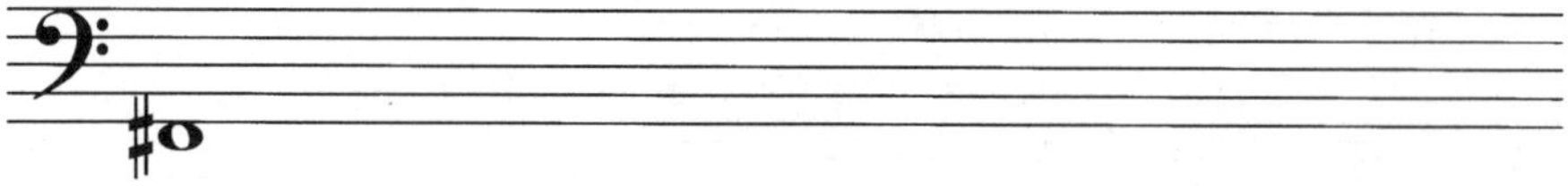

Although there are a few isolated examples of the whole-tone scale in the classical literature, it is found most extensively in music of the early twentieth century. Because of the whole-tone scale's ambiguity and harmonic vagueness, composers such as Debussy employed it to weaken the hold of nineteenth-century tonal practices, which they felt dominated music. Today, music based solely on the whole-tone scale is seldom written except as background music for movies and television.

The following examples show whole-tone music from the early twentieth century.

Debussy: ***Prelude to "The Afternoon of a Faun"***

1.

Debussy: "Voiles," Preludes, Book I

2.

Debussy: ***La Mer***

3.

Musical Problem

Play the preceding examples of whole-tone music. Discuss the ways in which each example establishes its own center of gravity, and locate this center of gravity in each.

EXERCISE 9•3

Write the indicated mode, pentatonic scale, or whole-tone scale beginning on the given pitch.

Pentatonic

1. 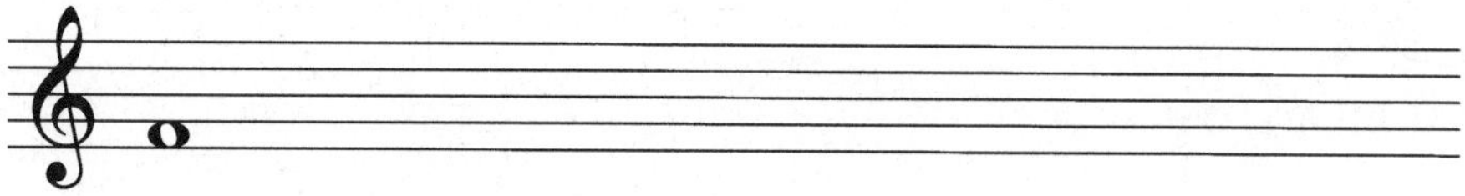

Whole tone

2. 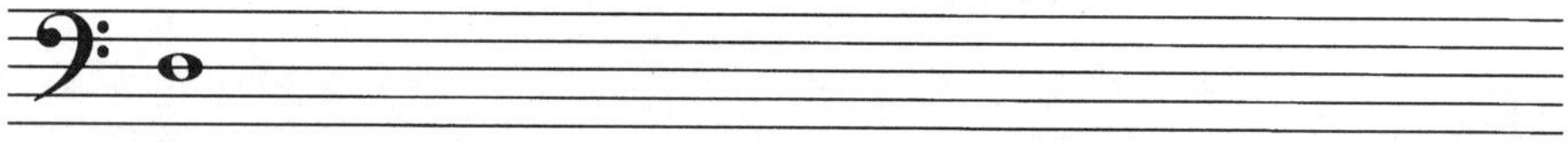

Lydian

3. 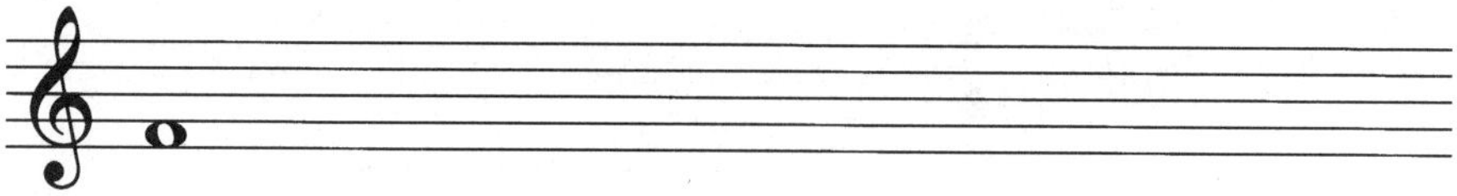

Mixolydian

4. 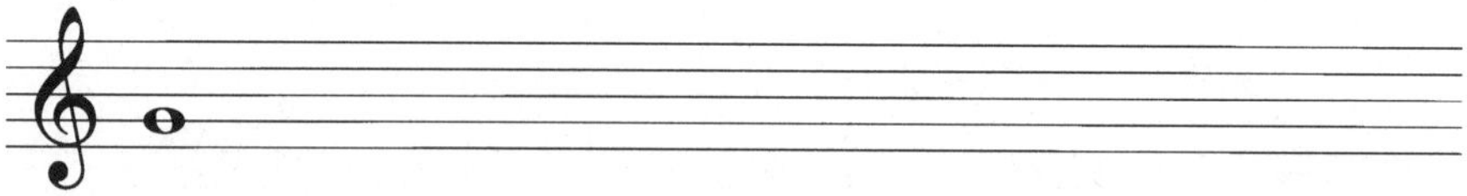

Pentatonic

5. 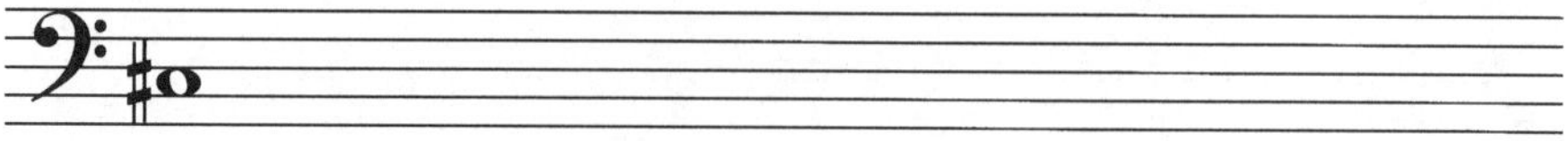

Phrygian

6. 

Pentatonic

7. 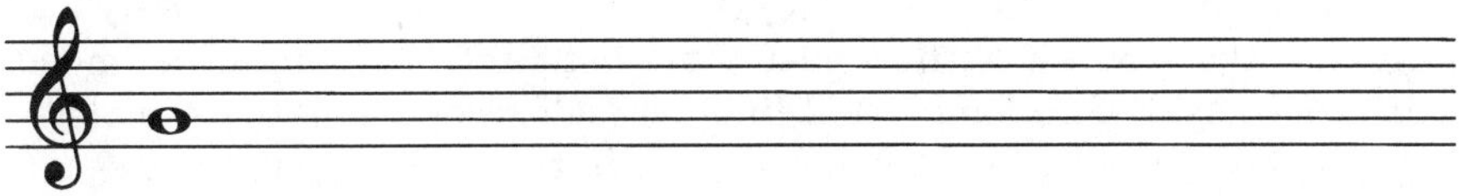

Dorian

8. 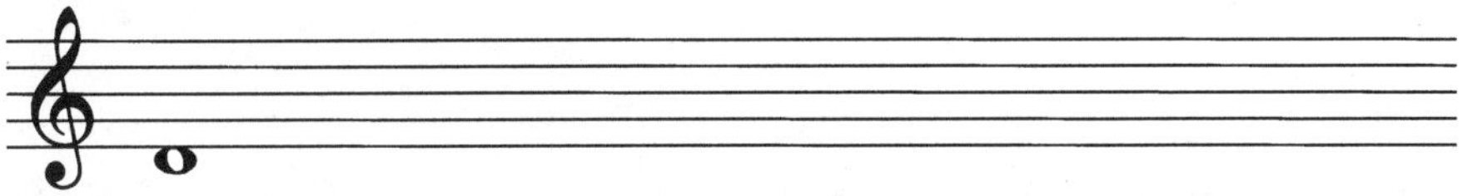

Whole tone

9. 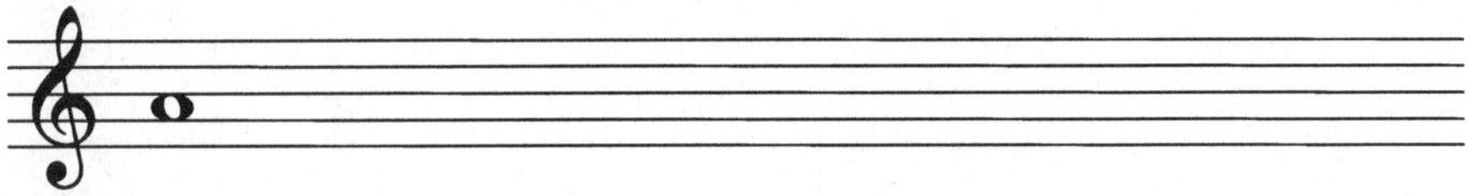

Pentatonic

10. 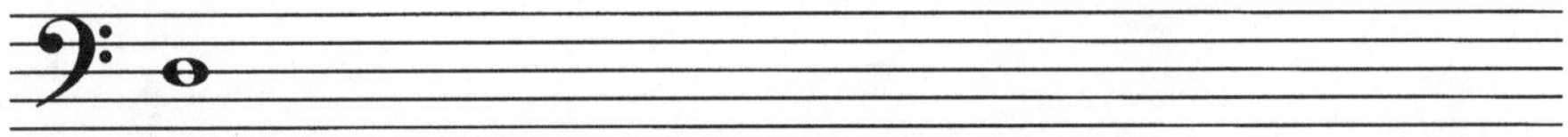

> ***Musical Problem***
>
> Ask someone to select scales randomly from Exercise 9-3 and to play each one several times. As they are being played, identify them by ear. (The modes will be less difficult to identify if you keep in mind that Dorian and Phrygian modes are similar to altered minor scales, and Lydian and Mixolydian modes resemble altered major scales.)

Focus

Major and minor scales have been the most important scales of Western music since the mid-1600s. They are still the most important today, although atonal, microtonal, and electronic music offer striking alternatives. But you would be wrong if you took this to mean that major and minor scales are the only ones that matter. As this chapter has shown, other types of scales can be found in the folk, popular, and classical music that you know. Keep in mind, too, that much of the world's music has *never* used major and minor scales.

The scales mentioned in this chapter represent only a small number of the many scales in use throughout the world today. For all musicians, and for anyone else interested in learning how music "works," some familiarity with these scales, and the music they produce, is essential. This chapter is only a beginning. Now that you know they exist, start listening for them in the music you hear every day. Before long, you'll find yourself recognizing these scales—particularly the modes and pentatonic scales—in the most unusual places.

Basic Structure of Triads

The triad is the basic chord of tonal music. Other chords—such as sevenths, ninths, and elevenths—are extensions of the triad. Four qualities of triads are possible: major, minor, augmented, and diminished. The quality of a triad is determined by the kinds of thirds it contains.

Triads are three-note chords built of two superimposed thirds. These two thirds, when stacked on top of each other, create the interval of a fifth between their two outside pitches. You will find that this interval of a fifth is as important to the harmony as it was to melody. When the triad is written in *root position*—that is, as two superimposed thirds—we identify the three notes of the triad, from the lowest to the highest, as *the root, the third,* and *the fifth.* In the following example, notice that the third of the triad is an interval of a third above the root, and the fifth of the triad is an interval of a fifth above the root.

F Major Triad, Root Position

If the triad appears in an altered form, the terms still apply to the pitches as if they were in root position, even though the intervals are no longer a third and a fifth:

F Major Triad, Altered Forms

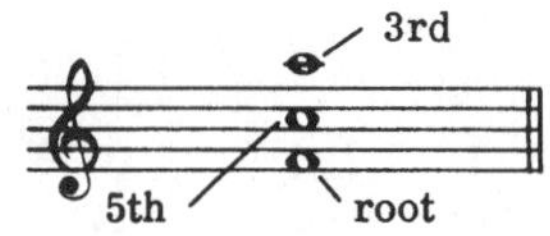

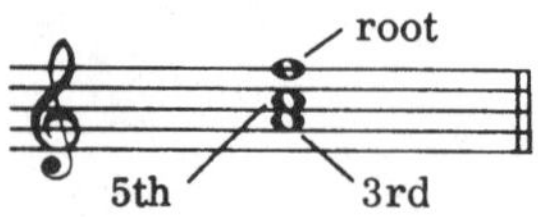

Triads take their name from the name of the root, that is, the lowest-sounding pitch when the triad is constructed as superimposed thirds. Notice that both examples above are F major triads, even though the second example does not actually have the F as the lowest sounding pitch.

Most beginning musicians can spell scales more easily than they can triads. This is because scales are based on the interval of a second while triads are based on the interval of a third. Until you get used to it, it's harder to think in thirds. The following exercise will help you begin to think in thirds. It deals only with the *arithmetic distance* of a third and not with the major, minor, augmented, or diminished qualities of triads.

EXERCISE 10•1

Practice reciting the following three-letter patterns until you can say them evenly.

ACE CEG EGB GBD BDF DFA FAC ACE

After you can say them evenly, work for speed. These patterns of three will help you think of triads from the root up.

Major and Minor Triads

The *major triad* (in root position) is built of two superimposed thirds. The lower third is a major third; the upper one is a minor third. The interval between the two outside notes—in this case, F and C—is a perfect fifth.

F Major Triad

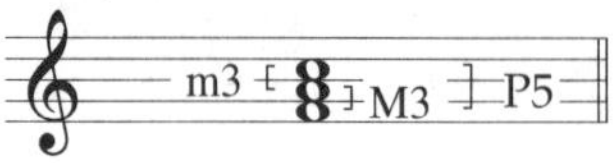

The *minor triad* is also built of superimposed thirds, but the order is reversed. In minor triads, the lower third is minor and the upper third is major. The outside interval remains a perfect fifth.

F Minor Triad

In both major and minor triads, the interval between the root and the fifth of the triad is always a perfect fifth. Some students find it easier to remember major triads as a major third plus a perfect fifth above the root, and minor triads as a minor third plus a perfect fifth.

F Major Triad

F Minor Triad

EXERCISE 10•2

Write major and minor triads in root position from the same given tonic note. Remember that major triads have a major third on the bottom while minor triads have a minor third as the lower third. Remember also that the interval between the root and the fifth must always be a perfect fifth.

1.

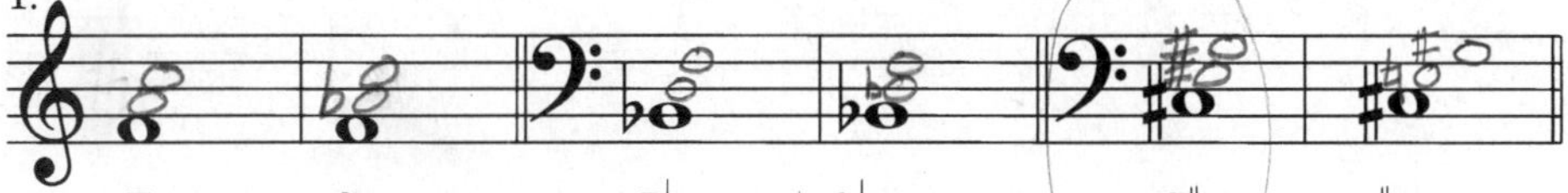

F fm B♭ b♭m C♯ c♯m

2.

A am D dm E em

3.

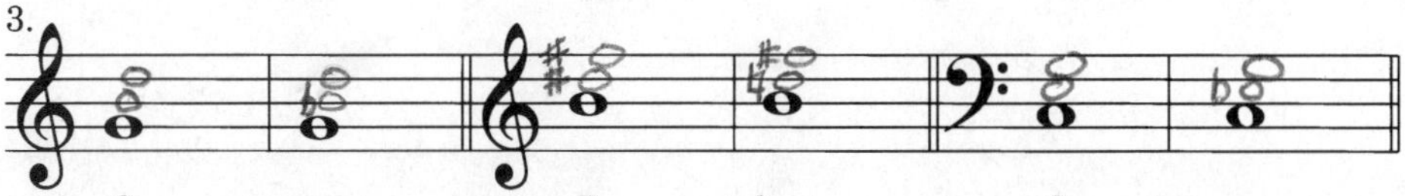

G gm B bm C cm

EXERCISE 10•3

Identify the root of each of the following triads, and label each as major (M) or minor (m) in quality.

EXAMPLE:

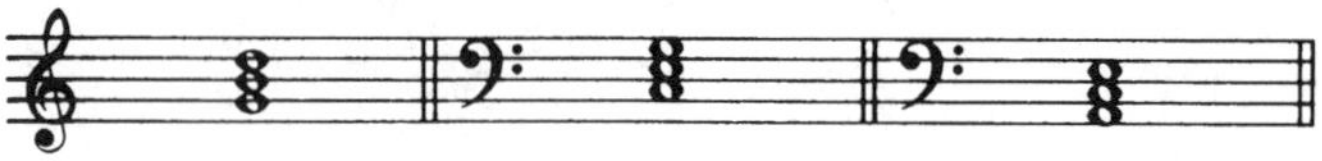

root	G	C	A
quality	M	M	m

1.

F	D	C	A
M	m	m	M

2.

B♭	E	A	F♯
m	M	m	M

BEAD

3.

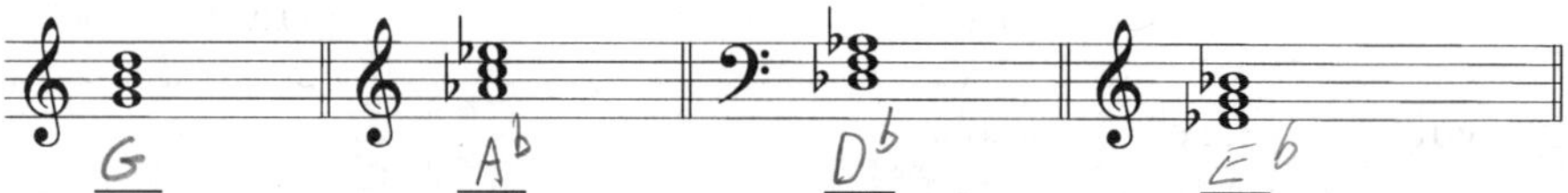

G	A♭	D♭	E♭
M	M	M	M

4.

D	F♯	D	G
M	m	m	M

5.

6.

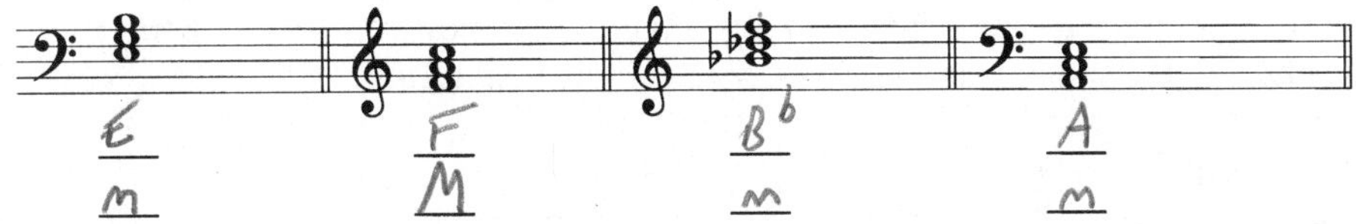

Musical Problem

Practice playing on the piano each of the triads you identified in Exercise 10-3. Play them with each hand separately, and then both hands together using the thumbs and third and fifth fingers. As you play, listen to the difference in sound between the major and the minor triads. Then ask someone to play the triads, and see if you can identify their quality by ear.

Close and Open Positions

When triads appear as two superimposed thirds, they are said to be in *close position.* When the notes of the triad are spaced farther apart than in close position, we call it *open position.*

Close Position

Open Position

Notice how open position skips one chord tone between each note.

D Minor Triad

Composers frequently employ open position to provide a change of musical color, and for reasons of voice leading. The following exercise will help you to recognize root-position triads in open position.

EXERCISE 10•4

The following are root-position triads in open position. The lowest note is the root of the triad. In each case, label the triad as major (M) or minor (m) in quality and, in the space provided, rewrite it in close position.

EXAMPLE:

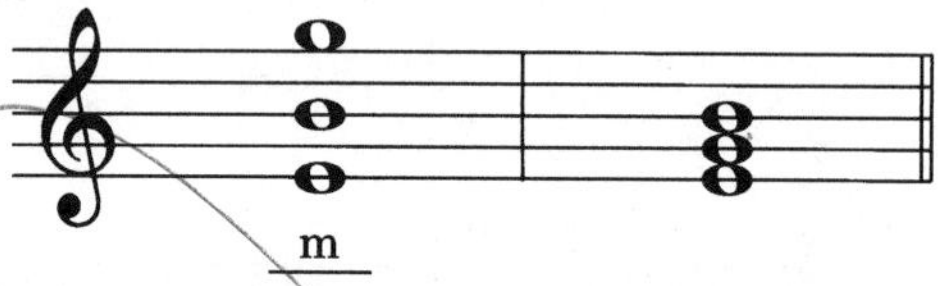

1.
2.
3.
4.

5. 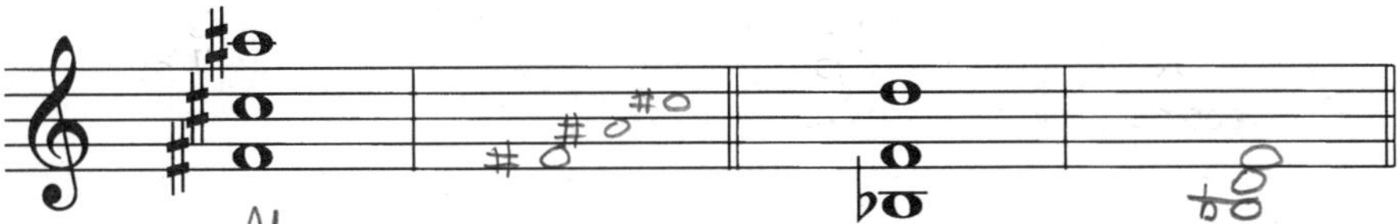

6. 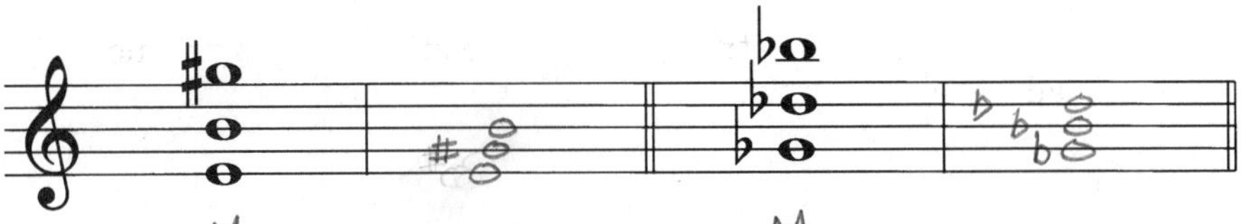

EXERCISE 10•5

Complete the indicated major or minor triad in close position, beginning on the root given. Remember: The interval between the root and the fifth of the triad should be a perfect fifth; the interval between the root and the third of the triad will be a major third for major triads, and a minor third for minor triads.

1. 

m M m M

2. 

m M M m

3. 

M M M m

4. 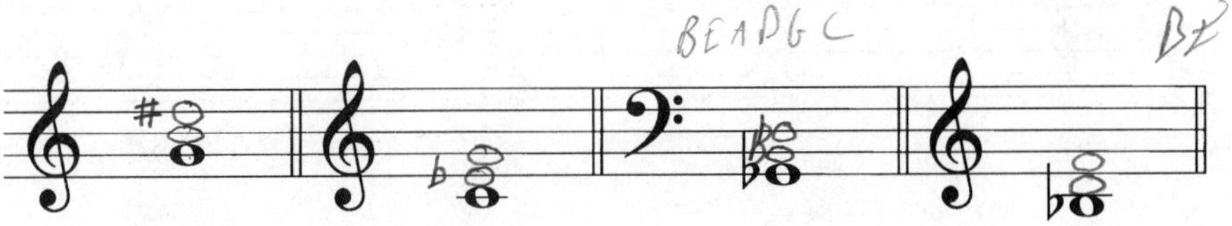

M m M M

5. 

m M M m

6. 

m m m m

Musical Problem

When you have completed Exercise 10-5, ask someone to play various lines of it on the piano, repeating each triad three times. As you listen, identify the triad as major or minor in quality.

EXERCISE 10•6

Complete the indicated close-position major or minor triads. In each case, the note given is the *third* of the triad.

1. 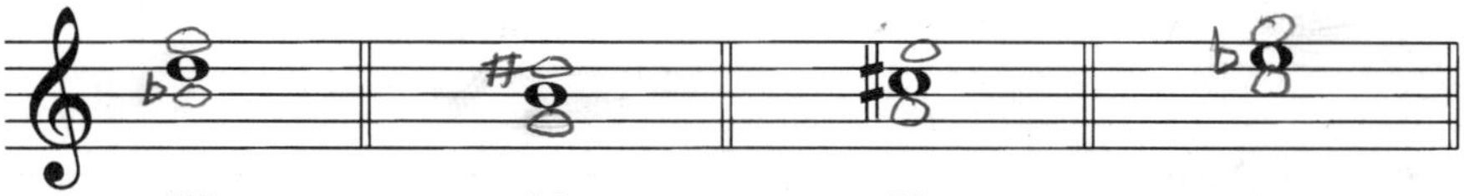

M M M m

2. 

M M m M

3. 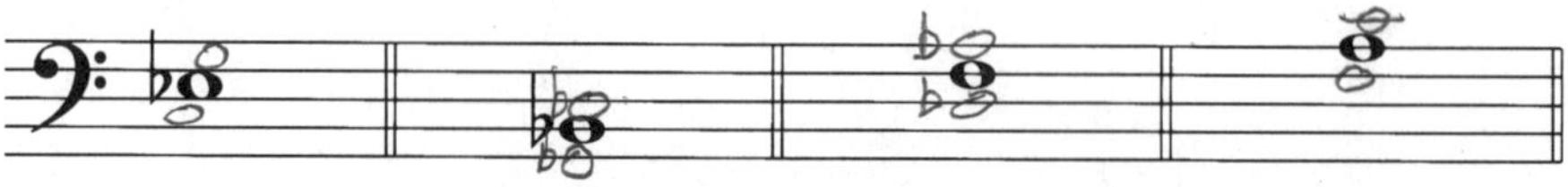

m m m M

4. 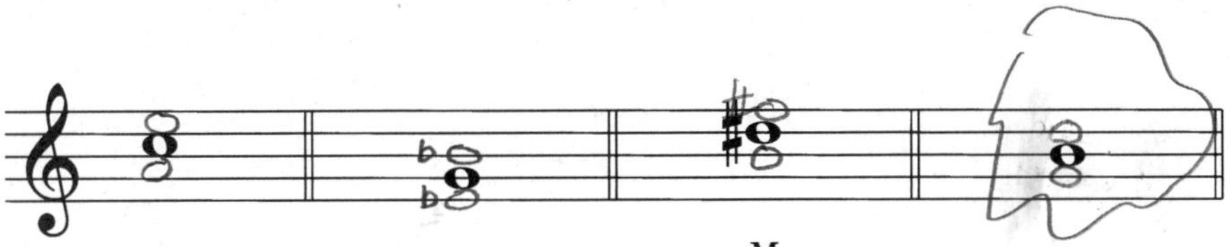

m m M m

5. 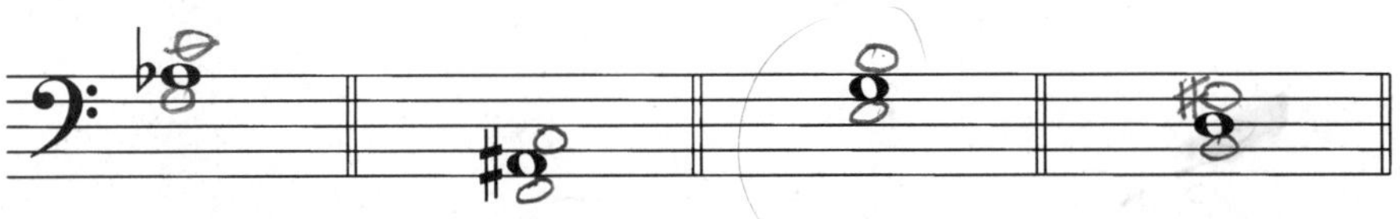

m M M m

6. 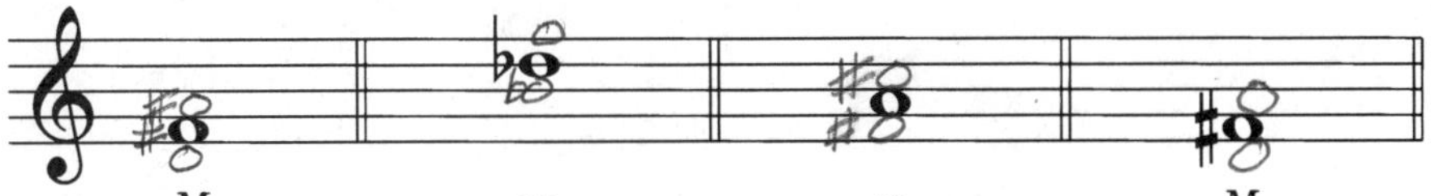

M m m M

EXERCISE 10•7

Complete the indicated close-position major or minor triads. In each case, the note given is the *fifth* of the triad.

1. 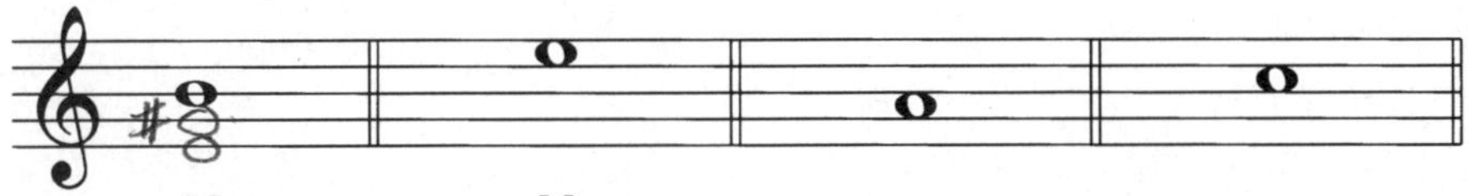

M M m m

2. 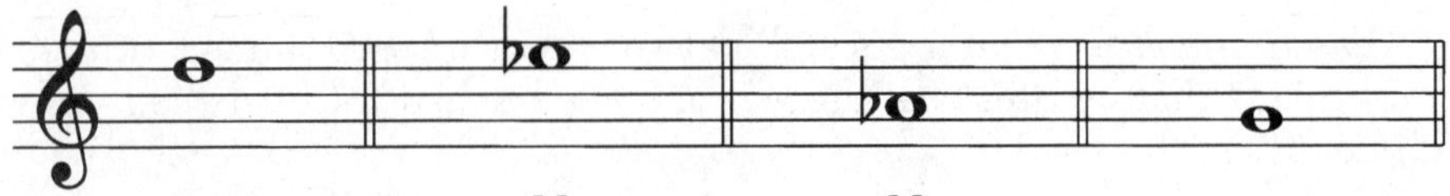

m M M m

3. 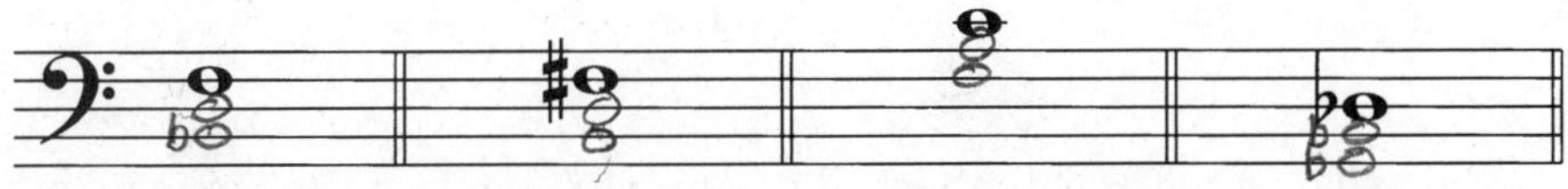

M m M M

4.
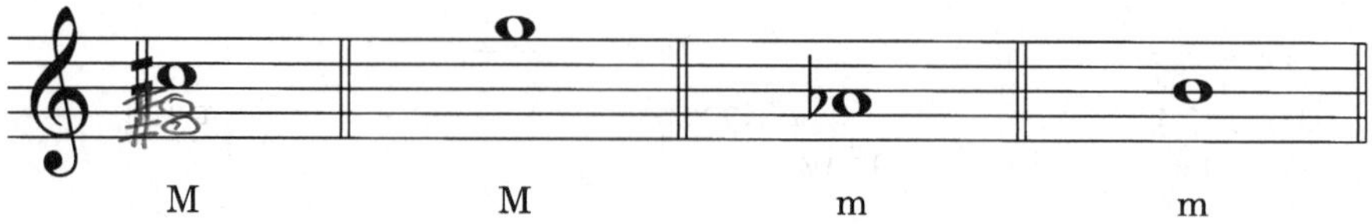

5.
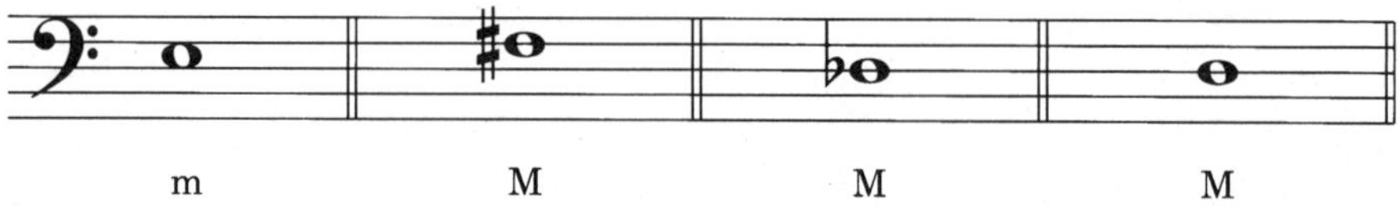

6.
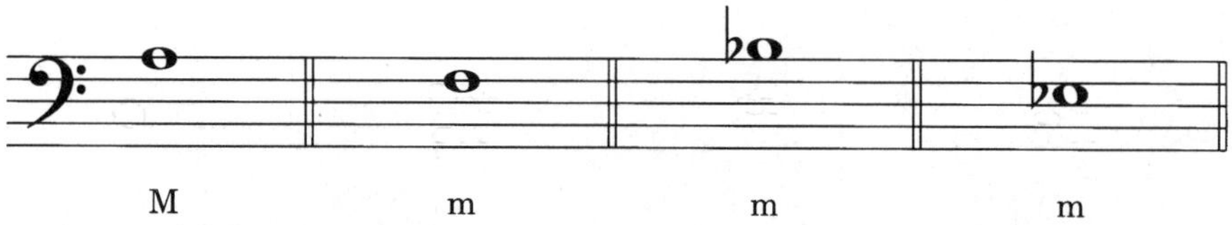

Augmented and Diminished Triads

The *augmented triad* consists of two superimposed major thirds. Notice that the resultant interval between the root and the fifth of the triad is an augmented fifth.

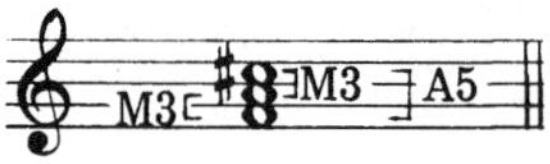

The *diminished triad* consists of two superimposed minor thirds, an arrangement that creates the interval of a diminished fifth between the root and the fifth of the triad.

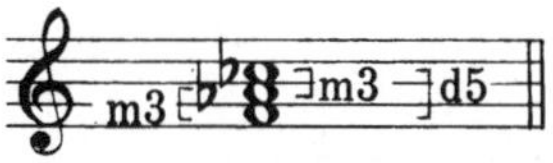

While augmented and diminished triads are found less often in tonal music than are major and minor triads, they can contribute a unique color and tension. Overuse, however, can weaken the tonal center of a piece.

EXERCISE 10•8

Identify the root of each of the following triads, and label the triads as augmented (A) or diminished (d) in quality.

EXAMPLE:

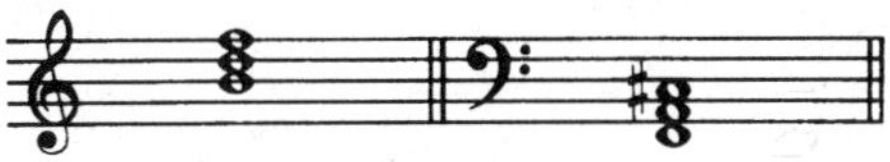

root	B	F
quality	d	A

1.

2.

3.

E   A

d   A

4.

C   G   [illegible]

d   a

5.

Musical Problem

Practice playing on the piano each of the augmented and diminished triads you identified in Exercise 10-8. Play them with each hand separately, and then both hands together. Pay particular attention to the sound of each kind of triad. Then, ask someone to play the triads, and see if you can identify their quality by ear.

EXERCISE 10•9

The following are root-position triads in open position. In the space provided, label each as augmented (A) or diminished (d) in quality.

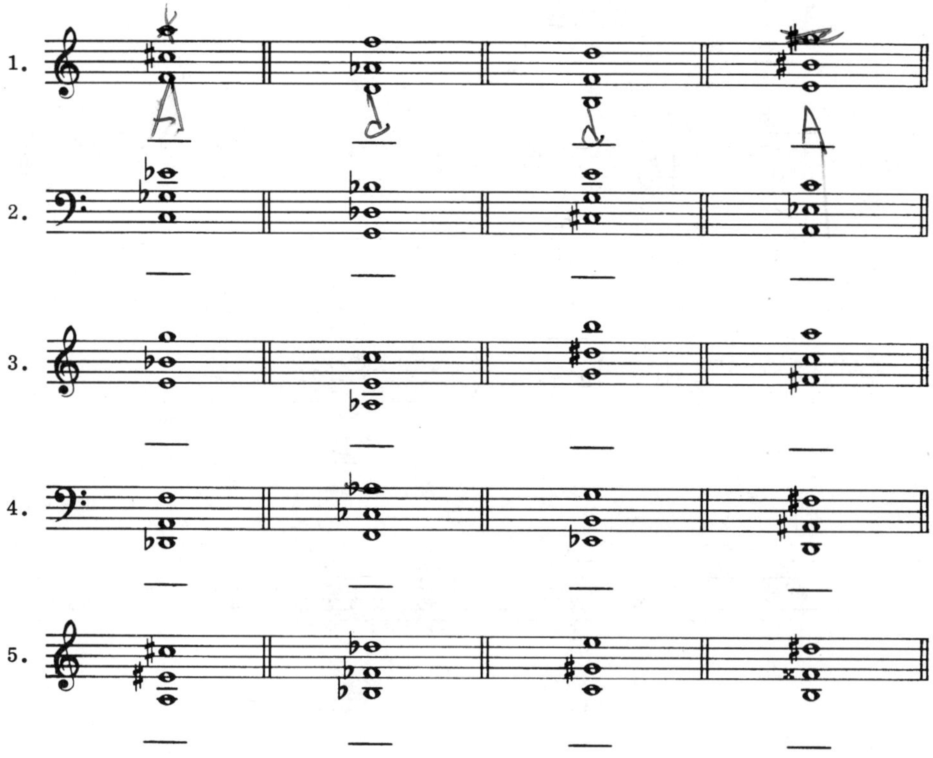

EXERCISE 10•10

Complete the indicated augmented or diminished triad starting from the given root. Remember that the augmented triad is a major third above the root plus an augmented fifth above the root, and that the diminished triad is a minor third above the root plus a diminished fifth above the root.

Musical Problem

When you have completed Exercise 10-10, ask someone to play various lines of it on the piano, repeating each triad three times. As you listen, identify each triad as augmented or diminished in quality.

EXERCISE 10•11

Complete the indicated close-position augmented or diminished triads. In each case, the note given is the *third* of the triad.

EXERCISE 10•12

Complete the indicated close-position augmented or diminished triads. In each case, the note given is the *fifth* of the triad.

Musical Problem

The following example is the Choral from Robert Schumann's *Album for the Young,* a set of forty-three piano pieces written in 1848. Listen to it as your teacher or a fellow student plays it several times. As you listen, try to identify the quality of each chord by its sound (major, minor, augmented, or diminished). Some chords will be more difficult to identify than others because they are *inverted* (the lowest note is not the root—see p. 248ff) or because they contain an extra pitch (a *seventh chord*—see p. 261ff. Still, you should be able to identify most of them after several hearings.

(continued)

Then, as a class, discuss the harmonic character of this piece. Which line has the melody? Is the melody more important, equally important, or less important than the harmony? Does the piece sound predominantly vertical (harmonic) or horizontal (melodic)?

Schumann: Choral from *Album for the Young*

Triads and Scales

Triads can be built on any note of the major and minor scales. Musicians often identify triads built on scale degrees by the same terms as the pitches of the scale:

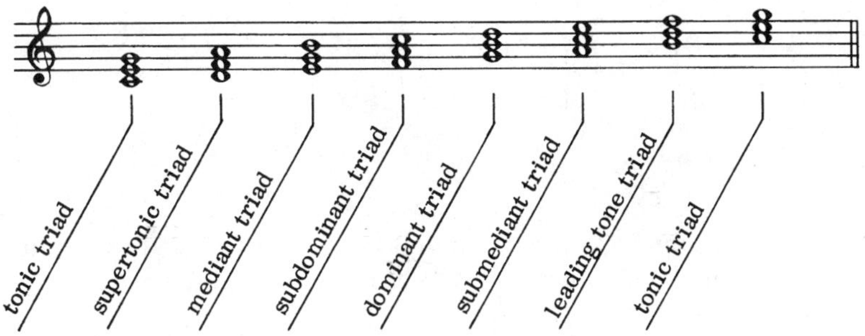

When triads are constructed on scale degrees, they must conform to the pitches of the scale. That is, if a scale has a B♭, all triads with a B will use a B♭.

Triads in F Major

Quality of triad: M m m M M m d M

Notice that the major scale produces three major triads, three minor triads, and one diminished triad.

The triads associated with the minor scale, because of its several versions, are a bit more confusing. The natural minor scale produces the following triads:

Triads in D Natural Minor

Quality of triad: m d M m m M M m

But since the scale itself contains a subtonic, a whole step away, rather than a true leading tone only a half step below the tonic, the harmony it produces is also without a leading tone. That, in turn, means that the dominant chord is minor rather than major in quality (because it contains a C natural rather than a raised C sharp). But by borrowing the leading tone from the parallel major, as the harmonic minor version of the scale does, we can raise the C to C sharp in the dominant (V) and leading-tone (vii°) chords, thus creating a stronger harmony. Notice that although true harmonic minor indicates that the mediant chord should also contain a C sharp as well, this would change the chord from a major triad to an augmented one, and composers do not always do that in actual music.

Triads in D Harmonic Minor

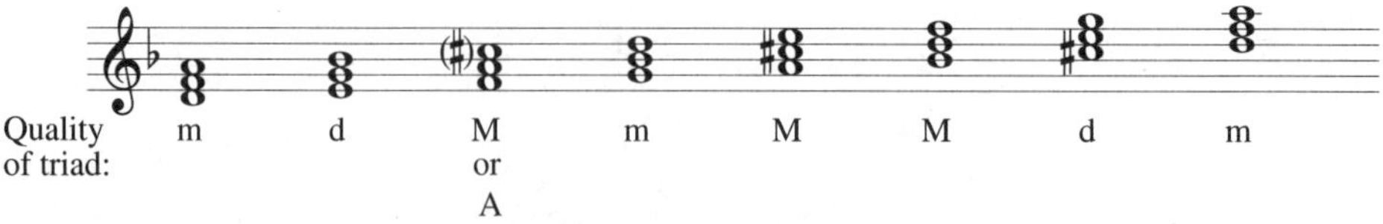

Although other alterations borrowed from major are possible, they are a little beyond the scope of this book. Here, we will limit ourselves to the leading-tone alterations discussed thus far.

Inversions of Triads

Triads do not always appear in root position. Quite often the third or the fifth of the triad is the lowest-sounding pitch. Nevertheless, the triad itself does not change; the root remains the root, and the quality remains the same.

Triads can appear in two positions other than root position: first inversion and second inversion. Triads in first and second inversions add variety to the harmony of a piece, and they also serve for voice leading.

In first inversion, the triad has the *third* of the root-position triad as the lowest-sounding pitch.

D Minor Triad

Root Position

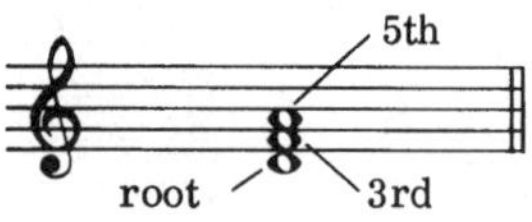

First Inversion

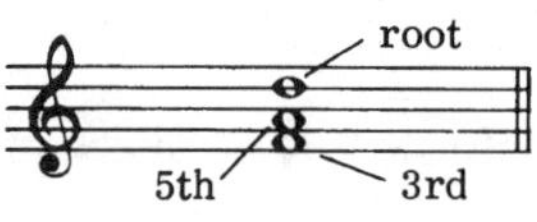

Remember that a triad in root position appears on the staff as two superimposed thirds. In first inversion, the triad consists of the same three pitches, but now there is the arithmetic interval of a fourth between the *upper* two pitches.

The triad in second inversion has the *fifth* as the lowest-sounding pitch.

D Minor Triad, *Second Inversion*

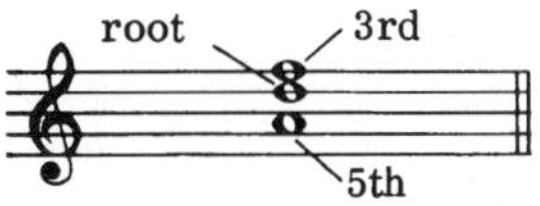

In second inversion, the triad has the arithmetic interval of a fourth between the *lower* two pitches.

As you begin the next exercise, keep in mind that the triad does not change simply because its notes change position. This is because we hear the identifying interval of the triad in root position (the perfect fifth) differently from the way we hear the identifying interval of the triad in first or second inversion (the perfect fourth). The perfect fifth directs our ear to hear the lower pitch as the root, while the perfect fourth directs our ear to the upper pitch. Therefore, the pitch we hear as the root of the triad doesn't change with inversion.

In the study of harmony, it is essential that you be able to identify triads correctly in an inversion. This means that you must first recognize the *kind* of inversion (first or second); otherwise you will identify the wrong pitch as the root.

EXERCISE 10•13

The following triads are in either first inversion or second inversion. Identify the inversion, the root of the triad, and the quality of the triad.

EXAMPLE:

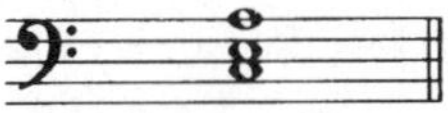

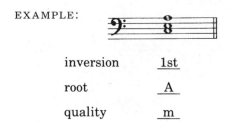

inversion 1st

root A

quality m

1.

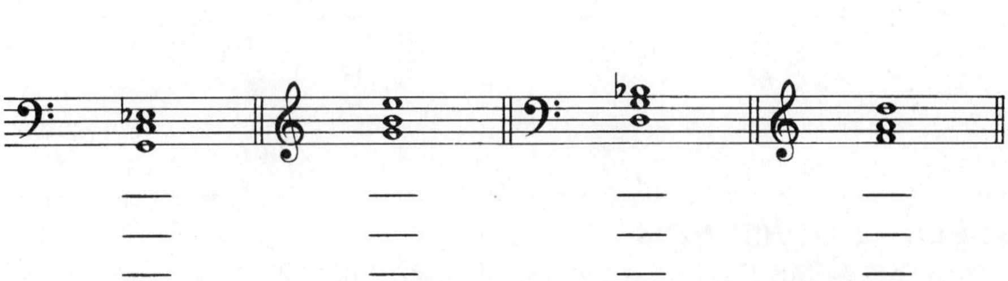

2. 

3. 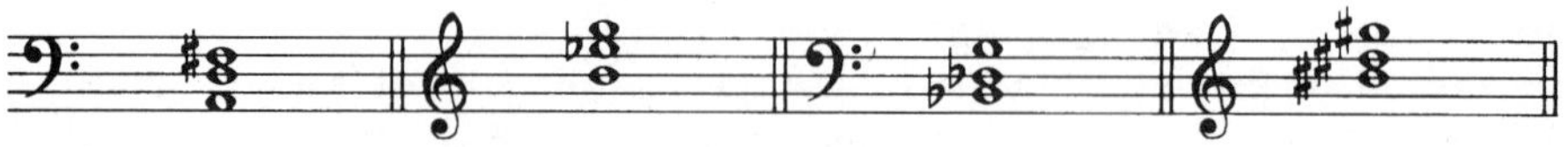

4. 

5. 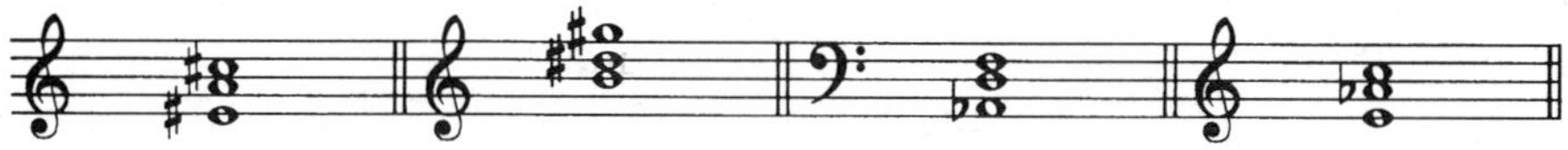

6. 

Labeling Inversions

In order to indicate whether a triad is in root position or in an inversion, a set of shorthand symbols has been developed. This shorthand system refers to the *arithmetic intervals above* the lowest-sounding pitch. Thus, a triad in *root position,* with intervals of a third and a fifth above the lowest-sounding pitch, could be shown as follows:

A triad in *first inversion,* with intervals of a third and a sixth above the lowest-sounding pitch, can be indicated by the following notation:

A triad in *second inversion,* containing intervals of a fourth and a sixth above the lowest-sounding note, can be shown as:

Notice that this shorthand system does *not* indicate the quality of the triad. Whether the triad is major, minor, augmented, or diminished is determined by how that triad functions in a particular key.

In practice, the shorthand system for labeling triad inversions has been abbreviated even further. For a triad in root position (the most common chord in tonal music), the numerals are omitted and the intervals of a fifth and a third are simply understood to be present.

Root Position

For a first-inversion triad, whose characteristic interval is a sixth above the lowest-sounding note, a 6 is indicated while the third, being understood as present, is not marked.

First Inversion

For a second-inversion triad, both of the numerals 6 and 4 are used so as to distinguish it from first inversion.

Second Inversion

Today, this system of labeling functions primarily in harmonic analysis. During the Baroque period (1600–1750), however, it was common for composers to write the keyboard part of an orchestral piece with only the bass line, plus subscript numerals to indicate inversions. This part was called *figured bass.* The keyboard musician was expected to play the written bass line, along with another instrument like cello or bassoon, and to fill in the harmonies according to the shorthand symbols. This practice, which persisted for almost 200 years, is similar to the technique of today's jazz pianists when they weave an appropriate musical fabric from a melody line and a set of chord symbols.

The following is an example of figured bass from the Baroque period. The top stave is the solo flute part. The bottom stave contains the figured bass part from which the keyboard performer was expected to create a suitable accompaniment.

Handel: "Siciliana" from Flute Sonata in F Major

EXERCISE 10•14

Write the indicated triad for each figured bass symbol. Each given note is the lowest-sounding pitch of a major triad. The subscript numerals indicate whether the triad is in root position or in an inversion.

1. 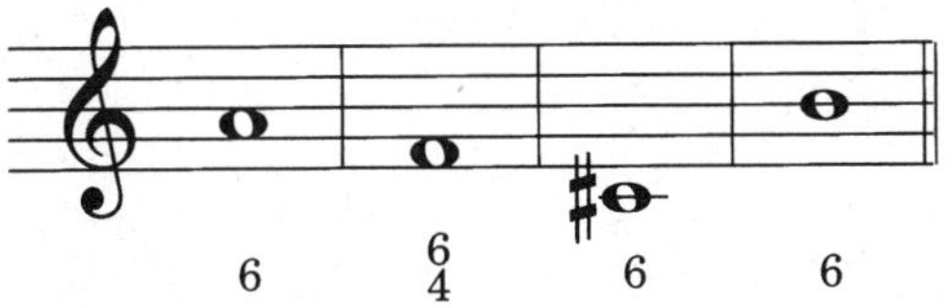

2. 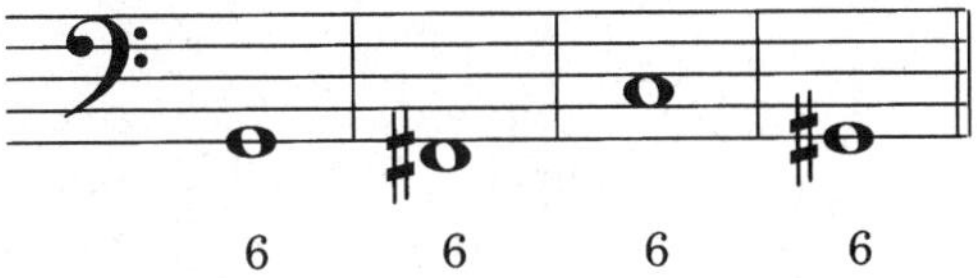

3. 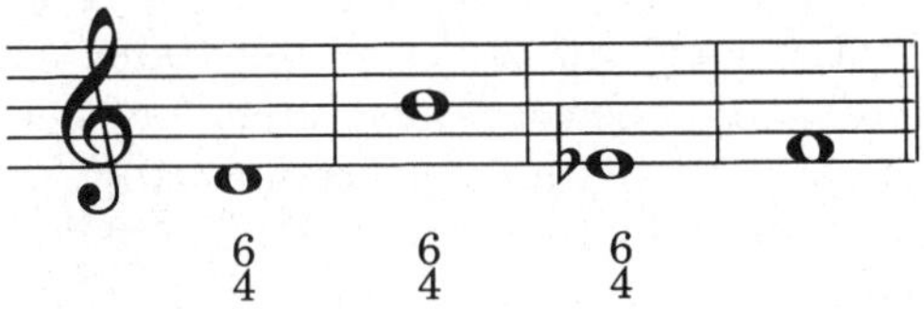

4. 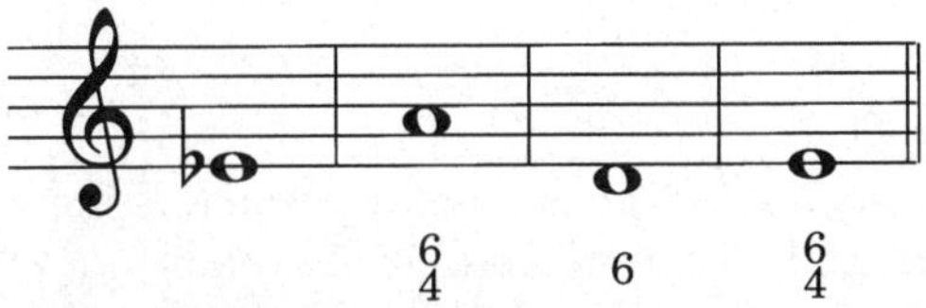

5. 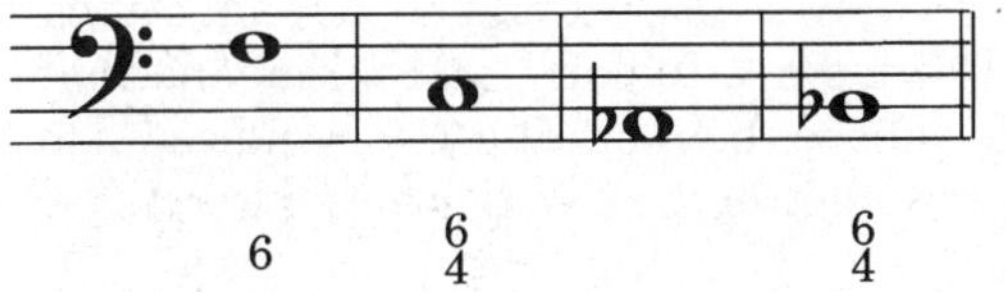

Musical Problem

Return to the Choral from Schumann's *Album for the Young* (p. 246). Locate and circle the inverted triads. Identify the inversion and the root of each triad you have circled. You will see that all of the triads in this work have one of the three pitches doubled; that is, the same letter name

(continued)

appears twice. This does not in any way change the nature of the basic triad. Ignore any chords that have four *different* pitches, because they are not triads.

After you have located the inverted triads, listen to the work again, paying particular attention to the triads. Remember that triads in inversion serve for both harmonic color and better voice leading.

Two Systems for Labeling Triads

There are two different ways of labeling triads in tonal music. Since each way gives important information about the harmony, musicians need to be familiar with both possibilities. *Roman numeral analysis* is the preferred method in theoretical discussions of music, when an understanding of the relationship between the triads is significant; if you continue the study of music theory, you will employ this system of labeling extensively. The other system, *pitch name identification,* appears most frequently as a performing system in popular music, jazz, and rock. If you expect to develop your performing skills, from singing folk songs to playing with a jazz or rock group, you will need to understand this type of labeling.

Roman Numeral Analysis

In roman numeral analysis, uppercase and lowercase roman numerals identify both the scale degree on which a triad is built as well as the quality of each particular triad. The uppercase roman numerals (I, IV, and V) identify the major triads; the lowercase roman numerals (ii, iii, and vi) identify the minor triads; and the symbol ° added to a lowercase number (vii°) identifies the diminished triad. A subscript 7 following the roman numeral means that the interval of a seventh has been added above the root. The key is indicated at the beginning of the analysis: an uppercase letter for a major key, a lowercase letter for a minor key.

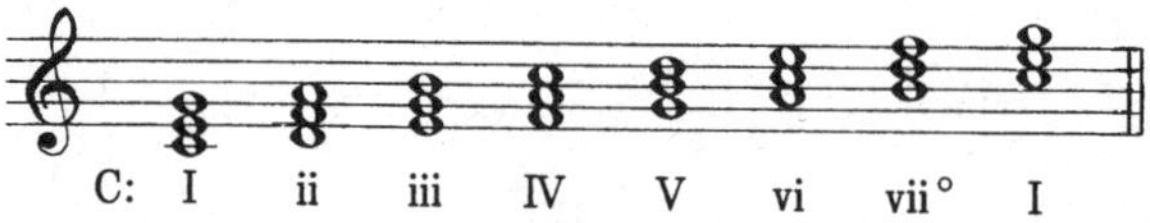

EXERCISE 10•15

Use roman numerals to label the triads in the following major keys.

1. 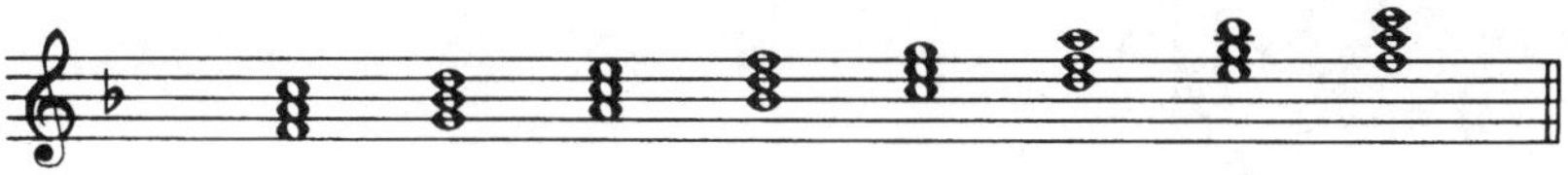

F: __ __ __ __ __ __ __ __

2. 

G: __ __ __ __ __ __ __ __

3. 

D: __ __ __ __ __ __ __ __

4. 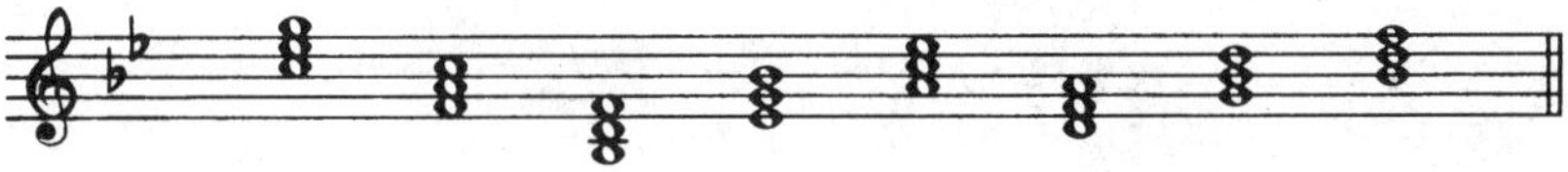

B♭: __ __ __ __ __ __ __ __

5. 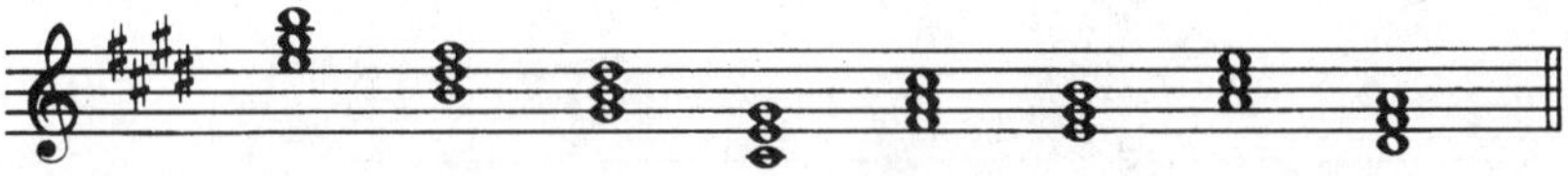

E: __ __ __ __ __ __ __ __

The triads built from the harmonic minor version of the minor scale (with the raised leading tone borrowed from major) are labeled as follows:

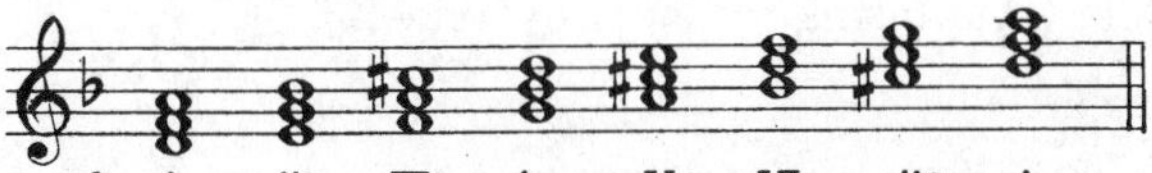

d: i ii° III or III+ iv V VI vii° i

The symbol + beside an uppercase roman numeral (III+) indicates an augmented triad. Although we need practice in writing this triad, remember that the augmented triad is not used that frequently by composers.

EXERCISE 10•16

Use roman numerals to label the triads in the following minor keys.

1. 

f♯: ___ ___ ___ ___ ___ ___ ___ ___

2. 

d: ___ ___ ___ ___ ___ ___ ___ ___

3. 

e: ___ ___ ___ ___ ___ ___ ___ ___

4. 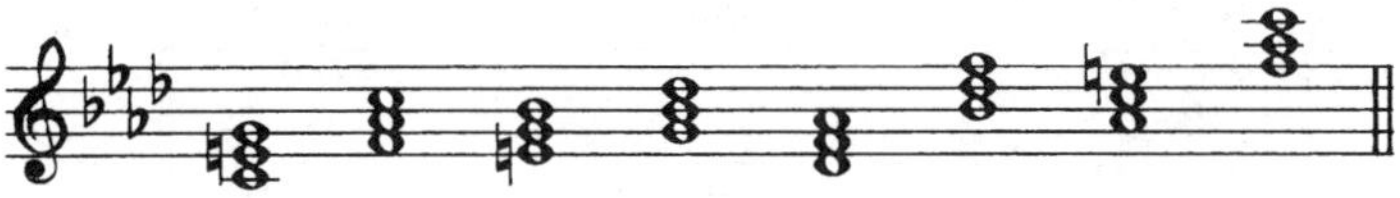

f: ___ ___ ___ ___ ___ ___ ___ ___

5. 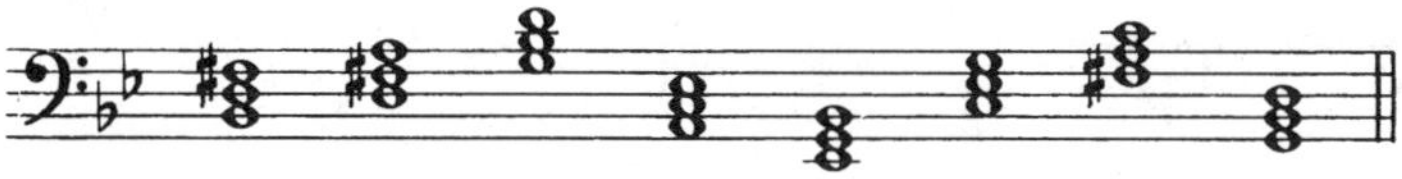

g: ___ ___ ___ ___ ___ ___ ___ ___

Every major scale and every minor scale produce the same patterns of triads; that is, the quality of each triad remains constant no matter what the key. The information given in the following chart will prove extremely useful in writing triads. Study it carefully before completing the next exercise.

Major Keys	*Quality of Triads*	*Natural Minor Keys*	*Changes to Natural Minor with a Borrowed Leading Tone*
I, IV, V	major	III, VI, VII	V
ii, iii, vi	minor	i, iv, v	
vii°	diminished	ii°	vii°
none	augmented		(possible III^{+} seldom replaces the major III)

EXERCISE 10•17

Write the indicated triads for each given key. Use accidentals rather than key signatures.

1. 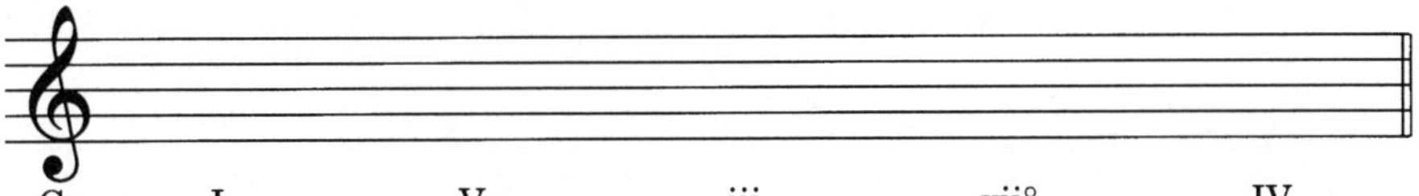

G: I V_6 iii vii° IV

2. 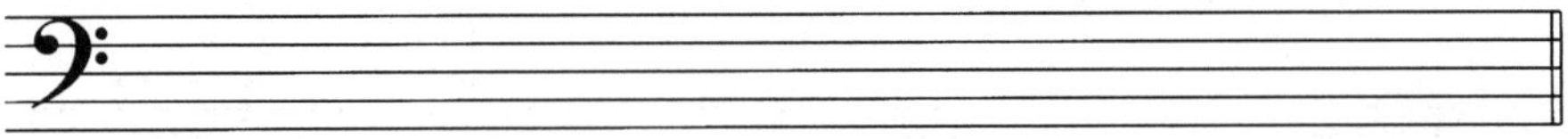

c: V i ii° III VI

3. 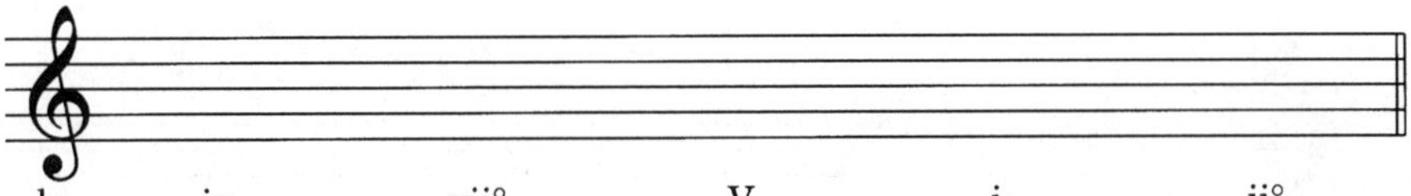

b: iv vii° V i_6 ii°

4. 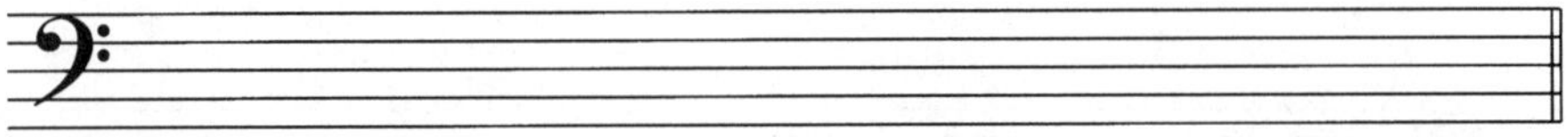

c♯: III VI ii° V iv

5. 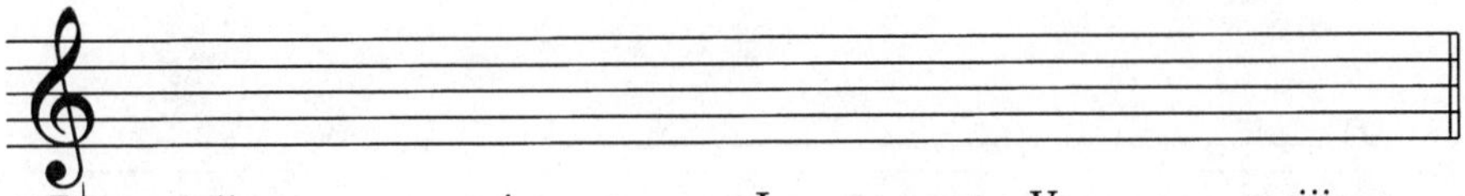

D♭: ii vi I^6_4 V iii

6. 

g♯: III VI ii° V iv

7. 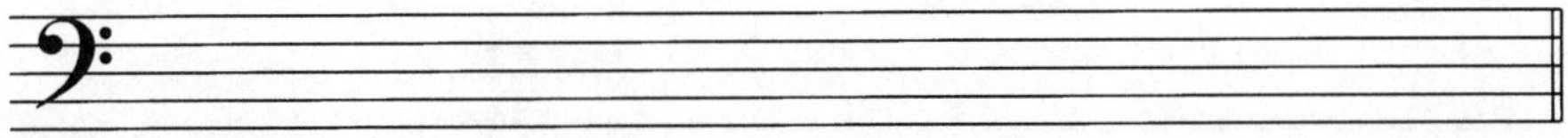

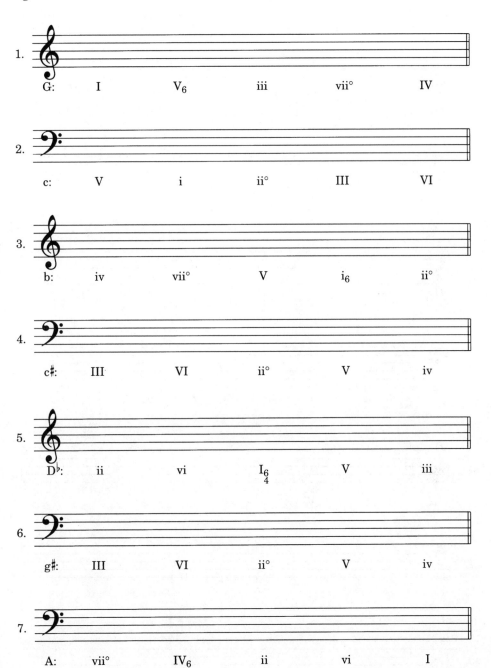

A: vii° IV_6 ii vi I

8. 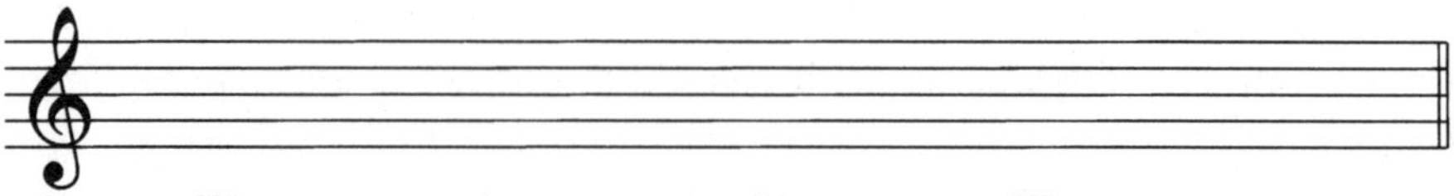

f: III i vii° VI ii°

9. 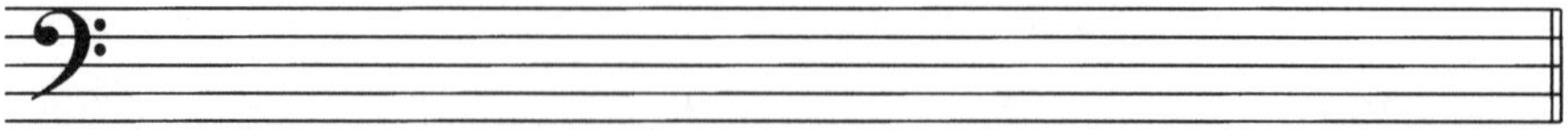

E♭: V vi IV iii I^{6}_{4}

10. 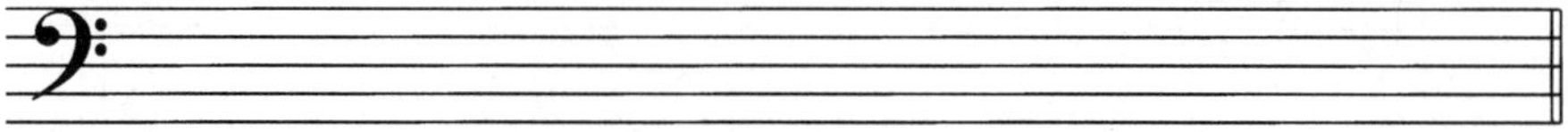

b♭: VI vii° i III+ iv

11. 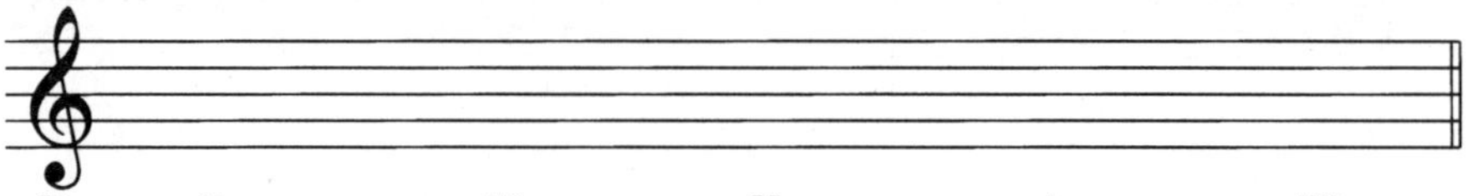

D: ii_{6} vii° V vi IV

12. 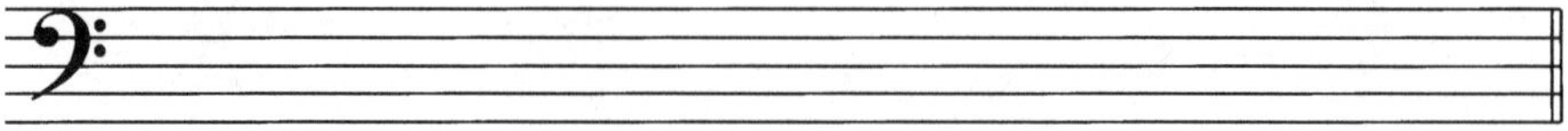

d♯: V ii° VI III iv

13. 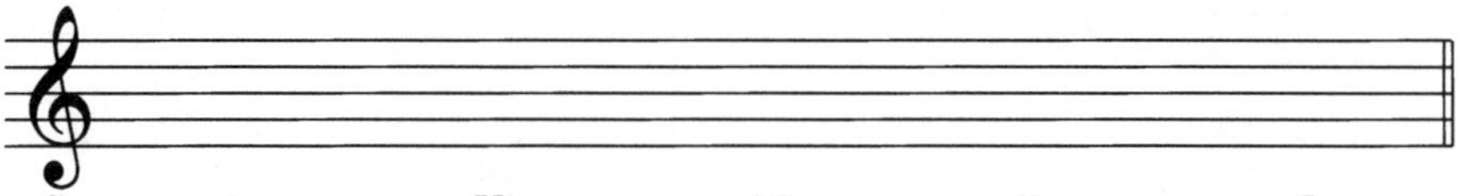

C: vi V vii° ii^{6}_{4} I

14. 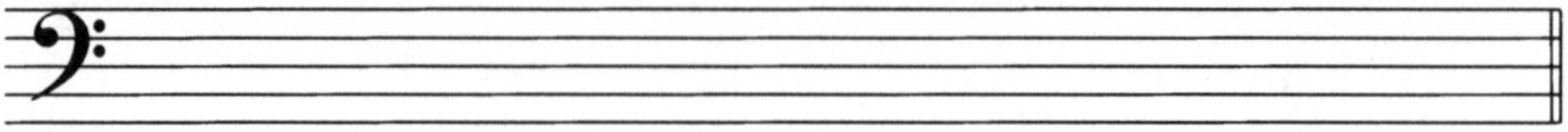

A♭: iii IV vi V vii°

15. 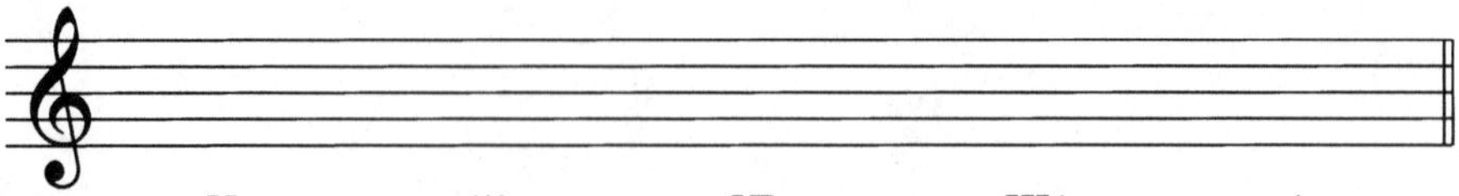

g: V ii° VI_{6} III+ iv

Pitch Name Identification

In the system of pitch name identification, the letter name of the triad is substituted for the roman numeral. While this no longer indicates the relationship of the various triads to the key, it does convey triad information more directly and, therefore, is useful in a variety of performing situations.

This system of labeling supplies both the name of the triad and its quality. An uppercase letter indicates major triads (D, G, A); an uppercase letter plus a lowercase *m* indicates minor triads (E*m*, F♯*m*, B*m*); an uppercase letter with a + or with the abbreviation *aug.* indicates augmented triads (G+); and an uppercase letter with a ° or with *dim.* indicates diminished triads (C♯°, F♯°, D♯°).

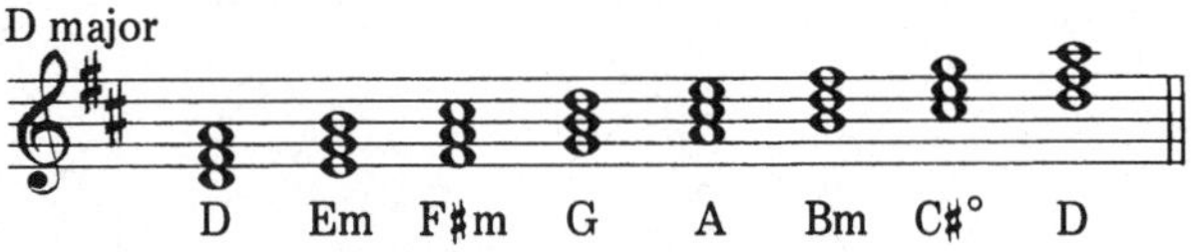

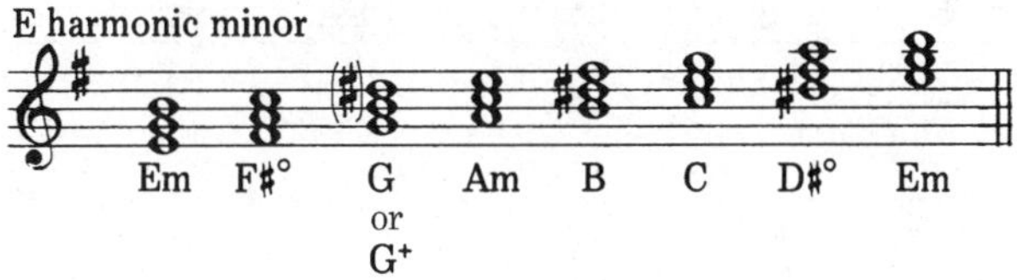

One current style of jazz notation indicates a minor chord with a minus sign (–) instead of a lowercase *m*. In this system, F♯–, B–, and A– are minor triads. The other chord symbols remain the same.

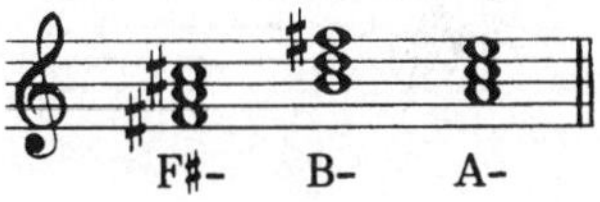

EXERCISE 10•18

Label the following triads using pitch name identification.

1. 

2. 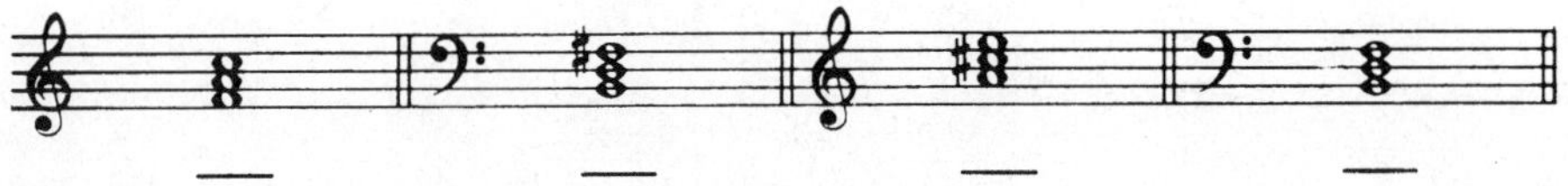

3. 

4. 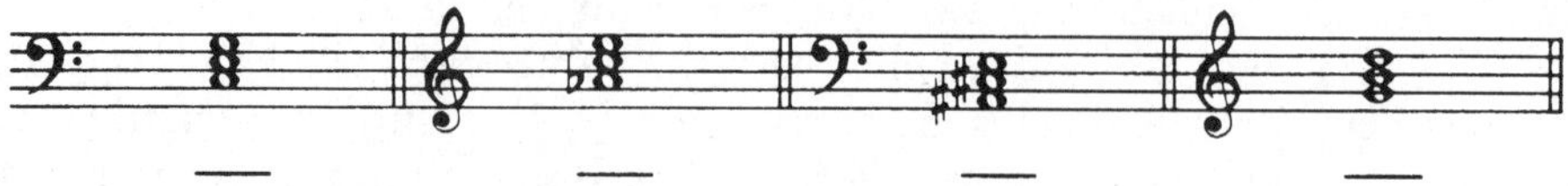

5. 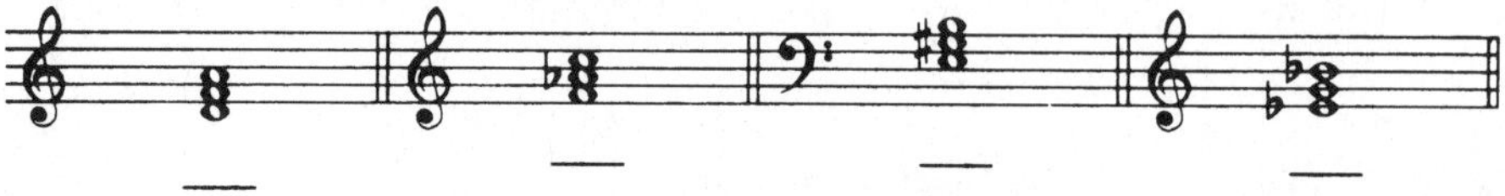

6. 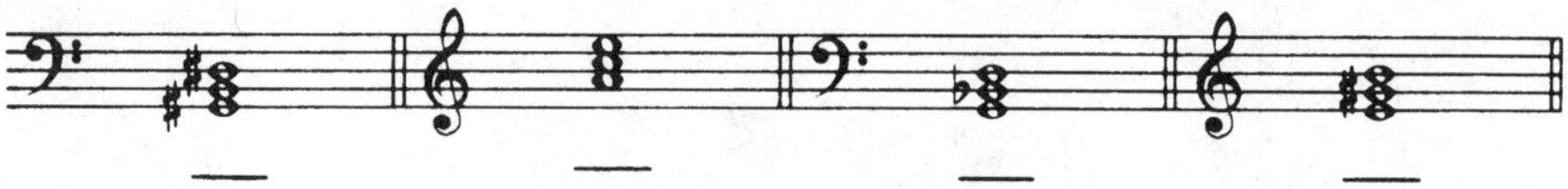

EXERCISE 10•19

Write the triads indicated below. All triads should be in root position.

1. 

2. 

3. 

4. 

G♯° | Fm | G♯m | Am

5. 

A♯° | A° | Bm | E°

Musical Problem

The following composition has been analyzed by the pitch name identification system. As a class, discuss the kinds of information this analytical system conveys to the performer.

"St. James Infirmary"

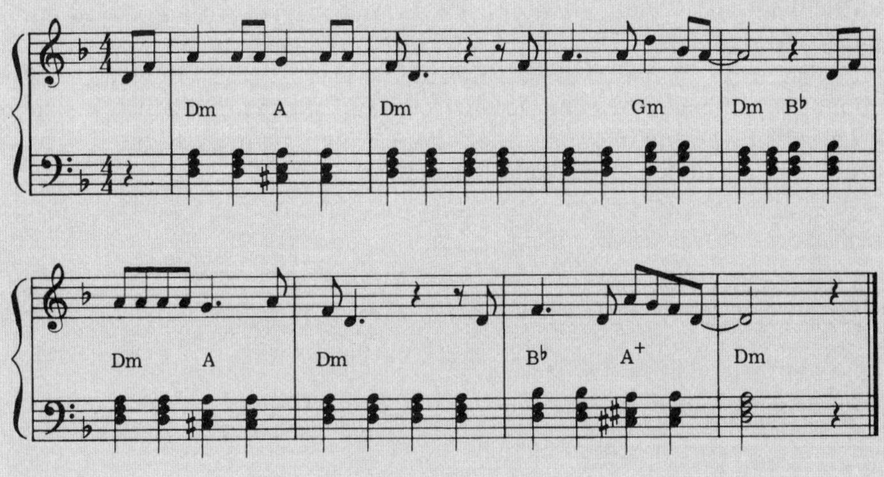

The Dominant Seventh Chord

So far we have dealt only with the triad—a three-note chord. The triad is, after all, the fundamental structure of tonal harmony. But music is not made up exclusively of triads. Composers of the past and of the present sometimes add a fourth pitch, and occasionally even a fifth and sixth pitch, to the triad. And while some styles of music, such as folk music or early rock-n-roll, function primarily with triads, other styles, such as recent jazz or the Romantic compositions of Chopin and Liszt, utilize four-, five-, and six-note chords extensively. But no matter what the style, when extra pitches are added to the triad it is always for the purpose of increasing the harmonic tension.

Even though the study of chords more complex than the triad is beyond the scope of this book, we need to take a brief look at the most frequently used four-note chord—the **dominant seventh chord**. Because it is used so extensively, it is sometimes difficult to find an example of tonal music that *doesn't* contain at least one dominant seventh chord. In this chapter, you will learn how to write it and recognize it.

All seventh chords are so called because the fourth note creates the arithmetic distance of a seventh above the root of the chord.

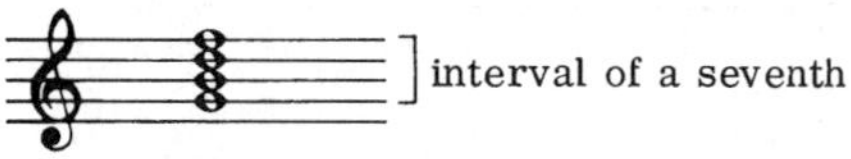

Although seventh chords can be built on any degree of the scale, the one built on the dominant, that is, the dominant seventh chord, is used more frequently than any of the other possibilities. This is because the additional note enhances the harmonic tension already inherent in the dominant triad.

The dominant seventh chord is *always* a major triad with an added minor seventh above the root. This is true for both major and minor keys. This constant structure—a major triad with an added minor seventh—is what gives the dominant seventh chord its characteristic sound. Notice in the following example that when working in a minor key, the leading tone must always be raised in order to create a major triad on the dominant.

Dominant Seventh Chord in B♭ Major

Dominant Seventh Chord in b♭ minor

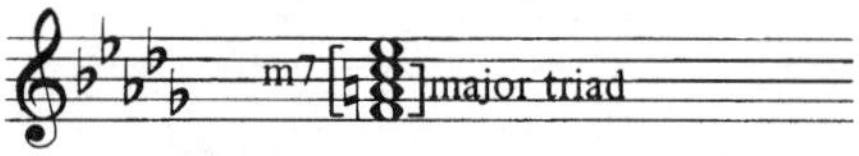

The dominant seventh chord is identified by the notation V_7, in which the roman numeral V indicates the triad built on the fifth, or dominant, note of the scale, and the subscript 7 indicates the interval of a seventh. In harmonic analysis, both symbols are necessary in order to identify correctly the dominant seventh chord. In pitch name identification, the symbol F_7 would be used for both of the previous examples.

Before beginning Exercise 10-20 and the Musical Problems that follow, play the following two patterns on the piano. Notice how the dominant seventh chord (V_7) produces an increase in harmonic tension. Listen to the difference between the V and V_7 several times. The dominant seventh sound is an extremely common sound in all styles of tonal music and one that you should begin to listen for and recognize.

C: V I

C: V_7 I

EXERCISE 10•20

Practice writing dominant seventh chords in root position in the keys indicated. When dealing with a minor key, remember to use the harmonic minor version. Remember also that the dominant seventh chord is always a major triad with an added minor seventh.

EXAMPLE:

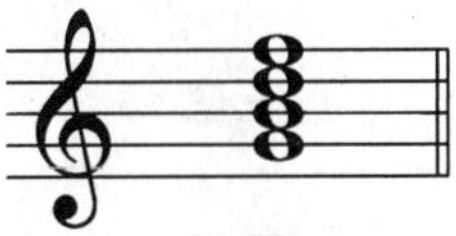

C: V_7

1. 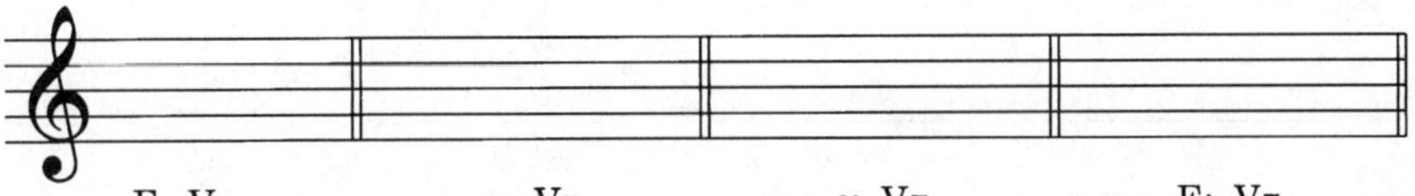

F: V_7 a: V_7 c: V_7 E: V_7

2. 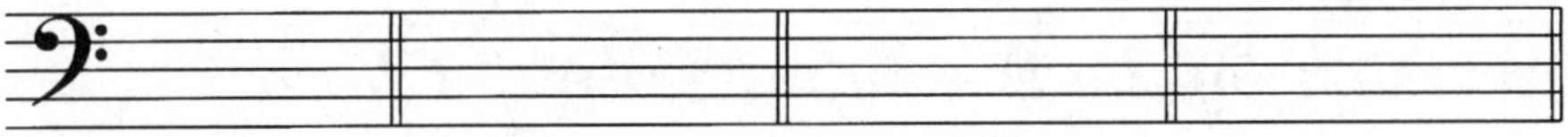

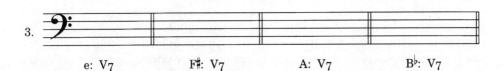

g: V_7 D: V_7 b: V_7 D♭: V_7

3. 

e: V_7 F♯: V_7 A: V_7 B♭: V_7

4. 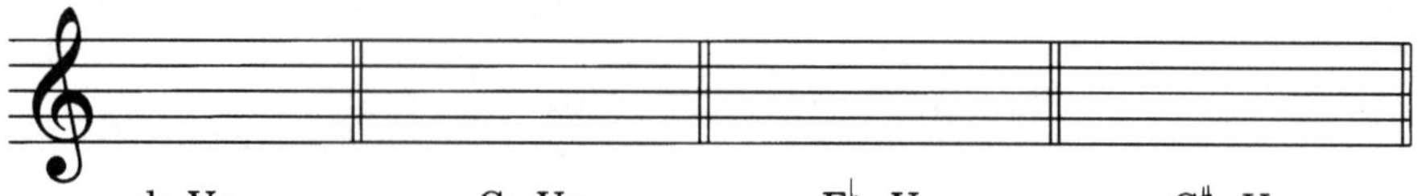

d: V7 G: V7 E♭: V7 C♯: V7

5. 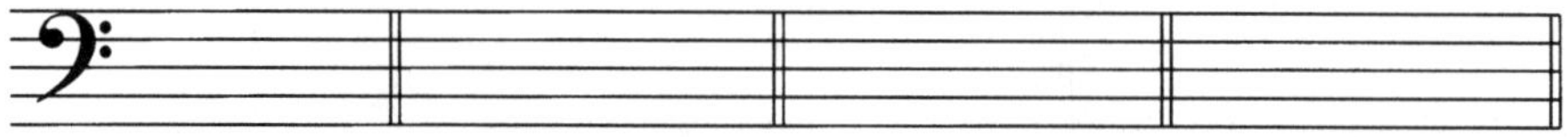

B: V7 A♭: V7 G♭: V7 f: V7

Musical Problem

You should learn to hear the difference between a seventh chord and a triad. Your instructor will play various lines from the preceding exercise. Some chords will be played as seventh chords, others as triads. In the following space, indicate whether you hear a seventh chord or a triad.

1. ____________ ____________ ____________ ____________

2. ____________ ____________ ____________ ____________

3. ____________ ____________ ____________ ____________

4. ____________ ____________ ____________ ____________

5. ____________ ____________ ____________ ____________

Inversions of the Dominant Seventh Chord

Although it is really beyond the scope of this book, you should be aware that dominant seventh chords can be inverted just as triads can. Knowing this will enable you to recognize these chords more easily in musical situations.

Remember that triads have two possible inversions beyond root position. But, since the dominant seventh chord has four notes, there are three possible inversions of it beyond root position. Notice in the following diagram that the name of the inversion is determined by the lowest sounding note just as in the inversion of triads. First inversion has the third of the chord as the lowest sounding note, second inversion has the fifth as the lowest sounding note, and third inversion has the seventh of the chord as the lowest sounding note. Notice also that the numbers refer to the intervals above the lowest note, as they do with triads.

Root position | 1st inversion | 2nd inversion | 3rd inversion

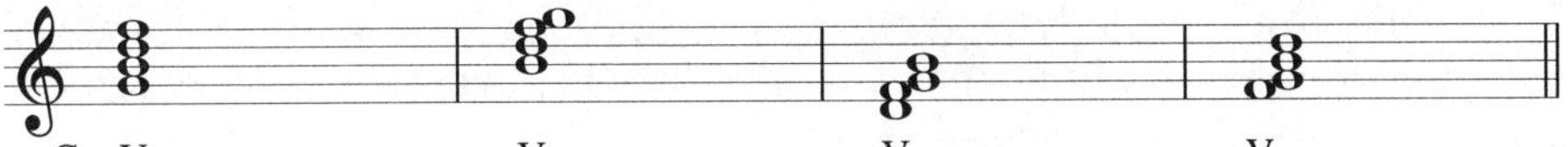

C: $V\begin{smallmatrix}7\\5\\3\end{smallmatrix}$ | $V\begin{smallmatrix}6\\5\\3\end{smallmatrix}$ | $V\begin{smallmatrix}6\\4\\3\end{smallmatrix}$ | $V\begin{smallmatrix}6\\4\\2\end{smallmatrix}$

And just as with triads, a shorthand system of labeling has developed that indicates only the essential intervals above the lowest note. In the actual analysis of music, or in figured bass, these are the numbers that you will see.

Root position | 1st inversion | 2nd inversion | 3rd inversion

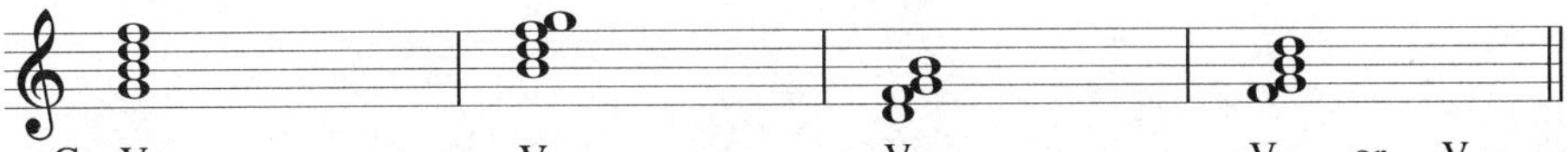

C: V_7 | $V\begin{smallmatrix}6\\5\end{smallmatrix}$ | $V\begin{smallmatrix}4\\3\end{smallmatrix}$ | $V\begin{smallmatrix}4\\2\end{smallmatrix}$ or V_2

EXERCISE 10•21

Practice writing inversions of the following dominant seventh chords. Remember that the dominant seventh chord is always a major triad with an added minor seventh. When working in minor keys, this means that you will have to use the harmonic minor version of the scale.

EXAMPLE:

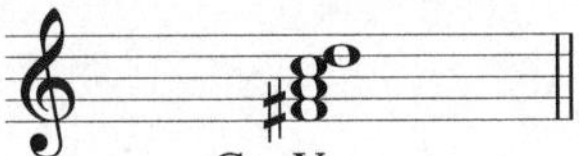

G: $V\begin{smallmatrix}6\\5\end{smallmatrix}$

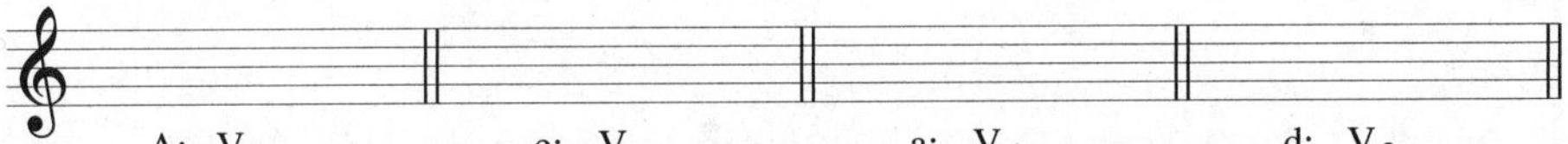

A: $V\begin{smallmatrix}6\\5\end{smallmatrix}$ | e: $V\begin{smallmatrix}4\\2\end{smallmatrix}$ | a: $V\begin{smallmatrix}4\\3\end{smallmatrix}$ | d: V_2

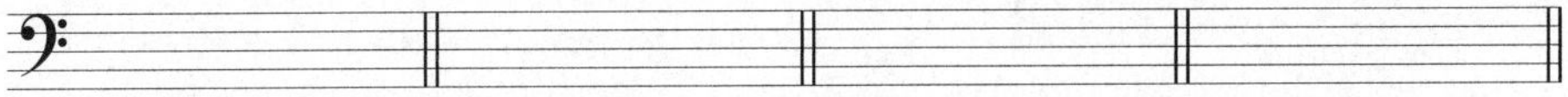

B♭: $V\begin{smallmatrix}4\\3\end{smallmatrix}$ | D: $V\begin{smallmatrix}4\\2\end{smallmatrix}$ | E: $V\begin{smallmatrix}6\\5\end{smallmatrix}$ | C♯: $V\begin{smallmatrix}4\\3\end{smallmatrix}$

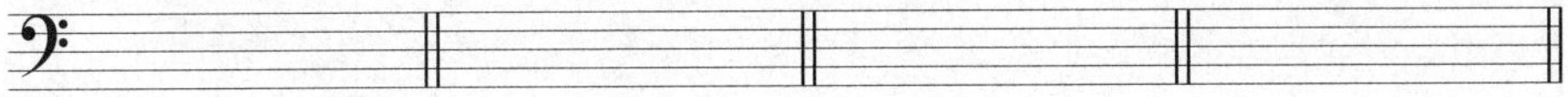

g: V_2 | F♯: $V\begin{smallmatrix}4\\3\end{smallmatrix}$ | c: $V\begin{smallmatrix}6\\5\end{smallmatrix}$ | F: $V\begin{smallmatrix}6\\5\end{smallmatrix}$

Musical Problem

The following two excerpts illustrate the roman numeral analysis of music. Pitches that are not part of the chord (i.e., nonharmonic pitches) are circled. Notice also that the chords occasionally occur in an inversion, rather than in root position, and that they can take several beats or even a measure to reveal all their pitches.

Listen to each example several times and study the analysis. What kind of information does it give you about the individual chords? About the progression of chords? About how the chords relate to the melody? In class, discuss the information that roman numeral analysis does and does not provide. How is this information useful to a performer?

"Blow Ye Winds in the Morning"

"Wayfaring Stranger"

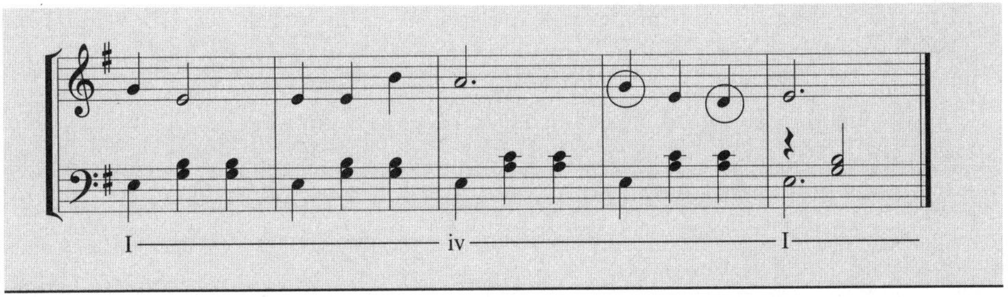

Triads in a Musical Context

In actual pieces of music, triads don't always appear as vertical chords. Composers often choose other types of settings for triads, particularly when they want the harmony to make a strong contribution to the horizontal motion of the piece. So, it is important for you not only to be aware that triads can appear in music in a variety of settings but also to be able to recognize the more common types. To help you begin, we will look briefly at the two most important ways in which composers have traditionally set triads: block chords and arpeggiations.

Block Chords

The following is an example of a composition using triads as block chords.

Schubert, *Valses nobles*

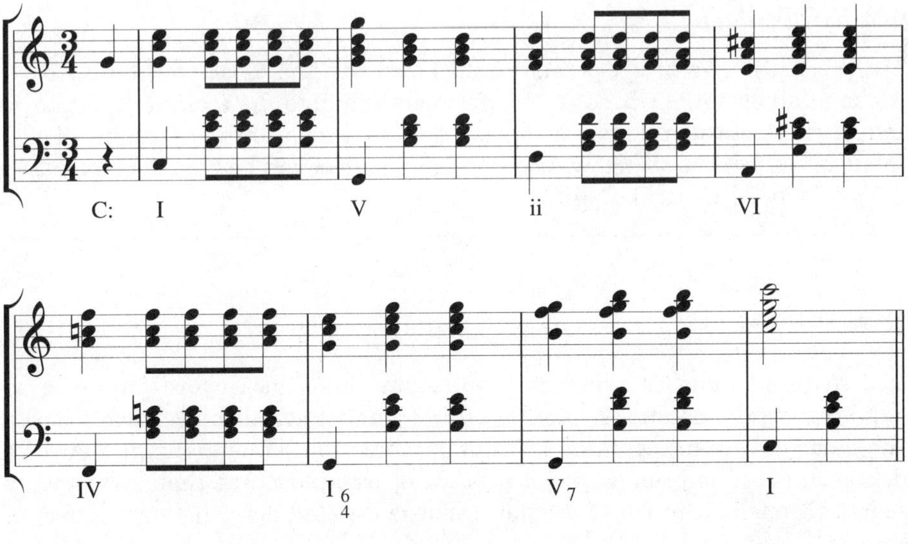

Notice in this example how vertical the harmony looks on the page. And, when listening to it performed, notice how your attention is drawn to this vertical quality more than to any horizontal motion. We hear these chords almost as separate entities even though, simultaneously, we are aware of their linear relationship to each other.

This special quality of block chords, to be able to emphasize both the vertical and the horizontal dimensions of the music, can be seen in the following pattern, which has been a staple in popular music since the 1950s. Notice how the vertical, almost percussive, qualities of the music are enhanced by the repetition of each chord.

> ### *Musical Problem*
>
> Make a list of five or six popular songs that use the block-chord style of accompaniment illustrated in the previous example. As a class, listen to two or three of them. Is you attention always drawn to the harmonic element in a similar way? How does the tempo affect the harmonic element, particularly its vertical qualities?

Arpeggiations

Often, composers choose arpeggiations rather than block chords in order to avoid directing the listener's attention too strongly toward the vertical aspects of the harmony. An arpeggiated accompaniment is an accompanying figure in which each chord is broken into a pattern of isolated notes that is generally repeated throughout much of the piece. These isolated notes have the effect of spreading the chord out over time, thus causing our attention to move linearly. Here are a few of the simpler arpeggiation patterns.

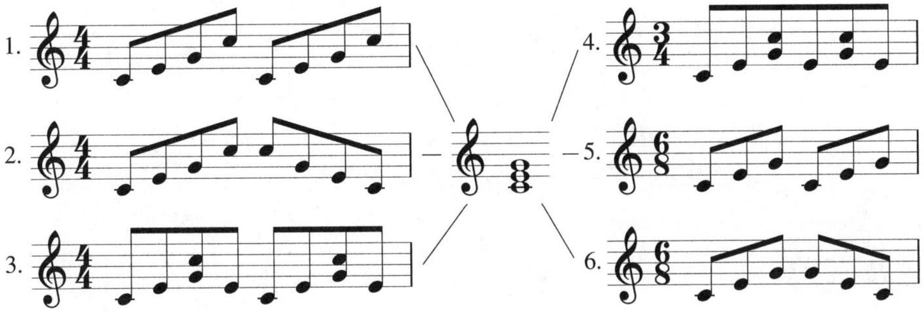

The following are several musical examples using some of these simple arpeggiations, or **broken chord patterns,** as they are sometimes called. The block chords on which these patterns are based are written below each line of music so that you can see more easily how each chord unfolds in time through the arpeggiations.

Clementi, "Rondo" from *Sonatina in G Major,* Op. 36, No. 5

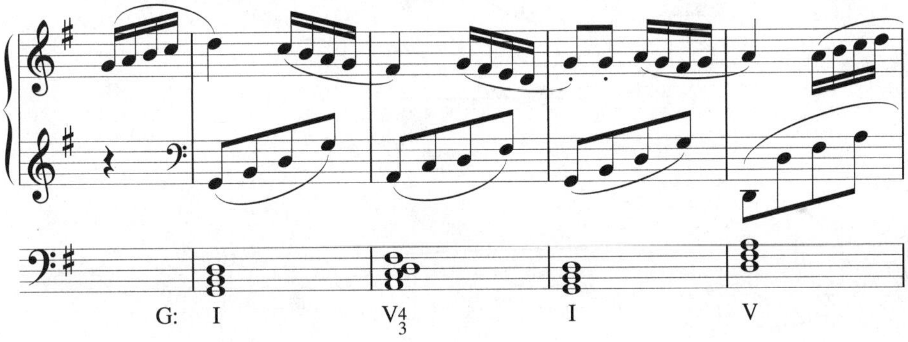

Beethoven, "Menuetto" from *Sonatina in D Major*

Clementi, "Rondo" from *Sonatina in F Major,* Op. 36, No. 4

EXERCISE 10•22

The chord progression that follows is written in block chords. In the space provided, create an arpeggiated version of this pattern suitable for piano or guitar. You may invent your own, or use one of the above examples as a model. If you don't play piano or guitar, ask someone who does to play your pattern for you.

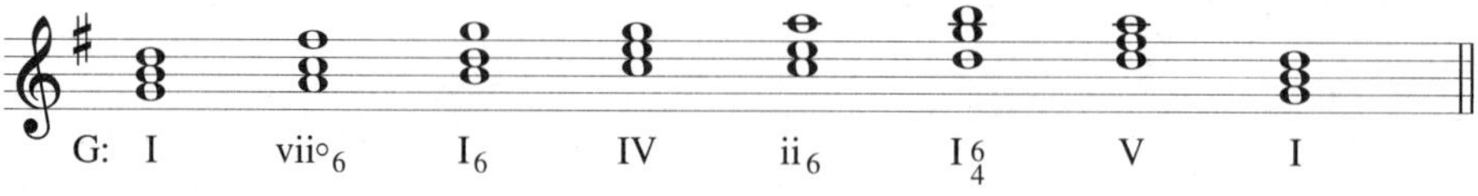

Composers throughout the centuries, both classical and popular ones, have used arpeggiated chords—and almost always for the same reason: it weakens the vertical qualities of the harmony, and replacess them with a linear quality that helps to move the music forward. This contribution is so important that chord arpeggiations appear in almost all musical styles and at almost any tempo.

Musical Problem

The ability to identify chord progressions, or even individual chords, by ear is extremely useful. But for people with little background or practice at this it can be extremely frustrating, particularly at first. Unless your ear is unusually well developed, it is unreasonable to expect that you could begin by taking the chords off a recording of your favorite piece. This is an extremely sophisticated skill that only comes to most people with consistent practice. While this may be one of your goals, it is not where you begin.

If you are just beginning, keep in mind these three points as you practice this musical problem.

1. You must practice consistently in order to improve. Ear training is not unlike preparing for an athletic event.
2. Success seems to come in plateaus; don't be overly concerned if you don't appear to show improvement every day or even every week.
3. It is better, and easier, to build on success. Ideally, your success rate should be in the area of 80 to 85 percent. If it is much lower, you are probably attempting material that is too difficult for you. This can actually slow your progress.

With this in mind, try the following:

Your teacher or another student from the class will play a major or minor scale as a reference. Then he or she will play a triad that is either the tonic or the dominant triad of that key. In the spaces provided, indicate which triad is being played.

1. ________________	5. ________________
2. ________________	6. ________________
3. ________________	7. ________________
4. ________________	8. ________________

Now try this using three triads—the tonic, dominant, and submediant. It helps to remember which triads are major and which are minor.

1. ________________	5. ________________
2. ________________	6. ________________
3. ________________	7. ________________
4. ________________	8. ________________

Finally, see if you can correctly identify one of four different triads—tonic, dominant, submediant, and subdominant.

1. ________________	5. ________________
2. ________________	6. ________________
3. ________________	7. ________________
4. ________________	8. ________________

Focus

The triad is the foundation of Western tonal music. On one level, the triad is a simple musical structure; it is this basic characteristic that has been the main subject of this chapter. On another level, however, the triad is a subtle and complicated musical pattern, for triads in combination can express a wide range of musical emotions. From before the time of Bach and up to the present, composers—of jazz and popular music as well as concert music—have conceived of and realized most of their musical ideas through the use of triads.

On one level, the triad is a simple musical structure that can be manipulated, as in this chapter's exercises, to produce simple right or wrong answers: You identify the triad correctly, or you don't; the triad is spelled correctly, or it isn't. This type of drill is absolutely essential for every musician, but don't mistake it for musical artistry.

On a musical level, there are no absolutely right or wrong answers. Most harmonic problems, for instance, have more than one correct solution. Composers faced with such ambiguous musical situations must often make choices that subtly affect the character of their work. Good composers seem to make the right choices consistently. Others write "theoretically correct" music that may seem good but is uninspired.

Chapter 11

Tonality

The first ten chapters of this book have focused, one at a time, on the individual elements of music. Essentially, our work so far has consisted of gaining an understanding of musical facts. Now, we need to begin the process of unifying this information—these facts about music—into an understanding of how "real" music works theoretically. Although, ultimately, this understanding of music is a lifetime goal, or at least several more semesters of work if you plan to continue studying music, we can begin to acquire this information and, at the same time, draw our work in this book to a logical conclusion.

The material covered in this chapter deals with tonality, that somewhat elusive concept whose definition most Western musicians take for granted. In its simplest sense, tonality is tonal music, that is, music in which both the melody and the harmony come from major or minor scales. But in a more subjective, personal sense, tonality is also that unique ability of musical tones, in both the scale and the actual music, to appear to relate themselves to one another. To our ears, these "tonal" pitches establish a hierarchy in which one tone becomes the focal point, the point of rest, the tonic, around which the other scale degrees rotate and interact, with varying degrees of tension and importance. This interrelationship of tonal scale degrees, as you will learn from future courses in music, regulates not only the details of music—consonance and dissonance, phrase structure, and cadences—but the overall form, or musical shape, of each work as well. For our work, we will concentrate on five of the most basic aspects of tonality: tendency tones, the dominant/tonic relationship, cadences, simple chord progressions, and harmonizing a melody.

Of course, we can only begin to explore these topics. The material covered in this chapter generally needs quite a bit more time to work through and absorb than any of the previous chapters. But if this is your *only* class in music theory, then this chapter will show you some practical applications for the information you have gained. If you plan further study of theory, then this chapter will introduce many of the concepts you will encounter in your later studies. Either way, it is important to remember that this is only the beginning.

Tendency Tones

In our earlier study of scales, you probably noticed that not all pitches of the major scale sound equal. That is, some pitches, like the tonic, appear completely at rest, while others, like the dominant or the leading tone, sound active and full of tension. You can experience this feeling of tension for yourself by singing an ascending major scale and stopping on the seventh scale degree. The desire you probably feel to complete the scale is strong because the leading tone is an active scale degree requiring, to our ears, resolution to another tone, in this case the more restful tonic.

You can experience a similar sensation by singing the major scale again, this time descending, and stopping on the supertonic. The second scale degree is also active, but to a lesser extent. Although not as powerful, it too appears to want to resolve, in this case also to the tonic.

If you wish, you can repeat this experiment, stopping on other tones of the scale and deciding their degree of activity and the direction of their attraction, or pull, toward other notes. What you will discover if you do this is that not all tones seem attracted directly to the tonic. Some, such as the subdominant, seem to pull equally toward the dominant. Others seem to pull toward other places, but not nearly as strongly as does the dominant-to-tonic attraction.

This apparent attraction of various scale degrees to one another is referred to as **tendency tones.** That is, certain pitches within a scale or melody have a *tendency* to move toward other tones. This idea is important, because it explains, in part, how melodies appear to move from one point in time to another. The sense of melodic motion we experience comes partially from melodic lines moving through differing levels of activity and tension toward a resolution on the tonic. The same concept holds true for pitches in the harmony. There, the "tendency" of pitches to pull in certain directions helps to give the harmony a feeling of movement between points of tension and places of rest.

At one time, some theorists believed that these tendencies, or tendency tones as they are usually called, were so strong that a chart could be made of how each scale degree above the tonic should move and resolve. But actual music is always more complicated and subtle than the charts that try to explain it, and these charts of tendency tones could never really be applied with much success to the melodies or harmonies composers had written. Nevertheless, the idea of tendency tones is still valid. What is important to remember is that there is a strong relationship between all the tones of the scale, both among themselves and with the tonic. Furthermore, this relationship allows the tonic to become the primary tone—the center of gravity—to which all the other tones seem to be related and to want, eventually, to resolve. Perhaps imagining an analogy with our solar system, with each planet at varying distances from the sun in the center, will be useful in understanding the unique part each scale degree plays in our perception of musical motion, as well as in the feeling of tension and resolution so important to tonal music.

Musical Problem

As a class, sing through any of the following melodies several times. Discuss the active pitches and the points of rest within each melody. To do this, try stopping at various places as you sing, and discussing what that particular tone contributes to the forward motion or resolution of the music. Remember that each scale degree contributes its own unique quality. Remember also that although this experience can be difficult to verbalize and discuss at times, our ears make these fine distinctions repeatedly and automatically.

1. "The Simpsons" TV show theme _____
2. "Titanic" theme _____
3. "South Park" TV show theme _____
4. "Star Wars" theme _____
5. "2001" theme _____
6. "Moon River" _____

The Dominant/Tonic Relationship

Beyond the tension and release inherent in the movement of all tonal melodies, a sense of forward motion and resolution also exists in tonal harmony. Nowhere is this more evident than in the simplest of chord progressions—the dominant to tonic relationship. This relationship—the dominant triad moving to the tonic triad—is, without doubt, the most frequently used progression in tonal music. The reason this is true is because of the strong gravitational attraction established between V and I. This relationship is so strong that these two triads, by themselves, can clearly establish the tonal center, or key, of a work.

To understand why this is true, it is important to consider the dominant triad for a moment. It includes not only the fifth degree of the scale, but also the leading tone and the supertonic. Remember from our discussion of tendency tones that these are all active scale degrees that, to our ears, appear to need resolution. Remember also from our work with triads that a fourth pitch—a minor seventh above the root—is often added to the dominant triad to make it sound even more active. Both the dominant triad and the dominant seventh chord, then, are active sounds, full of tension. All of this tension is released, or resolved, however, when the dominant triad (or dominant seventh chord) moves to the tonic triad, the point of rest in tonal music. This movement between tension and resolution gives the harmony, as it does the melody, a feeling of forward motion and a sense of centering within the key.

In the following example, a French folk song, notice that the entire melody can be accompanied by only tonic and dominant harmonies.

"Sur le Pont d'Avignon"

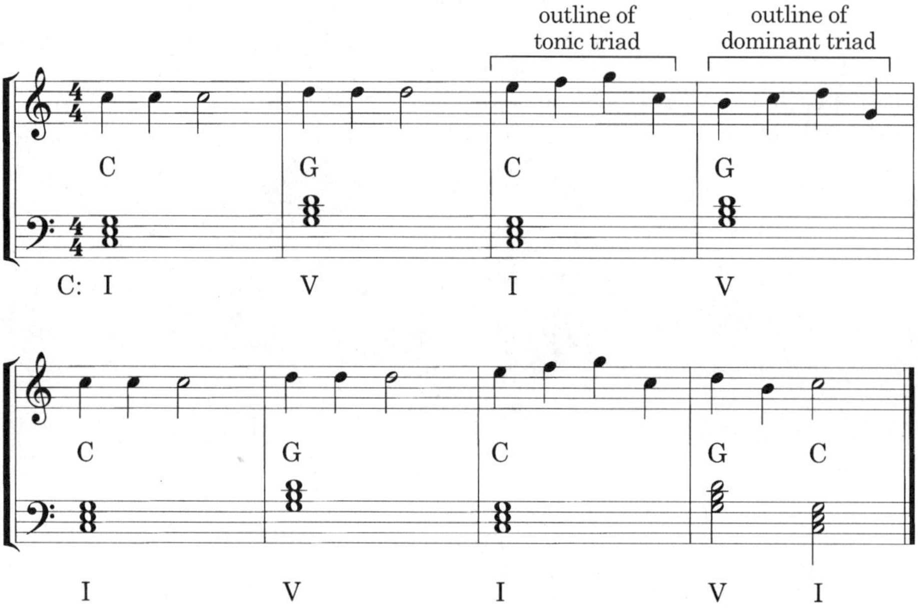

Notice also that both the melody and the harmony parallel each other. That is, when the triad changes, the melody also moves primarily to pitches that make up the triad (measures 3 and 4, for example). This movement between tonic and dominant in both the melody and the harmony, and the tension and resolution that are generated, are fundamental to the establishment of tonality and are the basis for all harmonic movement in tonal music, no matter how complicated.

Musical Problem

Ask someone in class to play or sing the melody of the previous example while you sing the root of each tonic or dominant triad. Can you feel the tension of the V chord resolve to the I?

Now try the opposite, with you singing the melody while someone else plays the I and V triads on the piano. Can you feel how the melody and harmony support each other?

Remember that this is a simple example with only one level of tension: the dominant triad. More complicated pieces of music will have many more subtle levels of tension, made possible by the availability of other chords (made with other scale degrees) from which to choose.

Cadences

Perhaps the most important thing to remember at this point is that chords do not move around randomly throughout a piece of music. Instead, they are arranged into phrases, following the outline of the melody, in much the same way that a paragraph of prose consists of several sentences, each made up of a complete thought. Furthermore, each phrase of the melody and harmony appears to come to its own point of rest, in the same way that sentences end with a period. And like a sentence, which can also end with a question mark or an exclamation point, these points of rest, or cadences as they are called, can vary in their strength and feeling of completeness. Understanding this concept of the cadence as a musical stopping point, and identifying the types of cadences that most frequently occur, is our next step toward understanding tonality.

A **cadence** is a momentary or permanent point of rest. Cadences occur both within a composition and at its conclusion; those that appear in the middle of a piece are always at the ends of musical phrases. A mistake many people make at first is to believe that V to I creates a cadence every time it occurs. This is not true. Cadences occur only at the ends of phrases.

Cadences can occur in both the harmony and the rhythm of a composition. (We will not go into rhythmic cadences here.) The **harmonic cadence** consists of two chords. There are four types of harmonic cadences that occur most frequently in tonal music: the *authentic cadence,* the *plagal cadence,* the *half cadence,* and the *deceptive cadence.* Each cadence is a different formula of two chords. And because this is so, each cadence can be heard as a *different* level of tension and resolution.

The Authentic Cadence

The **authentic cadence** in a major key is the chord pattern V–I; in a minor key it is the chord pattern V–i.

Authentic cadence, major key

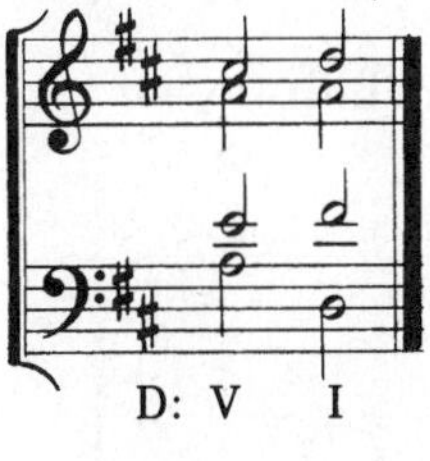

D: V I

Authentic cadence, minor key

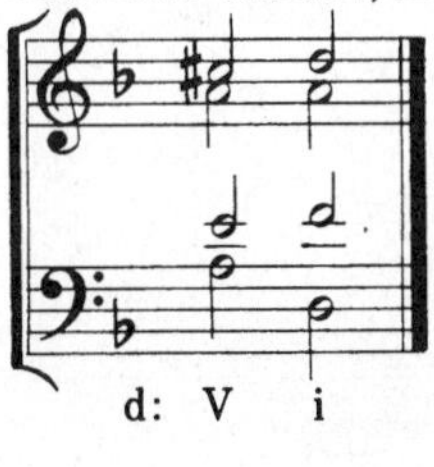

d: V i

What makes a cadence work? A cadence gives the impression of stopping musically because of the interaction of the melody, the harmony, and the rhythm. Notice that while the chord pattern V–I can occur many times, as it does in the previous example, "Sur le Pont d'Avignon," not all occurrences create a cadence. Notice in the following examples how the melody, harmony, and rhythm work together to produce a strong feeling of conclusion. The authentic cadence gives the strongest sense of conclusion of all the cadential patterns.

Hymn: Dundee

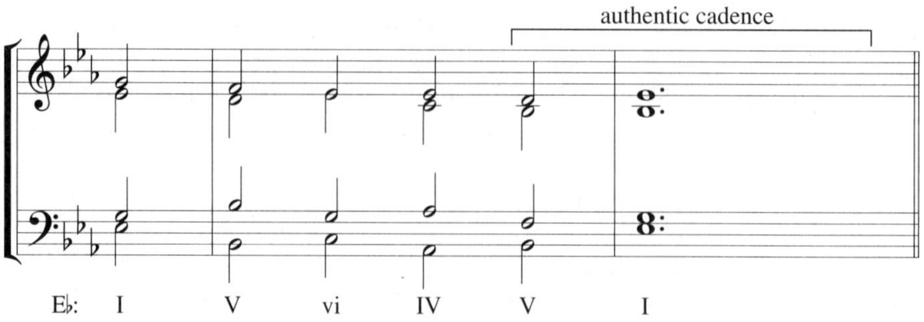

The authentic cadence is considered the strongest cadence because the sense of resolution—from the tension of the dominant triad to the restful nature of the tonic triad—feels most complete. This sense of resolution can be made to appear even stronger if the tension of the dominant triad is increased. As we learned in the previous chapter, this can be accomplished by the use of the dominant seventh chord. The additional note, located a minor seventh above the root, adds extra tension to the dominant sound which, in turn, is released with a stronger feeling of completeness when it moves to the tonic. Although dominant seventh chords can be used anywhere within a chord progression that seems appropriate, their most frequent use over the past three hundred years has been in the authentic cadence. Play and listen to the following two examples of authentic cadences that use the dominant seventh chords. Compare these examples to the previous one that used the dominant triad. Notice that the tension/release qualities of the cadence seem heightened when the dominant seventh chord appears.

Pay particular attention to the sound of the authentic cadence and try to remember it. If you are successful, you will begin to notice how frequently it occurs in the music you hear around you in the course of your day. The authentic cadence is the most frequently used cadence in rock, jazz, country, and classical music. You can hear it everywhere if you can remember what to listen for.

Hymn: Winchester New

Bach: Chorale, "Herr, ich denk' an jene Zeit"

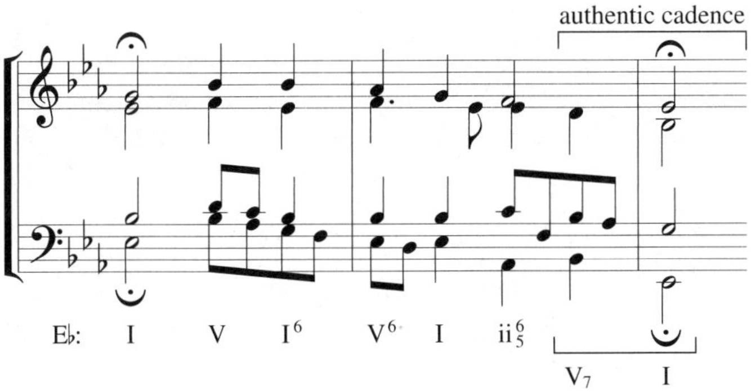

The Plagal Cadence

The **plagal cadence** is the chord progression IV–I in major or iv–i in minor.

Plagal cadence, major key

Plagal cadence, minor key

The plagal cadence is most familiar as the *Amen* ending of a hymn. This cadence, while also capable of producing a feeling of permanent rest, is not as strong as the authentic cadence. Consequently, it is used less frequently as the final cadence of a piece, except for hymns, where it has become commonplace.

Handel: "Lift up Your Heads" from *Messiah*

The Half Cadence

The **half cadence,** or **semi-cadence** as it is sometimes called, conveys a feeling of stopping that is only temporary. The half cadence never functions as a true conclusion to a whole section, or to an entire piece, because the half cadence formula ends on a dominant chord (V). The V in a half cadence can be preceded by any chord, but in practice it is most often preceded by the I, IV, or ii in major and the i or the iv in minor.

Half cadence, major key

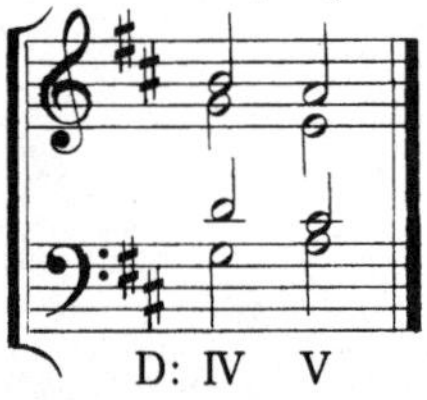

Half cadence, minor key

The half cadence gives the impression of a pause, not a complete relaxation of tension. As such, it sounds best when it appears in the middle of a musical statement rather than at its conclusion. The following example has two short phrases. Notice that the first phrase ends on a half cadence, while the second phrase ends on an authentic cadence. This is the most common two-phrase sequence of cadences in tonal music. So remember, more often than not, the first phrase ends on a half cadence; the second phrase answers with an authentic cadence. This information will help you when you try to harmonize a melody later in this chapter.

Kuhlau: Sonatina in C Major, Op. 55, No. 1, II

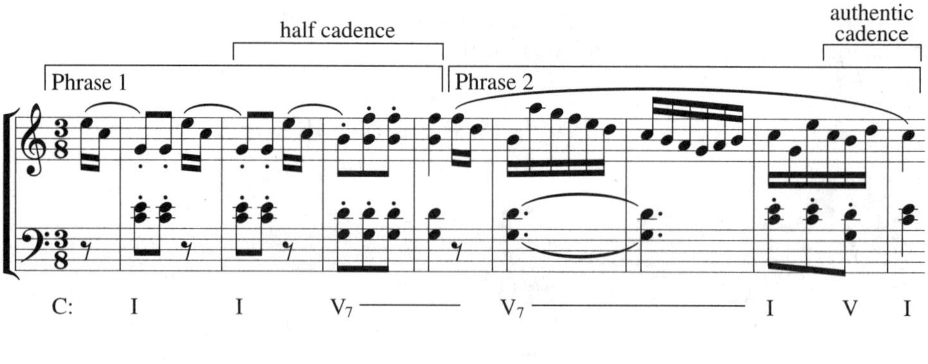

The Deceptive Cadence

The **deceptive cadence,** in its most common form, sounds at first as if it is going to be an authentic cadence. That is, the first chord of both the authentic and the deceptive cadence is a V or V_7, and our ear expects the final triad to be the tonic. Although this is true for the authentic cadence, it is not what happens in the deceptive cadence. Instead, the V or V_7 goes to an unexpected place, usually the vi, although other triads are possible. The result is that our ear has momentarily been deceived.

Deceptive cadence, major key

Deceptive cadence, minor key

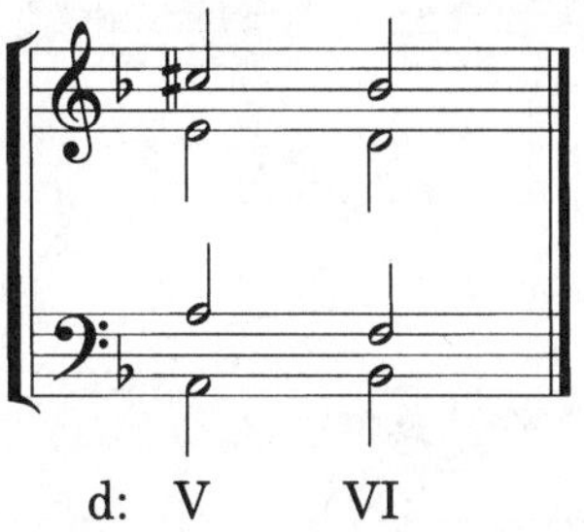

Ask someone to play the following example on the piano, first as written, and then a second time substituting the tonic triad for the submediant triad in the cadence.

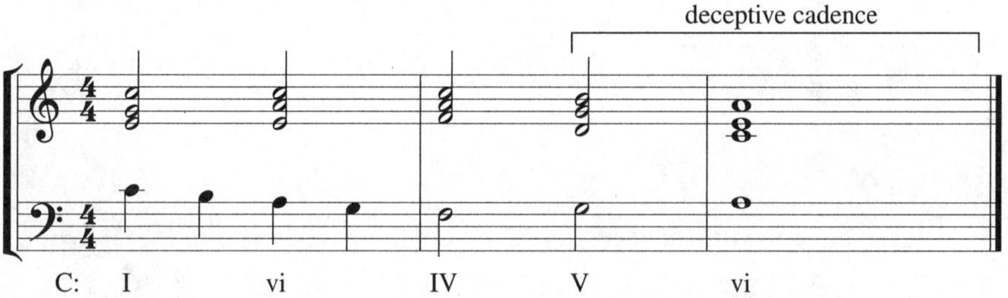

Notice that the authentic cadence created by the substitution of the I chord for the vi chord works well in this situation. In fact, our ear is led to expect it. This momentary deception of our ear allows the deceptive cadence to function as an *unexpected* point of repose. It cannot, however, function as the final cadence of a piece of music, since the purpose of the final cadence is to bring everything to an obvious conclusion.

Musical Problem

The following excerpts contain examples of the cadences we have studied in this chapter. Listen to each excerpt played several times, and identify by ear where the cadences occur. Then analyze each cadence as to type, first by ear, then with the music.

Clementi: Sonatina, Op. 36, No. 3, III

Schumann: "Soldiers' March" from *Album for the Young*

Bach: Chorale, "Ermuntre dich, mein schwacher Geist"

3.

Schumann: "The Poor Orphan Child" from *Album for the Young*

4.

Kuhlau: Sonatina in C Major, Op. 55, No. 1, I

5.

(continued)

Schumann: "The Wild Rider" from *Album for the Young*

Simple Chord Progressions

Exactly how do chord progressions function? As musical phrases move through various levels of tension and release, the alternation between activity and restfulness gives a feeling of movement to the music. This musical motion is supported by the melody, harmony, and rhythm; the interrelation of these three elements is what allows the V–I progression, for instance, to function as a cadence at the end of a phrase but not in the middle of one. Harmony contributes to a feeling of motion through the variety of chords (and their level of tension) that it has available. Every triad is, to some extent, active and tension producing, or passive and restful.

This alternation between harmonic tension and release can be heard in almost any example of tonal music. Pieces that use a large range of harmonic possibilities, however, are usually rather complicated and difficult to talk about; they are appropriate for more advanced theoretical study. Our discussion here will be limited to the concept of tension and release as it occurs in simple chord progressions.

Two-Chord Progression

The simplest chord progression consists of only two chords. In the majority of cases, these are the tonic triad and the dominant triad. The tonic triad, which is actually the center of gravity for *every* tonal chord progression, is the most restful sound. The dominant triad, on the other hand, is the most active sound. Therefore, a chord progression that simply alternates between the tonic and the dominant possesses a great deal of potential for musical tension and release.

Most folk songs, because they are intended to be sung and played by persons with little or no musical training, use relatively few chords. Take the following example, "Tom Dooley." It has only two chord changes for the entire song: I–V–I. Notice that although the chords change slowly, the broken-chord style of accompaniment in the bass supplies a continual feeling of motion. Listen to someone from your class play this piece, and concentrate on the accompaniment rather than the melody. Can you feel the change in tension when the V chord appears in measure 4? Notice how this level of tension is maintained for four measures before it resolves back to the I chord. It is this difference in tension level, and the harmonic motion between them, that allows such a simple chord progression to work musically.

"Tom Dooley"

Musical Problem

The following melodies can be harmonized with only tonic and dominant chords. As a class, sing the melodies that you recognize several times and decide, by ear, which parts of the melody require tonic chords and which parts need dominant chords. If you play piano, you may wish to pick the melody out at the keyboard and to add tonic and dominant chords to accompany it.

1. "Down in the Valley"
2. "London Bridge"

(continued)

3. "He's Got the Whole World in His Hands"
4. "Wayfaring Stranger"
5. "Don't Let the The Stars Get in Your Eyes"
6. "How Much Is That Doggie in the Window?"
7. "Jambalaya"
8. "O Tannenbaum"

Three-Chord Progression

When a third chord is introduced into a harmonic progression, it is often the subdominant chord. Remember that the plagal cadence (IV–I) is considered not as strong as the authentic cadence (V–I), because the tension created between IV and I is not as great as that between V and I. Similarly, the subdominant chord is also less tension producing than the dominant chord. Thus, in the three-chord progression I–IV–V, the IV chord stands intermediate in tension between the active V chord and the restful I chord.

The subdominant chord usually appears in one of two patterns: I–IV–V–I or I–IV–I–V–I. The following folk song has the I–IV–V–I progression.

"The Wabash Cannon Ball"

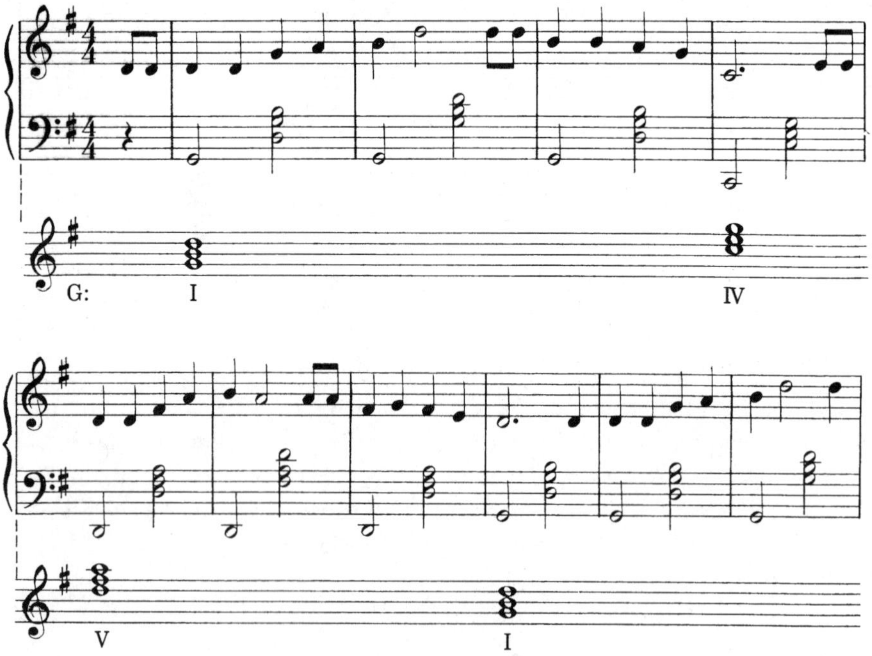

When used in this way, the subdominant chord contributes a first-level tension, which the dominant chord further increases to a second level. The harmonic tension is then resolved by the return to the tonic chord.

The next example of a three-chord progression uses the chord pattern I–IV–I–V–I.

"Michael, Row the Boat Ashore"

Here the subdominant chord establishes a first level of tension, which is resolved by the return of the tonic chord. Then, a second level of tension is introduced by the dominant chord, which is also resolved by the return of the tonic. Sing this example in class, with half the class singing the melody and the other half singing the root of each chord. Do you notice the different kinds of tension produced between I–IV–I at the beginning of the progression and I–V–I in the second half of the progression?

Musical Problem

The chord progressions for "The Wabash Cannon Ball" and "Michael, Row the Boat Ashore" are written in the previous examples as block chords in the treble clef in order to make them easier to see. In performance, however, they would never be played exactly this way. Ask someone in the class who plays piano and someone who plays guitar to perform one or both of these pieces, providing their own suitable accompaniment. As a class, discuss each accompaniment. What are the musical contributions of an accompaniment? Why do the block chords written in the examples not make a suitable accompaniment?

Harmonizing a Melody

As you may recall, the last musical problem asked you to harmonize a melody. The musical decisions you made for that are exactly the kinds of decisions you must make whenever you are choosing the most appropriate chords for a melody. Such decisions, however, will become more difficult as your vocabulary of chords grows to include all the diatonic as well as some of the chromatic possibilities. Other difficulties arise when you deal with unfamiliar melodies, or melodies that have a lot of scale passages in them. (Melodies that move in seconds obscure the chordal outlines.) We will leave the exploration of chromatic chords and difficult melodies to future study. We will also use only root position triads and not become involved with voice-leading procedures at this point. Here, however, are a few basic suggestions to help you get started. Once you get the idea, you'll be able to continue with new melodies on your own.

The first step in harmonizing a melody is obvious—become familiar with it. Play it. Sing it. Listen to it. Your goal is to locate the areas of tension and points of rest, to identify the musical phrases, and to decide where the cadences should go. Try to do as much of this by ear as possible; it's usually easier than trying to do it by looking at the written melody.

Let's begin with a melody that you may know, although you have probably never tried to harmonize it. It is by Stephen Foster, who lived between 1826 and 1864. Foster's contemporaries considered him the best songwriter America had ever produced. Today, some of his works have become the folksongs of America. The melody we are going to harmonize, "Old Folks at Home," was written in 1851 and was Foster's most popular song during his lifetime.

Whether you know this melody or not, the first step in harmonization is always the same. Become familiar with the melody before going on.

Foster: "Old Folks at Home"

Once you feel you know the melody well, the next decision to make (after you're sure you know what key it is in) is to decide where the cadences should occur. Remember, cadences happen only at the ends of phrases. Remember, too, that if you don't plan your cadences first, the chances are good that your harmony will wander aimlessly, and contribute little to the buildup of tension and the subsequent cadential release. Plan your cadences well, however, and the chord progression will not seem haphazard. Keep in mind that different kinds of cadences produce different levels of finality. And although the authentic cadence is the most final sounding of all the cadences, it should not be overused.

Our example, like many simple, diatonic melodies, is made up of four phrases, each of which is four measures long. Notice that the cadence points—measures four, eight, twelve, and sixteen—all contain whole notes, the longest note value of the melody. Another point to consider is that phrases one, two, and four of our example are similar in sound, while the third phrase is different. This creates an AABA format for the four phrases, something else we will need to take into consideration when we harmonize it.

Foster: "Old Folks at Home"

(continued)

Choosing cadences may seem difficult at first, but after you have harmonized several melodies you will begin to see the same cadence patterns emerge from piece to piece. A good place to begin is to remember that when two phrases sound related, you can try ending the first phrase on a half cadence and the second phrase on an authentic or plagal cadence. This pattern is not always the best choice, but it appears frequently, and if it fits it will make the first phrase sound somewhat incomplete and allow the second phrase to finish the musical idea.

In our example, the first phrase could end on a half cadence (the D can be a part of the G major triad), and the second phrase on an authentic cadence. The same is true of phrases three and four, although this type of symmetry is not always the best choice musically. Since we know we most likely want the piece to end with an authentic cadence, the only one we are unsure of is the cadence at the end of the third phrase. This could be a half cadence or an authentic cadence, since the G in measure twelve can be a part of both the G major and C major triads. In this particular case, however, the F major triad in measure eleven will allow us to use a plagal cadence, which will give us some variety and may be the best choice. Even though you should plan your cadences first, don't be concerned if you aren't certain which one to use at this stage. We know what our possibilities are with the third phrase of our example, and we can make a final decision when we fill in the other chords.

Foster: "Old Folks at Home"

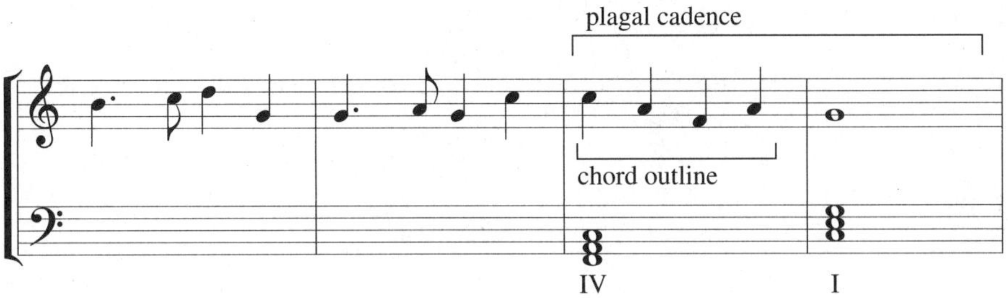

The next step in harmonizing a melody is to be certain that you correctly understand the **harmonic rhythm** of the melody—that is, how fast the chords change. Some pieces have a rapid, steady harmonic rhythm, with chord changes occurring almost every beat. Others change every two beats, or every measure, and sometimes less frequently. In the case of a piece with a slow, irregular harmonic rhythm, it is easy to make the chords change too rapidly, which is frustrating because it feels as if *no* chord is appropriate. In such a situation don't try to force a chord change where none is needed.

Once you have planned the cadences and understand the harmonic rhythm, you are ready to fill in the rest of the chords. Although a great number of melodies can be harmonized with only the I, IV, and V chords (and an even larger number if the vi chord is also included), many melodies seem to require additional chords. If you find yourself working with a melody of this type, keep in mind that any pitch can be a part of and harmonized in three different chords; for example, in the key of C, G can be the root of the V chord, the third of the iii chord, or the fifth of the I chord. If you have difficulty harmonizing a particular pitch in a new melody, begin by exploring these three diatonic possibilities.

Notice in the melody we are harmonizing that the harmonic rhythm changes about every measure. You can tell this by scanning the melody for chord outlines. Notice, for instance, that the melody spells a C major triad in measure three, an F major triad in measure eleven, and a G major triad in measure nine. Notice also in measures seven and fifteen that a C major triad is outlined in two beats, and the triad must change for beats three and four because D does not fit with the C major triad. Keep in mind also that chord changes will almost never occur in a perfectly symmetrical way. While this can seem a bit arbitrary and confusing at first, practice and your ear will help you decide the right choices.

Foster: "Old Folks at Home"

Now let us turn our attention to a different kind of melody. This is a "Dance" for piano by Beethoven.

Beethoven: "Dance"

The process of harmonizing a melody by Beethoven is, fundamentally, no different from harmonizing a song by Stephen Foster. They are, after all, both tonal melodies. So, if we follow the steps we took in the previous harmonization, we should be successful here. As you will recall, these steps were as follows:

1. Become familiar with the melody.
2. Plan the cadences.
3. Become familiar with the harmonic rhythm.
4. Fill in the remaining chords.

As you look at Beethoven's melody, notice that it seems to be divided into two separate parts, each of which is repeated. This pattern creates a binary, or two-part, form consisting of an A section of eight measures (sixteen when repeated) followed by a contrasting B section, also of eight (sixteen) measures. In completing our harmonization, we must take this formal structure into account.

As we continue looking at the melody, two problems appear that may need extra attention. The first is that, while some measures outline triads and will be easy to harmonize correctly, others contain scale passages moving in seconds. Choosing the proper harmony for these sections will require some thought. The second potential difficulty concerns the chromatic pitches in measures nine, ten, thirteen, and fourteen. Our problem here is to determine how these pitches relate to the diatonic chords that will occur in these measures.

In beginning to plan the cadences, another problem arises unexpectedly. How long are Beethoven's phrases? Is the first phrase eight measures long, as it appears to be, or does measure four contain an implied cadence, as we might expect it to? The same problem also arises in the B section, where the end of the phrase appears to be measure sixteen, although measure twelve may be an implied cadence as well. In a case such as this, the proper thing to do is to plan the cadences you are certain of and wait for the others until you know more about the harmonic rhythm and how you intend to fill in the remaining chords. And so, at this point, the only two cadences we can be certain of are the ones that end sections A and B, both of which will be authentic cadences (V_7–I).

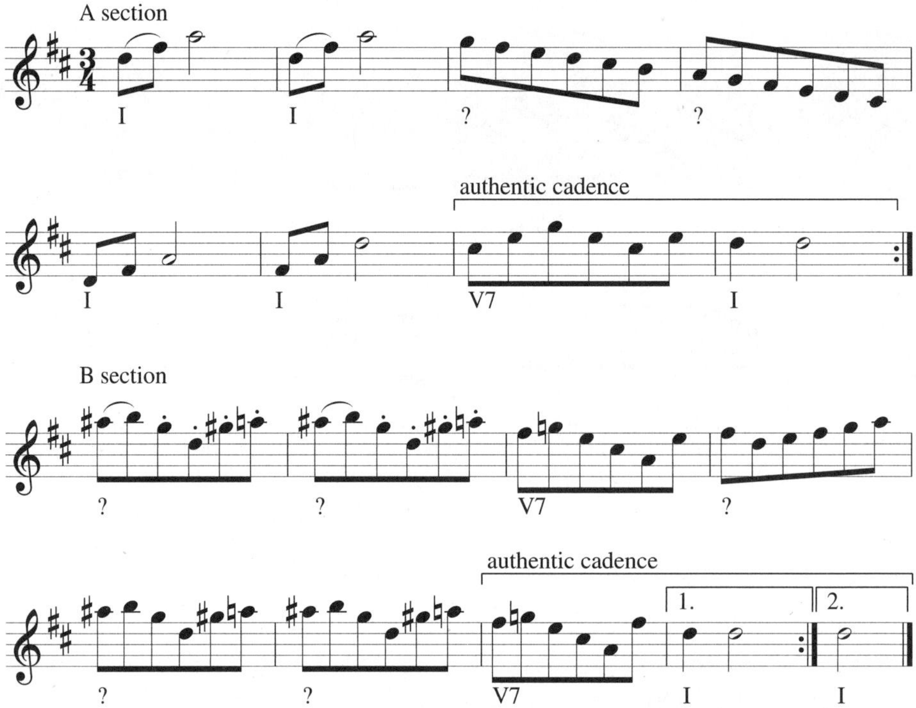

When looking at scale-like passages it is often difficult to recognize the outlines of chords, but they are still there. The chords are just obscured by all the intervals of a second. So when harmonizing these passages, we must decide which are the chord notes. Sometimes this is easy. The chord tones in scalar passages often occur on the beat, while the non-chord tones occur off the beat. When this is not so, and we must use our imagination to decide which chord is most likely to occur at this point in the phrase or in the structure of the piece.

With our scale passages in measures three and four, notice how the dominant seventh chord (a, c♯, e, g) is outlined on the beat in measure three, and reinforced by four of the six pitches in measure four. Pitches that are not part of the triad are circled.

Meas. 3-4

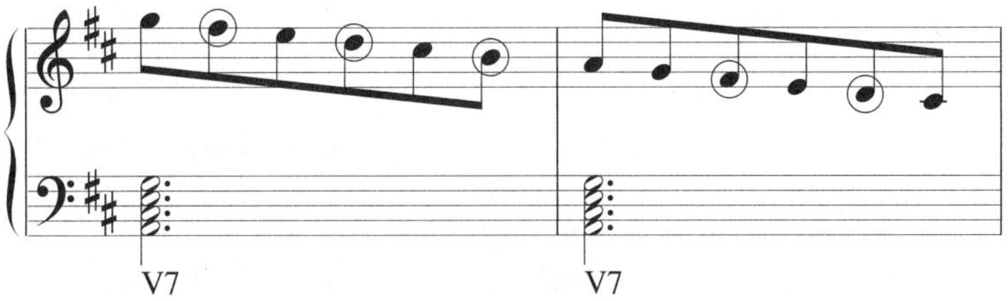

Similarly, the scale passage in measure twelve outlines the tonic triad (d, f♯, a) with four of its six pitches, three of which occur on the beat.

Meas. 12

As for the chromatic pitches in measures nine, ten, thirteen, and fourteen, a careful look will tell us that the measures are identical. This would seem to imply that the harmony will be the same for each measure. But why are the a♯ and g♯ there to begin with? What purpose do they serve? In general, if a pitch that is not a part of the key occurs once and is then canceled for the corresponding pitch that is in the key, the nonharmonic pitch is considered to be color. That is, it supports and reinforces the pitch that comes after it. In this case, both the a♯ and the g♯ act as leading tones to the pitches that follow them (a♯-b, g♯-a), giving the b and the a new colors, and making them temporarily more important than they ordinarily are.

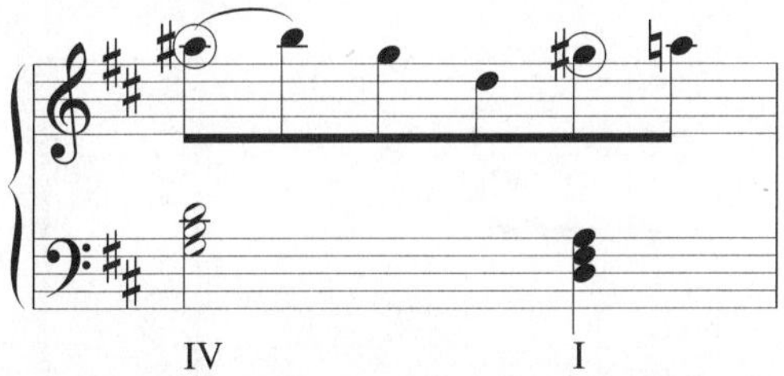

An interesting point worth noting is that the harmonic rhythm of the B section moves faster than that of A. In the A section the harmonic rhythm generally moves at the rate of one chord every two measures. In the B section, there is a new chord every measure, and sometimes two chords per measure.

Here, then, is the completed harmonization. Notice that Beethoven sustains the harmonic interest and achieves the contrast he is seeking by varying both the chord progression and the harmonic rhythm of the two sections. Section A is oriented around a tonic-dominant progression, while section B is tonic-subdominant oriented. Also, the faster harmonic rhythm in the B section further differentiates the two sections, as does the introduction of chromatic pitches in the second part.

Beethoven: "Dance"

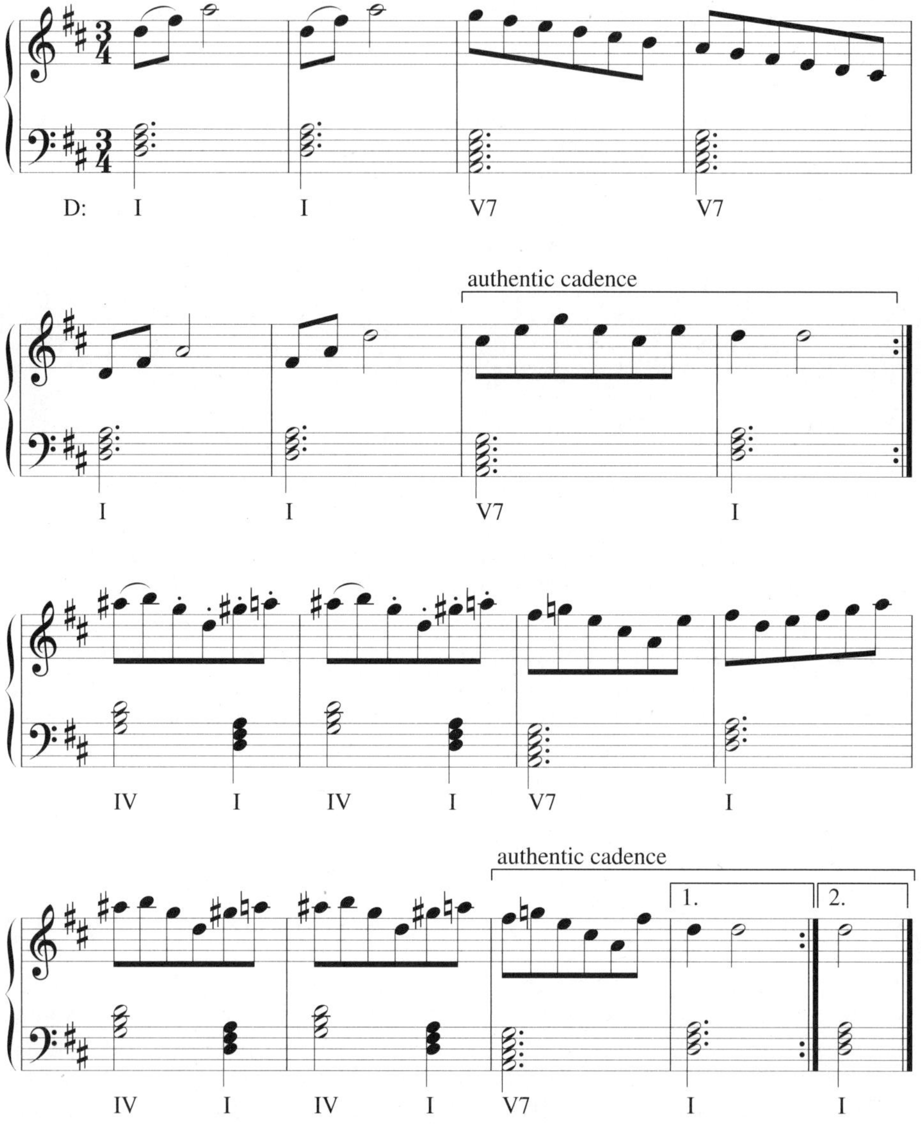

As mentioned earlier, our work with harmonizing melodies has been limited to the use of block chords. We have not concerned ourselves at this point with proper voice leading procedures and with making our harmonization more musical. But it might be a good idea, as we end our work with tonality, to look at how Beethoven balanced the technical and the musical aspects of harmonizing his own melody. Here is how Beethoven actually wrote "Dance."

Notice that not only was Beethoven concerned with choosing the proper chords but he also wanted to use each chord in a way that supported and reinforced the melody. In section A for instance, where the harmonic rhythm moves slowly, Beethoven arpeggiated each chord to create momentum and provide a constant forward motion. In the B section, where the harmonic rhythm moves faster, he ends the arpeggiation and uses quarter-note chords to punctuate the continually moving melody.

In your own work, keep in mind that some melodies are easier to harmonize than others. Don't become discouraged if you run across a difficult one. Just follow the steps we have been using and remember that the skill of harmonizing a melody, like everything else, improves with practice.

Musical Problem

Choose one or more of the following melodies to harmonize. Use only block chords in root position (as in the previous example), and don't worry at this point about creating a suitable accompaniment. Begin by listening to the melody, planning the cadences, and establishing the harmonic rhythm. As you work, keep in mind that there is no one absolutely correct harmonization for most melodies. Some chord progressions do, however, sound more interesting than others.

"Mockingbird Hill"

1.

"New River Train"

2.

"Red River Valley"

3.

Focus

Here we are at the end of this book. Hopefully, you have discovered that the study of tonal music and how it works is a fascinating topic full of many surprises and intriguing concepts. And, while we have spent most of our time exploring the various fundamental components that make up music, it is important always to keep in mind that these individual components go together in some mysterious way to create an art form that is rewarding, imaginative, and never-ending. In music, there is always something more to learn and experience. So, as you go forward, keep in mind that this book has given you a good beginning but it is only that, a foundation. If you are to continue to grow as a musician, you must build on what you have learned here. The fundamentals of music don't change, but the ways composers have used them through the centuries have changed, and an understanding of musical style will be essential to your continued development.

For some of you, the next step is a formal theory class; for others, it is independent work and study. To be successful, everyone must understand the material contained in this final chapter. Chord progressions are the essence of tonal music. Their significance cannot be overstated. If you understand the concept of the simple chord progression that is presented in this chapter, it will be easier to handle the more complicated progressions you will encounter later on. And, if you understand that all chord progressions (and their cadences) create varying levels of tension and release, then the chromatic patterns you encounter later will not seem so confusing or ambiguous.

This book began by drawing a distinction between musical talent and musical knowledge. Let me now remind you that the task of balancing your talent and your knowledge of music will be with you for the remainder of your musical life. Look at it as both a challenge and an opportunity; all good musicians find their own unique ways of maintaining the balance. Good luck.

Focus on Skills IV

The following questions cover material presented in Chapters 10 and 11. If you have difficulty with any of these questions, review the relevant sections.

1. Identify the root of each of the following triads, and label each as major (M), minor (m), augmented (A), or diminished (d) in quality.

a.

root

quality

b.

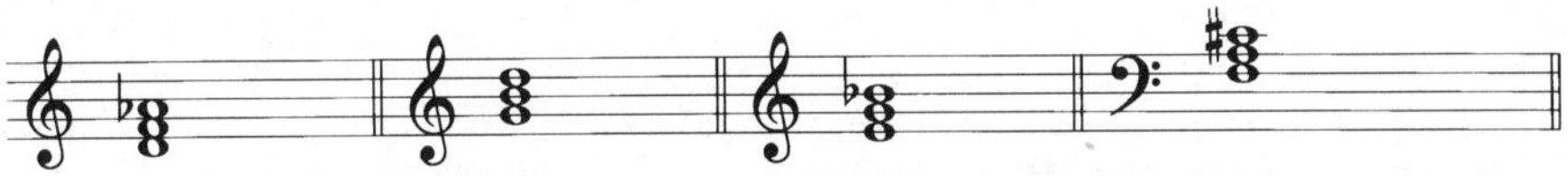

c.

d.

e. 

2. The following triads are in either first or second inversion. Identify the inversion, the root of the triad, and the quality.

a. 

inversion ___ ___ ___ ___

root ___ ___ ___ ___

quality ___ ___ ___ ___

b. 

c. 

d. 

3. Write the following triads in close position.

a.
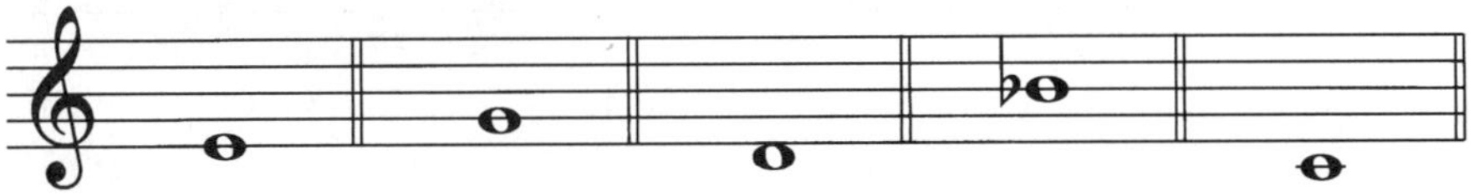

b.
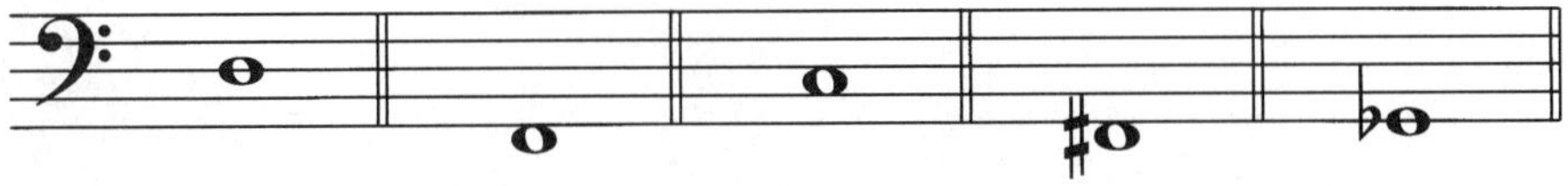

c.
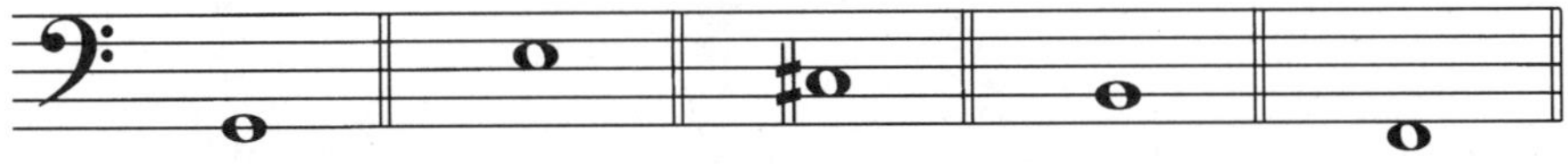

4. Write the following triads in open position.

a.
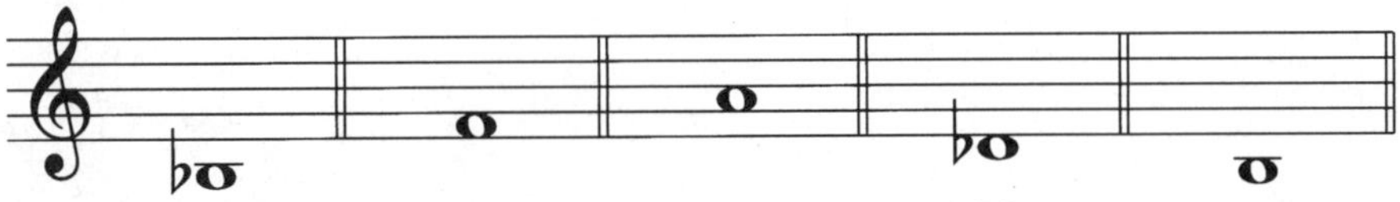

b.

5. Complete the following triads and dominant seventh chords in close position.

a.
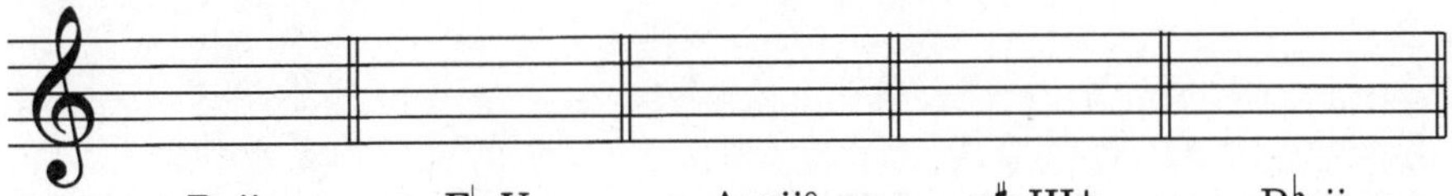

b.

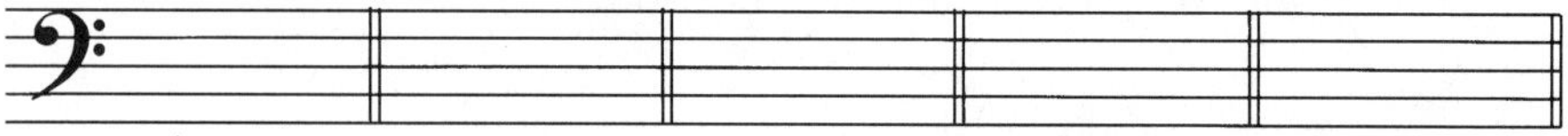

b: iv c♯: V_7 B♭: ii E♭: iv b♭: vii°

c.

g: V_7 F: vii° C♭: vii° e♭: V_7 F♯: IV

d.

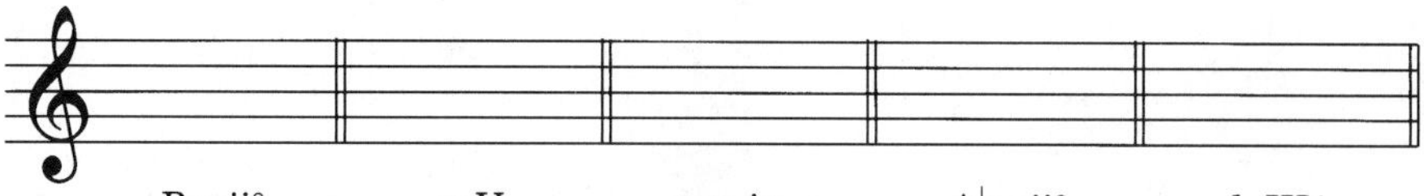

B: vii° a: V_7 g: iv A♭: vii° d: III+

6. The following melody can be harmonized with only the I, IV, and V chords. Using block chords, write your harmonization below the melody in the staff provided.

"Wildwood Flower"

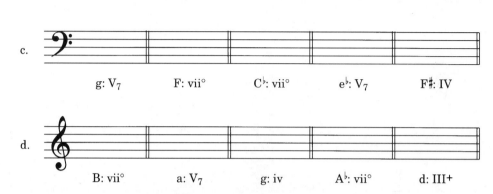

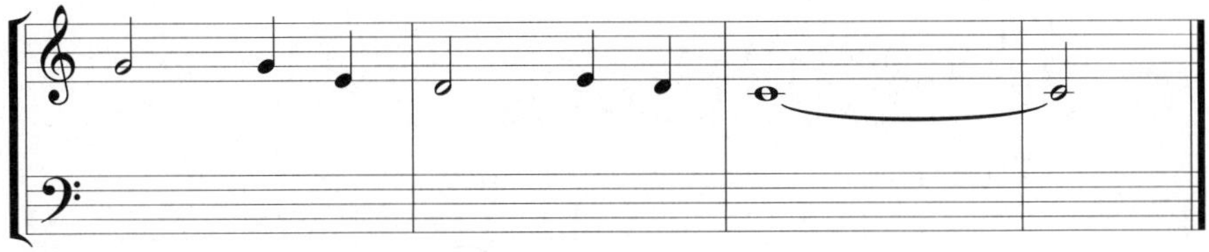

A Appendix

Graded Rhythms for Counting and Performing

Simple Meters

1. 

2. 

3. 

4. 

5. 

6. 

7. 

8. 

9. 

10. 

11. 

12. 

13. 

14. 

15. 

16. 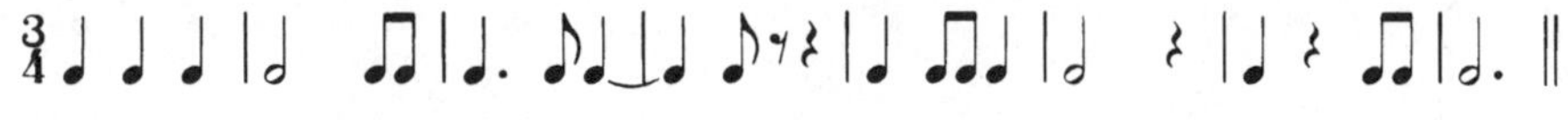

17. 

18. 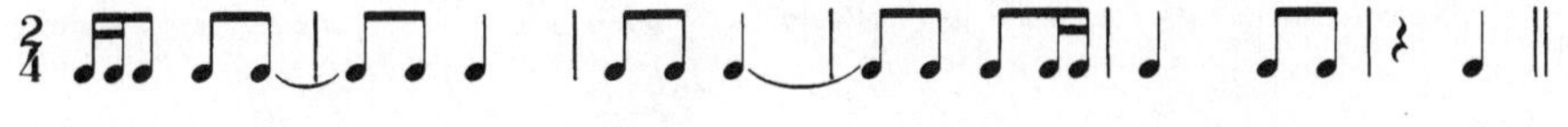

19. 

20. 

Compound Meters

21. 

22. 

23. 

24. 

25. 

26. 

27. 

28. 

29. 

30. 

31. 

32. 

33. 

34. 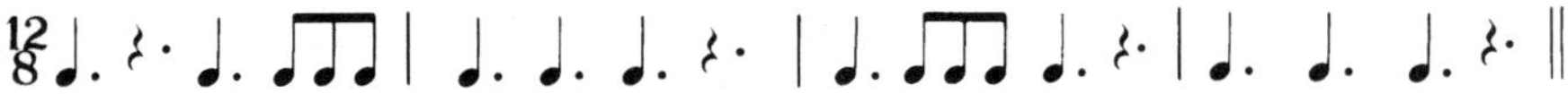

35. 

36. 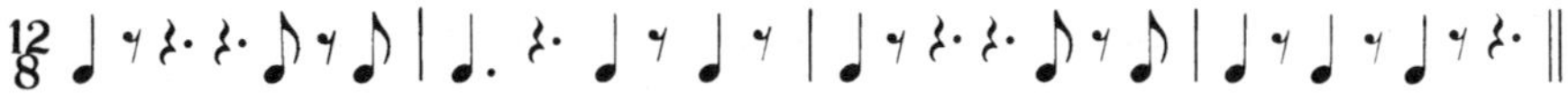

37. 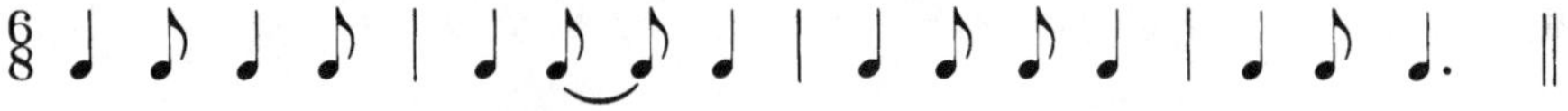

38. 

39. 

40. 

41. 

42. 

43. 

Less-Familiar Meters (Simple and Compound)

44. 

45. 

46. 

47. 

48. 

49. 

50. 

51. 

52. 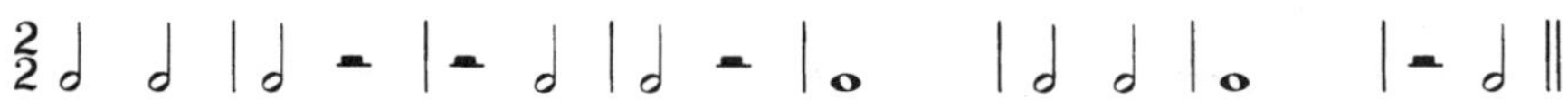

53. 

54. 

55. 

56. 

57. 

58. 

59. 

60. 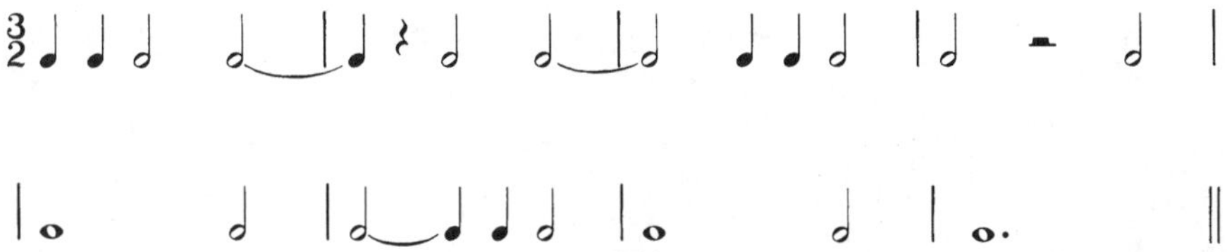

61. 

62. 

63. 

64. 

65. 

66. 

67. 

68. 

69. 

70. 

71. 

72. 

73. 

74. 

75. 

Appendix B

Graded World Rhythms in Two and Three Parts

The following two- and three-part rhythmic excerpts are adapted from a variety of musical styles and traditions throughout the world. They can be practiced with hand clapping or performed with "found" percussion instruments that students bring to class. Notice that many of the three-part patterns can be repeated a number of times. In these cases, adding or subtracting a voice on each repetition will increase the musical interest.

Two-Part Rhythms

Vivace **Western Europe**

1.

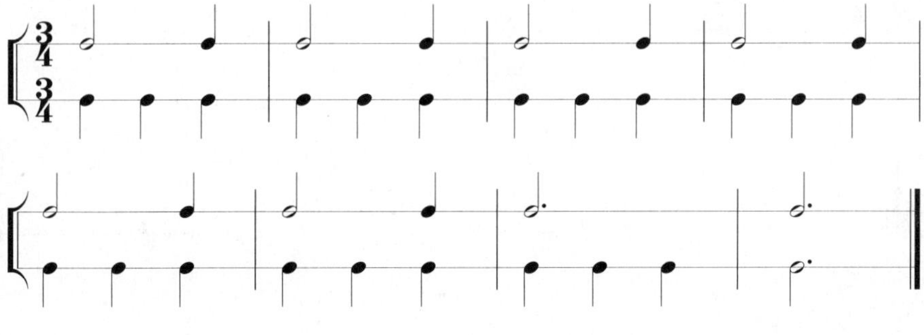

Fast **Asia**

2.

Moderate **Asia**

3.

Moderate **Western Europe**

4.
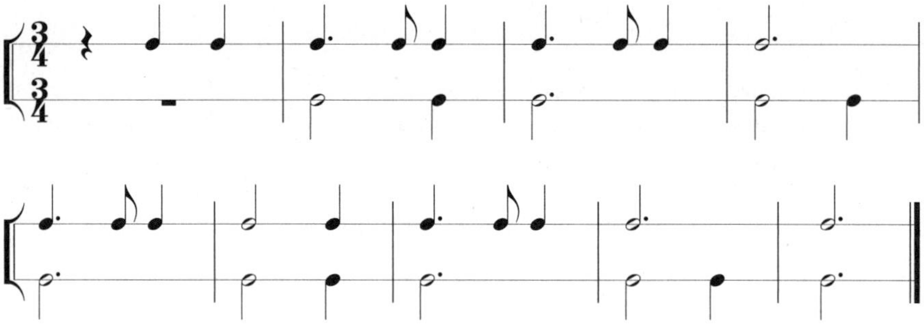

Slowly **Asia**

5.

Fast **Western Europe**

6.
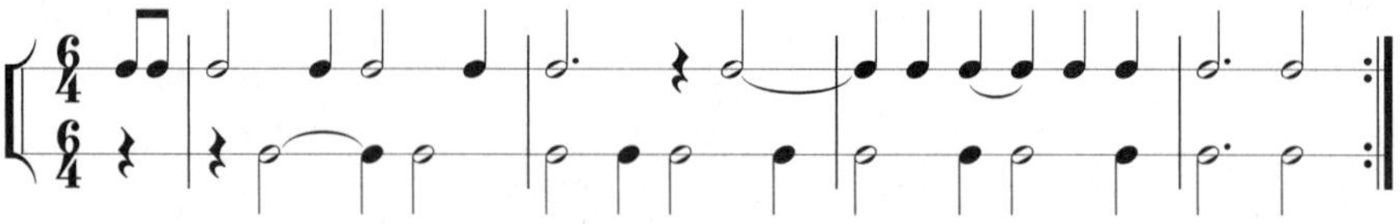

Moderate **Western Europe**

7.

Moderate **Western Europe**

8.

Moderate **African**

9.

Slowly **Western Europe**

10.

Fast (in 5) — Eastern Europe

11.

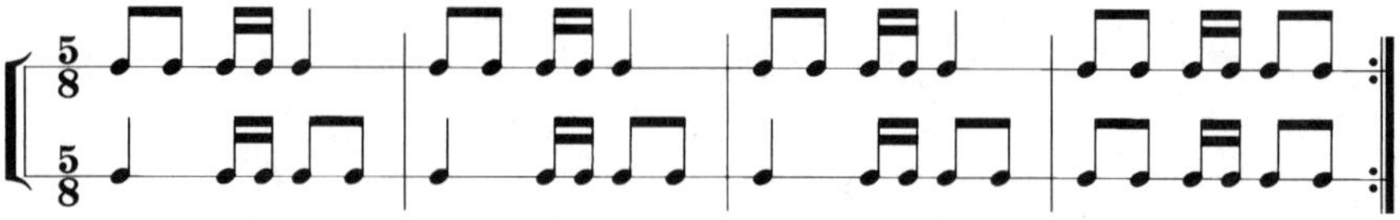

Spirited (in 7) — Eastern Europe

12.

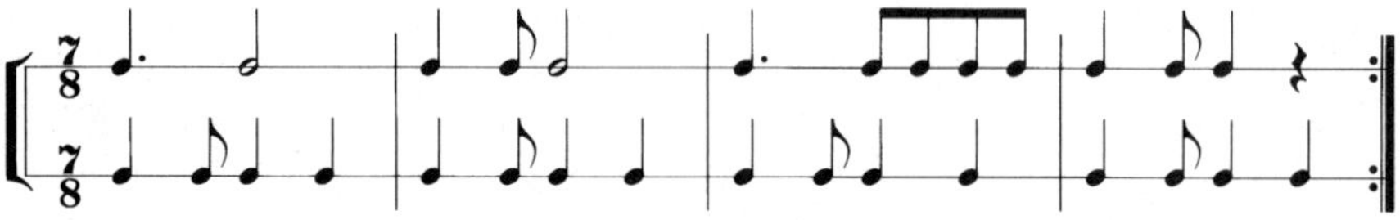

Slowly (in 4) — Western Europe

13.

Stately — Eastern Europe

14.

Three-Part Rhythms

Fast — African

15.

Fast **South America**

16.
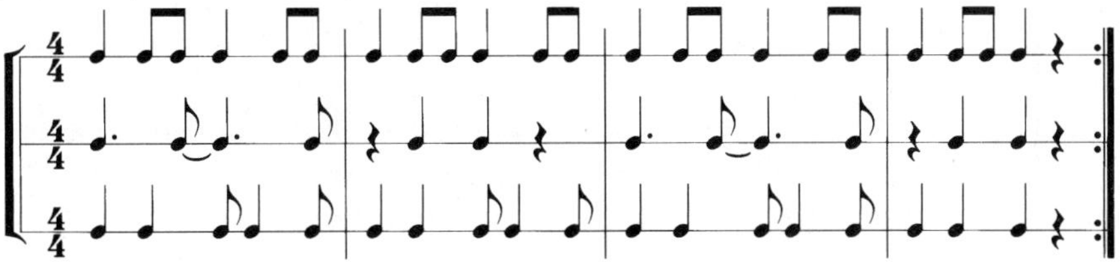

Fast **African**

17.

Slowly **Western Europe**

18.

Moderate **South America**

19.

Moderate **Africa**

20.

Appendix **C**

Syllables for Sight-Singing Scales and Modes

1. Chromatic scale—ascending:
   do, di, re, ri, mi, fa, fi, sol, si, la, li, ti, do

   Chromatic scale—descending:
   do, ti, te, la, le, sol, se, fa, mi, me, re, ra, do
2. Major scale:
   do, re, mi, fa, sol, la, ti, do
3. Natural minor scale:
   do, re, me, fa, sol, le, te, do
4. Harmonic minor scale:
   do, re, me, fa, sol, le, ti, do
5. Melodic minor scale—ascending:
   do, re, me, fa, sol, la, ti, do

   Melodic minor scale—descending:
   do, te, le, sol, fa, me, re, do
6. Dorian mode:
   do, re, me, fa, sol, la, te, do
7. Phrygian mode:
   do, ra, me, fa, sol, le, te, do
8. Lydian mode:
   do, re, mi, fi, sol, la, ti, do
9. Mixolydian mode:
   do, re, mi, fa, sol, la, te, do
10. Pentatonic scale—version one:
    do, re, mi, sol, la, do

    Pentatonic scale—version two:
    do, re, fa, sol, la, do
11. Whole-tone scale:
    do, re, mi, fi, si, li, do

D *Appendix*

Graded Melodies for Sight-Singing and Playing

Major Keys

1. 

2. 

3. 

4. 

5. 

6.

7.

8.

9.

10.

11.

12.

13. 

14. 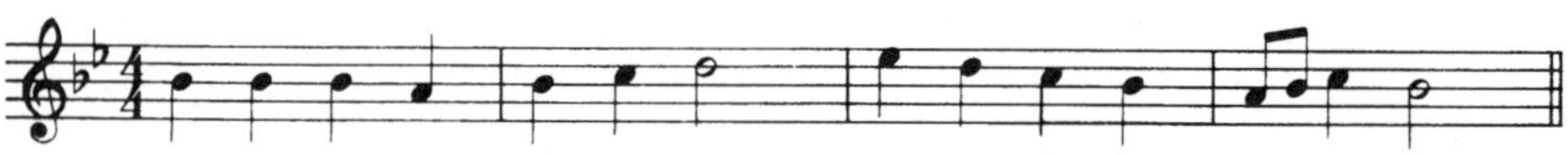

15. 

16. 

17. 

18. 

19. 

20. 

21. 

22. 

23. 

24. 

25. 

26. 

27. 

28. 

29. 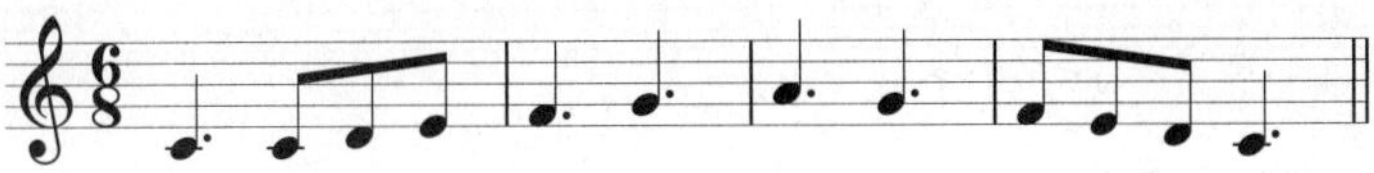

30.

31.

32.

33.

Minor Keys

34.

35.

36.

37.

38.

39. 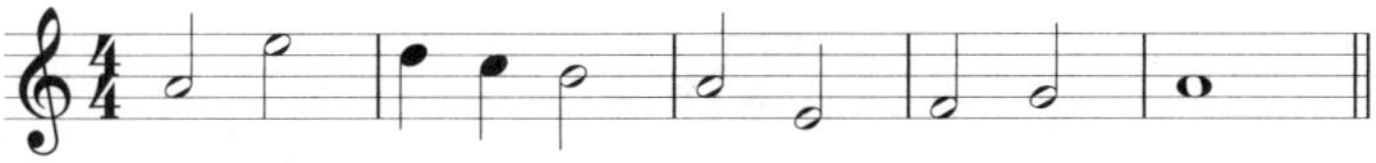

40. 

41. 

42. 

43. 

44. 

45. 

46. 

47. 

48. 

49. 

50. 

51. 

52. 

53. 

54. 

55. 

56. 

Appendix E

Major-Scales Fingerings for Keyboard Instruments

In the following staves, the top line of numbers gives the fingering for the right hand, and the bottom line for the left hand. The numeral 1 always indicates the thumb.

C major

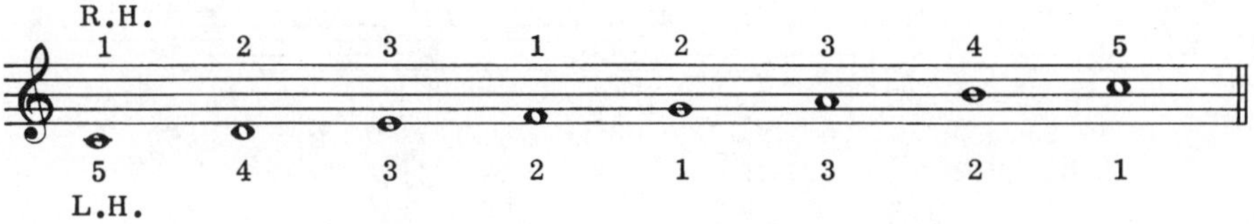

G major

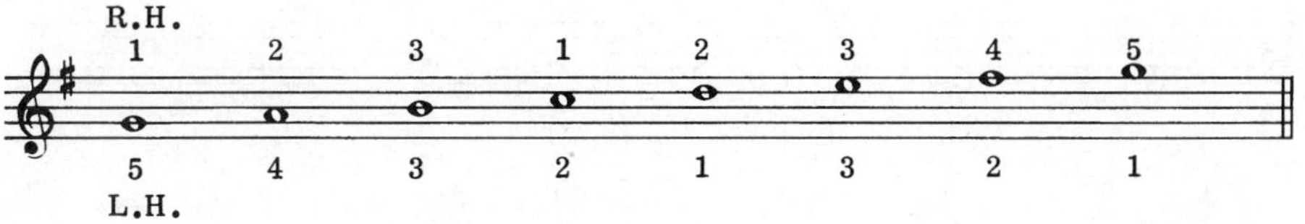

D major

A major

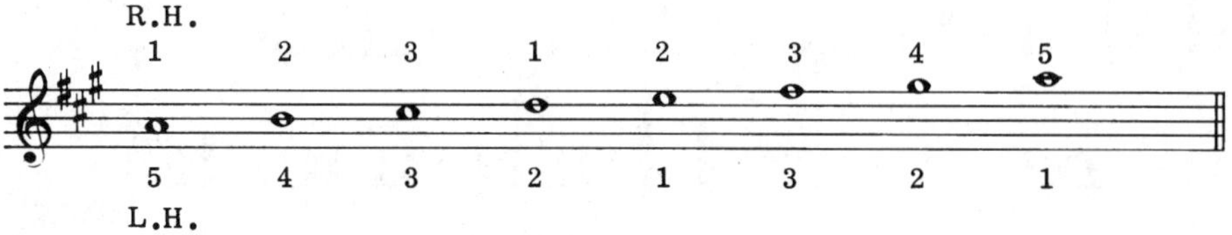

E major

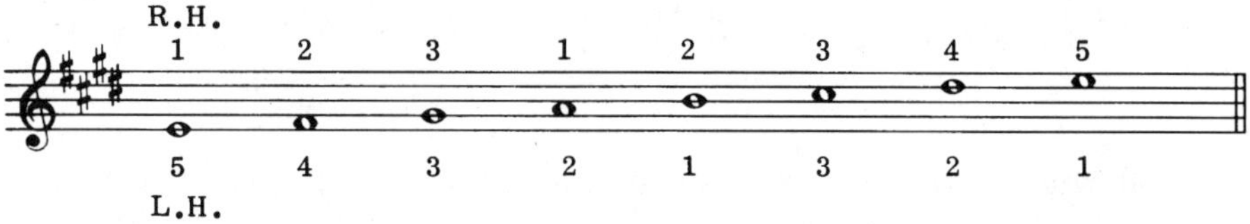

B major

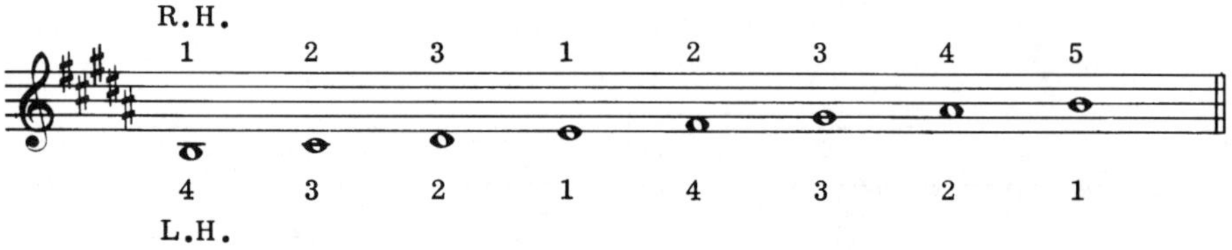

C♭ major

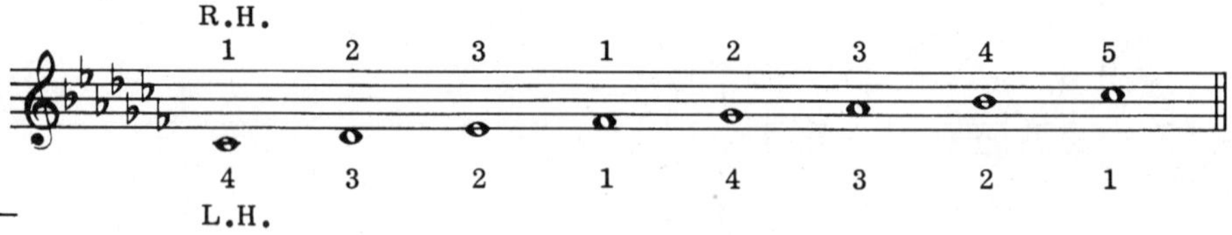

F♯ major

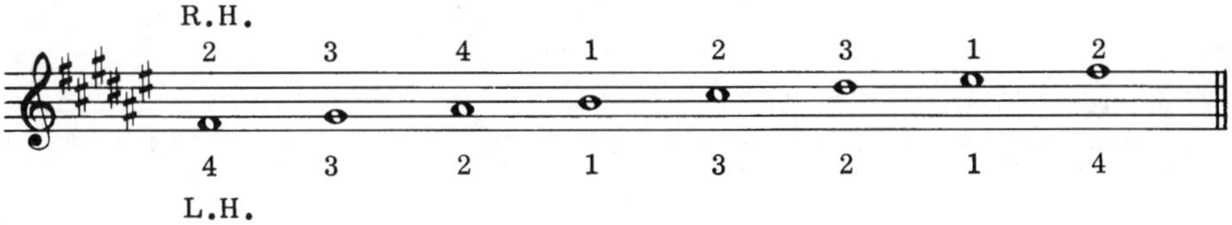

G♭ major

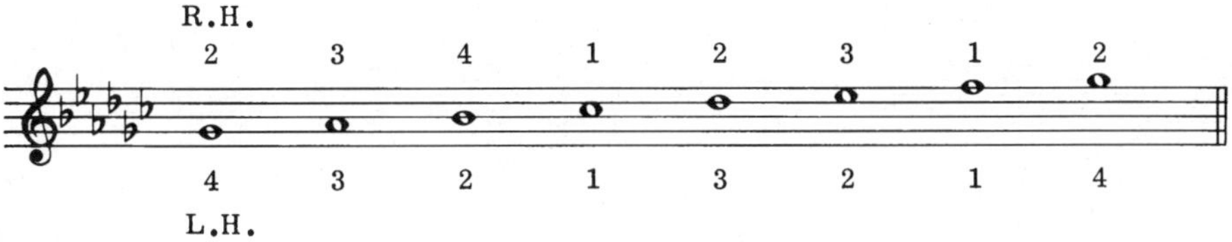

C♯ major

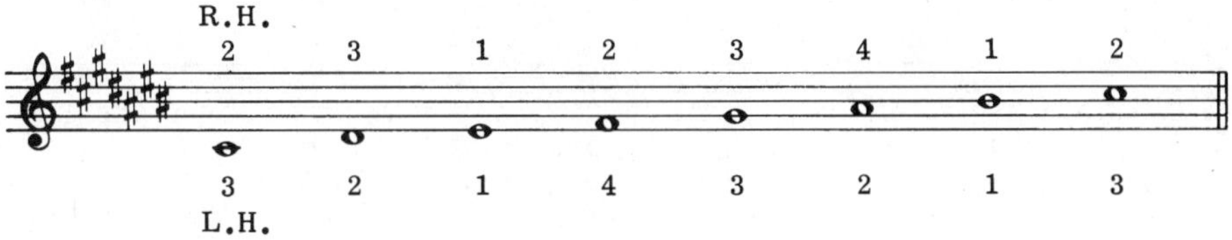

D♭ major

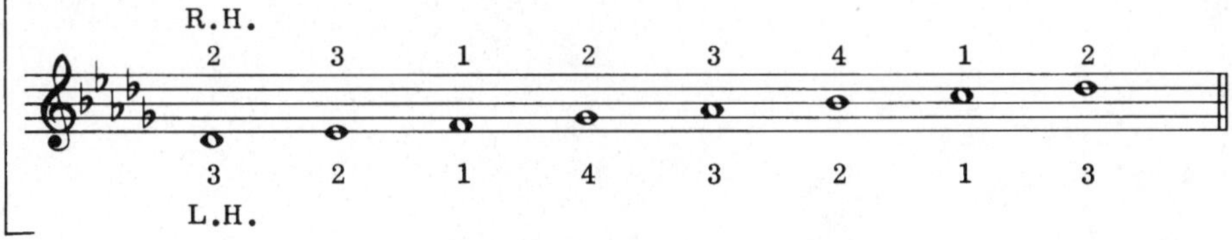

A♭ major

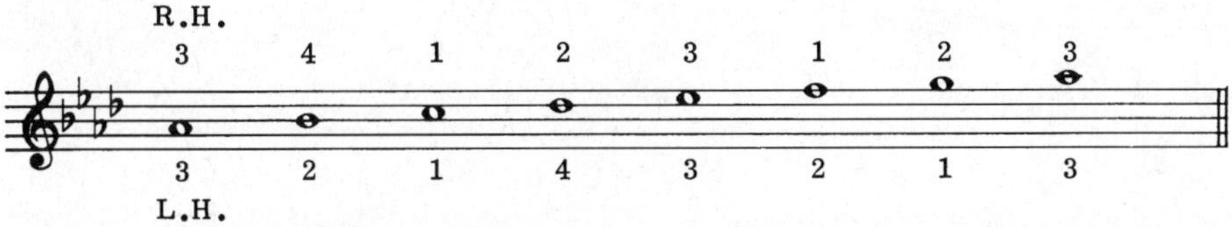

E♭ major

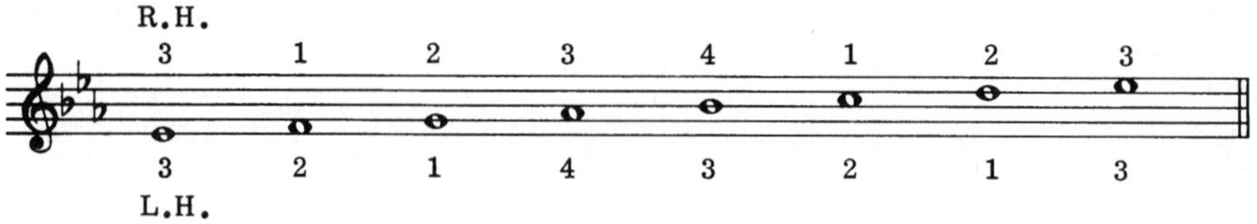

B♭ major

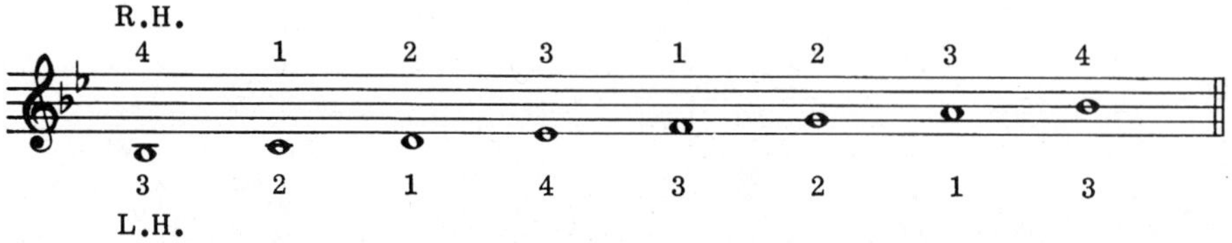

F major

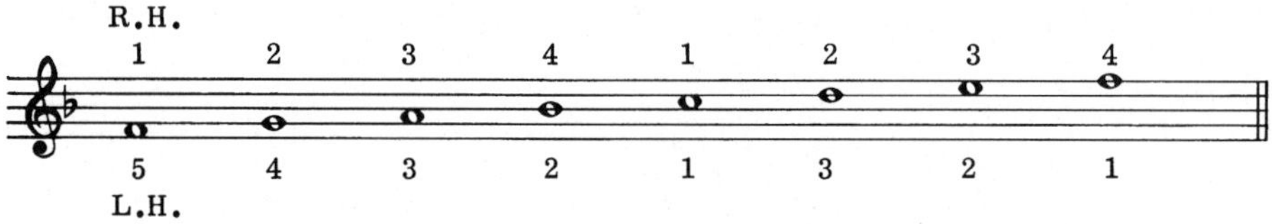

Appendix F

The C Clef

The C Clef

Although the treble clef and the bass clef are widely used, they are not the only clefs that appear in music. Several hundred years ago most music, both vocal and instrumental, was written in the **C clef.** Today, such instruments of the modern orchestra as the viola, cello, bassoon, and trombone either use the C clef exclusively or employ it frequently. It is also vital for the study of counterpoint. If you expect to study and perform early music, to work with orchestral instruments, or to continue your study of music theory, you will need to be able to read the C clef.

Unlike the treble or bass clef, the C clef does not always appear in the same location on the staff. It is movable and may be used on any line of the staff.

C clef positions

Today, however, it is most commonly found in one of two positions. When located on the third line of the staff, it is referred to as the **alto clef;** when located on the fourth line, it is known as the **tenor clef.**

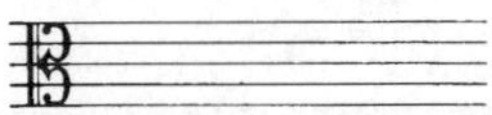

alto clef

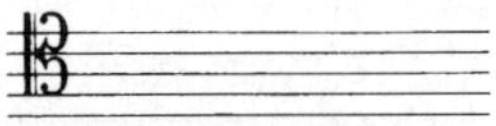

tenor clef

In all cases, whether in the alto or tenor or some other position, the C clef identifies the location of the note C. Furthermore, this C is always middle C—that is, the C in the middle of the great staff. In the following example, this same C is indicated in four different clefs:

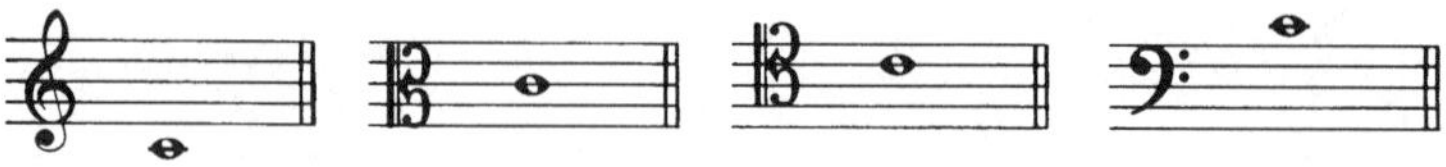

Practice drawing the C clef in the alto and tenor clef positions. The C clef is made by (1) drawing two parallel vertical lines as long as the depth of the staff and (2) drawing two curved lines to the right of the vertical lines that meet the right-hand vertical lines above and below the third or fourth line of the staff, depending on which of the positions is being drawn.

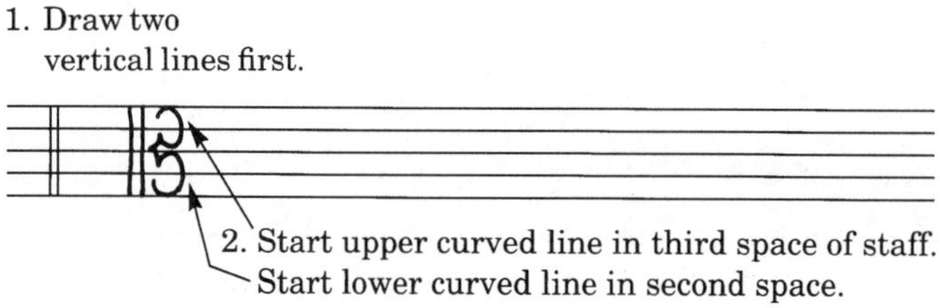
1. Draw two vertical lines first.
2. Start upper curved line in third space of staff.
Start lower curved line in second space.

Now identify by letter names the following pitches in the alto and tenor clefs. Remember that both alto and tenor clefs identify middle C.

1. 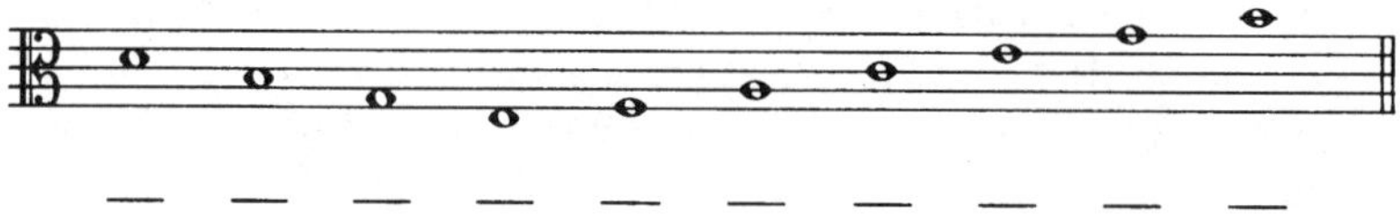

2. 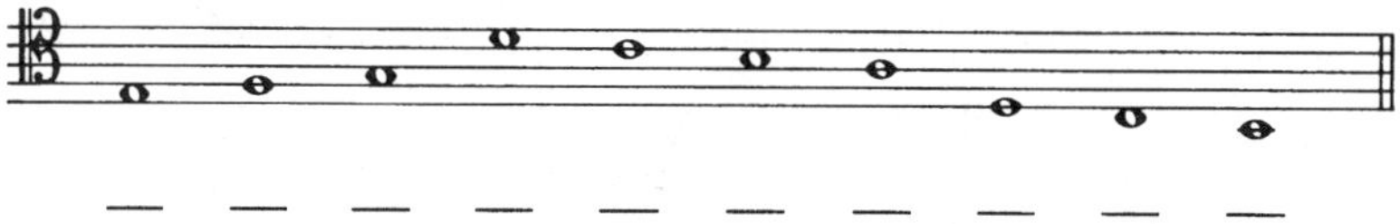

3. 

4. 

5. 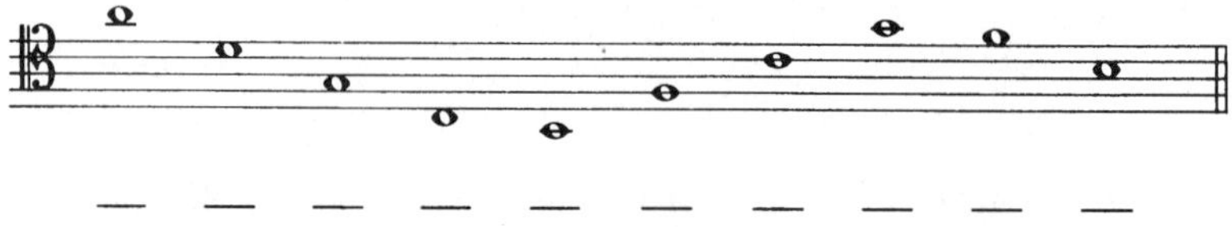

6. 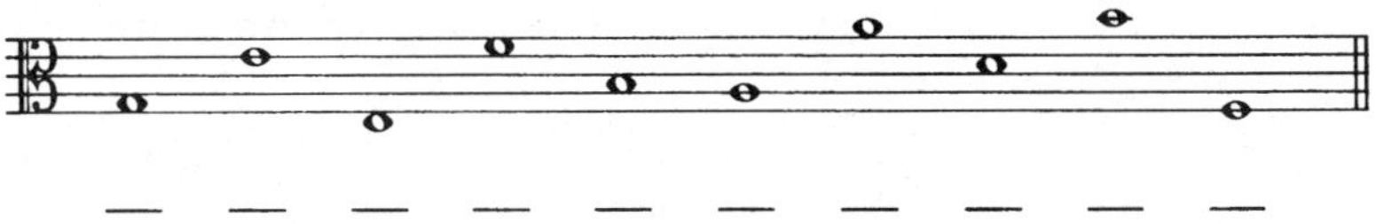

Now try the following. First identify the given pitch. Then rewrite the same pitch, but in the other clef.

1. 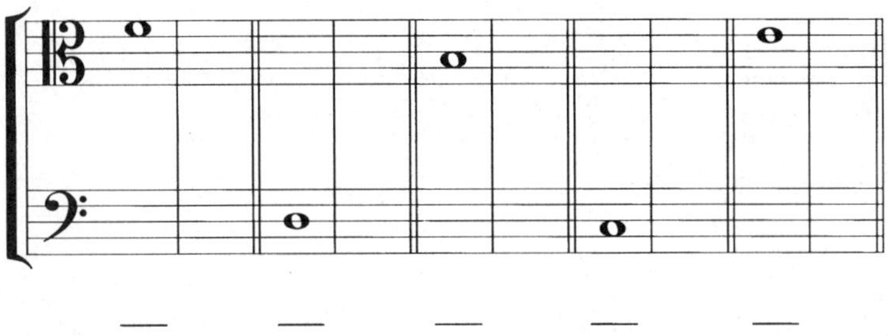

2. 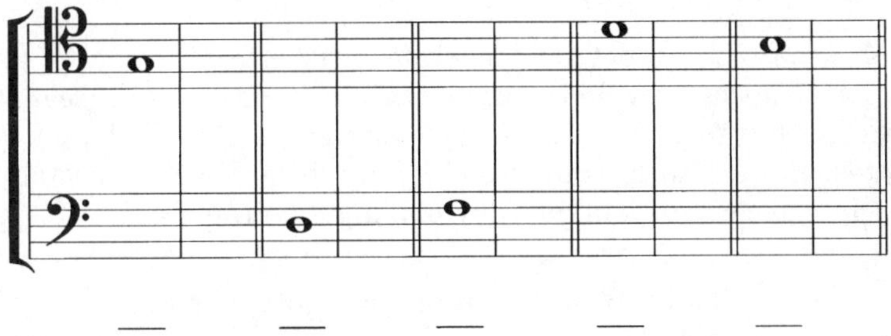

3. 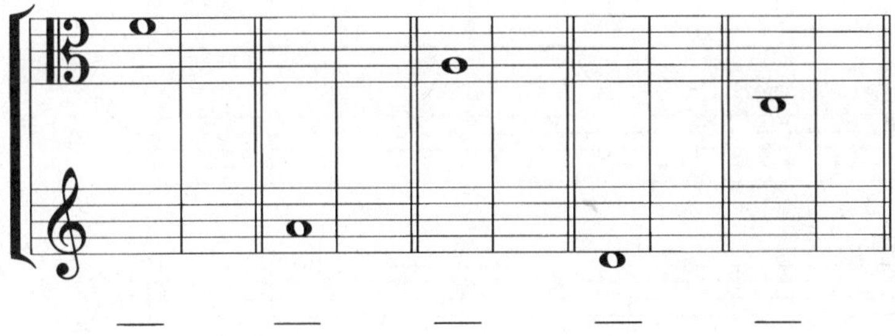

The following musical example is the opening of the chorale "Ein' Feste Burg" from Cantata No. 80 by Bach. Notice that in this excerpt the soprano, alto, and tenor voices all employ various positions of the C clef. The soprano voice uses a position of the C clef known as the *soprano clef,* while the alto and tenor voices use the two positions you have been working with. The variety of positions in which the C clef appears here is the result of the composer's interest in keeping all the voice parts on or near the staff.

Bach: "Ein' Feste Burg" from Cantata No. 80

Here is a phrase from another Bach chorale, written in treble, alto, tenor, and bass clefs. In the space provided, rewrite the phrase in a single great staff, transferring the pitches from the alto and tenor clefs to the treble and bass clefs, as indicated. Be careful in your use of ledger lines. Your instructor or a member of the class can check your work by playing it on the piano.

Bach: "Heut' Triumphieret Gottes Sohn"

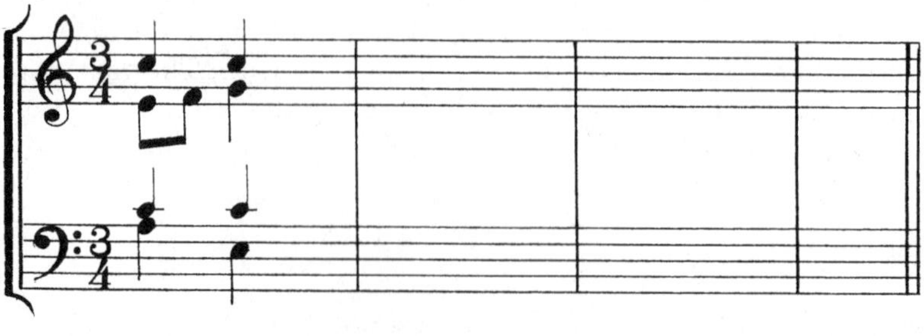

Appendix G

Transposing the Modes

In transposing the modes, we will concentrate only on the authentic ones: Dorian, Phrygian, Lydian, and Mixolydian. These are the ones in which the *finalis,* or tonic, coincides with the first note of the scale. These four modes are easy to recognize when they occur on the white keys. But if transposed to another beginning pitch, as they often are today, recognition becomes more difficult. Let's begin our study with the following example.

"Scarborough Fair"

A hasty glance at this piece might lead you to believe that it is in A natural minor (the key signature and last note are clues). Notice, however, that the eighth measure contains an F♯. If we begin on A (the beginning and ending pitch of the song) and construct a scale based on the pitches of the melody, we find that "Scarborough Fair" is, in fact, in Dorian mode:

One way of learning and recognizing the modes in their transpositions is to remember where the half steps are:

Mode	*Half Steps*
Dorian	2–3, 6–7
Phrygian	1–2, 5–6
Lydian	4–5, 7–1
Mixolydian	3–4, 6–7

If it is still difficult to distinguish the modes, it may help to relate the modes to the major and minor scales, with which you are already familiar. Thus, *Dorian mode* is similar to the natural minor scale but with a *raised sixth degree*:

D natural minor

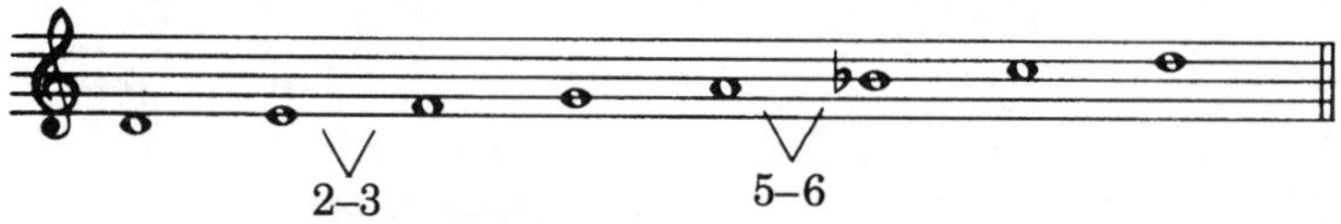

Dorian mode on D

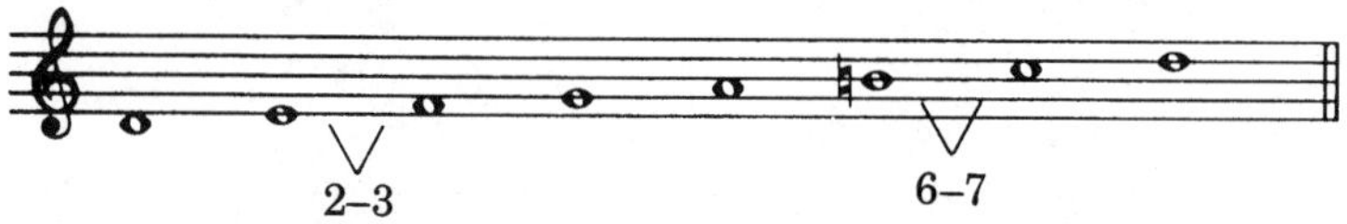

To write Dorian mode on A, we write the A natural minor scale but with a raised sixth degree:

Dorian mode on A

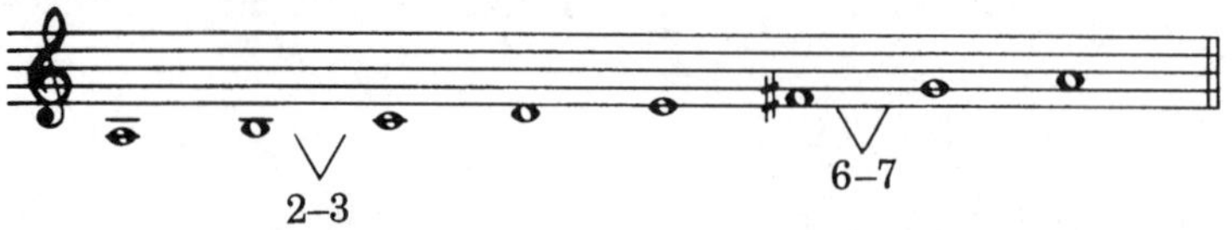

Phrygian mode is similar to the natural minor scale but with a *lowered second degree*:

E natural minor

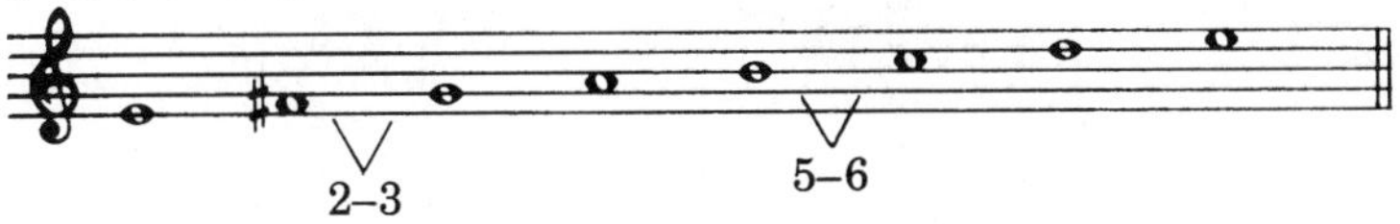

Phrygian mode on E

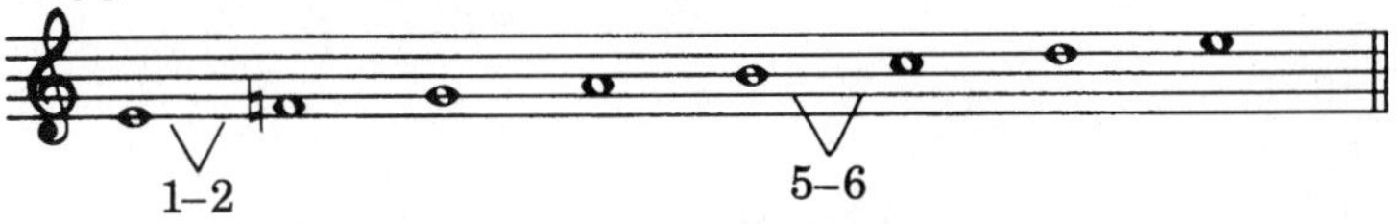

To write Phrygian mode on A, we think of the A natural minor scale, but we lower the second degree:

Phrygian mode on A

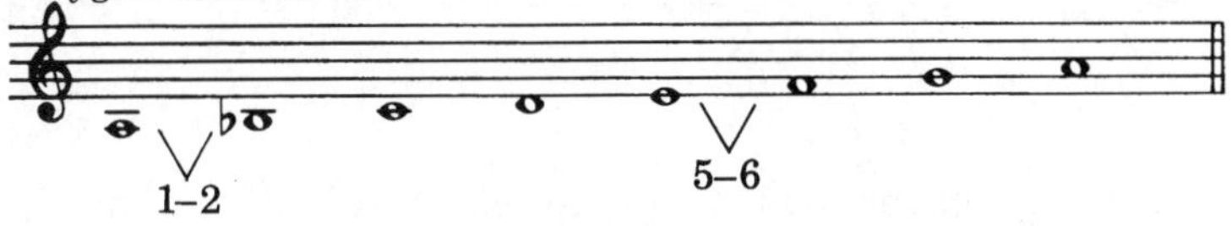

Lydian mode is similar to the major scale but with a *raised fourth degree*:

F major

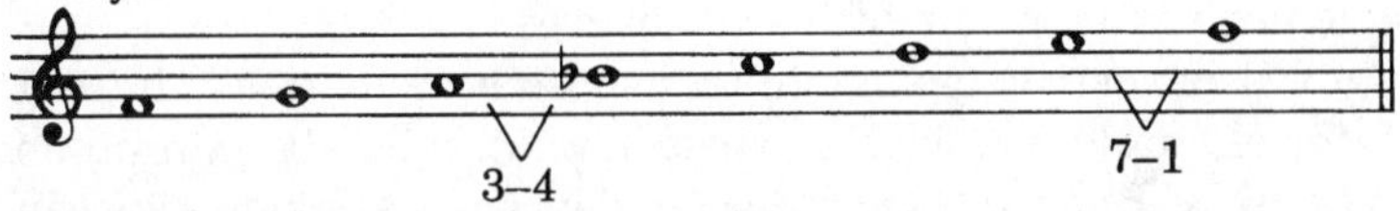

Lydian mode on F

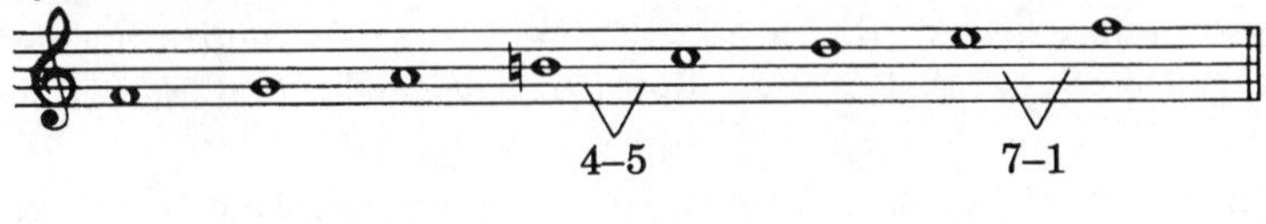

To write Lydian mode on C, we think of the C major scale but with a raised fourth degree:

Lydian mode on C

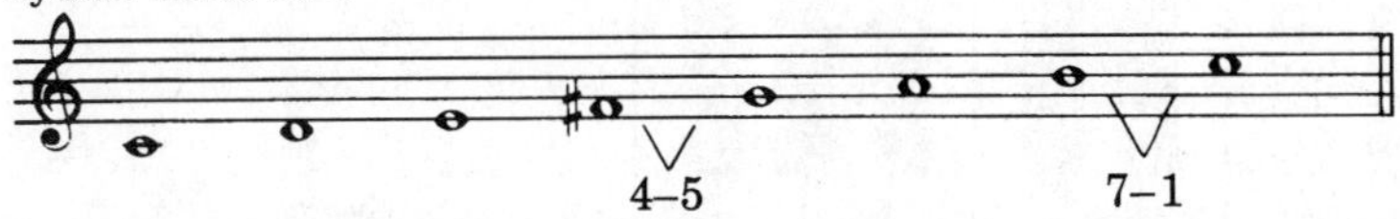

Mixolydian mode is similar to the major scale but with a *lowered seventh degree*:

G major

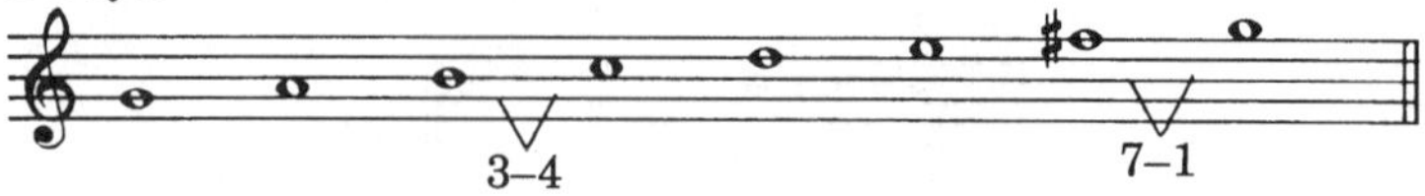

Mixolydian mode on G

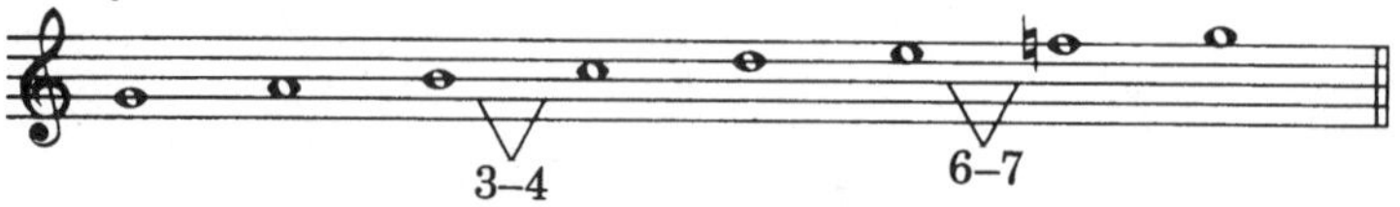

To write Mixolydian mode on C, we think of the C major scale, but we lower the seventh degree:

Mixolydian mode on C

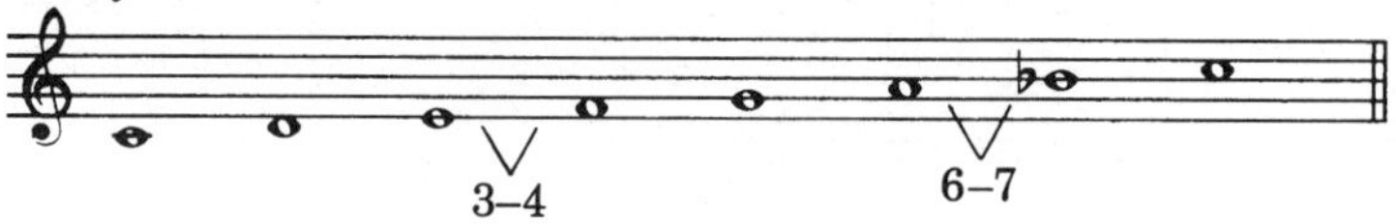

An alternative way to remember the modes is to relate each of them to the major scale. In this system, Dorian mode uses the pitch content of the major scale, but uses the second scale degree as the beginning pitch. Phrygian mode, likewise, can be thought of as a major scale beginning on the third scale degree; Lydian mode as a major scale beginning on the fourth degree; and Mixolydian mode as a major scale beginning on the fifth scale degree.

Using this system, it is relatively easy to transpose a mode to a different beginning pitch. If, for example, we wish to write Dorian mode beginning on B♭, we need only to think of B♭ as the second scale degree of a major scale, in this case the A♭ major scale, and then use the accidentals of that scale. Since the accidentals for A♭ major are A♭, B♭, D♭, and E♭, Dorian mode beginning on B♭ would be B♭–C–D♭–E♭–F–G–A♭–B♭. A similar process works for the other modes.

Write the indicated modes starting from the given pitch. Before beginning, mentally note the relationship of each mode to the major or natural minor scale. Mark the half steps in each mode you write. A keyboard is provided to help you visualize each scale.

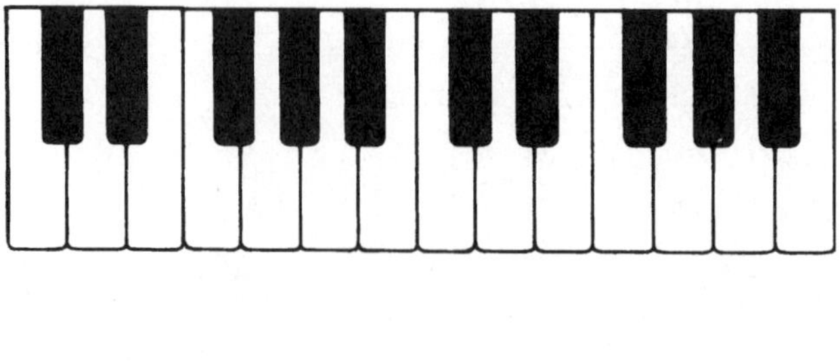

Dorian mode

1. 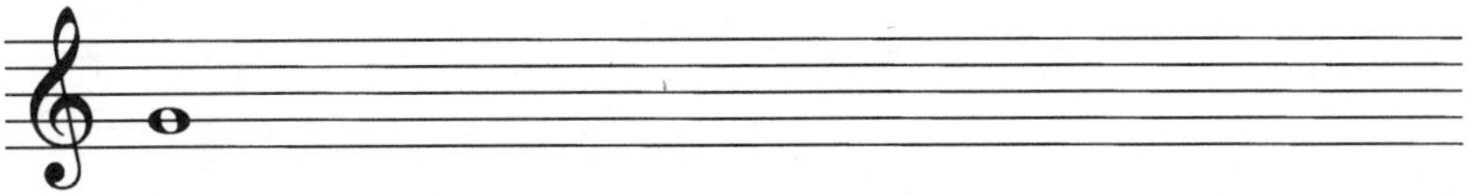

Dorian mode

2. 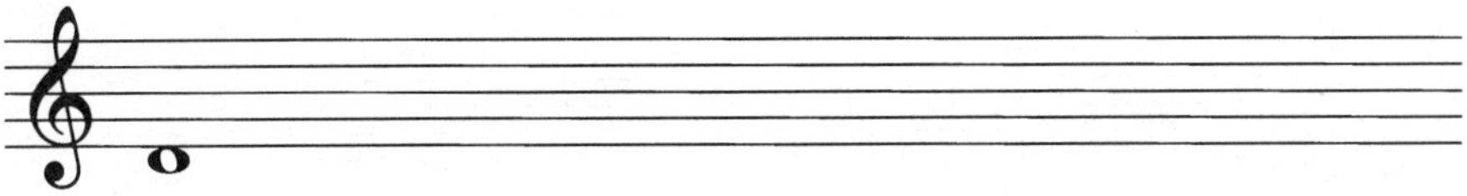

Dorian mode

3. 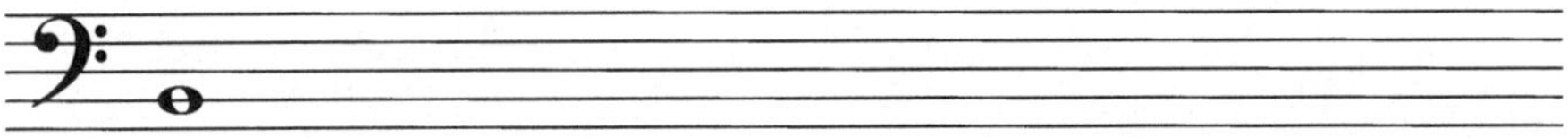

Dorian mode

4. 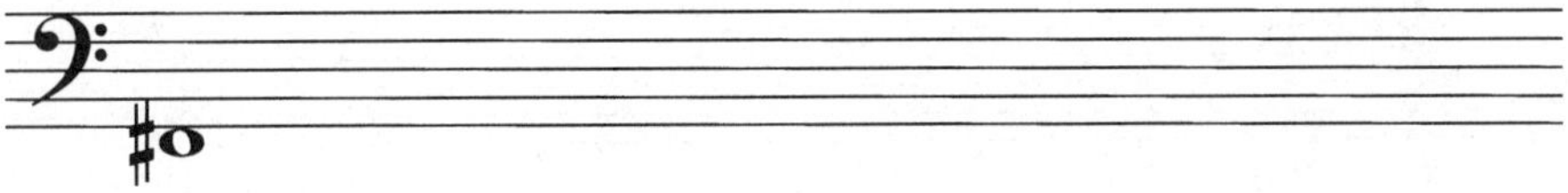

Phrygian mode

5. 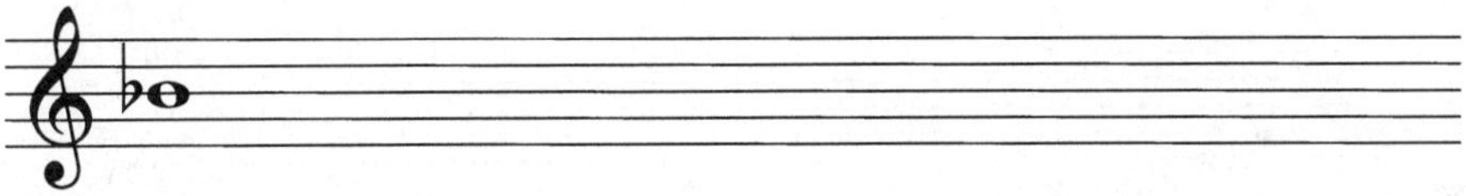

Phrygian mode

6. 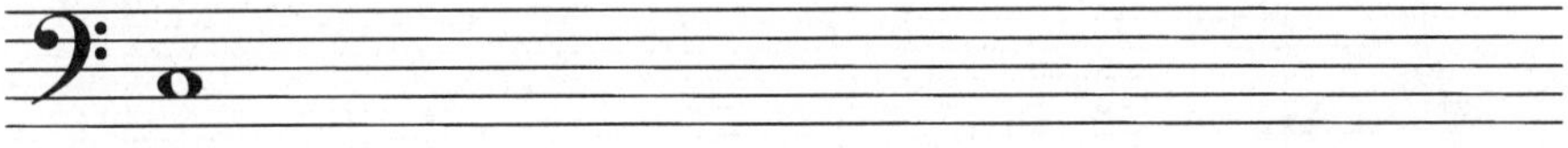

Phrygian mode

7. 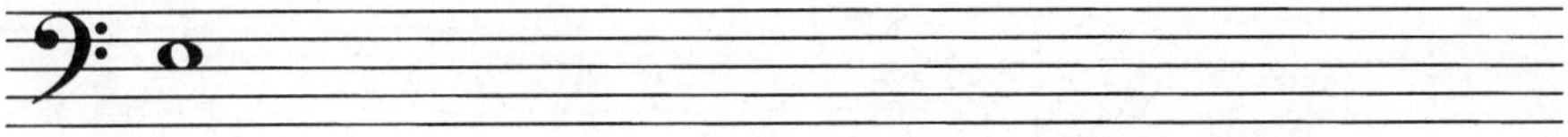

Phrygian mode

8. 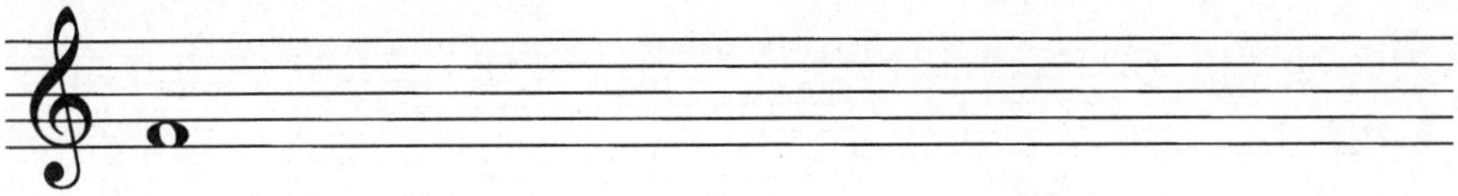

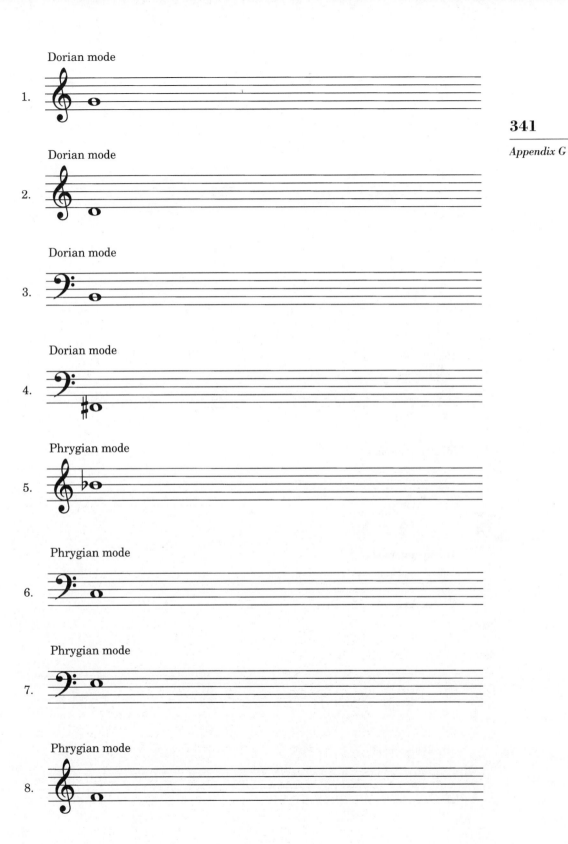

Lydian mode

9. 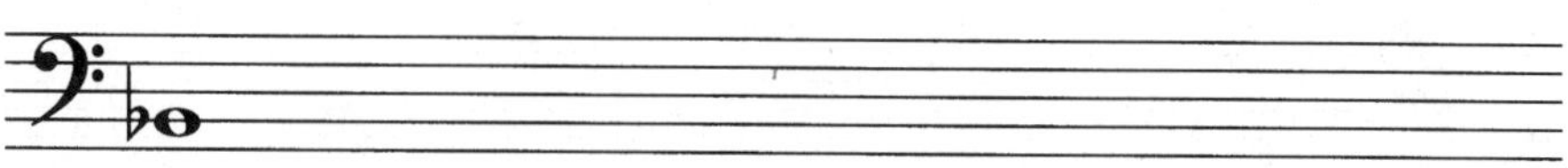

Lydian mode

10. 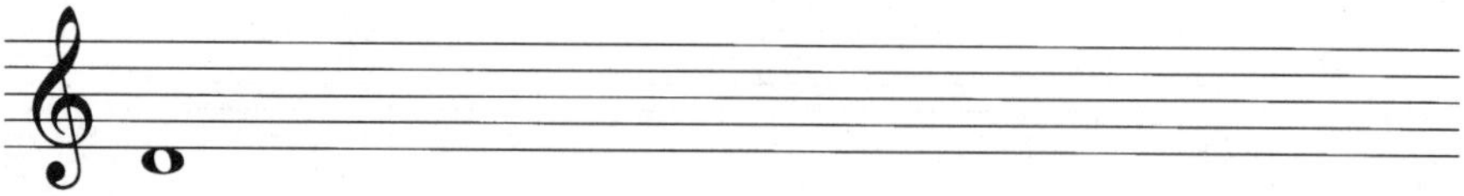

Lydian mode

11. 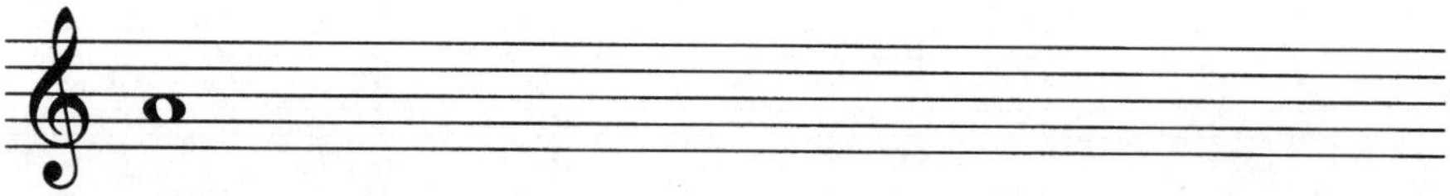

Lydian mode

12. 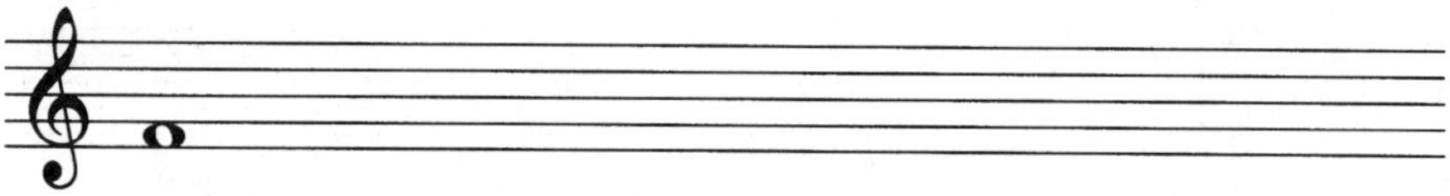

Mixolydian mode

13. 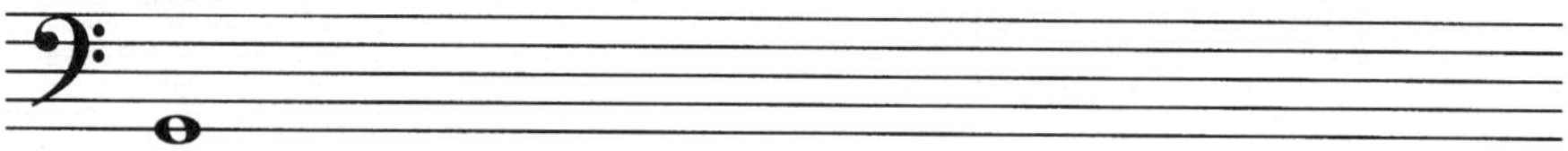

Mixolydian mode

14. 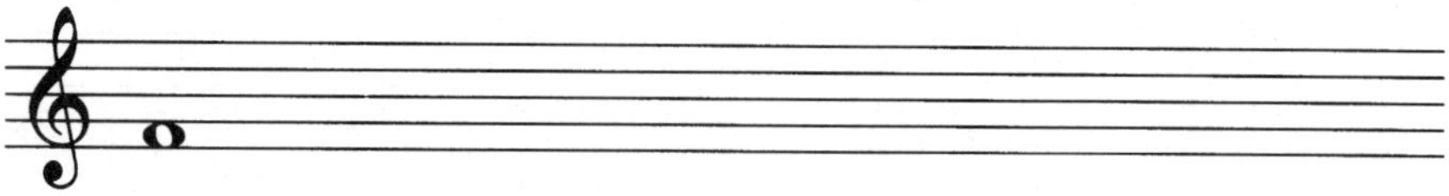

Mixolydian mode

15. 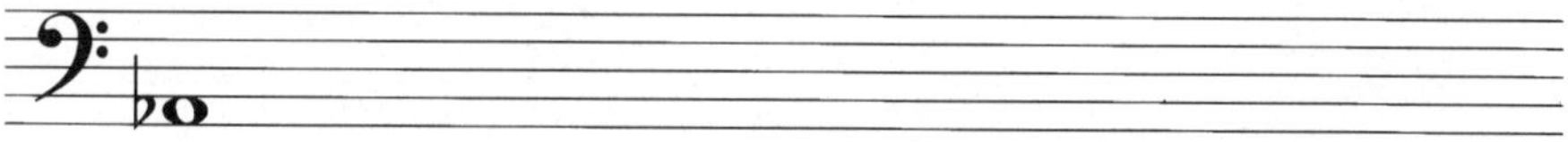

Mixolydian mode

16. 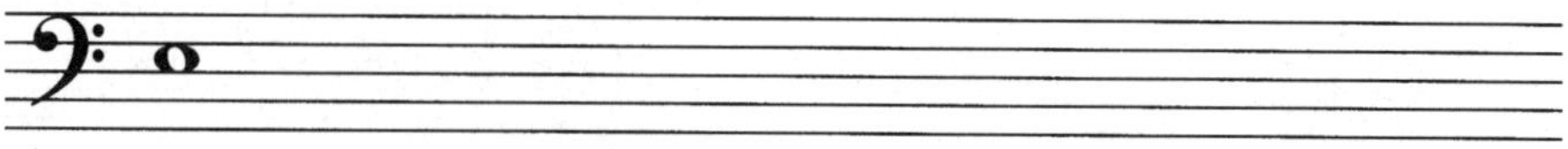

Appendix H

A Brief Discussion of Dynamics

Composers indicate degrees of loudness and softness (called **dynamics**) by annotating their music with specific words and abbreviations, most often Italian, occasionally French or German.

Volume in music is usually either maintained at steady levels or gradually changed. The standard words and symbols for a *steady volume* are:

English	*Italian*	*Abbreviation*
very soft	**pianissimo**	***pp***
soft	**piano**	***p***
moderately soft	**mezzo piano**	***mp***
moderately loud	**mezzo forte**	***mf***
loud	**forte**	***f***
very loud	**fortissimo**	***ff***

Occasionally, extremes in volume are desired, particularly in contemporary music. In such cases, the symbols ***ppp***, ***pppp***, ***fff***, and ***ffff*** are used.

Gradual changes in volume are indicated by the following words and symbols:

English	*Italian*	*Abbreviation*	*Symbol*
become softer	**diminuendo** **decrescendo**	*dim.* *decresc.*	>
become louder	**crescendo**	*cresc.*	<

Where the symbols for *diminuendo* or *crescendo* are used, the length of the symbol indicates the relative length of time in which the volume change is to occur. For example, ***p*** < ***f*** indicates a gradual change from *piano* to *forte* and taking approximately twice as long as ***p*** < ***f***. Furthermore, the change in the latter example will sound more obvious to the listener, because it will move through *mezzo piano* and *mezzo forte* more quickly than the first example.

Whereas the symbols that dictate gradual volume changes suggest the time in which the change is to occur, the Italian terms or abbreviations are less specific unless the Italian terms **subito** (suddenly) or **poco a poco** (little by little) are added to the volume indicator. *Subito **f***, for example, means suddenly loud, while *dim. poco a poco* means gradually softer.

Appendix **I**

A Brief Introduction to Timbre

Timbre refers to the unique sound quality of an instrument or voice that allows us to distinguish it from other instruments playing the same pitch. Timbre is determined, in part, by the way in which the sound is produced, the size of the instrument, and the design of the instrument.

When an instrument or a voice produces a tone, we hear it as a single pitch. In actuality, the tone is a composite of a fundamental frequency and a series of **overtones.** We hear a single pitch because the overtones are not as loud as the fundamental. This phenomenon is known as the **harmonic series,** and it consists of a fundamental pitch plus its first fifteen overtones.

The term **partials** refers to all the pitches within a harmonic series, including the fundamental. When the reference is to *overtones,* however, the fundamental is considered a separate element. Thus, the following example, showing the harmonic series for the pitch C, is said to have either a fundamental and fifteen overtones or sixteen partials.

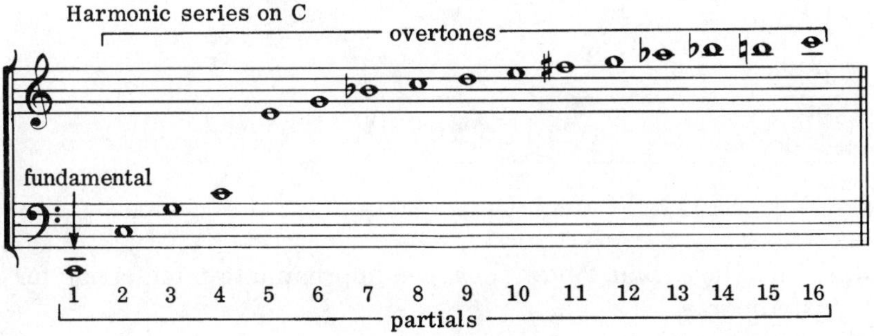

For instance, when a violin string is played, it begins to vibrate. Not only does the entire string vibrate, but shorter vibrations occur simultaneously over various lengths of the string. The vibration of the entire string produces the fundamental pitch we hear, while the shorter vibrations (the overtones) color the sound.

One instrument differs from another in timbre because each instrument is designed to amplify certain overtones and suppress others. It is, therefore, the design of an instrument that accounts, in large part, for its characteristic timbre.

Two other factors influence instrumental timbre: the size of the instrument and the way in which the sound is produced. In general, the larger the instrument the lower the pitch range. Mentally compare the pitch ranges of a violin and a string bass, or a trumpet and a tuba. Both sets of instruments produce pitches in the same way. In each case, it is the size of the instrument that gives one a soprano range and the other a bass range.

Orchestral instruments are grouped into families according to how the sound is produced (strings, woodwinds, brass, and percussion). Members of each family of instruments sound related because their similar way of producing sound helps create a similarity in timbre.

Strings: Violin, Viola, Cello, String Bass

A string instrument produces sound when a string is set in motion by a bow or is plucked by a finger. The vibration of the string is amplified by the body of the instrument. Pitch is determined, in part, by the length of the string—the longer the string, the lower the pitch. The diameter and the tension of the string also affect pitch.

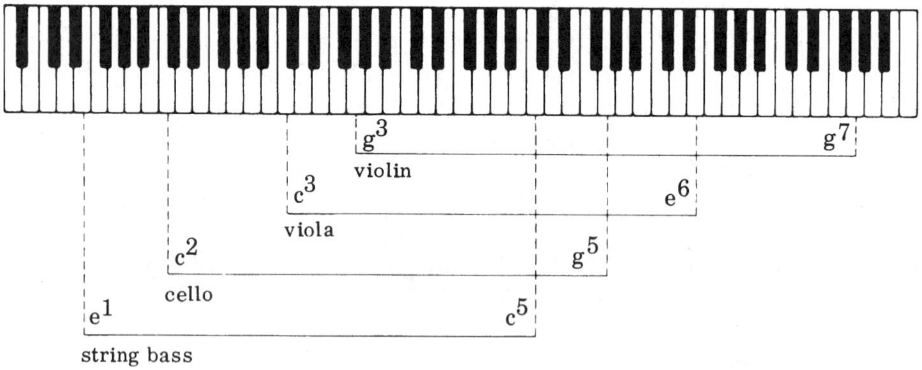

This illustration and those that follow show the approximate pitch range for each family of instruments.

Woodwinds: Piccolo, Flute, Oboe, English Horn, Clarinet, Bass Clarinet, Bassoon, Contra Bassoon

A woodwind instrument produces sound when the column of air inside the instrument is set in motion. Since this is done in a variety of ways, the sound of the woodwind family is less homogeneous than that of other families of instruments. The air column in a flute or a piccolo is set in motion by blowing across an air hole; in a clarinet or a bass clarinet by blowing against a single cane reed; and in an oboe, an English horn, a bassoon, or a contra bassoon by blowing against a double cane reed. The pitch on all woodwind instruments is controlled by finger holes on the instrument, which allow the performer to control the length of the air column—the longer the air column, the lower the pitch.

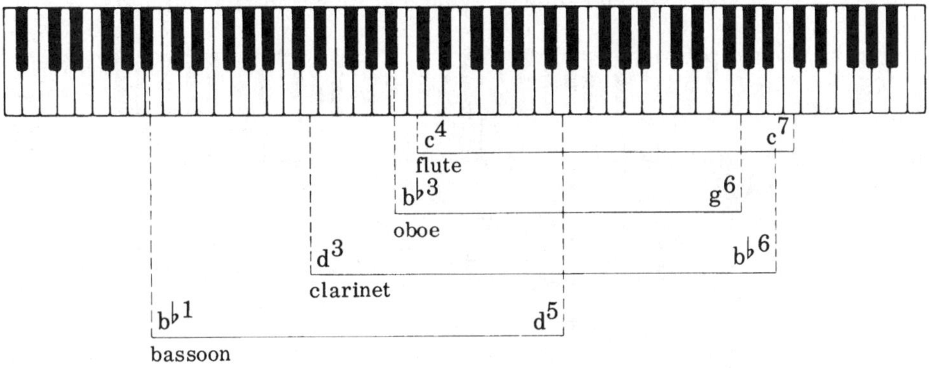

Brass: Trumpet, French Horn, Trombone, Tuba

The air column inside a brass instrument is set in motion when the performer buzzes his or her lips into a cup-shaped mouthpiece. Pitch on the trumpet, French horn, and tuba is controlled by three valves that open and close various lengths of tubing, thereby making the air column longer or shorter. Pitch on the trombone is controlled by the slide, which varies the length of the air column.

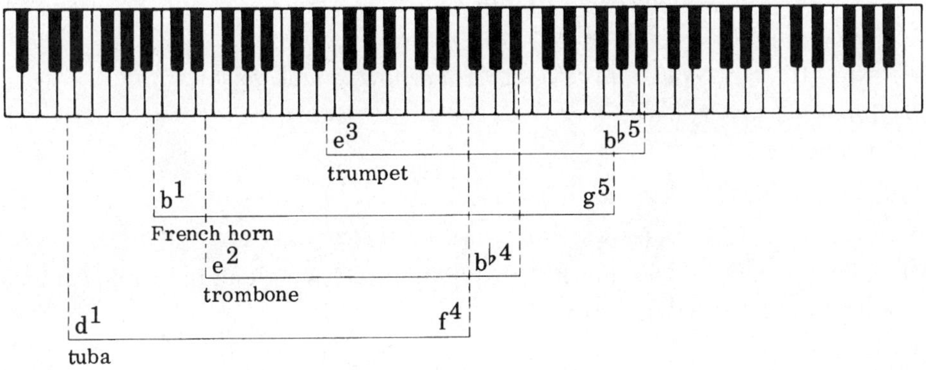

Percussion

Sound is produced on percussion instruments by striking them, usually with a wooden stick or a felt- or yarn-covered mallet. Some percussion instruments produce definite pitches, among them timpani (kettledrums), marimba, vibraphone, xylophone, chimes, and orchestra bells. The percussion instruments that produce an indefinite pitch include snare drum, bass drum, cymbals, and gong.

Voices

Human voices are classified into four main categories, by range: soprano, alto, tenor, and bass. The average range for each classification is as follows:

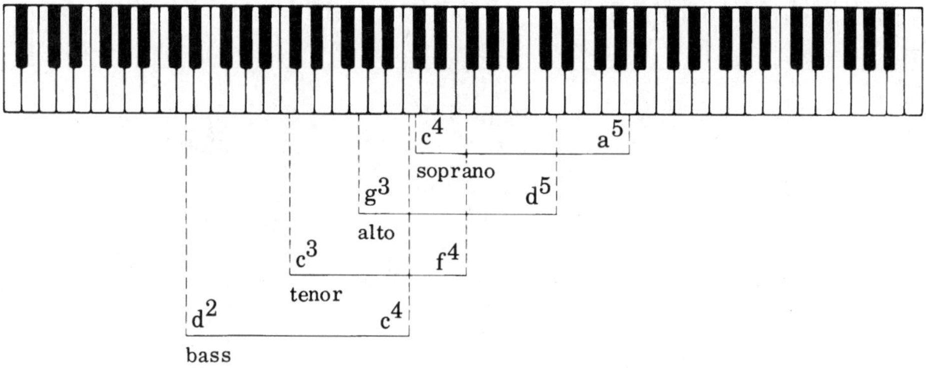

A further subdivision of voice types, shown here, is often made, particularly in opera, in order to indicate which vocal technique and which portion of the range are stressed.

I. Soprano
   A. coloratura—emphasizes agility and range
   B. lyric—emphasizes a more gentle voice quality
   C. dramatic—emphasizes dynamic range

II. Mezzo-Soprano—a high alto/low soprano

III. Alto—the term *contralto* refers to a very low female voice

IV. Tenor
   A. lyric
   B. dramatic (*Heldentenor* in German)

V. Baritone

VI. Bass-Baritone—has some of the baritone's high tonal qualities and some of the bass' low tonal qualities

VII. Bass

Appendix J

A Brief Discussion of Acoustics

Acoustics may at first appear an unlikely topic for a book concerned with music fundamentals. But acoustics is becoming more relevant every year. The dramatic increase in the number of synthesizers and in the use of home computers to make music has brought the study of acoustics to the forefront.

Every musical sound has four characteristics: pitch, volume, duration, and timbre. On a mechanical level, these are the components manipulated when we play an instrument or sing. The same is true on an electronic level for synthesizers and the music programs of computers. Sounds are created on these instruments by altering and adjusting the four basic characteristics of sound. If you plan to become involved with programming synthesizers, or in composing with computers, you will need a solid understanding of acoustics.

Frequency

Musical sounds, in fact all sounds, are made up of physical vibrations of air molecules. The air molecules themselves do not move forward. Instead, they vibrate back and forth in repeated patterns called oscillations. These patterns in the air are similar to the ripples in a pond created by throwing in a stone.

Air molecules are set into motion in a number of ways. Saxophone players do it by causing their reed to vibrate; string bass players pluck a string; trombone players buzz their lips inside the mouthpiece. Once the sound is begun, air molecules near the vibrating source are set into motion, and they, in turn, transfer this pattern of motion to adjacent molecules. This is how sound travels through the air.

It may be difficult at first to think of a musical pitch as a vibrational pattern of air molecules, but that is what it is. Furthermore, the faster the vibrating pattern, the higher the pitch; the slower the pattern, the lower the pitch. When thought of this way, the more accurate term for pitch is frequency.

Frequency is the number of times a vibrational pattern repeats itself. This repetition is generally measured in vibrations per second, and the term for this is Hertz (normally abbreviated Hz). When musicians talk about the pitch the orchestra tunes to as A-440 (the A above middle C), they are actually referring to a frequency of 440 Hz, that is, an air displacement of 440 vibrations per second.

Another interesting characteristic of pitch is that when the frequency is reduced by one-half, the pitch we hear descends by one octave. While the A above middle C vibrates at 440 Hz, the A directly below middle C vibrates at only 220 Hz, and the A below that at 110 Hz. The vibrating frequencies for all the As on the piano follow.

3,520 Hz
1,760 Hz
880 Hz
440 Hz
(middle C)
220 Hz
110 Hz
55 Hz
27.5 Hz

Amplitude

The pitch or frequency of a sound is determined by the speed of the vibrational patterns. But the speed of the vibration does not determine how loud a sound is. In other words, the dynamics can change without affecting the pitch. Loudness, known as amplitude, is controlled by how far each air molecule is displaced. That is, the more air movement in the initial displacement, the farther the displacement will carry through the air, and the louder the sound will appear. Scientists measure amplitude in decibels; musicians use less precise terms like *mezzo piano* and *forte.*

An important point to remember is that excessive volume, particularly when listening on headphones, can cause permanent hearing loss. This has been thoroughly documented. Although many people enjoy loud music, it is important to use caution when listening at high volume, since a loss of hearing can never be corrected.

Duration

Musical sounds have three distinct parts—attack, sustain, and decay. The initial attack describes how the sound begins. It can be quite sudden and forceful, as when a trumpet player moves his or her tongue and releases air into the instrument. Or it can be more gentle, as when a pianist lightly touches the keys. Most instruments are capable of a variety of attacks.

Once a sound is begun, the second stage is the sustain stage. Some instruments, such as the organ, can sustain a sound indefinitely. Others, such as a clarinet, can sustain only as long as the breath of the performer holds out. And other instruments, such as the xylophone, have a sharp attack but almost no sustain time at all.

Once a sound begins to fade it is considered to be in the decay stage. Musical sounds normally come to an end in one of two ways: There is a gradual loss of amplitude until the sound is no longer audible, or the sound is cut off abruptly by stopping the air or muting the string.

Synthesizers and the music programs of computers work by controlling the attack—sustain—decay characteristics of a sound. By manipulating one or all of these elements, well-known sounds, such as the sound of a flute, can be created electronically, or new sounds can even be invented.

Timbre

You will remember from Appendix H that every instrumental sound is really a composite consisting of the fundamental pitch plus the overtones of the harmonic series. Each instrument, including the human voice, emphasizes certain overtones and suppresses others. This creates a unique vibrational pattern for each instrument, but it does not alter the frequency. Therefore, two instruments, such as the flute and the oboe, can play the same pitch (frequency) but still maintain their own characteristic and distinct tone color (timbre).

K Appendix

Using the *Focus on Fundamentals* Enhanced CD

The enhanced CD that accompanies this book offers yet another way for you to practice and improve. Called *Focus on Fundamentals,* it contains hundreds of audio files and supplementary practice exercises. These exercises are keyed to individual chapters of the book and focus on the basic skills that you will need in order to master music fundamentals. There is also instant feedback of your progress, and a way to test yourself and e-mail the results to your instructor.

The Audio Files

There are two kinds of files on your enhanced CD. The first kind is a set of 25 audio files that allow you to hear musical examples from both the text and the Musical Problems. You can use your CD player to listen to these files; you can also hear them using your computer.

The audio files are indexed as follows:

1. Bach: Minuet in G Minor
2. Russian Folksong
3. Clementi: Sonatina, Op. 36, No. 1, I
4. Schumann: Siciliana from *Album for the Young*
5. *Estampie* (Thirteenth-Century Dance)
6. "Nowel Syng We" (Medieval Carol)
7. Landini: *Ecco la Primavera*
8. Scarlatti: Sonata in C Minor
9. "Molly Malone"
10. "Joshua Fit the Battle of Jericho"
11. W. F. Bach: Praeludium from the *Little Piano Book* (natural minor)
12. W. F. Bach: Praeludium from the *Little Piano Book* (harmonic minor)

13. "Lavender's Blue"
14. Schumann: Chorale from *Album for the Young*
15. "Blow Ye Winds in the Morning"
16. "Wayfaring Stranger"
17. Clementi: Sonatina, Op. 36, No. 3, III
18. Schumann: Soldiers' March from Album for the Young
19. Bach: Chorale, *Ermuntre dich*
20. Schumann: The Poor Orphan Child from Album for the Young
21. Kuhlau: Sonatina in C Major, Op. 55, No. 1, I
22. Schumann: "The Wild Rider" from *Album for the Young*
23. "Mockingbird Hill"
24. "New River Train"
25. "Red River Valley"

The Application Files

The application file, *Focus on Fundamentals,* is a set of exercises designed to help you learn the fundamentals of music. To use it successfully, you must install it on your computer. If you try to run the exercises from the enhanced CD, the speed will be too slow to be useful, and several features will be unavailable.

As you start each new topic, begin with the text—the exercises and musical problems. Once you are familiar enough with them to understand the basic concepts of the new material, you can then use the enhanced CD for additional practice. It is not a good idea to start a new topic with the enhanced CD since it will not contain the factual information found in the book.

Installing Focus on Fundamentals *on Your Computer*

Minimum System Requirements

PC	Mac
Windows 98, ME, 2000, XP	MAC OS 8.1 (or later)
Pentium II 233 Mhz	PowerPC processor (or later)
64-MB RAM	64-MB RAM
16-bit sound card	16-bit sound card
800 X 600, 16-bit high color display	800 X 600, 16-bit high color display
Speakers or headphones	Speakers or headphones
4× CD-ROM	4× CD-ROM

This is an enhanced CD that contains both audio and application files. The audio files can be heard on both your CD player and your computer and the application must be installed on your hard drive before it will run.

PC Installation

From My Computer on the Windows screen, open the CD-ROM drive.

Select Focus.exe and follow the on-screen instructions.

On Windows XP

From My Computer on the Windows screen, select the CD-ROM drive.

Choose Open from the file menu.

Select Focus.exe and follow the on-screen instructions.

When installation is complete, launch the *Focus on Fundamentals* application from your Start Menu Programs folder.

Mac Installation

Open the *Focus on Fundamentals* CD icon.

Double click on Focus Installer and follow the on-screen instructions.

When installation is complete, launch the *Focus on Fundamentals* application from your hard drive.

General Outline of Focus on Fundamentals

When you have opened the program you will notice that the exercises are arranged in chapters identical to those of the book. Each *Focus on Fundamentals* chapter contains one or more groups of practice exercises that stress the most important and necessary skills found in that chapter. The *Focus on Fundamentals* practice material you will find on the enhanced CD is as follows:

Chapter 1: Basics

1. Clap and Count
2. Identify Pitches
3. Name the Keys

Chapter 2: Rhythm

1. Recognizing Meters
2. Hearing Rhythms

Chapter 3: Pitch

1. Name and Rewrite Pitches
2. Locate Notes

Chapter 4: Major Scales

1. Writing Ascending Scales
2. Writing Descending Scales

Chapter 5: Major Key Signatures

1. Identify Key Signatures
2. Write Key Signatures

Chapter 6: Intervals

1. Identify Intervals
2. Write Intervals
3. Hearing Intervals

Chapter 7: Minor Key Signatures

1. Identify Key Signatures
2. Write Key Signatures

Chapter 8: Minor Scales

1. Write Natural Minor Scales
2. Write Harmonic Minor Scales
3. Write Melodic Minor Scales

Chapter 9: Other Scales and Modes

1. Write Pentatonic Scales
2. Write Modal Scales
3. Write Whole-Tone Scales

Chapter 10: Triads

1. Complete the Triad
2. Identify Inverted Triads
3. Write Triads
4. Write Dominant 7th

Chapter 11: Tonality

1. Recognize Progressions

Testing Yourself and E-mailing Your Results to Your Instructor

It is possible at any time to check your progress and to send your quiz results to your instructor. By choosing Quiz from the Mode menu, you can quiz yourself on the material and the answers will not be shown. When you have answered the desired number of questions, press Submit. Your score will be calculated and presented to you in the form of an e-mail that you can forward to your instructor. This requires an active Internet connection.

It is also possible to save and send your quiz results at a later time. Choose Quiz Report from the Progress menu to see your quiz history and change status.

Glossary

Terms appearing here are **boldfaced** in text.

Accelerando A tempo marking indicating a gradual change to a faster tempo.

Accent mark (>) A sign that indicates that the note above or below it receives more stress than the surrounding notes.

Accidentals A set of signs that, when placed in front of a notehead, alter the pitch of that note chromatically. See also **Sharp sign; Flat sign; Double sharp sign; Double flat sign; Natural sign.**

Adagio A tempo marking indicating a slow tempo.

Allegro A tempo marking indicating a fast tempo.

Alto clef See **C clef.**

Andante A tempo marking indicating a moderate tempo, about walking speed.

Arithmetic distance The letter-name distance between two pitches. The arithmetic distance identifies the interval (third, fourth, and so on), but not the interval quality (major, minor, and so on).

Augmented interval The increasing of a perfect interval or a major interval by one half step.

Authentic cadence A momentary or permanent point of rest in a harmonic progression created by the two-chord progression V–I in major or iv–i in minor.

Bar lines Vertical lines, placed immediately before the accented pulse, that divide written music into measures. The meter is more easily read when music is divided into measures. Compare with **Double bar lines.**

Bass clef (F clef) (𝄢) A sign that locates the note f on the fourth line of the staff. This f is then used as a reference point for locating other pitches.

Cadence A temporary or permanent point of rest at the end of a musical phrase.

C clef (𝄡) A sign that locates the note middle c on the staff. This sign is movable and may appear on any of the staff's five lines. Today it is commonly found on the third line (alto clef) or the fourth line (tenor clef). In either position the c becomes a reference point for locating other pitches.

Chord The major component of tonal harmony; three or more pitches sounding simultaneously. See **Triad.**

Chromatic half step A half step that involves two pitches of the same letter name and staff location, such as G to G♯, A to A♭, or E to E♯. See also **Diatonic half step.**

Chromatic scale A scale formed by the division of the octave into twelve equal half steps.

Clef A sign that locates a particular pitch on the staff. This pitch is then used as a reference point for other pitches on the staff. The commonly used clefs are treble clef, bass clef, and C clef.

Compound interval Any interval greater than an octave in arithmetic distance.

Compound meter Any meter in which the basic pulse is normally subdivided into three equal parts.

Crescendo (*cresc.* or $<$) A dynamics marking indicating that the musical passage is to grow louder.

Deceptive cadence A temporary point of rest in a chord progression, in which an unexpected chord, usually vi, follows a V or V_7 instead of the tonic triad that is expected.

Decrescendo (*decresc.* or $<$) A dynamics marking indicating that the musical passage is to grow softer.

Diatonic half step A half step that involves two pitches with adjacent letter names and staff locations, such as A to B♭, G♯ to F, or B to C. See also **Chromatic half step.**

Diminished interval The decreasing of a perfect interval or a minor interval by one half step.

Diminuendo (*dim.* or $>$) A dynamics marking indicating that the musical passage is to grow softer.

Dominant The fifth tone or triad of a major or minor scale.

Dominant seventh chord (V_7) The chord formed by adding a fourth note, a minor seventh above the root, to the dominant triad.

Dotted note A dot placed beside a note increases the value of the original note by one half. Thus, a dotted half note is equal to three quarter notes. Any note can be increased by half its value by adding a dot.

Double bar lines Two vertical lines used in written music, most commonly to indicate the beginning of a new section in a large work or to mark the end of a work.

Double flat sign (𝄫) An accidental that, when placed in front of a note, lowers the pitch of that note by two half steps (one whole step).

Double sharp sign (×) An accidental that, when placed in front of a note, raises the pitch of that note by two half steps (one whole step).

Downbeat The strongest beat of any meter, always written as the *first* beat of the measure.

Duple meter A division of the musical pulse into a recurring pattern of one strong and one weak beat.

Duplet A borrowed division in compound meter, in which a note normally subdivided into three equal parts is subdivided into two equal parts.

Dynamics A characteristic of musical sound involving degrees of loudness and softness. In written music, volume is indicated by specific words and abbreviations.

Enharmonic pitches The use of two different letter names for the same pitch. C♯ and D♭, F♯ and G♭, E♯ and F are examples of enharmonic pitches.

F clef See **Bass clef.**

Flat sign (♭) An accidental that, when placed in front of a note, lowers the pitch of that note by a half step.

Form The organizing principle, or structure, of a piece of music. Form in music can be compared to the blueprint of a building. It controls how music unfolds in time. Most musical forms that are used to any extent have been given their own identifying names. These include binary, ternary, strophic, and sonata forms, as well as fugue, theme-and-variation, and rondo forms.

Forte (*f*) A dynamics marking indicating *loud.*

Fortissimo (*ff*) A dynamics marking indicating *very loud.*

G clef See **Treble clef.**

Great staff A treble clef staff and a bass clef staff joined together by a vertical line and a brace. It is employed in music that requires a range of pitches too wide for a single staff, such as piano music.

Half cadence A temporary point of rest in the harmony of a piece of music created by a momentary pause on the dominant chord. The half cadence itself is a two-chord progression, the most common being IV–V or I–V in major, and iv–V or i–V in minor.

Half step The smallest interval in tonal music. On the piano, it is the distance between any key and the key immediately above or below it.

Harmonic cadence A momentary or permanent point of rest in the harmony of a piece. There are several types, each a different formula of two chords. See also **Authentic cadence; Plagal cadence; Half cadence.**

Harmonic interval The musical distance between two pitches sounded simultaneously. See also **Interval.**

Harmonic minor scale An altered version of the natural minor scale. The seventh degree is raised a half step to create a leading tone. This, in turn, creates the interval of an augmented second between the sixth and seventh degrees of the scale.

Harmonic rhythm The rate of change—fast or slow, steady or irregular—of the chords in a piece of music.

Harmonic series A fundamental frequency plus a series of overtones, heard as a single pitch. All musical pitches contain the harmonic series, or parts of the series.

Harmony Harmony generally refers to the horizontal progression of chords that takes place throughout a piece of music. The harmony is generated directly from the scale, or scales, on which a piece is based.

Interval The musical distance between two pitches. Intervals may be harmonic (sounding simultaneously) or melodic (sounding successively). Interval quality may be perfect, major, minor, augmented, or diminished.

Key signature A grouping, at the beginning of a composition, of all the accidentals found in the major or natural minor scale on which the piece is based.

Largo A tempo marking indicating a broad, very slow tempo.

Leading tone The seventh tone or triad of a major, melodic minor, or harmonic minor scale; a half step below the tonic.

Ledger lines Short lines above or below the staff that function to extend the pitch range of the staff.

Lento A tempo marking indicating a slow tempo.

Major scale A seven-note scale based on an interval pattern of five whole steps and two half steps, the half steps occurring between the third and fourth, and the seventh and first tones.

Measure A division in written music that allows the meter to be seen more clearly. Measures are created by bar lines placed immediately before the accented pulse.

Mediant The third tone or triad of a major or minor scale.

Melodic interval The musical distance between two pitches sounded in succession. See also **Interval.**

Melodic minor scale A scale developed to avoid the augmented second of the harmonic minor scale. In the ascending form, the sixth and seventh degrees of the natural minor scale are raised; in the descending form, they are lowered to their position in natural minor.

Melody A consecutive horizontal line of pitches that contains a contour (or shape), rhythmic motion, and cadences (or arrival points of rest). The interaction of these elements can produce an infinite number of melodic possibilities.

Meter The division of the musical pulse into a recurring pattern of strong and weak pulses. The most common patterns or meters are duple meter, triple meter, and quadruple meter.

Meter signature Two numbers, one above the other, that appear at the beginning of a piece of music. The top number indicates the meter of the music; the bottom number tells which note value represents one beat.

Metronome An instrument invented in the early 1800s that produces a certain number of clicks per minute. Since each click can represent one beat, it is a more precise way of indicating tempo than the Italian terms also commonly used to mark tempo. The metronome marking in written music is given by the symbol M.M., which stands for *Maelzel's metronome.*

Mezzo forte (*mf*) A dynamics marking indicating *moderately loud.*

Mezzo piano (*mp*) A dynamics marking indicating *moderately soft.*

Minor scale A seven-note scale, of which there are three versions. See also **Harmonic minor scale; Melodic minor scale; Natural minor scale.**

Moderato A tempo marking indicating a moderate tempo.

Modes A group of seven-note scales consisting of five whole steps and two half steps. By changing the placement of the two half steps, seven modes were created (Ionian, Dorian, Phrygian, Lydian, Mixolydian, Aeolian, and Locrian). These scales, from which the present-day major and natural minor scales were drawn, were the basis of Western music until the early 1600s.

Modulation The act of moving from one key center to another within a composition. Sometimes this is done by using a double bar and a change of key signature. Other times, the key signature remains the same, but accidentals are introduced into the music that actually change the key.

Motive A motive is a part of a melody, and is a short arrangement of pitches that is identifiable as a melodic unit. The motive usually lends itself well to further transformation or development. Some melodies consists of several short motives.

Movable *do* A system of sight-singing in which the tonic of any scale is always *do,* and the subsequent syllables are assigned to each succeeding pitch of the scale.

Natural minor scale A seven-note scale consisting of five whole steps and two half steps. The half steps occur between the second and third tones and the fifth and sixth tones.

Natural sign (♮) An accidental that, when placed in front of a note, cancels (for that note) any existing sharp, flat, double sharp, or double flat.

Noteheads The small oval shapes drawn on the staff to represent particular pitches.

Octave sign (8va) A sign indicating that the notes below it are to be performed one octave higher than written (8va‒‒‒┐), or that the notes above it are to be performed one octave lower than written (8^va^___┘).

Overtones The pitches above the fundamental pitch in the harmonic series.

Parallel keys A major key and a minor key with the same tonic but different key signatures.

Partials All the pitches of the harmonic series, including the fundamental.

Pentatonic scale A scale with five pitches per octave. A variety of pentatonic scales exists; the most well-known version contains no half steps.

Perfect pitch The ability to always recognize by ear any pitch when it is sounded. See also **Relative pitch.**

Period A combination of two or more melodic phrases. If a period consists of two phrases, the first generally ends with a feeling of incompleteness that the second phrase acts to complete.

Phrase The phrase is the basic building block of a melody. It gives a feeling of completeness. Historically, phrases have tended to be symmetrical in length, that is, two, four, or eight measures in length. Melodies are often built of two or more phrases.

Pianissimo (*pp*) A dynamics marking indicating *very soft.*

Piano (*p*) A dynamics marking indicating *soft.*

Pitch The frequency at which a given sound vibrates.

Plagal cadence A momentary or permanent point of rest in the harmony of a piece of music created by the two-chord progression IV–I in major or iv–i in minor.

Poco a poco A dynamics marking meaning *little by little,* as in *dim. poco a poco* (gradually softer).

Presto A tempo marking indicating a very fast tempo.

Pulse The constant, regular beat in music. It can be represented visually by a line of quarter notes, half notes, eighth notes, and so on; it is felt as the beat to which you tap your foot.

Quadruple meter A division of the musical pulse into a recurring pattern of one strong and three weak pulses.

Related keys A major key and a minor key with the same key signature but different tonics.

Relative pitch The ability to identify a second pitch or pitches once a reference-point pitch is known. See also **Perfect pitch.**

Repeat sign (𝄆 𝄇) A sign consisting of double bar lines plus two large dots either before or after the bar. This sign occurs in written music at the beginning and the end of measures that are to be immediately repeated.

Rest A musical sign used to indicate duration of silence. Every note value has a corresponding rest sign.

Rhythm Rhythm organizes musical sounds into patterns of time duration. Strictly speaking, *meter* refers to a recurring pattern of strong and weak beats, while *rhythm* means the various arrangements of irregular durations within the metrical pattern.

Ritardando A tempo marking indicating a gradual change to a slower tempo.

Scale A group of pitches, generally in patterns of whole steps and half steps, that form the basic pitch material for a composition. See **Major scale, Minor scale, Modes, Pentatonic scale,** and **Whole-tone scale.**

Semi-cadence See **Half cadence.**

Sharp sign (♯) An accidental that, when placed in front of a note, raises the pitch of that note by a half step.

Simple interval Any interval that is one octave or smaller.

Simple meter Any meter in which the basic pulse can be normally subdivided into two equal parts.

Slur A curved line, extended over two or more notes of different pitch, used to indicate a smooth, connected style of playing or singing.

Staff (pl.: staves) A set of five parallel lines on which music is notated. The five lines, the four spaces between the lines, and the spaces above and below the staff are used to indicate pitch. Normally, the higher on the staff a symbol is located, the higher the pitch.

Subdominant The fourth tone or triad of a major or minor scale.

Subito A dynamics marking meaning *suddenly,* as in *subito **p*** (suddenly soft).

Subject The melodic material of contrapuntal compositions such as inventions and fugues.

Submediant The sixth tone or triad of a major or minor scale.

Subtonic The seventh tone or triad of a natural minor or descending melodic minor scale; a whole step below the tonic.

Supertonic The second tone or triad of a major or minor scale.

Syncopation Occurs when an accent is placed on what would otherwise be a weak beat.

Tempo The speed at which a piece of music moves; the speed of the pulse. In written music, Italian terms or a metronome marking are used to indicate the tempo.

Tendency tones The apparent attraction of various scale degrees to one another. In general, the need for active tones, that is, the fifth, seventh, and second, to resolve to less active tones, that is, the tonic.

Tenor clef See **C clef.**

Texture Indicates the density (thickness or thinness) of a musical line. There are three primary musical textures: Monophonic texture is one melodic line without accompaniment. *Homophonic texture* is one predominant melody with accompaniment. *Polyphonic texture* is two or more equally important melodic lines occurring simultaneously (also called *contrapuntal texture*).

Theme The melodic material used for classical works such as sonatas, symphonies, theme-and-variations, and other generally homophonic compositions.

Tie A curved line connecting two notes of the same pitch, and used for creating notes of long duration.

Timbre The unique sound or tone color of an instrument or voice. The timbre is determined, in part, by the size and design of the instrument, and by the way in which its sound is produced.

Time signature See **Meter signature.**

Tonal music Music in which both the melody and the harmony are derived from major or minor scales.

Tonic The first note or triad of a major or minor scale; the pitch to which the other tones of the scale seem to be related.

Transposition The act of moving a piece, or a section of a piece, from one key level to another. Often, singers will transpose a piece to another key in order for it to be in a range better suited to their voice.

Treble clef (G clef) (𝄞) A sign that locates the note g^1 on the second line of the staff. This g^1 is then used as a reference point for locating other pitches on the staff.

Triad The basic chord of tonal music. A three-note chord constructed of two superimposed thirds. Four qualities of triads are possible—major, minor, augmented, and diminished.

Triple meter A division of the musical pulse into a recurring pattern of one strong and two weak beats.

Triplet A borrowed division in simple meter, in which a note normally subdivided into two equal parts is subdivided into three equal parts.

Upbeat The beat before the downbeat, that is, the final beat of a measure.

Vivace A tempo marking indicating a quick and lively tempo.

Whole step An interval consisting of two half steps.

Whole-tone scale A scale consisting of six pitches per octave, each a whole step apart.

Subject Index

This index includes topics discussed in text. See *Glossary* for specific terms, and *Index to Musical Examples* for names of composers and titles.

Index to Musical Examples

LICENSING AND WARRANTY AGREEMENT

Notice to Users: Do not install or use this CD-ROM until you have read this agreement. You will be bound by the terms of this agreement if you install or use this CD-ROM or otherwise signify acceptance of this agreement. If you do not agree to the terms contained in this agreement, do not install or use any portion of this CD-ROM.

License: The material in the CD-ROM (the "Software") is copyrighted and is protected by United States copyright laws and international treaty provisions. All rights are reserved to the respective copyright holders. No part of the Software may be reproduced, stored in a retrieval system, distributed (including but not limited to over the www/Internet), decompiled, reverse engineered, reconfigured, transmitted, or transcribed, in any form or by any means—electronic, mechanical, photocopying, recording, or otherwise—without the prior written permission of Wadsworth (the "Publisher"). Adopters of Duckworth's *A Creative Approach to Music Fundamentals,* 8th Edition, may place the Software on the adopting school's network during the specific period of adoption for classroom purposes only in support of that text. The Software may not under any circumstances, be reproduced and/or downloaded for sale. For further permission and information, contact Wadsworth, 10 Davis Dr., Belmont, CA 94002.

U.S. Government Restriction Rights: The enclosed Software and associated documentation are provided with RESTRICTED RIGHTS. Use, duplication, or disclosure by the Government is subject to restrictions as set forth in subdivision (c) (1) (ii) of the Rights in Technical Data and Computer Software clause at DFARS 252.277.7013 for DoD contracts, paragraphs (c) (1) and (2) of the Commercial Computer Software-Restricted Rights clause in the FAR (48 CFR 52.227-19) for civilian agencies, or in other comparable agency clauses. The proprietor of the enclosed software and associated documentation is Wadsworth, 10 Davis Dr., Belmont, CA 94002.

Limited Warranty: The warranty for the media on which the Software is provided is for ninety (90) days from the original purchase and valid only if the packaging for the Software was purchased unopened. If, during that time, you find defects in the workmanship or material, the Publisher will replace the defective media. The Publisher provides no other warranties, expressed or implied, including the implied warranties of merchantability or fitness for a particular purpose, and shall not be liable for any damages, including direct, special, indirect, incidental, consequential, or otherwise.